FORM AS ARGUMENT IN CICERO'S SPEECHES

AMERICAN PHILOLOGICAL ASSOCIATION
American Classical Studies

Series Editor

Matthew S. Santirocco

Number 31

Form as Argument in Cicero's Speeches
A Study of Dilemma

by
Christopher P. Craig

Christopher P. Craig

FORM AS ARGUMENT IN CICERO'S SPEECHES
A Study of Dilemma

Scholars Press
Atlanta, Georgia

FORM AS ARGUMENT IN CICERO'S SPEECHES

by
Christopher P. Craig

© 1993
The American Philological Association

Library of Congress Cataloging in Publication Data
Craig, Christopher P.
　Form as argument in Cicero's speeches/ by Christopher P. Craig.
　　p. cm. — (American classical studies; no. 31)
　　Includes bibliographical references and index.
　　ISBN 1-55540-878-8 (hard). — ISBN 1-55540-879-6 (pbk.)
　　1. Cicero, Marcus Tullius. Orationes. 2. Speeches, addresses, etc., Latin—History and criticism. 3. Persuasion (Rhetoric)
4. Rhetoric, Ancient. 5. Literary form.　　I. Title. II. Series.
PA6357.C73　　　1993
875'.01—dc20　　　　　　　　　　　　　　　　93-4254
　　　　　　　　　　　　　　　　　　　　　　　　　CIP

Printed in the United States of America
on acid-free paper

for Ann

TABLE OF CONTENTS

Preface..ix

CHAPTER ONE: INTRODUCTION...1

CHAPTER TWO: *PRO ROSCIO AMERINO*...................................27

CHAPTER THREE: *DIVINATIO IN CAECILIUM*..........................47

CHAPTER FOUR: *PRO ROSCIO COMOEDO*..........................67

CHAPTER FIVE: *PRO SULLA*...89

CHAPTER SIX: *PRO CAELIO* 105

CHAPTER SEVEN: *PRO PLANCIO*..123

CHAPTER EIGHT: THE *SECOND PHILIPPIC*..........................147

CHAPTER NINE: SOME GENERALIZATIONS..........................169

APPENDIX ONE: DILEMMA FORMS IN CICERO ORATIONS.....181

ALPHABETIZED LIST OF DILEMMA FORMS
IN CICERO'S ORATIONS..211

TABLE OF CONTENTS

APPENDIX TWO: SYNTAX AND FUNCTION OF
DILEMMA FORMS IN CICERO'S ORATIONS...........................213

BIBLIOGRAPHY...219

GLOSSARY OF RHETORICAL AND LEGAL TERMS..................235

INDEX OF NAMES..239

INDEX OF PASSAGES CITED..245

Preface

Among his many achievements, Cicero is the greatest orator of Roman antiquity. The study of the ways in which he persuades began while he was still alive and has persisted, with more or less energy and penetration, for two millennia. Today, Cicero's speeches continue to engage students of persuasion, whether classicists, renaissance experts, or scholars in departments of Rhetoric and of Speech Communication.

Yet there is an important question about Ciceronian persuasion that has not heretofore been fully addressed. Given that a large part of the orator's audience shared with him an education in the art of persuasion, how does Cicero use that common education, his audience's very knowledge of rhetoric, in order to influence their perceptions of his arguments?

The commentaries on the orations contain many observations about Cicero's persuasive use of his audience's rhetorically educated expectations in specific passages. But there has not yet been any attempt to approach this question in a systematic way. The purpose of this book is to offer such a systematic approach.

My method, set forth in the introductory chapter, is to select an argument form for which the ancient rhetorical tradition establishes very clear expectations, then to examine the ways in which Cicero, in his use of that form in specific orations, brings those expectations into play to persuade the rhetorically educated segment of his audience. While this method does finally generate a typology of uses, it has the benefit of insisting that statements about Ciceronian arguments must be grounded in the careful study of the contexts that surround them; there is no substitute for close reading.

I would stress that this work will certainly not be the definitive and final systematic treatment of the ways in which Cicero uses the expectations of his rhetorically educated audience in order to persuade them; I hope that it will be judged a sound beginning.

For this study I envision a primary audience of classicists, both specialists in Cicero and others. But some non-classicists may also find this approach of interest. I would especially hope that this project will be useful for our colleagues in departments of Rhetoric and of Speech Communication who are specialists in the history and in the theory of argumentation.

Since there are two different prospective audiences for this work, I should make clear exactly what I do and do not expect the reader to know. I assume that any reader of this study already knows who Cicero was, is at least generally familiar with the times in which he lived, and has read, in Latin or in English translation, the speeches that I discuss prior to reading my discussions of them. The reader will want to know that all dates are B.C.E. unless otherwise specified, and that all abbreviations of Latin works are those used in the *Oxford Latin Dictionary*. While the footnotes give titles of most periodicals in abbreviated form, generally following *l'Année Philologique*, all of these titles are given in their full form in the bibliography.

I do not assume a knowledge of Latin except for the Latin names of Cicero's works and the most basic traditional rhetorical vocabulary. With the exception of these most obvious terms (e.g, *exordium, argumentum*), I have translated in the text all Latin words and phrases that can be rendered easily and accurately in English. A brief glossary of rhetorical and legal terms (below pp. 235-238) translates terms which could not conveniently be brought into English in the body of the text. This glossary also further explains the most important Latin terms used, and repeats the definitions of English phrases that have been used in any special sense. For all extended Latin passages, I quote English translations. A list of the texts and translations quoted comprises the first section of the bibliography. For Cicero's works and the *Rhetorica ad Herennium*, translations are taken from editions in the *Loeb Classical Library* unless otherwise noted. The one exception is the *Philippics*, for which quotations are taken from the fine translation of Shackleton Bailey unless otherwise noted. In several cases a minor adjustment of a *Loeb* translation has been necessary. On rare occasion, when an English translation changes substantially the syntax of an important Latin text, I provide my own translation, marked as such. For texts other than Cicero's works and the *Rhetorica ad Herennium*, I specify the translation that I have used. In the absence of such a notice, the translation is my own. Largely for mechanical reasons, Greek texts are not given in the original but are quoted only in English translation.

In writing this book, I have become indebted to many scholars. While I cannot possibly acknowledge them all in this brief space, there are a few individuals whom I must thank *nominatim*. This project grew out of discussions with my mentor in all matters rhetorical, Professor George A. Kennedy. The work has profited both from his initial interest and from his subsequent insights. Professor Michael C. Leff introduced me to works on persuasion that classicists usually do not read. Professor Thomas Heffernan helped to shape the initial presentation of my approach. Professor Harold C. Gotoff read an earlier draft of chapters one, two, six and eight, and made them better. Dr Jon Hall revealed to me several misleading obscurities in the introduction. Professor Joseph J. Hughes read critically chapter eight, and provided valuable suggestions. Professor John T. Kirby read an earlier draft of the whole with a jeweller's eye, and saved me from many errors both of content and of presentation. Finally, the reports of the two referees for the Association were excellent. From very different perspectives, both of these scholars revealed remarkable learning and lavished exquisite care on a task that is usually both anonymous and thankless. I have since learned their identities, and must acknowledge a special debt to Professors Jane W. Crawford and Ann Vasaly.

I hope that this distinguished and generous group of scholars will be happy to see how many of their suggestions I have incorporated. More fervently, I hope that they will not be saddened that I have persisted in so many disagreements. Whatever errors and infelicities remain are my sole responsibility.

I must also thank the Association's editorial board for monographs, and especially the series editor, Professor (now Dean) Matthew Santirocco has been a model of efficiency and patience. Mr. Dennis Ford of Scholars Press has given impeccable technical advice. My colleague Professor

James E. Shelton has demonstrated remarkable generosity by proofreading every Latin and English word of the final text with his customary care.

I am indebted as well to many other members of the University of Tennessee community. All of my colleagues in the Classics Department have been uniformly supportive of this work in ways both intellectual and personal. My fellow charter members of the University Studies interdisciplinary faculty colloquy on rhetoric ("the IDCOR") have helped me to understand the place both of Cicero and of this project in the larger landscape of rhetorical studies. The Graduate School of the University of Tennessee, Knoxville, generously provided a Professional Leave Award in 1989-90 that allowed time to place this work on a firm foundation. Ms. Nancy Laemlein and the rest of the staff of the Interlibrary Services section of the Hodges Library have provided invaluable service. Mrs. Bobbie Owenby, our departmental secretary, typed the tables for the second appendix, and cheerfully accommodated my lengthy stays before her computer while I grappled with the mysteries of camera-ready copy.

In a broader sense, I must thank my fifteen-month-old daughter Sarah for continually exploring with me both the art of persuasion and the limits of argument. Finally, Ann Robinson-Craig, my wife, has for ten years placed me in a debt that no words can properly acknowledge and no action can requite. I dedicate this book to her.

C.P.C.
Knoxville
March, 1993

CHAPTER ONE: INTRODUCTION

Cicero's *De Inventione* is rightly considered a virtual textbook of an important part of the Hellenistic rhetorical theory to which an educated Roman of the early first century B.C.E. would be exposed.[1] While we cannot measure what portion of the audiences for Cicero's speeches was composed of such educated Romans, we can be confident that that portion will have included many members of the juries who decided Cicero's legal cases, and many members of the senate who heard his deliberative speeches. For this important group of educated Romans, the young Cicero's full treatment of the "reasoned discovery of the sorts of true or apparent factors that render a case probable"[2] is a valuable indication of the types of arguments that an orator is expected to choose. Scholars of Ciceronian persuasion regularly use it for just that purpose.

But there is a kindred aspect of the teaching embodied in *De Inventione* that is equally useful, and virtually unexplored. It is striking that Cicero, while he provides an abundance of *loci*, or patterns, from which individual arguments may be drawn,[3] also speaks of several forms

---

[1] Cf. S.F. Bonner, *Education in Ancient Rome* (Berkeley: University of California Press, 1977) 68-69; George A. Kennedy, *The Art of Rhetoric in the Roman World* (Princeton: Princeton University Press, 1972) 114-38. Citations and translations from *De Inventione* are from the *Loeb* edition of H.M. Hubbell, *Cicero II: De Inventione, De Optimo Genere Oratorum, Topica* (Cambridge, MA: Harvard University Press, 1949, reprinted 1976.)
[2] *Inv.* 1.9: Inventio est excogitatio rerum verarum aut veri similium quae causam probabilem reddant.
[3] For the influences on *De Inventione*, see Kennedy (above, n.1) 103-106, 126-138.
  Cicero indiscriminately mixes different notions of the *loci* from which individual arguments are drawn. Empirically, one can differentiate two broad types of *locus*: First is the *locus* with some general content that gives rise to appropriate arguments for certain circumstances. In the Hermagorean scheme, for example, the *constitutio*

that are not concerned with finding individual arguments at all. In a way that we would associate with style rather than with invention, Cicero prescribes procedural or syntactical forms in which arguments may be *presented* in the most forceful or polished manner. For irrefutable arguments, these forms are the dilemma, enumeration, and simple conclusion. For arguments both necessary and probable, stylistic embellishment may be achieved through reasoning by analogy and forms that derive from the rhetorical syllogism.[4]

---

coniecturalis requires *loci* of prescribed general content concerning motive, character, and the act itself (*Inv.* 2. 16-51; cf. the *loci ex persona* and *ex negotio*, *Inv.*1. 34-43). The speaker need only tailor these *loci* of generalized content to his specific task.

The other broad type of *locus* is that of the certain form or procedure that will yield apposite arguments. For example, the entire status of definition is taken up with a procedure, the defining of the nature of the act itself (*Inv.* 1.11; 2.52-56). Another example is the treatment of *adiunctum negotio* with the completely formal topics of the more and the less, of contraries, negatives, genus, species and result at *Inv.* 1.41. This approach approximates the Aristotelian use of *topoi* which we see, *mutatis mutandis*, in *De Orat.* 2.162-173 and in Cicero's *Topica*, where *loci* are no longer content-specific, but have become the *sedes argumentorum* (*Top.* 8) in the sense of formal patterns. For what little we know of the history of the initially Aristotelian redefinition of topics as formal, see F. Solmsen, "The Aristotelian Tradition in Ancient Rhetoric," *AJP* 62 (1941) 36-50, 169-190, pp. 40-41, 172-73.

It is important to note that these *loci*, whether of generalized content or abstracted form, are prescribed patterns for *finding* arguments, not for *presenting* them. In this sense, they are fundamentally different from the argument forms discussed below.

[4] For dilemma, *Inv.* 1.44-45 ("*complexio*") 79, 83-84 ("*comprehensio*"); *Rhet. Her.* 2.38 ("*duplex conclusio*"), cf. 4.52 ("*divisio*"). For *enumeratio*, *Inv.* 1.44-45, 79, 84-85; *Rhet. Her.* 2.33-34. For *simplex conclusio*, *Inv.* 1.44-45, 79, 86. For stylistic embellishment of arguments both necessary and probable, *Inv.* 1.50. For reasoning by analogy ("*inductio*"), *Inv.* 1.51-56; (cf. "*similitudo*," *Top.* 41-45). For forms that derive from the rhetorical syllogism, *Inv.* 1.57-77 ("*ratiocinatio*"); cf. *Rhet. Her.* 2.28-30; cf. *Top.* 53-57).

With the *inductio* and *ratiocinatio*, Cicero forcefully emphasizes his primary concern with style: "Nam argumentatio nomine uno res duas significat, ideo quod et inventum aliquam in rem probabile aut necessarium argumentatio vocatur et eius inventi artificiosa expolitio....Nos autem de expolitionis partibus loquimur. (*Inv.* 1.74-75) ["For the one word 'argument' has two meanings, because a thought on any matter that is either probable or certain is called an argument, and the same term is applied to the artistic embellishment of this thought....But we are talking about the methods of embellishment."]

H.M. Hubbell (above, n.1) p.90 and n.a, gives the mistaken impression that Cicero, at *Inv.* 1.79ff, treats as stylistic features the various arguments from probability. Cicero says of his types of probability arguments, "Horum exempla et descriptiones in praeceptis elocutionis cognoscentur." (*Inv.* 1.49) [Instances and descriptions of these will be given with the rules for style.] Hubbell takes this as a reference to the discussion of the various probability arguments in Cicero's discussion of refutation at *Inv.* 1.79ff. But this treatment contains no rules for style for these arguments. Cicero,

INTRODUCTION

I propose to examine the uses in Ciceronian oratory of one of these presentational argument forms, the dilemma, with an eye to the following questions: How does Cicero use highly recognizable argument forms to emphasize strong arguments and to mask weak ones? What effects does the orator achieve by deploying these ostentatious argument forms within longer lines of argument? How can these argument forms advance the entire persuasive strategy of an individual speech? In short, how does Cicero manipulate his audience through the use of presentational argument forms?

I want to ask these questions because their answers can shed important light on the larger question of how Cicero persuades, and because they have not heretofore been pursued in any systematic way.

To make clear exactly what I hope to accomplish, it will first be useful to make explicit the relationship of this work to the major trends in the scholarship on Ciceronian persuasion. The rest of this introductory chapter will then briefly explain my choice of dilemma over other argument forms as a primary focus, and locate this argument form in the rhetorical and oratorical heritage that Cicero shared with his peers.

I

C.J. Classen, in his 1982 essay "Ciceros Kunst der Überredung," enumerates three approaches to understanding Ciceronian oratory as persuasive art:[5] 1) We may examine each speech in terms of its unique situation, including specific legal aspects, political ramifications, and the public opinion of the time. 2) We may detail the extent to which Cicero's practice corresponds with rhetorical theory by collecting examples from the speeches that reflect the precepts of the handbooks or the traditional techniques of oratorical practice.[6] 3) We may notice tactics that Cicero uses repeatedly in the speeches without trying to connect these tactics with rhetorical theory.

---

at *Inv.* 1.49, is surely looking forward to treating probability arguments in a future general treatment of *elocutio* (cf. *Inv.* 1.9), a treatment that in fact he was not to write.

[5] C.J. Classen, "Ciceros Kunst der Überredung," in W. Ludwig, ed., *Rhétorique et Éloquence chez Cicéron, Fondation Hardt Entretiens*, vol. 28, (Vandoeuvres-Genève: Fondation Hardt, 1982) 149-184, 149-150.

[6] That Classen would include in this approach the charting of correspondences between Cicero's practice and earlier oratory I infer from his p. 149, n.2, citing R. Preiswerk, *De Inventione Orationum Ciceronianarum*, (Basel diss., 1905). Preiswerk's work is concerned to find in Cicero's works the conventional *loci* of Roman practice.

The first approach justly lies at the base of most modern work on Ciceronian persuasion. Scholars with a variety of agendas take an exposition of the unique circumstances of each *causa* as the key to understanding Cicero's persuasive strategies. This concentration on the individual *causa*, already occasionally emphasized,[7] was canonized by Christoff Neumeister in his attempt to describe the real wellsprings of effective forensic oratory.[8] In the same vein, the essential work of W. Stroh[9] bases the understanding of Cicero's persuasive arrangement of arguments on the demands of the individual case. Classen's own work explicitly pursues the understanding of Ciceronian persuasion through the careful study of individual speeches in their unique circumstances.[10] Most recently, J.M. May[11] structures his discussion of the development of Ciceronian ethical argumentation around an analysis of Cicero's response to the special circumstances of each of fifteen speeches. Generally, the analysis of arguments within the unique contexts of specific orations is the dominant thread in the current study of Ciceronian persuasion.

The second of Classen's categories, the collection of examples in Cicero's speeches of his adherence to rhetorical theory, has properly been subordinated to the concern for understanding the organic function of the individual speech. Certainly Hellenistic rhetorical theory informs Cicero's works.[12] Further, *loci* that are not reflected in Hellenistic theory, but that are part of the Roman tradition of public speaking, can usefully be noted in Cicero's speeches.[13] Finally, Cicero's acquaintance with the Attic orators

---

[7] Thus, e.g., R. Heinze's classic "Ciceros Rede Pro Caelio," *Hermes* 60 (1925) 193-258. Cf. C.J. Classen, *Recht-Rhetorik-Politik* (Darmstadt: Wissenschaftliche Buchgesellschaft, 1985) 9 and nn.20-21.
[8] Chr. Neumeister, *Grundsätze der forensischen Rhetorik gezeigt an Gerichtsreden Ciceros* (*Langue et parole, Sprach- und Literaturstrukturelle Studien*, 3), Munich: M. Hüber, 1964.
[9] W. Stroh, *Taxis und Taktik: die advokatische Dispositionskunst Ciceros Gerichtsreden* (Stuttgart: Teubner, 1975).
[10] C.J. Classen (above n.7).
[11] J.M. May, *Trials of Character: The Ethos of Ciceronian Eloquence* (London and Chapel Hill: University of North Carolina Press, 1988).
[12] F. Rohde, *Cicero quae de inventione praecepit quatenus secutus sit in orationibus generis iudicialis* (Koenigsberg diss., 1903), is the fullest catalogue of such correspondences.
[13] See esp. R. Preiswerk (above n.6). For traditional Roman *loci* of invective, see I. Opelt, *Die lateinischen Schimpfwörter und verwandte sprachliche Erscheinungen: Eine Typologie* (Heidelberg: Carl Winter, 1965); N.W. Merrill, *Cicero and Early Roman Invective* (U. of Cincinnati diss., 1975).

leaves perceptible marks in his work.[14] But the real interest for us as students of persuasion is in the ways in which the orator uses these elements creatively to attain a specific goal.[15] Most important is the fact that rhetorical teachings and traditions of Roman practice reveal the audience expectations that constrain Cicero, and that he can manipulate for his purpose. For this reason, one now seldom sees catalogues of Ciceronian correspondences to a list of rhetorical prescriptions.[16] Instead, useful observations about correspondence with rhetorical precepts and traditional practice are imported into discussions of the persuasive process in specific speeches.[17]

But there is still a place for catalogues, and this is Classen's third approach. Without regard to rhetorical theory, Classen makes a list of actual tactics that recur in Cicero's speeches, along with collections of the citations where they occur. This approach moves towards an empirically based general description of Ciceronian persuasive tactics. This general understanding is, implicitly or explicitly, a complementary and equally important goal of all those who attempt to understand the argumentation of individual speeches.

The study of presentational argument forms will both require and advance each of the three major approaches described by Classen. These approaches will be juxtaposed, and in a sense integrated, to yield a better understanding of the role of argument forms in Ciceronian persuasion.

First, in order to understand Cicero's use of argument forms both to express arguments and to create the appearance that these arguments are forceful, it will be necessary to treat these argument forms within the specific contexts of individual speeches where they occur. I have chosen six speeches that are rich in argument forms, interesting in themselves, and reflective of the four different periods in Cicero's oratorical career. These speeches are the *Divinatio in Caecilium, Pro Roscio Comoedo, Pro Sulla,*

---

[14] See esp. A. Weische, *Ciceros Nachahmung den Attischen Redner* (Heidelberg, 1972). See also C.W. Wooten, *Cicero's Philippics and Their Demosthenic Model: The Rhetoric of Crisis* (London and Chapel Hill, 1983), and the other works on the Demosthenic influence on Cicero cited at chapter eight, n.1 (below, p. 147).
[15] Cf. Classen, (1985) (above, n.7), 11-12.
[16] There are exceptions. See most recently B.P. Wallach, "Cicero's *Pro Archia* and the Topics," *RhM* 132 (1989) 313-331.
[17] See., e.g., A.D. Leeman, "The Technique of Persuasion in Cicero's Speech for Murena," in W. Ludwig, ed., *Rhétorique et Éloquence chez Cicéron, Fondation Hardt Entretiens*, vol. 28, (Vandoeuvres-Geneva: Fondation Hardt, 1982) 193-228, esp. 221-22 (on *status*), 224-25 (on *genus causae*), 207-215 (on the *contentio dignitatis*).

Pro Caelio, Pro Plancio, and the *second Philippic*. As a preliminary to treating these speeches, I will note in a more general way the forms and uses of presentational argument forms in Cicero's first criminal case, *Pro Roscio Amerino*. This will establish the tools and strategies available to Cicero near the beginning of his oratorical career. My treatment of *Pro Roscio Amerino*, together with the more detailed analyses of the other six speeches, will establish the unique contexts for Cicero's use of argument forms, and their role in individual lines of argument and persuasive processes.

Classen's second approach, documenting the correspondence of practice to rhetorical theory, is in one sense vitally important for this study. It is only through rhetorical theory that we may securely determine the argument forms that Cicero and his audience would take as markers of forceful reasoning. On the other hand, the fact that Cicero does use such forms, that his practice does correspond to rhetorical theory, is foundational rather than final. Building upon this documented correspondence of practice with theory, we may then explore the ways in which Cicero deploys these forms, with the audience expectations that attach to them, to persuade in specific circumstances. Thus, despite the catalogue of examples of dilemma in the appendix, this study is not primarily concerned with the intervening step of documenting the correspondence of Cicero's practice to rhetorical theory, but with the ways in which the orator uses elements of rhetorical theory in actual persuasive processes.

Classen's third approach, the isolation of Cicero's recurring tactics, irrespective of the prescriptions of rhetorical theory, gives a model for the type of generalization that this work must attempt. In the conclusion, I will identify the use of dilemma with a set of empirically observed persuasive tactics. While these tactics may depend upon audience expectations grounded in rhetorical theory, Cicero uses these expectations to achieve effects that are not contemplated in the handbooks.

It is noteworthy that Classen divides the catalogue that exemplifies his third approach into persuasive tactics not only of invention and of arrangement, but also of style.[18] He makes the important point that word choice and simple repetition can establish themes and tone that function independently of the substance of a case, and create a climate in which the

---

[18] Classen (1982) (above, n.5), 177-183.

audience is more easily persuaded.[19] Classen further shows how two syntactical forms, exclamations and questions, are integral to one of Cicero's tactics for confusing his audience about the thoroughness and reliability of his account of events.[20] The point I want to underscore is the unsurprising one that style, in the sense of word choice and syntactic forms, with their repetitions and internal variations, has a vital role in the persuasive process.[21] There is a real sense in which form not only reinforces content, but actually becomes co-equal with content in effecting persuasion. In this sense, form *is* argument.

Given that form, in the sense of word choice, syntax, repetition and variation, can constitute a type of extra-rational argument, the recognized presentational forms of argument in classical rhetorical theory take on a different value. Of course they have a certain mechanical validity which both speaker and audience will find compelling. But they also function as discrete, recognizable verbal or syntactic patterns that create certain effects. Argument forms thus can be used in the same way that individual words or other syntactical patterns are used, to create extra-rational persuasive effects within the context of an individual discourse. An argument form, then, may express the mechanical relationship of its

---

[19] Classen (1982) (above, n.5), 180: Sie (sc. die Sprache) wird zum grundlegenden Element der rhetorischen Strategie, die sich unabhängig von den Sachproblemen auf Wörter mit hohem emotionalen Gehalt stützt und diese in psychologisch überlegter und wirksamer Form verwendet, d.h. gern frühzeitig, aber nicht immer gleich betont, einführt und dann haüfig wieder verwendet und ihnen damit den Character des Selbstverstandlichen, Natürlichen, Angemessenen gibt, um das subjective, wertende, polemische Element nicht spürbar werden zu lassen.
[20] Classen (1982) (above n.5) 181-2 and 167.
[21] Thus Classen devotes a chapter (pp. 120-179) of *Recht-Rhetorik-Politik* (above, n.7) to the ways in which style reinforces invention and arrangement in the speech for Murena. The study of the relationship of style to persuasive goal has seldom been systematically undertaken, despite an enormous body of work on Cicero's style (for which see the fine survey of M. von Albrecht, "M.T. Cicero, Stil und Sprache," *RE* Supplementband 13 (Munich, 1973) cols 1237-1347, with lit.) A notable exception is J. Axer, *The Style and Composition of Cicero's Speech Pro Q. Roscio Comoedo* (Warsaw: Wydawnictwa Uniwersytetu Warsawskiego, 1980). Commentators regularly make occasional observations about the interrelation of style and content. Among these, the unique stylistic commentary of H.C. Gotoff, *Cicero's Elegant Style: An Analysis of the Pro Archia* (Urbana: University of Illinois Press, 1979), provides an abundance of such observations; Lacey's commentary on the *Second Philippic* (Warminster: Aris & Phillips, 1986) consistently emphasizes the ways in which language reinforces sense; similarly, F.P. Donnelly's wonderful Jesuit school commentaries on *Pro Milone* (New York: Bruce, 1935) and *Pro Lege Manilia* (New York; Fordham University Press, 1939) have many careful observations about the interrelation of style and argument.

contents, and in that sense it is the culmination of the process of invention of arguments. But the same argument form, if recognized as presentational, can give by the very fact of its use or repetition the extra-rational impression of forceful argument. This impression is a means of persuasion grounded in style. It is exactly this double and simultaneous persuasive function of argument forms that I want to examine.

This inquiry is then a logical extension of current work on Ciceronian persuasion. The time has come systematically to view the role in actual Ciceronian persuasive processes of the rhetorically sanctioned presentational argument forms that the orator and the educated members of his audience would have in common.

II

But why focus upon dilemma? Since the types of argument forms that Cicero describes in his rhetorical works and uses in his speeches are quite diverse, considerations of time and space made it prudent to impose some limit upon this study. The wisest course seemed to be to concentrate upon one argument form. For the sake of clarity, that chosen form should meet these criteria: It should be highly recognizable, unambiguous, and common. By highly recognizable I mean simply that Cicero's original audience and we would all know it when we heard it. By unambiguous, I mean that the argument form must permit consensus about its constituent elements, including any implicit assumptions on which it is based.

These unexceptionable criteria quickly narrow the possibilities. Syllogistic forms, the *ratiocinatio* that Cicero discusses as a form of embellishment of argument (*Inv.* 1.57-77), supplemented by his mature treatment of the forms of syllogistic arguments at *Topica* 53-57, fall prey to ambiguity. Aristotle himself had already pointed out that his enthymeme, or rhetorical syllogism (*Rhet.*1.1. 1355a3-14), will often have a term suppressed, since long and explicit chains of reasoning were inappropriate for the usual audience of public speaking (*Rhet.* 1.1.1357a1-4; 2.22.1395b21-27). In this tradition, Cicero records the debate concerning which of the five parts of his *ratiocinatio*, major and its "proof," minor and its "proof," and conclusion, may be suppressed; in practice, Ciceronian argumentation makes little use of the full *ratiocinatio*, and is seldom systematically and explicitly syllogistic.[22] Supplying implicit terms

---

[22] How greatly the expectations for rhetorical argument forms in Cicero's time diverged from the syllogistic may be seen in the treatment of the five-part argument at

is then a purely subjective exercise, and one can seldom be confident of achieving consensus. Equally problematic, for one who will supply suppressed premises, every argument can potentially be viewed as syllogistic. This leads away from the analysis of the role of highly recognizable, unambiguous argument forms in persuasion and back to a broader model for the criticism of arguments based upon their formal validity in syllogistic terms. Whether such criticism is appropriate for Ciceronian argumentation is an open question.[23] In any case, syllogistic forms provide a poor purchase to begin the present study.

Inductio, or argument by analogy, also presents problems. The form that Cicero describes in *Inv.* 1.51-56 is not simply induction, nor analogy of one case with another, nor is it apparently the drawing of conclusions from historical examples. As a presentational form, this *inductio* seems to involve assertion of at least two propositions as preface to a final proposition that holds true by analogy, and that attacks or refutes the opponent. This form is cumbersome enough to make it too uncommon for our purpose.[24]

There remains *Inv.* 1.44-45, where Cicero discusses the most forceful ways of expressing irrefutable arguments:

> Necessarie demonstrantur ea quae aliter ac dicuntur nec fieri nec probari possunt, hoc modo: "Si peperit, cum viro concubuit." Hoc genus argumentandi, quod in necessaria demonstratione versatur, maxime tractatur in dicendo aut per complexionem aut per enumerationem aut per simplicem conclusionem. (45) Complexio est in qua, utrum concesseris, reprehenditur, ad hunc modum: "Si improbus est, cur uteris? si probus, cur accusas?" Enumeratio est in qua pluribus rebus expositis et ceteris infirmatis una reliqua necessario confirmatur, hoc pacto: "Necesse est aut inimicitiarum causa ab hoc esse occisum aut metus aut spei aut alicuius

---

Rhet. Her. 2.28-30. For the fate of Aristotle's enthymeme in the later rhetorical tradition, see esp. F. Solmsen, "The Aristotelian Tradition in Ancient Rhetoric," *AJP* 62 (1941) 36-50, 169-190, pp. 39-42, 196-78. See also W. Kroll, "Das Epicheirema," *Sitz. der Wissenschaftlichen Akademie in Wien, phil.-hist. Klasse*, 116.2 (1935) 4-28.

Preiswerk (above, n.6), 101-106, attempts to catalogue instances of *ratiocinatio* in Cicero's speeches.

[23] An attempt to view the speeches in this way is C.P. Craig, *The Role of Rational Argumentation in Selected Judicial Speeches of Cicero*, U. of North Carolina diss, 1979. On the other side, I find compelling the argument of Stephen Toulmin, *The Uses of Argument* (Cambridge: Cambridge University Press, 1958), that the analytical, syllogistic model is inappropriate to analyze most everyday arguments. Whether Toulmin's own model is acceptable is another question. See the critique by C. A. Willard, *Argumentation and the Social Grounds of Knowledge* (Tuscaloosa: University of Alabama Press, 1983), esp. 146ff.

[24] Rohde (above n.12) 79, notes that he has found no examples of *inductio* in the judicial speeches.

amici gratia aut, si horum nihil est, ab hoc non esse occisum; nam sine causa maleficium susceptum non potest esse: si neque inimicitiae fuerunt nec metus ullus nec spes ex morte illius alicuius commodi neque ad amicum huius aliquem mors illius pertinebat, relinquitur igitur ut ab hoc non sit occisus." Simplex autem conclusio ex necessaria consecutione conficitur, hoc modo: "Si vos me istuc eo tempore fecisse dicitis, ego autem eo ipso tempore trans mare fui, relinquitur ut id quod dicitis non modo non fecerim, sed ne potuerim quidem facere." Atque hoc diligenter oportebit videre, ne quo pacto genus refelli possit, ut ne confirmatio modum in se argumentationis solum habeat et quandam similitudinem necessariae conclusionis, verum ipsa argumentatio ex necessaria ratione consistat.

Those things are proved irrefutably which cannot happen or be proved otherwise than as stated; for example, "If she has borne a child, she has lain with a man." This style of argument which is used for rigorous proof, generally in speaking takes the form of a dilemma, or of an enumeration or of a simple inference. A dilemma is a form of argument in which you are refuted, whichever alternative you grant, after this fashion: "If he is a scoundrel, why are you intimate with him? If he is an honest man, why accuse him?" Enumeration is a form of argument in which several possibliities are stated, and when all but one have been disproved, this one is irrefutably demonstrated; the following is an example: "He must have been killed by the defendant either because of his enmity to him, or through fear or hope or to gratify a friend; if none of these statements is true, he cannot have been killed by the defendant. For a crime cannot be committed without a motive. If there was no enmity, and no fear, and no hope of any advantages from his death and his death was of no interest to any friend of the defendant, it therefore follows that the defendant did not kill him." A simple inference arises from a necessary consequence, as follows: "If you say that I did this at that time, but at that particular time I was overseas, it follows that I not only did not do what you say, but that I was not even in a position to do it." And it will be necessary to keep a sharp watch that this kind of argument cannot be refuted in any way, so that the proof may not contain in itself only a form of argument and a mere appearance of a necessary conclusion, but rather that the argument may rest on rigorous reasoning.

Of these three argument forms, *simplex conclusio*, simple inference, is ubiquitous; if the orator is doing his job, every inference will seem simple. If one maintains that some inferences are not examples of *simplex conclusio*, the criteria again become purely subjective.[25] Thus ambiguity is again a problem. *Enumeratio*, on the other hand, is quite unambiguous, but is not very common.[26] The present *enumeratio* has now revealed disadvantages in the choice of every presentational argument form except

---

[25] Rohde (above n.12) 96-98, who attempts to limit the category, finds only 13 examples of *simplex conclusio* in the judicial speeches.
[26] Rohde (above n.12) 68-70, finds seven examples in the judicial speeches, and none in the speeches after Cicero's consulship.

one. *Complexio*, dilemma, is at once highly recognizable, unambiguous, and occurs more than eighty times in Cicero's speeches.[27] It thus seemed the most productive choice for a study of the use of presentational arguments.

III

For the sake of simplicity, I have adopted the Greek-derived English name for this device, dilemma. We will see that the name varies widely among Latin authors, and that the concept of the device itself requires some clarification. This is not to say that Cicero's example at *Inv.* 1.44-45 is not revealing; he uses this form for presenting irrefutable arguments with the special function of *ad hominem* attack, apparently against a prosecutor or a witness, arguing that the target's actions betray a lack of self-consistency. While this is a large amount of information, the discussion at *Inv.* 1.44-45 does not give a complete sense of the range of recognizable forms and uses that might be associated with dilemma. So it will be useful to locate this argument form in the traditions of ancient rhetorical theory and oratorical practice.

In extant rhetorical writings, dilemma first appears in Aristotle's *Rhetoric*. In his catalogue of the sources of the premises for enthymemes, Aristotle gives this example of an argument from opposite consequences (*Rhet.* 2.23.1399a19-29):[28]

> For example, a priestess did not allow her son to engage in public debate: "for," she said, "if you say what is just, the people will hate you; but if what is unjust, the gods will." [She then continued:] "You should then engage in public debate; for if you speak what is just, the gods will love you, if what is unjust, the people will." This is the same as what is said about buying the marsh with the salt. This "twist" occurs whenever good and evil follow either of two opposites.

Then, further on, at *Rhet.*2.23.1400b5-8, dilemma serves as the example of a different topic:

> Another, when something is about to be done that is contrary to what has been done, is to look at them together [*hama skopein*]. For example, when the people of Elea asked Xenophanes if they should sacrifice and sing dirges to Leucothea or not, he advised them not to sing dirges if they regarded her as a god, and if as a human being not to sacrifice.

---

[27] A full list of citations will be found in the appendix. Rohde (above n.12) 70-76, lists forty examples, of which two (*Div. Caec.*, 17; *Clu.*, 64) are not dilemmas at all.
[28] Translations of Aristotle are those of George A. Kennedy, *Aristotle on Rhetoric: A Theory of Civic Discourse* (New York: Oxford University Press, 1991).

In both these examples, Aristotle is establishing general *topoi* that give rise to enthymemes. Although each of his enthymemes takes the form of dilemma, he has no name for the device. The nature of Aristotle's examples is revealing. While the story of the priestess and her son may be one that he has invented, it has the sound of a well known tale. In any case, Aristotle's second example is simply ascribed to Xenophanes, and clearly had a currency that was not confined to oratory. Dilemma (and perhaps one type of retort to dilemma) then occurs as an argument form in non-oratorical contexts, and is memorable enough that Aristotle can cite it in illustration of the *topoi* he formulates, and thus bring it into formal rhetoric. Still, the two *topoi* are quite distinct arguments in deliberative oratory.[29] One concerns a future choice between two courses of action, the other the choice to commit a future act that contradicts past actions. The first depends upon the unevenness of external circumstances, the second on a lack of consistency in the attitudes of the target, viz. the people of Elea. While dilemma will do to illustrate both, Aristotle does not discuss the defining qualities of the device.

Dilemma next appears in the rhetorical literature in the Hellenistic rhetorics of the early first century B.C.E.. In *De Inventione* 1.44-45, as we have seen (pp. 9-10 above), it is treated as a form in which irrefutable conclusions can be cast as *ad hominem* argument underscoring the inconsistency of the target's actions in a judicial context. The emphasis on the judicial context is of course characteristic of Hellenistic rhetorics. The naming of the device, *complexio*, and its association with irrefutable argument are new. In *De Inventione*, dilemma has become completely conceptualized. The importance of the irrefutable quality of a true dilemma is underscored when the young Cicero later explains the means of refuting a flawed dilemma, one that does not depend upon an irrefutable conclusion (*Inv.* 1.83-84):

> Quae vero sicuti necessaria dicentur, ea si forte imitabuntur modo necessariam argumentationem neque erunt eiusmodi, sic reprehendentur: primum comprehensio (= dilemma) quae utrum concesseris debet tollere, si vera est, nunquam reprehendetur; sin falsa, duobus modis, aut conversione aut alterius partis infirmatione; conversione, hoc modo:
>
> Nam si veretur quid eum accuses qui est probus?
> Sin inverecundum animi ingenium possidet,
> Quid autem accuses qui id parvi auditum aestimet?

---

[29] Cf. G.P. Palmer, *The Topoi of Aristotle's Rhetoric as Exemplified in the Orators* (University of Chicago diss., 1934), esp. 44-49, 76-77.

INTRODUCTION 13

Hic, sive vereri dixeris sive non vereri, concedendum hoc putat ut neges esse accusandum. Quod conversione sic reprehendetur: "Immo vero accusandus est. Nam si veretur, accuses, non enim parvi auditum aestimabit. Sin inverecundum animi ingenium possidet, tamen accuses; non enim probus est." Alterius autem partis infirmatione hoc modo reprehendetur: Verum si veretur, accusatione tua correctus ab errato recedet."

Statements which are made with the implication that they are necessarily true can be attacked in the following way if they only imitate a rigorous argument and are not really such: in the first place the dilemma, which ought to be a decisive argument no matter which alternative you choose, if it is true, can never be answered, but if it is false, it can be answered in two ways, either by conversion or by denial of one part: by conversion in this way: "For if the man is modest, why should you attack so good a man? And if the temper of his mind be shameless, then what avails your accusation of one who recks little of such a charge?" Here it is expected that whether you say he is modest or not, you will have to grant that you should not accuse him. This can be answered by conversion thus: "On the contrary, he ought most certainly to be accused. For if he is modest you should accuse him, for he will not reck little of such a charge. But if the temper of his mind be shameless, you still should accuse him, for he is not an upright man." It can be answered by denial of one alternative, as follows: "But if he is modest, he will be reformed by your accusation and abandon the error of his way."

It is noteworthy that Cicero considers the true dilemma invincible. It is also noteworthy that the flawed dilemma that he offers here differs from the example at *Inv.* 1.44-45 in that it does not demonstrate the target's inconsistency. This example itself is taken not from oratory but from drama reflecting oratory.[30] We get a sense both of the popularity and of the highly recognizable nature of the device. Finally, dilemma, although burdened with different names, *complexio* in *Inv.* 1.44-45 and *comprehensio* here, is well enough conceptualized that Hellenistic rhetoric already prescribes two tactics for answering it. (The first of these, *conversio*, strongly resembles the procedure we saw in the first example in Aristotle's *Rhetoric* 2.23.1399a19-29.)[31]

---

[30] The fragment is anonymous. See E.H. Warmington's *Loeb* edition, *Remains of Old Latin*, 4 vols. (Harvard University Press, 1936), vol. 2, p. 614.
[31] While Cicero does not discuss dilemma in his other rhetorical works, he has Caesar place Crassus in a dilemma at the end of the second book of *De Oratore*. Crassus complains that Antonius has explained the matter of persuasion, and left him only the words. "Tum Caesar, 'si, quod difficilius est, id tibi reliquit, est nobis' inquit 'causa, cur te audire cupiamus; sin, quod facilius, tibi causa non est, cur recuses.'" (*De Orat.* 2. 367.) ["Then Caesar said, 'If he has left to you that which is more difficult, we have a reason to want to hear you. But if he has left to you that which is easier, you have no reason to refuse.'"] What more urbane way to urge a master orator to talk about oratory? It would have perhaps hurt Crassus' characterization, and would

The *Rhetorica ad Herennium*, contemporary with *De Inventione* and our first complete Hellenistic rhetoric,[32] also treats dilemma, but by yet another name, *duplex conclusio* (2.38). The anonymous author's rather elliptical discussion comes in his exposition of the faulty argumentation (*vitiosae argumentationes*, 2.31) of the third of the the five parts of his full rhetorical argument:

> In confirmatione rationis multa et vitanda in nostra et observanda in adversariorum oratione sunt vitia, proptereaque diligentius consideranda quod adcurata confirmatio rationis totam vehementissime conprobat argumentationem.
> Utuntur igitur studiosi in confirmanda ratione duplici conclusione (= dilemma), hoc modo:
>
> Iniuria abs te adficior indigna, pater;
> Nam si inprobum esse Cresphontem existimas,
> Cur me huic locabas nuptiis? Sin est probus,
> Cur talem invitam invitum cogis linquere?
>
> Quae hoc modo concludentur aut ex contrario convertentur aut ex simplici parte reprehendentur. Ex contrario, hoc modo:
>
> Nulla te indigna, nata, adficio iniuria.
> Si probus est, te locavi; sin est improbus
> Divortio te liberabo incommodis.
>
> Ex simplici parte reprehendetur si ex duplici conclusione alterutra pars diluitur, hoc modo:
>
> "Nam si inprobum esse Cresphontem existimas,
> Cur me huic locabas nuptiis?" "Duxi probum;
> Erravi; post cognovi, et fugio cognitum."
>
> Ergo reprehensio huiusmodi conclusionis duplex est; auctior illa superior, facilior haec posterior ad excogitandum. (*Rhet. Her.* 2.38-39)

> In the Proof of the Reason, there are many faults to be avoided in our discourse and also to be watched for in that of our adversaries. These must be considered the more carefully because an accurate Proof of the Reason supplies the most cogent support of the whole argument.
> Students in the rhetorical schools, therefore, in Proving the Reason, use a Dilemma, as follows: "You treat me, father, with undeserved wrong. For if you think Cresphontes wicked, why did you give me to him for wife? But if he is honourable, why do you force me to leave such a one

---

abruptly have halted the dialogue, had he replied, "If the task is more difficult, I may embarrass myself in front of my friends. If it is easier, I risk boring you with observations that require no great talent."

[32] See the admirable *Loeb* edition of Harry Caplan, *[Cicero] ad C. Herennium De Ratione Dicendi*, (Cambridge, MA: Harvard University Press, 1954); G. Kennedy (above n.1) 111-138, with lit.

against his will and mine? Such a Dilemma will either be reversed against the user or be rebutted in a single term. Reversed, as follows: "My daughter, I do not treat you with any undeserved wrong. If he is honourable, I have given him you in marriage; but if he is wicked, I shall by divorce free you from your ills." It will be a rebuttal in a single term if one or the other alternative is confuted, as follows: "You say: 'For if you think Cresphontes wicked, why did you give me to him for wife?' I thought him honourable. I erred. Too late I came to know him, and knowing him, I fly from him." Thus the rebuttal of a dilemma of this type is twofold: the first fuller, the second easier to invent.

From this account, it is clear that dilemma is considered a very strong argument form, appropriate to that part of the presentation that supplies the strongest support for the whole argument. The anonymous author takes issue not with the use of dilemma, but with the use of a faulty dilemma. We certainly cannot infer that the author believes that all dilemmas, whether sound or faulty, can be refuted in one of the two ways he details. So the treatment in the *Rhetorica ad Herennium* has much in common with that of the young Cicero. Despite the difference in the name of the device, the example shows it to be the same. And again, the example is taken from drama rather then from earlier Greek or Roman oratory.[33] Finally, like the dilemma at *Inv.* 1.44-45, this example attacks the inconsistency of the target's behavior, although it is in a familial rather than judicial context, and so is not an aggressive *ad hominem* attack.

It is however worth noting that the annoymous author's simpler strategy for refuting a dilemma differs from Cicero's in denying the validity of one of the alternate protases, rather than the validity of one of the alternate conclusions. This difference has an interesting consequence; using the author's form of simpler refutation, Cicero's own example of an irrefutable dilemma could conceivably be refuted. Thus "Si improbus est, cur uteris? si probus, cur accusas?" (*Inv.* 1.45) [If he is a scoundrel, why are you intimate with him? If an honest man, why do you accuse him?] might be answered in this way: "I thought that he was a good man, and so was intimate with him. I erred, and when I saw my error I accused him." This does not mean that Cicero, or the author of the *Rhetorica ad Herennium*, would see Cicero's example as a false or weak dilemma. But it does underscore that Cicero's true dilemma is irrefutable only because of the context, now lost to us, which would render such a refutation unviable. This is only to say that dilemma, like all other rhetorical arguments,

---

[33] For the origin of the anonymous author's example, see the note of Caplan (above n.32) *ad loc.*

derives its viability from its context. So a dilemma, however refutable *in vacuo*, may still carry with it the powerful impression of strong or even invincible argument, provided that the premises on which it is based are not, within the context of the oration, so obviously jarring, specious, or otherwise unacceptable to the audience that a refutation strategy will be invoked, and will then yield a useful result.

Finally, despite the difference in the form of the simpler refutation of dilemma, the differences in name, and the fact that Cicero's true dilemma is absolutely irrefutable, while the anonymous author does not properly discuss true dilemma, it is clear that both writers represent a tradition in which the device is well conceptualized, viewed as particularly appropriate to strong argument, and answerable by two particular tactics when it is faulty.

Interestingly, the author of the *Rhetorica ad Herennium* also uses dilemma forms as his first two examples of the stylistic figure *divisio*:

> Divisio est quae rem semovens ab re utramque absolvit ratione subiecta, hoc modo: "Cur ego nunc tibi quicquam obiciam? Si probus es, non meruisti; si improbus, non commovebere." Item: "Quid nunc ego de meis promeritis praedicem? Si meministis, obtundam; si obliti estis, cum re nihil egerim, quid est quod verbis proficere possim?" Item: "Duae res sunt quae possunt homines ad turpe compendium commovere: inopia atque avaritia. Te avarum in fraterna divisione cognovimus; inopem atque egentem nunc videmus. Qui potes igitur ostendere causam maleficii non fuisse?" (*Rhet. Her.* 4.52)
>
> Division separates the alternatives of a question and resolves each by means of a reason subjoined, as follows: "Why should I now reproach you in any way? If you are an upright man, you have not deserved reproach; if a wicked man, you will be unmoved." Again: "Why should I now boast of my deserts? If you remember them, I shall weary you; if you have forgotten them, I have been ineffective in action, and therefore what could I effect by words?" Again: "There are two things which can urge men to illicit gain: poverty and greed. That you were greedy in the division with your brother we know, that you are poor and destitute we now see. How, therefore, can you show that you nad no motive for the crime?"

Divisio does not mean dilemma, for the third example is not a dilemma at all. Still, the inclusion of dilemma forms under one of the figures of thought (*sententiarum exornationes*) shows that in Cicero's time an audience could be sensitive to the formal, stylistic dimension of such arguments. It is also noteworthy that both of the dilemma forms used to characterize *divisio* are not true dilemmas in that they do not seem to attack an opponent, but to give reasons for the speaker's failure to pursue a topic.

INTRODUCTION

Thus Hellenistic rhetoric teaches other uses for the form besides the presentation of forceful arguments.

It is worthwhile to follow dilemma through Quintilian, the great judge and summarizer of the rhetorical tradition. For Quintilian, dilemma has no special name, but is one type of *divisio*. Here, however, *divisio* is an argument form rather than a stylistic figure.[34] Quintilian's great virtue is that, while other authors have provided examples, he finally offers a succinct definition:

> Fit (sc. divisio) autem ex duobus, quorum necesse est <esse> alterum verum, eligendi adversario potestas. efficiturque ut utrum elegerit noceat. Facit hoc Cicero pro Oppio: 'Utrum, cum Cottam appetisset, an cum ipse sese conaretur occidere, telum e manibus ereptum est?' et pro Vareno: 'Optio vobis datur, utrum velitis casu illo itinere Varenum usum esse an huius persuasu et inductu.' Deinde utraque facit accusatori contraria. (Quintilian 5.10.69)
>
> Or we may give our opponent the choice between two alternatives of which one must necessarily be true, and as a result, whichever he chooses, he will damage his case. Cicero does this in the *pro Oppio*: "Was the weapon snatched from his hands when he had attacked Cotta, or when he was trying to commit suicide?" and in the *pro Vareno*: "You have a choice between two alternatives: either you must show that the choice of this route by Varenus was due to chance or that it was the result of this man's persuasion and inducement." He then shows that either admission tells against his opponent.[35]

It is important that every example that we have noted in earlier authors, except the overtly stylistic example at *Rhet. Her.* 4.52, conforms with Quintilian's definition. There are two choices, one must be valid, the opponent has the power to choose, and either choice hurts him. Since this type of *divisio* is clearly dilemma, the examples provide more information about how the ancients conceptualized the device. While both of Quintilian's examples are from speeches that are not preserved, and so can give us no context to understand any special function of the device, it is clear enough that both are couched in the form of alternative questions, direct or indirect. Now all the earlier examples in rhetorical writings are in the form of two alternative conditions: If p then x, but if q then y. In light of Quintilian's definition, and his examples from Cicero, we ought

---

[34] The third example of *divisio* at *Rhet. Her.* 4.52, which is clearly not a dilemma, could also be labelled *distributis subiecta oratio*, which Quintilian, 9.3.93, doubts is really a figure. Thus Quintilian seems to move the auctor's entire category of *divisio* from the realm of style to that of invention. Cf. Caplan's note on *Rhet. Her.* 4.52.

[35] I quote from the four-volume *Loeb* translation of H.E. Butler (Cambridge, MA: Harvard University Press, 1921, reprinted 1960).

also to include forms that meet the definition whether they are couched as alternative conditions or not.

A final Latin author who deserves mention is Servius. In his late fourth or early fifth century commentary on Vergil's *Aeneid*, he is the first to bring the word *dilemma* with an attendant definition into Latin.[36] He does so in order to characterize two arguments. The first is Creusa's appeal to Aeneas as he leaves his home to join in the fighting within Troy:

>   Si periturus abis, et nos rape in omnia tecum;
>   sin aliquam expertus sumptis spem ponis in armis,
>   hanc primum tutare domum. cui parvus Iulus,
>   cui pater et coniunx quondam tua dicta relinquor?
>   (*Aen.* 2.675-678)
>
> If you are going to die, take us, too, into all things with you; but if having learned something you place some hope in the taking up of weapons, first defend this home. to whom is little Iulus, to whom is your father, to whom am I, once called your wife, being left?

Servius comments, "argumentum dilemma, id est, conplexio, quae adversarium ab utraque parte concludit." ["The argument is a dilemma, that is a *complexio*, which shuts in the opponent from either side."]

While this definition is not as full as that offered by Quintilian in his discussion of *divisio*, example and definition together show that it is identical. So the device finally assumes in Latin the Greek-derived name that still serves in English.

Servius also cites one other dilemma, this one initially puzzling. As Pallas goes to meet his death against Turnus, he proclaims to his opponent:

>   'aut spoliis ego iam raptis laudabor opimis
>   aut leto insigni: sorti pater aequus utrique est.
>   tolle minas.' fatus medium procedit in aequor;
>   (*Aen.* 10.449-451)
>
> "I will now be praised either for the spoils taken from the enemy general or for my glorious death: my father is equal to either fate. Dispense with threats." Having spoken, he advances into the middle of the plain.

---

[36] *TLL*, s.v. "dilemma" lists only the two citations in Servius and one example at Jerome, *contra Rufinum*, 3,3, which dates to 402 C.E. Since Servius' work cannot be dated with precision, it is possible that Jerome first brought the word itself into the Roman alphabet. For the evidence on the dates, see M. Schanz (rev. C. Hosius), *Geschichte der Römischen Literatur*, five volumes (Munich: C.H. Beck, 1959 reprint of 1927 edition), volume 4, part 1, p. 174 (Servius) and p. 478 (*contra Rufinum*).

Servius comments, "dilemma argumentum, quod est ab utraque parte firmissimum et concludit adversarium." ["A dilemma argument, which is very strong in each of the two alternatives and shuts in the opponent."]

Another reader might take this argument as Pallas's attempt to muster his own courage, and would in any case question how it foils his opponent at all. But Servius' language, echoing his comment on the earlier passage, makes clear that he sees this argument as qualitatively like that at *Aen.* 2.675-678. He seems to think that Turnus wants Pallas to feel afraid, and that either choice that Pallas offers vitiates his opponent's goal. While this may not be the most satisfying response to the text, Servius' example, and his comment upon it, do not indicate a conception of the device that goes beyond Quintilian's definition.

Recurring to the Greek rhetorical tradition, we have no extant discussion of dilemma after Aristotle until perhaps the second century C.E. From that period, a treatise on invention has come down to us, incorrectly ascribed to Hermogenes.[37] This treatise contains a well considered treatment (*Inv.* 4.6),[38] with examples drawn from Demosthenes. It deserves full quotation:

> Dilemma, while it is a figure of speech, yet has the appearance of keenness and of truth. It is of this sort: whenever we ask the opponent two questions and are prepared to refute him concerning either. It is necessary that the questions be opposites of each other on the assumption that the opponent must certainly answer one or the other; if we should be able to refute both answers, it is fitting to ask in dilemma form, but if not, not to introduce the figure. For if one of the questions is easy for the opponent to answer, but difficult for you to refute, you will be completely beaten; for you ask either on the assumption that he will not be able to answer or so that, even if he should answer, you refute him; if he should vanquish you by answering, you yourself are to blame for the defeat. And indeed it is not necessary to ask simple questions, much less anything in dilemma form, except when the opponent does not have an answer, or when he is going to give an answer that is helpful to you; for generally the questioner asks as one confident in attaining victory by means of the question.
> An example of dilemma is, "Were you present when these things happened and did you join in the celebration, or were you not present?" [Cf. Demosthenes, *De Corona*, 217] For if the opponent says, "I was present and I joined in the celebration," the orator is prepared to say,

---

[37] On the problem of authorship, see H. Rabe's comments in the *praefatio* of his edition of Hermogenes (Stuttgart: Teubner, 1969 reprint of 1913 edition) VI-IX.

[38] Besides Pseudo-Hermogenes, L. Spengel, *Rhetores Graeci*, 3 vols. (Leipzig: Teubner, 1854-56) notes only two brief later mentions of the device, by Apsines (Spengel I.376.25), and by an anonymous author who quotes one of Pseudo-Hermogenes' examples (Spengel III.115.19).

> "How then do you accuse those with whom you joined in the celebration?" But if he says, "I was not present," he will answer him that "you deserve to be punished since you do not share in the good fortunes of the city." And again, "Did you know what was going to happen or not?" [Cf. Demosthenes, *De Corona*, 196] For if the opponent says, "I knew," he answers, "Why then did you not give a warning?" And if he says, "I did not know," "Why then do you accuse us for not knowing? For if you knew, you should have given a warning; but if you did not know, why do you accuse others for not knowing, since ignorance of the future is the common condition of all mankind?"
> Dilemmas indeed arise from two questions asked towards one conclusion, for example, "Whether you married a beautiful woman or an ugly woman, you should not have married." For one conclusion is derived from both, that one should not marry, because on the one hand a beautiful woman is promiscuous, while on the other hand an ugly woman is a punishment. And the common dilemmas are these. Or, whenever each of the questions requires its own apodosis, this too is styled a dilemma and is a Demosthenic figure.

In keeping with the presentational aspect of the device that we note in *Inv.* 1.44-45 and see clearly underscored at *Rhet. Her.* 4.52, Pseudo-Hermogenes treats *dilemmaton* simply as a figure of speech.[39] He recognizes the forms of alternative questions, each with its own answer, which he in fact calls a Demosthenic use of the device. This confirms Quintilian's earlier evidence on the Latin side that alternative questions are an appropriate form for dilemma. Since dilemma took this form in Demosthenes, and is conceived in this way not only in the Greek tradition but also by Quintilian, with examples from Cicero, it seems likely that dilemma was already conceived in the alternate question form by Cicero and his audiences.

The testimony of Pseudo-Hermogenes also clarifies Quintilian's definition in another way. The Greek rhetorician gives an example taken from *De Corona*, 217, in which Demosthenes addresses his opponent. In our text of *De Corona*, the passage is somewhat different:[40]

> I should like to ask Aeschines a question: when all that was going on, when the whole city was a scene of enthusiasm and rejoicing and thanksgiving, did he take part in the worship and festivity of the populace, or did he sit still at home, grieving and groaning and sulking over public successes? If he was present as one of the throng, surely his behaviour is scandalous and even sacrilegious, for after calling the gods to witness that certain measures were very good, he now asks a jury to vote that they

---

[39] Thus in the later Latin tradition, the fourth century rhetorician Victorinus, in his commentary on Cicero, *Inv.* 1.44-45, calls *complexio* a "forma dictionis." C. Halm, *Rhetores Latini Minores* (Leipzig: Teubner, 1863) p.233.11.

[40] I quote from the *Loeb* translation of C.A. and J.H. Vince (London: Heineman, 1926).

were very bad -- a jury that has sworn by the gods! If he was not present, he deserves many deaths for shrinking from a sight in which everyone else rejoiced. (Demosthenes, *De Corona*, 217)

One critical difference from Pseudo-Hermogenes' version is that here Demosthenes addresses the jury rather than Aeschines, explaining to them the dilemma in which he is placing his opponent. This narration to the audience of the opponent's two choices and their results, while conformable to Quintilian's definition, does not conform in one particular with any of the examples in the rhetorical literature. In all of those examples where the addressee is clear, the opposition is addressed directly.[41] So we might question whether an argument such as that in our text of *De Corona* 217 would be perceived as a dilemma by an ancient audience. One could argue that the fact that Pseudo-Hermogenes (or his source) recast this argument so that the opponent would be addressed directly may indicate that direct address was felt to be an essential feature of the device. On the other hand, it seems equally likely that Pseudo-Hermogenes (or his source) felt that this argument was a sufficiently striking example of dilemma to use it as one of his two examples of the Demosthenic form of the device. The recasting is then due to simplification for paedogogical purposes; Pseudo-Hermogenes not only cites but explains the argument. However one accounts for the recasting, the choice of this passage as an example would not have occurred if the original argument were not perceived as a dilemma.

On balance, the probability that the ancients would perceive *De Corona* 217 in its unchanged form as dilemma seems stronger; as long as the opponent is the target, the opponent need not be addressed directly for the ancient audience to perceive that a dilemma is being used.

Finally, it should be noted that Pseudo-Hermogenes also includes as dilemmas statements with compound protases and one apodosis. His example is this: "Whether you married a beautiful woman or an ugly woman, you ought not to have married." This use of alternative protases with a single apodosis is unparalleled among the examples in the rhetorical literature. There is a choice of mutually exclusive alternatives. Did the target marry a beautiful woman or an ugly woman? But it is not the case that one of the choices must be valid. It is an extreme position to hold that all women who are not beautiful are ugly. So Quintilian's definition is

---

[41] The examples from *pro Vareno* and *pro Oppio* at Quintilian 5.10.69 (above, p. 17) do not have sufficient context to indicate clearly whether the prosecution or the jury is being addressed.

technically not satisfied. Further, this form does not conform to any of the earlier examples in the rhetorical literature. So it is simply impossible to know whether Cicero's audience would conceive of this unparalleled form as a dilemma. Accordingly, caution must be exercised in citing arguments of this type to generalize about the role of the dilemma form as argument for Cicero and his initial listening and reading audiences.

As Quintilian (5.10.120-121) observes, the theoretical prescriptions of rhetoric are based upon the actual practice of earlier speakers. Dilemma appears in Greek oratory already in Andocides, and becomes a standard technique of conjoining proof or refutations with personal attack in the Attic orators.[42] While these attacks are largely conformable to the discussion in the later rhetorical tradition, I would extract three generalizable types that are ill matched to the examples in the handbooks, but that will prove important for Cicero's practice. Unlike the examples in *De Inventione* and the second book of the *Rhetorica ad Herennium*, some personal attacks in dilemma form need not focus upon the inconsistency of the target's behavior. They may instead simply postulate that the target is guilty of some inappropriate belief or action, then offer variant explanations for the target's axiomatically wrongful behavior. The earliest example of this type is Andocides 2.2-3:[43]

> "Indeed I am completely at a loss to understand why the question of your receiving a benefit from me should cause such excitement among our friends here. They must either be the most stupid of all mankind or the worst public enemies. If they hold that when the state is prospering they are better off individually, they are showing extreme stupidity in advocating to-day a policy which directly conflicts with their own interests; while if they do not identify their interests as individuals with yours as a community, they can only be public enemies.

The key difference between this type of dilemma and that at *Inv.* 1.45, for example, is that it does not focus upon an inconsistency of behavior, but builds both of its alternate conclusions on the same presumption, that the target is in the wrong. While this contribution of the

---

[42] I note these examples (Instances concerned with simple refutation rather than personal attack are in parentheses.): Andocides 2.2-3, (cf. 2.22); Lysias 13.75-76, (25.14); Isaeus 1.21, 6.58; Isocrates 11.42-43 [properly a dilemma that makes target offensive to audience], (15.94-96), 19.32, cf. 17.27-28; (Aeschines 2.163); Demosthenic corpus (16.30), (18.24), 139, 196, 217, (20.24), 102, 113, 145, 22.40-41 (*bis*), 62, 23.133-34, 24.122, 188-89, 25.38, 64-66, 26.14, (27.55), (29.47), 32.16, 37.8, 49.41, 51.16, 56.32, 58.12 & 45-47, cf. (4.18), 15.24 & 28; Hyperides, *For Euxenippus* 14-15, 17; Lycurgus, *Against Leocrates* 34, 63, 75-76.

[43] *Loeb* translation of K.J. Maidment, *Minor Attic Orators*, volume 1 (Cambridge, MA: Harvard University Press, 1941).

Greek practical tradition is not exemplified in the later rhetorical discussions, it certainly accords with Quintilian's definition, and clearly contributes to the understanding of the dilemma that Cicero and the best educated of his contemporaries would share.

The other two noteworthy Attic types do not conform to Quintilian's definition, but will still be important in Cicero's practice. The first of these is a narrative rather than a directly argumentative technique. The speaker tells of a dilemma in which the opponent found himself in the past, and so has no present choice. Thus Isocrates, in the *Trapeziticus*:[44]

> ...he understood that if he should deliver his slave to torture, he would be convicted of an act of rascality, and, on the other hand, if he failed to do so, he would lose his case; ... (17.27-28)

Finally, the speaker may narrate a dilemma in which he found himself in the past:[45]

> Owing to -- shall I say my own youthful folly, or the influence of others who persuaded me into such a piece of madness? -- I was luckless enough to be forced to choose between two of the most painful alternatives imaginable. On the one hand, I could refuse to disclose the authors of the outrage. In that case I not only trembled for my own fate, but caused the death of my father, who was entirely innocent, as well as my own -- he was inevitably doomed if I refused to speak. On the other hand, I could purchase my own life and liberty and avoid becoming my father's murderer -- and what would a man not bring himself to do to escape that? -- but only by turning informer.
>
> Of the alternatives before me, then, I chose that which meant years of sorrow for myself, but immediate release for you from the distress of the moment. (Andocides 2.7-8)

Such a self-professed dilemma, completely different in time, target, and function from the device defined by Quintilian, actually serves to justify the speaker's own past actions.[46]

Of the Roman tradition of eloquence before Cicero we know much less.[47] Among the sparse remains, there is only one example of dilemma. The younger of the famous Gracchi, C. Sempronius Gracchus, attacked P. Popillius Laenas (cos. 132) for his role in executing supporters of his older brother in 132. C. Gracchus passed a law that no one could be sentenced on a capital charge without the assent of the plebs, and charged Laenas

---

[44] *Loeb* translation of G. Norlin, *Isocrates*, 3 vols. (London: Heinemann, 1929).
[45] Trans. Maidment, above, n.43.
[46] Cf. also Antiphon, *Tetralogies* 1.beta.3; Isocrates 17.6 & 10.
[47] The remains of Roman republican oratory, excluding Cicero, are collected by Enrica Malcovati, *Oratorum Romanorum Fragmenta Liberae Rei Publicae*[4] (Torino: Paravia, 1976).

retroactively under this law. Our brief fragment apparently refers to this hard-won right of the plebs:[48]

> quae vos cupide per hosce annos adpetistis atque voluistis, ea si temere repudiaritis, abesse non potest quin aut olim cupide adpetisse aut' nunc temere repudiasse dicamini.

> If you rashly reject those things that you have eagerly sought and desired for all these years, it is unavoidable that you be said either to have once sought these things greedily or to have now rejected them rashly.

It is noteworthy that the immediate target of this dilemma form is not the opponent, but the audience itself. Further, C. Gracchus only places the audience in a dilemma in the future, in the event that they do not do as he urges. In this the argument does not conform with any of the examples in the rhetorical literature after Aristotle (the Xenophanes example at *Rhet.* 2.23.1400b5-8), nor with Quintilian's definition. Thus we cannot be confident that the ancients would perceive Gracchus' argument as a proper dilemma. Nonetheless, the dilemma form which takes the audience rather than the opponent as its target does have antecedents in the Attic orators,[49] and will be worth noting in Cicero.

C. Gracchus also provides a justly famous example of a "dilemma," in the sense of a personal predicament, that is not technically a dilemma at all. Cicero quotes with approval the younger Gracchus' emotionally charged exclamation: "Quo me conferam, quo vertam? In Capitoliumne? at fratris sanguine madet. An domum? matremne ut miseram lamentantem videam et abiectam?" ["Where shall I go? Where shall I turn? To the Capitol? But it is wet with my brother's blood. Or to my home? so that I may see my wretched mother weeping and prostrate?"] (*De Orat.* 3.214)[50] This exclamation, which can be traced back, *mutatis mutandis*, to Euripides' *Medea*, has been called the dilemma of C. Gracchus.[51] One notes immediately that Gracchus' plaint is very different from the example of dilemma at *Inv.* 1.44-45. There the device underscores irrefutable argument by confronting an opponent with mutually exclusive choices such that he must choose one and either choice hurts him. On the other hand,

---

[48] Quoted by Aulus Gellius, *NA* 11.13.1 = Malcovati (above n.47) p.184, no.32. A convenient discussion of the law is D. Stockton, *The Gracchi* (Oxford U.P., 1979) 117-26, with lit. For the speech, Stockton, 220 and P. Fraccaro, "Studi sull' eta dei Gracchi," *Studi Storici per l'Antichità Classica*, nuova serie 1, 42-136, esp. 88-97.
[49] Demosthenic Corpus 20.121, 23.43 & 195; Hyperides, *Against Philippides* 10; Cf. Lysias 15.8, 27.6.
[50] Malcovati (above n.47), p.196, no. 61.
[51] M. Bonnet, "Le Dilemme de C. Gracchus," *REA* 8 (1906) 40-46.

the target of Gracchus' "dilemma" is not an opponent, but Gracchus himself. His two choices, while powerfully pathetic, are not mutually exclusive in any logical sense; going to the Capitol does not preclude then going to his mother's home. Finally, he is not compelled to choose one or the other, since of course neither choice is considered as anything other than a vehicle for pathos. This pathetic, self-inflicted choice of emotionally charged alternatives that are neither mutually exclusive nor exhaustive is thus fundamentally different from Cicero's device.[52] While a famous example of cultured and effective pathos, it is not an example of that highly recognizable, unambiguous form of irrefutable argument that is our present concern.

To summarize: The presence of dilemma, under whatever name, in *De Inventione* and the *Rhetorica ad Herennium* indicates its status as a fixture of Hellenistic rhetorical teaching. That teaching was based on imitation, as well as theory and practice, and the device occurs in the Attic orators as well.[53] In short, dilemma is a device known to the educated Romans who were a crucial group within Cicero's primary listening and reading audiences. Their conception of the device can be reconstructed from the rhetorical tradition. Dilemma is the offering to the opponent (not necessarily in direct address) of two choices such that he must choose one or the other, and either choice hurts him. From the examples in the rhetorical literature, supported by examples in the Attic orators, we note that the situation that gives rise to the dilemma may be some fixed circumstance, some presumable error of the target, or a fundamental inconsistency in the target's behavior.[54] While the definition will accommodate any syntax that offers the two alternatives and their two results, the two syntactical patterns that seem most conformable with the

---

[52] Isocrates 14.46-7 is the only good parallel to Gracchus' pathetic "dilemma" in the Attic orators, and there the choices are at least exhaustive and mutually exclusive.
[53] It was common enough in the Greco-Roman educational tradition that in the next century it finds a place in the accounts of three of the four evangelists (Mt. 21.23-27; Mk. 11.27-33; Lk. 20.1-8).
[54] Aristotle's example at *Rhet.*2.23.1399a19-29 depends upon a fixed circumstance. "If you say what is just, men will hate you; if you say what is unjust, the gods will." In actual oratory, the fixed circumstance may be founded upon the opponent's ostensibly mistaken view or action, as at Antiphon 2.2-3. Cf. also Demosthenes 20.102; 22.40-41; 23.133-134; 24.122. The opponent's inconsistency is the basis of the examples at Aristotle *Rhet.* 2.23.1400b5-8; Cicero, *Inv.* 1.45; *Rhet. Her.* 2.38. In oratorical practice, cf. e.g., Demosthenes 26.14; C. Gracchus, Malcovati (above n.47), p.184, no.32.

ancient understanding of the device are alternate conditions and alternate questions, direct or indirect. Finally, to return to Cicero's *De Inventione*, we note that dilemma is apparently invincible, fundamentally presentational, and useful for *ad hominem* attacks.

We have also noted that there are examples in the practice of Cicero's Greek and Roman predecessors, and in at least one theoretical treatment of style, of dilemma forms that do not satisfy Quintilian's definition, but that are still clearly recognizable as dilemma structures. These other dilemma forms fail to meet Quintilian's definition in one of two ways. First, they may be directed at someone other than the opponent. So C. Gracchus could warn his audience not to fall into a dilemma. So also, at *Rhet. Her.* 4.52, the speaker finds that following a course of action, boasting, will place him in a dilemma.[55] More generally, a dilemma in which a speaker finds himself may serve as an excuse for an action, or for a failure to act (*Rhet. Her.* 4.52). Second, in the Attic orators, we find narration of a dilemma in which the opponent or some other target has found himself in the past.[56] These narrative dilemmas do not meet Quintilian's definition, since no present choice is offered to the opponent. Both of these types of dilemma form are obviously related to true dilemma and can make a strong impression in their own right; we will do well to examine them, as well as true dilemmas, if we are to understand the uses of this argument form in Ciceronian persuasion.

For the sake of clarity, we will use these terms: "Dilemma" and "true dilemma" conform in all regards with Quintilian's definition. "Dilemma structures" are not true dilemmas in that the target is not the opponent and/or the time frame is past and so permits no choice. These dilemma structures applied to the past we will also call "narrative dilemma." Finally, as a convenient phrase to include examples of both true dilemma and other dilemma structures, we will use simply "dilemma form."

Now let us investigate how Cicero actually uses this highly recognizable, presentational form of invincible argument, this common legacy of rhetorical education, to persuade in specific contexts.

---

[55] On rare occasion, an Attic orator finds himself in a dilemma as well: Antiphon 1.1; Isocrates 6.70, 14.46-47, 15.83; Demosthenes 18.4 and 27.53.
[56] Isocrates 17.27-28 (against opponent); Antiphon *Tetralogies* 1.beta.3 and Isocrates 17.6 & 10 (against speaker himself).

CHAPTER TWO: *PRO ROSCIO AMERINO*

Cicero's defense of Sex. Roscius of Ameria on a charge of parricide in 80 is the orator's first speech in a criminal proceeding.[1] Along with his civil plea *Pro Quinctio* of the year before, it is the earliest Ciceronian oration we have. Although dilemma forms are not frequent in either work,

---

[1] See R. Heinze, "Ciceros politische Anfänge" (1909) in *Vom Geist des Römertums*[3], ed. E. Burck (Darmstadt: Wissenschaftliche Buchgesellschaft, 1960), 87-140, esp. 98-103; J. Humbert, Les *plaidoyers écrits et les plaidoiries réelles de Cicéron*, (Paris: Presses Universitaires de France, n.d. [1925]) 100-111; W.B. Sedgwick, "Cicero's Conduct of the Case *Pro Roscio*," *CR* 48 (1934) 13; Solmsen, "Cicero's First Speeches: A Rhetorical Analysis," *TAPA* 69 (1938) 542-556; A. Afzelius, "Zwei Episoden aus dem Leben Ciceros," *C & M* 5 (1942) 209-217; E.S. Gruen, *Roman Politics and The Criminal Courts*, 149-78 B.C. (Cambridge, MA: Harvard University Press, 1968), 265-271; G.A. Kennedy, *The Art of Rhetoric in the Roman World* (Princeton: Princeton University Press, 1972), 151-154; W. Stroh, *Taxis und Taktik* (Stuttgart: Teubner, 1975), 55-79; V. Buchheit, "Chrysogonus als Tyrann in Ciceros Rede für Roscius aus Ameria," *Chiron* 5 (1975) 193-211; "Ciceros Kritik an Sulla in der Rede für Roscius aus Ameria, " *Historia* 24 (1975), 570-591; T.E. Kinsey, "A dilemma in the Pro Roscio Amerino," *Mnemosyne* 19 (1966) 270-271; "Cicero's speech for Roscius of Ameria," *Symbolae Osloenses* 50 (1975) 91-104; "Cicero's Cases against Magnus, Capito, and Chrysogonus in the *Pro Sex. Roscio Amerino* and Its Use for the Historian," *LAC* 49 (1980) 173-190; "A Problem in *Pro Roscio Amerino*," *Eranos* 79 (1981) 149-150; "The Case against Sextus Roscius of Ameria," *LAC* 54 (1985) 188-196; P.M. della Morte, *Studi su Cicerone Oratore, Studi e Testi dell' Antichità VIII*, Naples, Società Editrice Napolitana, 1977; A. Vasaly, "The Masks of Rhetoric: Cicero's *Pro Roscio Amerino*," *Rhetorica* 3 (1985) 1-20; J.M. May, *Trials of Character* (Chapel Hill and London: University of North Carolina Press, 1988), 21-31.

The most useful commentaries are G. Landgraf[2] (Leipzig and Berlin: B.G. Teubner, 1914, reprint Hildesheim: G. Olms, 1966); E. Osenbrüggen (Braunschweig: Vieweg, 1844); K. Halm[10], rev. G. Laubmann (Berlin: Weidmann, 1886); F. Richter and A. Fleckeisen[4] (Leipzig and Berlin: Teubner, 1906). The *Loeb* edition is that of J.H. Freese, New York: G.P. Putnam's Sons, 1930.

With the exception of the several articles by Kinsey, these works will hereafter be referenced by the authors' last names.

those in the speech for Roscius of Ameria are more plentiful, and so reveal more fully the range of presentational roles that arguments in dilemma form embody at the beginning of Cicero's oratorical career. Unlike the other six speeches which we will examine, *Pro Roscio Amerino* is useful primarily for its chronological position at the beginning of Cicero's speeches, and not for any remarkably frequent or integral use of dilemma forms to meet the special demands of the rhetorical challenge. So a highly detailed analysis of the argumentation will not be useful for our purpose. Rather it will suffice to examine the role of each use of the device within its immediate argumentative context. Still, in order to understand the roles of these dilemma forms in their individual contexts, it will be useful to establish the circumstances of the speech, the rhetorical challenge that Cicero must answer, and the general shape of the argumentation.

According to Cicero, these are the facts: A certain Roscius, a wealthy citizen of Ameria and an enthusiastic supporter of Sulla (15-16), was murdered in Rome (18). We are not told the date, but the murder will have happened after 1 June of 81 (128). The victim's fellow townsman T. Roscius Magnus was responsible for the murder, and immediately sent a messenger to Ameria to announce Roscius' death to his crony T. Roscius Capito (19, 96-98). Four days later, Magnus and Capito sent to Sulla's camp at Volaterrae to inform Chrysogonus, Sulla's powerful freedman, of Roscius' death. At the instigation of Magnus and Capito, and without Sulla's knowledge, Chrysogonus inserted the victim's name on the list of the proscribed so that his property could be auctioned (20-22, 105-107). Chrysogonus then purchased the estate, valued at some 6,000,000 sesterces, for the token sum of 2,000 sesterces (6, 21). He rewarded Capito with possession of three of the victim's farms, and compensated Magnus by making him his agent to administer the property (21, 108). Magnus then went to Ameria and evicted the victim's son, Cicero's client, from his home. The people of Ameria, who knew the victim as an enthusiastic supporter of the *nobiles*, were shocked at this apparent mistake. By a decree of their town council, they sent an embassy of ten leading citizens to Sulla at Volaterrae to explain that the elder Roscius should not have been among the proscribed (23-26). One of this party was Capito. Chrysogonus, aided by Capito, persuaded this delegation that he would correct the mistake and see that young Roscius' property was restored to him. Satisfied, the delegates naively returned home without ever seeing Sulla (26, 109-110). Chrysogonus and Magnus and Capito, after various delays, finally decided that the only way they could enjoy the property in peace was to kill the victim's son and heir (26). After they had tried in vain to kill him, the young Roscius fled to Rome, where he received help from a friend of the family, Caecilia (27). Chrysogonus and Magnus and Capito, unable to kill the young man themselves, hit upon the expedient of judicial murder. Acting through a paid prosecutor (55, 58), one C. Erucius, they had young Roscius charged with murdering his father. If found guilty, the young man would be killed, and Chrysogonus and company left to enjoy the property. The prosecution could be confident because this was the first murder trial in some time, and a conviction would signal a desirable return to normalcy after the civil war and the proscriptions. More important, Chrysogonus' interest in the case would seem to many to show Sulla's wish for a conviction (28-29a). This implication was strong enough that no one of the prominent *patroni* could be prevailed upon to defend Sex. Roscius (1-4). And so that role fell to the young Cicero.

The prosecution's version of events is understandably different.[2] Erucius argues that the elder Roscius and his son did not get along (40). The younger Roscius had a brother, since deceased, whom the father kept with him in Rome, while he relegated Cicero's client to the countryside around Ameria (42). The defendant, Erucius argued, believed that his father was going to disinherit him (52). So there was a strong motive for murder. There was also opportunity. Although Erucius does not seem to have maintained that the defendant was in Rome at the time of the murder, the crime took place during a violent period; a murder would have been simple enough to arrange (80). Finally, there were other indications of the defendant's criminal nature (82).

Erucius, while making clear that Chrysogonus favors the prosecution (132), does not mention that the elder Roscius had been placed among the proscribed, or that his property had been auctioned (5-6, 28).[3] Indeed, for the prosecutor to mention the alleged proscription of the elder Roscius

---

[2] For a fuller attempt to reconstruct the prosecution's arguments and the most extreme account of the possible weaknesses of Cicero's case, see Kinsey, "The Case Against Sextus Roscius." On those weaknesses, see also E. Lincke, "Zur Beweisführung Ciceros in der Rede für Sextus Roscius aus Ameria," *Commentationes Fleckeisenianae* 1 (1890) 187-98.

[3] Chrysogonus' own explanation of his behavior, supplied by the scholiast (p. 314 Stangl), will not have been mentioned in the course of the trial. See Kinsey, "Cicero's Speech for Roscius," 96-97.

would imply that the victim had been legally killed, and thus would vitiate the murder charge. To mention the sale of Roscius' property without admitting that the victim was among the proscribed would imply that the sale was illegal, and that the victim's property should be restored to the young Roscius. So the prosecution must proceed as if the alleged proscription and the sale of the elder Roscius' property had never transpired.

These strictures on the prosecution point to the most vexing problem of the speech. Why do Chrysogonus and company construct a situation that is bound to hurt them? They leave Cicero two choices regarding the question of whether the elder Roscius had been proscribed. The orator can argue that the victim had been legally considered among the proscribed, and thus demolish the legal ground for a murder charge. On the other hand, Cicero can accept the position of the prosecution that there is no notion that the victim was among the proscribed, and that a murder has been committed. But the contention that the elder Roscius was murdered, not legally killed, means that his property could not legally have been auctioned, and thus Chrysogonus and his cronies have in effect stolen the defendant's inheritance. So the prosecution leaves Cicero with a choice that either vitiates the accusation or demonstrates that those behind it have acted illegally and rapaciously.[4]

The simplest explanation for this apparent stupidity is that Chrysogonus and company genuinely believed that intimidation would prevail; the defense would not dare to mention the fact that Chrysogonus was in possession of the victim's estate, indeed would not dare to criticize Chrysogonus at all, since an attack on Sulla's freedman would seem a perilous attack on Sulla. Add to that the fact that such remarks might be taken to attack the claims of those who had bought at auction the property of the proscribed, a group that would include many members of the jury.

The only countervailing reason for the defense to mention the fate of the elder Roscius' property would be to support the case that there had been no murder because the victim was among the proscribed. But the prosecution could feel secure that the defense would not try to make the case that the victim had been proscribed.[5] Anyone could see that such a legalistic defense of patricide, however judicially correct, would be

---

[4] Cf. Richter-Fleckeisen ad sec. 126; Sedgwick, 13; Heinze, 99-100; Stroh, 61; Kinsey, "A Problem in *Pro Roscio Amerino*," 149-150.

[5] *Per contra*, Heinze, 99-100. See the appendix to this chapter on pp. 44-45.

dangerously repugnant to the jury.[6] The compromise claim, that the elder Roscius had been among the proscribed but that the younger Roscius had not killed him, might likewise seem a transparent and damning defense of a patricide. In any case, neither does the prosecution anticipate nor does Cicero advance this argument.[7]

The choice that Cicero makes is of course to treat the elder Roscius' death as murder and to dwell upon the illegality of Chrysogonus' acquisition of the estate. Cicero chooses this strategy because of political considerations within the Sullan faction. The young Roscius is supported by some of the most prominent members of the Sullan establishment.[8] If he, or they, had believed that Sulla were staunchly behind Chrysogonus, their support and Cicero's defense would likely not have been offered. But this case provides the testing ground for the extent to which those minions of Sulla, unchecked in the time of the proscriptions, are going to be allowed to abuse Sulla's power now that the proscriptions are over. Sulla established the primacy of the senate both in the government and in the courts, including his new *quaestiones perpetuae*. Now, is the system to be allowed to work? Cicero's political role is to serve as the mouthpiece for some of the most prestigious supporters of Sulla to make their case against Chrysogonus and his ilk.[9]

This role, while hardly the heroic stand against Sulla that Cicero would later claim (*Off.* 2.51), is not without danger. The absence of eminent *patroni*, and of the most prominent members of the families who support Roscius, shows that there is some uncertainty about how Sulla will perceive an attack on his freedman.[10]

One obvious outcome of Cicero's choice of strategy is that he must actually defend his client on the murder charge. His principal response here is to destroy Erucius' arguments, all drawn from probability, by arguing that Magnus and Capito are more likely to be responsible for the murder than is the defendant. (*antikategoria.* Cf. Quintilian 7.2.9, 18-25

---

[6] Cf. Segwick, 13, who believes that Cicero could not use this argument because the victim's name had already been removed from the proscription list before the trial.
[7] *Per contra*, Stroh, 61-62.
[8] See esp. Afzelius, 213-217; Gruen, 265-271, with lit..
[9] Whether Cicero, true to his later anti-Sullan feelings, here censures the dictator in a veiled way must remain an open question; irony is in the eye of the beholder. The strongest case for Cicero's censure of Sulla in the speech is Buchheit, esp. 576-591.
[10] Gruen, 271. *Per contra* Kinsey, "Cicero's Case against Magnus," 183-190, concludes that Cicero took the case because it was too trivial for a more prominent *patronus*.

and 3.10.4.) Cicero's allegations against Magnus and Capito are so weak and inconsistent that they are surely insubstantial.[11] But they only need to show the weakness of Erucius' arguments in order to succeed.

In these probability arguments, the danger of Cicero's position is again revealed. The orator declines to make the most straightforward probability argument, that Chrysogonus masterminded the murder as well as subsequent events.[12] Cicero clearly feels that it would be too inflammatory simply to accuse Chrysogonus of plotting to murder the victim then claim him as one of the proscribed. To attribute such an action to Sulla's creature would be to attack the consistency, and thus the validity, of the principles under which all of the proscribed were killed. Instead, Magnus and Capito are brought into play. While unlikely murderers as individuals, they combine to form an appropriate composite murderer, an alternative to the defendant that is not too close to Sulla.[13]

To summarize, Cicero's goal is twofold. He must damn Chrysogonus' actions as anti-Sullan and he must counter the charges against his client. Although he has strong support within the Sullan faction, he still runs the risk of offending Sulla, or the jury. The rhetorical challenge he faces is that he must tailor his defense in such a way that it accomplishes his two goals while at the same time disavowing Sulla's knowledge or approval of his freedman's acts, claiming his own strong support for Sulla and his program, avoiding the implication that abuses under Sulla's tenure had actually extended to murder for profit, and assuaging any discomfort among the jury, many of whom will have profited from the proscriptions, that their support of his position might weaken their claim to their newly acquired wealth.

While the rhetorical challenge has not heretofore been comprehensively formulated in this way, Cicero's answers to the various aspects of this challenge have been well and frequently analyzed. For our purposes, it will suffice to review the general shape of his speech, and the roles of dilemma and other dilemma structures in his argument. From what has been said, it will be clear that true dilemmas may be directed not only against Erucius, but against the orator's other *adversarii*, Magnus, Capito, and Chrysogonus.

---

[11] Cf. Kinsey, "Cicero's Case against Magnus," 173-181; "Cicero's Speech for Roscius," 100-102; Stroh 57-59, with lit.
[12] Cf. Stroh, 59-60; Kinsey, "Cicero's Speech against Magnus," 182-183.
[13] Stroh, 67-68.

The *exordium* (1-14) sounds the themes of Cicero's inexperience, and of the apprehension of more qualified *patroni*. Cicero then drops his bombshell, stating explicitly that Chrysogonus is the reason for that apprehension, and Chrysogonus' greed the reason for the accusation.[14] Finally, the orator asserts that he wants the jury to be severe, in order to stop the real murderers who are attacking his client.

The *narratio* (15-34) gives the version of events rendered above (pp. 28-29). The emotional conclusion of the *narratio* (29b-34) includes the first dilemma form in the speech:

> Pater occisus nefarie, domus obsessa ab inimicis, bona adempta, possessa, direpta, fili vita infesta, saepe ferro atque insidiis appetita. Quid ab his tot maleficiis sceleris abesse videtur? Tamen haec aliis nefariis cumulant atque adaugent, crimen incredibile confingunt, testis in hunc et accusatores huiusce pecunia comparant; **hanc condicionem misero ferunt ut optet utrum malit cervices *T*. Roscio (sc. Magno) dare an insutus in culleum per summum dedecus vitam amittere.** (30)

> "The father atrociously murdered, his house besieged by enemies, his property taken away, seized, and plundered, his son's life endangered, often assailed by treachery and the sword -- what kind of crime seems to be missing among so many misdeeds? Yet they crown and aggravate them by other impious acts. They invent an incredible charge, bribe with my client's own money witnesses and accusers to appear against him, and **reduce the wretched man to the alternative of choosing whether he prefers to offer his throat to Titus Roscius [sc. Magnus] or to be sewn up in a sack and lose his life by a most infamous death.**"

In this passage of pathetic argument, we see the defendant himself confronted with a harsh dilemma in which either alternative leads to death. Technically, this is not a true dilemma, since it is not directed at the opponent. Rather it harnesses the dilemma form to elicit pity for Cicero's client. Already we see the young orator using the form as an emotional argument in a way that he does not imagine in *De Inventione*.[15]

The *partitio* (35-36) lists three heads for the coming *argumentatio*: the refutation of Erucius' charge of parricide, the brazenness of Magnus and Capito, and the influence of Chrysogonus.[16]

---

[14] Cf. Kennedy, 152-53; Stroh 68-69.
[15] And in a way unexampled in the remains of previous Roman oratory. In function, this type of dilemma form is similar to the "dilemma" of C. Gracchus. It differs, obviously, in that the speaker's client, not the speaker himself, is the target. More fundamentally, it differs in that the two alternatives really are exhaustive, and the consequences of each really is materially harmful. Thus, unlike the "dilemma" of C. Gracchus (pp. 24-25 above), it may properly be considered a dilemma form.
[16] Throughout the *argumentatio*, and the speech as a whole, we will see that Cicero's arguments are largely grounded in assumptions drawn from his depiction of the

The first section of the *argumentatio* (37-82) refutes Erucius' charges largely on the basis of the categories of argument *ex persona, ex causa*, and *ex negotio* (from character, motive, and circumstances surrounded the crime) that we find described in De Inventione (2.16-51; cf. 1.34-43). Cicero's dominant theme is that parricide is the most enormous of crimes, and so requires a most powerful motive, which Erucius has not demonstrated. Having amplified this basic argument at remarkable length (including the famous purple passage on parricide in secs. 71-73a), the orator generously allows that, although he has already won, he will dwell on Erucius' inability to show motive. He is content to explore the means by which Roscius might do the deed.

> Quo modo occidit? ipse percussit an aliis occidendum dedit? Si ipsum arguis, Romae non fuit; si per alios fecisse dicis, quaero quos? Servosne an liberos? Si liberos, quos homines? indidemne Ameria an hosce ex urbe sicarios? Si Ameria, qui sunt ei? cur non nominantur? si Roma, unde eos noverat Roscius qui Romam multis annis non venit neque umquam plus triduo fuit? ubi eos convenit? qui conlocutus est? quo modo persuasit? ~Pretium dedit'; cui dedit? per quem dedit? unde aut quantum dedit? Nonne his vestigiis ad caput malefici perveniri solet? (74)
> How did he kill him? Did he strike the blow himself, or entrust the task to others? If you maintain that he did it himself, I answer that he was not in Rome; if you say that he did it by the hands of others, I ask you, who were they? Slaves or free men? If free men, who are they? from the same place Ameria, or some of these assassins from Rome? If from Ameria, who are they? why are their names not given? if from Rome, how did Roscius, who for several years did not come to Rome and never stayed there more than three days, make their acquaintance? When did he meet them? how did he get an interview with them? how did he persuade them? He gave them a bribe. To whom, and through whom, did he give it? where did the money come from, and how much was it? Is it not by following up all such traces that the starting point of a crime is usually reached?

Thus Cicero begins his arguments *ex negotio* with an overpowering series of three sets of alternatives. Did Roscius commit the murder himself or hire it done? The first alternative is immediately dismissed as impossible, and the second divided into two further alternatives. Did he have it done by slaves or free men? The possibility that free men were his agents is then further subdivided into consideration of free men from Ameria or from Rome, and dismissed in a further hail of questions.[17]

---

various characters involved. Vasaly gives the most thorough description of the dynamics of these ethical arguments.
[17] In this diaeretical chain Landgraf, *ad loc.*, would count three examples of dilemma. For the hail of questions as a distracting tactic, cf. C.J. Classen, "Ciceros Kunst der

Cicero's treatment of the final alternative, that Roscius had had the murder done through slaves, nicely elucidates the relationship between the show of invincible reasoning and premises founded on ethical argument. Within this entire section of the argument, the idea that Roscius has hired the murder done is unsubstantiable, but it is certainly not impossible. Yet it is not enough, given the sensational nature of the charge, for Cicero to show that it cannot be proven. He must persuade the jury that the charge cannot even be plausibly advanced. The only support for such a demonstration is the audience's acceptance of Cicero's portrayal of Roscius' upright, rustic character. Cicero thus treats the final alternative, that Roscius' agents were slaves (77-78) largely with a *praeteritio* stressing that planning a murder does not accord with the rustic ways that the prosecution has assigned to Roscius (77, 'Et simul'- 78), and an amplification of the contention that Roscius, given the prosecution's picture of him, could know no one whom he could employ to commit the murder in Rome (79).

The treatment of this possibility after the contention that free men were the agents, a reversal of the original order of the alternatives given in section 74, allows Cicero to finish on his strongest point. Sliding adroitly from slaves as murderers to slaves as witnesses, he points out that the slaves of Roscius senior were apparently the only witnesses to the murder, and Chrysogonus refuses to surrender them for interrogation. Finally, turning from Chrysogonus and Magnus and Capito back to Erucius, the orator recapitulates his series of alternatives:

> Nunc, Eruci, ad te venio. Conveniat mihi tecum necesse est, si ad hunc maleficium istud pertinet, aut ipsum sua manu fecisse, id quod negas, aut per aliquos liberos aut servos. Liberosne? quos neque ut convenire potuerit neque qua ratione inducere neque ubi neque per quos neque qua spe aut quo pretio potes ostendere. Ego contra ostendo non modo nihil eorum fecisse Sex. Roscium sed ne potuisse quidem facere, quod neque Romae multis annis fuerit neque de praediis umquam temere discesserit. Restare tibi videbatur servorum nomen, quo quasi in portum reiectus a ceteris suspicionibus confugere posses; ubi scopulum offendis eius modi ut non modo ab hoc crimen resilire videas verum omnem suspicionem in vosmet ipsos recidere intellegas. (79)

> "Now, Erucius, I come to you. We must needs agree that, if my client is connected with this crime, he either committed it with his own hand, which you are unable to prove, or by the agency of others, free men or slaves. Free men? You are unable to show how he was able to meet

---

Überredung," in W. Ludwig, ed., *Rhétorique et Éloquence chez Cicéron, Fondation Hardt Entretiens*, vol. 28, (Vandoeuvres-Genève, 1982) 149-184, esp. 168 (with n.6)-171.

> them, by what means he persuaded them, where, by whose agency, what expectations he raised, what bribe he offered. I, on the contrary, prove that Sextus Roscius not only did not do, but could not have done, any of these things, seeing that for several years he had neither been in Rome nor had ever left his farm without good reason. It seems that the only thing left to you was to name the slaves; this appeared a kind of harbour where you might take refuge when driven from your other false allegations, instead of which you have struck upon such a sort of rock that you not only see the charge rebound from Sextus Roscius, but also understand that every suspicion recoils upon yourselves.

The idea that Roscius did the deed with his own hand is here briefly dismissed. The orator now treats only the choice of free men or slaves as agents. The ethical arguments folded into the earlier statement of this chain of reasoning, the simple fact of repetition, and the stress on Chrysogonus' refusal to surrender the slaves, make Cicero's demonstration seem unassailable. The prosecution's assertions have been transmogrified from the unsubstantiated to the impossible. Of course this is an illusion. A man who would come to Rome and stay in the house of Caecilia, a woman related to both of the consuls-elect, would not be completely ignorant of how events might be made to happen in the City.

The entire treatment of the arguments *ex negotio* takes its structure from the offering of alternatives that would make the opponent's story acceptable. Each alternative is then shown to be unsubstantiated. While this is not the form of the device that Cicero presents in *Inv.* 1.44-45, this argumentative structure certainly conforms with Quintilian's definition of dilemma, and with his example from *pro Vareno*. Still, it is noteworthy that the argument is not irrefutable. Cicero, through reliance on arguments from character, emphasis on the opponent's suppression of evidence, and simple repetition, adds an extra-rational component of persuasion to the logic of his demonstration. He converts "unsubstantiated" to "impossible." The apparent rigor of the argumentative structure helps to conceal the extra-rational nature of that shift, and to lend an air of irrefutability to a conclusion that is at least debatable. Dilemma forms play a key role in creating that impression of rigor.[18]

The second section of the *argumentatio*, deals with the *audacia* of Magnus and Capito (83-123). Using again the topics of motive, character and arguments *ex negotio*, Cicero will show that the Roscii are more likely suspects than is his client. It is noteworthy that this section opens with Cicero's insistence that he does not wish to play the prosecutor (83). The

---

[18] Contrast Stroh, 72-73.

fact that Cicero stops short of making a decisive case against Magnus and Capito is strong evidence that he simply cannot. Whatever the circumstances leading to the sale of the victim's property, there is no substantial link between Magnus or Capito and the murder itself. Fortunately, Cicero need only compare Magnus and Capito to his client, and show that they are more probably suspect than is the younger Roscius.

Unfortunately, this comparative weighing of probabilities is also weak. The orator begins with the basic question of motive, "Who stood to gain?" (86). But in Cicero's own version of events, Magnus could not have foreseen his profit at the time of the murder, while Roscius might have thought to secure his inheritance by his father's death.

Thus Cicero's only hope is to rely upon presuppositions about character, and to mask the inconsistency of his account through the contrasting portrayal of the avaricious, impoverished, hostile Magnus and the honest, rustic, loving son (86-88).

Cicero pursues this strategy even further beyond the pale of coherence in the following attack on Erucius (89-91). That remarkable ramble has this broad train of thought: Magnus is wicked and easy to accuse. Erucius could accuse him at length, and Erucius is a good accuser only because the better accusers were killed in the civil war. During these troubled times, many were killed with seeming impunity, although the leaders (i.e. Sulla) knew nothing about it. Still these killers will finally be brought to justice. But Cicero must stress that he is not here acting as an accuser.

This virtual exercise in free association offers no further evidence that Magnus had a special motive for the murder. So Cicero concludes (92 ad init.) that there were then many motives to drive Magnus to murder! The sounding of themes and the sheer volume of words have completely replaced coherent argument.

Having ostensibly considered motive, the orator can now move to means. As with the earlier argument *ex negotio*, the notion that Roscius is not a creature of the City, and, implicitly, could not get anyone in the City to do the deed, is fundamental. When the murder was committed, Magnus was in Rome while Roscius was not. One can then infer that Magnus was the more likely murderer. The logical objection to this, that Roscius was perfectly capable of having the murder committed from afar, Cicero addresses in this way:

> Erat tum multitudo sicariorum, id quod commemoravit Erucius, et homines impune occidebantur. Quid? ea multitudo quae erat? **Opinor,**

38 FORM AS ARGUMENT

> aut eorum qui in bonis erant occupati, aut eorum qui ab eis conducebantur, ut aliquem occiderent. Si eos putas qui alienum appetebant, tu es in eo numero qui nostra pecunia dives es; sin eos quos qui leviore nomine appellant percussores vocant, quaere in cuius fide sint et clientela; mihi crede, aliquem de societate reperies; (93)
>
> As Erucius has told us, at that time there was a crowd of assassins, and men were killed with impunity. Well, of whom was this crowd composed? I imagine either of those who were occupied in buying properties, or of those who were hired by them to murder somebody. If you think the criminals were those who coveted the property of others, you are one of the number, you who are enriched by our wealth; but if you think they were those who are called by the milder name of bandits, inquire under whose protection, whose dependants they are, and believe me, you will find one of your associates.

Cicero's entire argument is based upon the depiction of the characters of Roscius and Magnus. The orator need not underscore again Roscius' (improbable) inability to have the deed done. Rather he confronts Magnus with a dilemma of which the first prong is founded on the question of who stood to gain, and the second, marvelously, on the assumption that since bloodthirsty criminals were active in the City (91), and Magnus is a resident of the City, Magnus is in league with these bloodthirsty criminals. Here the argument is based merely upon previous characterization and a simple thematic resonance with the virtual free association of sections 89-91. In this context, the dilemma has a double function. First it adds the appearance of rigor to a virtually incoherent argument based upon assumptions finally grounded in character depiction. Second, and equally important, it is also a vehicle to reinforce that negative character depiction.

The fifth instance of dilemma form in this speech is not a true dilemma, but differs from the dilemma of the rhetorics in an especially useful way. At the end of Cicero's treatment of Magnus and Capito (119-123), he again pointedly raises the matter of the victim's slaves whom Chrysogonus, and Chrysogonus' agent Magnus, refuse to surrender for interrogation. The best men in the state had asked that they be handed over. They had asked on behalf of a son prostrate with grief and eager to find the truth of his father's murder.

> Res porro abs te eius modo postulabatur ut nihil interesset, utrum eam rem recusares an de maleficio confiterere. Quae cum ita sint, quaero abs te quam ob causam recusaris. (120)
>
> Further, the request made to you was of such a kind that it made no difference whether you refused it or confessed the crime. This being so, I ask you why you refused it.

The fact that the slaves were not surrendered for interrogation is, along with the disposition of Roscius senior's property, the most damning evidence that Cicero offers against his opponents. Accordingly, the orator makes the most of it in the first two of the three main divisions of his argument (77-79, 119-123). In this latter passage, Cicero strengthens that emphasis with a dilemma form that narrates two choices offered to his opponent *in the past*. Whichever one Magnus chose would have demonstrated his guilt in the murder of Roscius senior. This form, a recounting of a dilemma that had confronted the opponent, differs from the device described in the rhetorical handbooks exactly because it offers no real choice in the present. Further, it is fundamentally different from the one narrative dilemma directed at an opponent that we noted in the Attic orators (Isocrates 17.27-28). There the narrative dilemma explains the target's action. Here the form simply emphasizes the target's presumed guilt. Such a narrative dilemma seems as emphatic as a normal dilemma, but dismisses even the possibility that the opponent might reply.

We have seen that the defendant as well as the opponent may be the target of a dilemma form, with very different results (sec. 30, above, p. 33). At the beginning of the third main division of the argumentation, that dealing with Chrysogonus (124-142), we find that it can also be useful for Cicero to find himself in a dilemma:

> Venio nunc ad illud nomen aureum Chrysogoni sub quo nomine tota societas latuit; de quo, iudices, neque quo modo dicam neque quo modo taceam reperire possum. Si enim taceo, vel maximam partem relinquo; sin autem dico, vereor ne non ille solus, id quod ad me nihil attinet, sed alii quoque plures laesos se putent. Tametsi ita se res habet ut mihi in communem causam sectorum dicendum nihil magno opere videatur; haec enim causa nova profecto et singularis est. (124)

> "I come now to that golden name of Chrysogonus, under which the whole association is concealed. **I am at a loss gentlemen, how to speak of this name, or how to remain silent about it. If I remain silent, I omit a most important part of my argument; if I mention it, I am afraid that not Chrysogonus alone -- that is a matter of indifference to me -- but several others may consider themselves insulted.** Nevertheless, the case is of such a nature that it does not seem that I need say much against "brokers" generally: for this case is assuredly of a novel and remarkable character.

The orator must deal with the delicate topic of Chrysogonus' acquisition of the elder Roscius' property. The topic is delicate because many, perhaps all, in the senatorial jury will have profited from the proscriptions. The faintest hint that Cicero questions the legality of such acquisitions can make the jury extremely hostile, no matter what their predisposition towards Chrysogonus or their desire to honor the juror's oath. Since the jurors may be pulled in different directions by the claims of duty and self-interest, Cicero defuses this tension by making it explicit, and proclaiming that it is a problem for him. By showing that he is sensitive to the jurors' concerns in a way that does not offend them for having those concerns, the orator makes clear that he will be a threat to no one except his opponents. This gives him a license to treat the awkward topic of Chrysogonus' purchase of the elder Roscius' property, assuring the jury that it is a unique case that will not affect their own acquisitions. Thus, unsurprisingly, Cicero's self-professed dilemma proves useful for his case.

The final dilemma form in the speech is interesting primarily for the way in which its position holds the argument together. In the attack on Chrysogonus, Cicero first argues that it is illegal for the elder Roscius' property to have been sold because he does not fit either category of those to be proscribed. If the killing was not legal, then the sale of the victim's property cannot be legal (125-126). After again emphasizing that he is not criticizing Sulla, only Chrysogonus, the orator goes on to stress again that the sale of the property was illegal, and to question whether an auction actually even took place.

> opinor enim esse in lege quam ad diem proscriptiones venditionesque fiant, nimirum Kalendas Iunias. Aliquot post mensis et homo occisus est et bona venisse dicuntur. **Profecto aut haec bona in tabulas publicas nulla redierunt nosque ab isto nebulone facetius eludimur quam putamus, aut, si redierunt, tabulae publicae corruptae aliqua ratione sunt; nam lege quidem bona venire non potuisse constat.** (128)

> Now I believe that the lateste date on which proscriptions and sales may take place is stated in the law -- namely, the first of June. Some months afterwards Roscius was slain and his property is said to have been sold. **In any case, either this sale was not entered on the public registers, and we are being cheated by this rascal more cleverly than we think, or, if it was, the registers have been tampered with in some way, for it is evident that the property could not have been sold by virtue of the law.**

Cicero, with the aid of Roscius' good Sullan supporters, could certainly have discovered whether there was a public record of the auction of Roscius' property. The absence of such a record would be grist for his mill. If the record did exist, he could label it a fraud. But why raise both possibilities only to answer each, and thus construct a dilemma?

The dilemma that Cicero constructs marks a break in his attack on Chrysogonus. The orator immediately proceeds to explain that he is now speaking for himself, not for Roscius. Roscius has no desire to question any settlement of property (thus even remotely to threaten any juror's profits from the proscriptions). All he desires is acquittal. But Cicero, not now speaking as an advocate but as a concerned Roman, must attack Chrysogonus' abominable behavior (128 "Intellego" - 129).[19] But how can Cicero introduce this shift? He cannot make the distinction between his own views and those of Roscius at the beginning of his treatment of Chrysogonus without losing a real advantage. One part of that useful self-professed dilemma with which this treatment begins is the demand that Cicero plead the defendant's case (124). To separate his interests from those of his client in this environment would muddy his attempt to reassure the jurors; he and Roscius must be as one in the desire not to threaten the jurors' property claims arising from the proscriptions. Thus Cicero must find a way to introduce the division between his sentiments and those of Roscius later in his argument. Strictly speaking, he must interrupt his line of argument in order to make this adjustment. How to bridge this necessary interruption? Cicero casts the last argument before the interruption in dilemma form. This leaves the attack on an exceptionally forceful note. Thus Cicero's return to that attack with the volley of questions in sec. 130, now speaking for himself rather than for his client, has a memorable, natural point from which to continue.

From this overview it is clear that Cicero at the beginning of his career capitalizes upon the presentational aspect of the dilemma form as a symbol of memorable and irrefutable argument. The dilemma forms in the diaeretical reasoning of sections 74-79 create an impression of forceful argument that helps conceal the weakness of conclusions based largely upon characterization. The perfectly plausible assertion that the defendant could have hired the murder done is answered only by pleading his rustic inexperience. But this explanation is offered within a framework that is so apparently rigorous that the weak argument derives an aura of irrefutability from the pattern within which it is presented. This effect is a direct result of the stylistic, presentational aspect of the argument form that Cicero employs.

---

[19] For this early use of the rhetoric of advocacy, see G.A. Kennedy, "The Rhetoric of Advocacy in Greece and Rome," *AJP* 89 (1968) 419-436, 431; Stroh, 76-77 and n.77; May, 28.

Similarly, Cicero's assertion that Magnus is a more likely murderer than Roscius is based completely upon character delineation, and given the appearance of argumentative rigor through the use of a dilemma form (93). This appearance of argumentative rigor, by seeming to validate argument based on assumptions about character, also reinforces the apparent validity of those assumptions.

The other use that Cicero makes of the presentational aspect of dilemma in this speech is as a type of punctuation within the flow of the argument. Since dilemma is a means of emphasis, the orator may use it as a memorable marker at a break in a line of argument that he will later resume (128).

It is also clear that Cicero the orator redirects the dilemma form in ways that Cicero the young rhetorician does not discuss. These dilemma forms are dilemma structures, but not true dilemmas according to the examples in *De Inventione* or the definition of Quintilian; either in their time frame or in their target they diverge from the standard device. Thus we must be very cautious in speaking of their stylistic, presentational value. Still, the three examples of dilemma structures in this speech are worth noting as examples of Cicero's creative and practical expansion of the uses that the basic mechanics of dilemma may serve. 1) By changing the temporal reference of the device from present to past, Cicero shapes an argument form that has all the offensive impact of dilemma, yet does not allow the opponent even the possibility of a reply (120).[20] 2) By changing the target of the dilemma form, Cicero converts a weapon of forceful reasoned attack to more overtly extra-rational ends. Thus he may depict his own client as caught in a dilemma, and so stir pity for the defendant in a way that assumes, and so underscores, his client's innocence (30). 3) More interestingly, he may confess that he himself is in a dilemma (124). While this is a tactic for gaining indulgence already in the Attic orators,[21] Cicero's use of it is especially penetrating. Unlike Demosthenes at *De Corona* 4, for example, Cicero explicitly declares the conflicting feelings of his audience. He can then announce a course that will resolve this conflict, and thus obtain a license to speak in a way that could otherwise incite the audience's hostility.

---

[20] We have already noted the difference between Cicero's form and that at Isocrates 17.27-28.
[21] Antiphon 1.1; Isocrates 6.70; Demosthenes 18.4; 27.53.

Finally, while the ethical argumentation of the case has been well analyzed,[22] we may note in a summary way the relationship between that argumentation and Cicero's uses of dilemma forms. We have seen that Cicero's arguments using true dilemmas are built upon, and thus extra-rationally validate, assumptions about the character of the defendant or of his opponents. These assumptions, while ethical, are integral to arguments that bear directly upon the question at issue: Did Roscius kill his father or not? All characterizations of the defendant are part of the *argumenta ex persona* that Cicero and his audience would expect in a question of fact (*Inv.* 2.28-37 and 1.34-36). By extension, characterizations that lead to the argument that some other party is more likely to have committed the crime are similar exercises of these *argumenta ex persona*. The role of dilemma is then both to build upon and retroactively to validate ethical assumptions in arguments that are relevant in the narrowest way to the question at issue. On the other hand, the orator's description of the dilemma confronting his client is simply foundational, helping to establish his characterizations of the parties without directly building any such arguments upon them. Lastly, Cicero's profession that he is in a dilemma in order to speak in a way that would otherwise perturb the audience affects the question at issue only indirectly. Rather it functions primarily in the arena of the orator's own relationship with the audience, and so is an example of the dilemma form used in the service of the rhetoric of advocacy.

Already in Cicero's earliest criminal pleading, we see the orator's appreciation of the value of dilemma as both a vehicle and a symbol of forceful argument. The young orator understood well the interrelationship of the mechanical and presentational aspects of this highly recognizable argument form. He also understood the possibility of variations on the form, both to make arguments, especially ethical arguments, more forceful and to develop useful ethical appeals.

With this background, we may now examine the ways in which a more mature Cicero will systematically harness the special symbolic and extra-rationally persuasive properties of this argument form.

---

22 See esp. Vasaly; May, 21-31.

APPENDIX TO CHAPTER TWO:
DID THE PROSECUTION WANT AN ACQUITTAL?

I adopt the position that the prosecution miscalculated. Despite the fundamental contradiction of claiming that Roscius was a murder victim while enjoying the victim's property as though he were among the proscribed, the Roscii and Chrysogonus expected to prevail through intimidation. A radically different possibility is that argued by Heinze, 99-100; the prosecution wanted the defendant acquitted. Overwhelmed by the opposition of Chrysogonus, which would intimidate any would-be *patronus*, Roscius would be left defenseless, and would himself have to answer the murder charge. Finally, his only tool would be to claim that his father had been among the proscribed, and thus that he could not be convicted of the murder. It is in the interest of the prosecution to allow him this plea, since it would confirm Chrysogonus' property rights. Further, Roscius' plea would be held a legalistic evasion of conviction for parricide. His reputation would be ruined, and his further claims to recover his property would not find the support of any decent person.

Stroh, 61-66, claims to agree substantially with Heinze, with one important refinement. He points out that the law provided that people could be killed with impunity either if they were among the proscribed or if they had been killed in the camps of the opposing side during the civil war. Cicero tells us (127) that the victim is reckoned as one of those who had simply been killed in the camps of the opposing side. This piece of information, not mentioned by the prosecution, was still accessible to the defense. Thus the orator would not have to make the judicially correct but highly inflammatory plea that the defendant had legally killed his father. His client would be acquitted, and the verdict would demonstrate that the elder Roscius had been proscribed, and so would buttress Chrysogonus' claim to his property.

The text certainly supports Stroh's refinement of Heinze's idea. Unfortunately, the resulting thesis cannot stand. In Heinze's view, any legal precedent that might come from arguments based on the idea that the victim had been proscribed is complemented by the idea that the defendant, while legally innocent, is apparently guilty of the moral outrage of parricide. It is this ignominy, as well as the admission that his father was among the proscribed, that would destroy any further support for his property claims. Stroh's argument removes the ignominy and leaves only the legal precedent. T.E. Kinsey, "A Problem in *Pro Roscio Amerino*," 149-50, rightly objects that an acquittal obtained with the argument that the victim had been among those killed in the opponents' camp would not decisively vitiate a future suit by Roscius to recover his inheritance from Chrysogonus. Once acquitted, Roscius could disown Cicero's line of reasoning that led to the acquittal. After all, the jury might have acquitted on some other grounds. For that matter, Cicero himself could disown his own reasoning as a bit of temporizing. The good people of Ameria, and the good *nobiles* in Rome, would then have no reason to slacken their support for the young Roscius' attempt to recover his property.[1]

So Heinze's position, clarified through the support of Stroh and the opposition of Kinsey, is finally unconvincing. Still, one can appreciate why Heinze would have found the alternative explanation, the apparent stupidity of the prosecutors, so singularly unsatisfying.

---

[1] Kinsey offers another, less convincing argument against the positions of Heinze and Stroh. Kinsey argues that the proscriptions, including posting of names, killing, and auction of property, legally stopped completely on June 1 of 81. So, even if Cicero wished to give the prosecutors the admission they wanted in return for an acquittal, he could not risk it. Erucius had only to mention the date of the crime, after June 1 of 81, to demolish the defense.

Kinsey's time argument depends upon his interpretation of two passages, *S. Rosc.* 21 and 128, that need not be read as he wants them to be. It is entirely possible that the end of the proscriptions on 1 June 81 meant the end of adding names to the lists of the proscribed, *not* granting amnesty to those who were proscribed before that time. Since "proscriptiones venditionesque" (128) function as one idea for Cicero, he says that all that would stop on 1 June. But it is possible that the killing of those proscribed before that date, and the sale of their property, would still be legal.

CHAPTER THREE: *DIVINATIO IN CAECILIUM*

Cicero's speech arguing that he rather than Q. Caecilius Niger will be a more effective prosecutor of Verres is the only example of the genre of *divinatio* that has survived.[1] It presents a unique environment in which dilemma forms are remarkably prominent (true dilemma at secs. 12, 31, 33, 58, 60, other dilemma structures at secs. 4 and 14). We must discover the elements of Cicero's strategy that render dilemma such a useful form, both of argument and of presentation, in our only extant *divinatio*.

The circumstances of the speech are inseparable from the political climate in Rome in 70.[2] Ten years before, Sulla's reform had made the

---

[1] For analyses of the speech, see W. Sternkopf, "Gedankengang und Gliederung der 'Divinatio in Caecilium,'" *Gymnasium Dortmund Jahresbericht* 1904-5, 4-17 (reprinted with insignificant abridgement in B. Kytzler, ed., *Ciceros literarische Leistung*, Wege der Forschung vol. 240 [Darmstadt: Wissenschaftliche Buchgesellschaft, 1973] 267-299); C. Neumeister, *Grundsätze der forensichen Rhetorik*, Langue et parole, Sprach- und Literaturstrukturelle Studien, 3. Munich: M. Hüber, 1964) 35-41; W. Stroh, *Taxis und Taktik* (Stuttgart: Teubner, 1975) 174-187 (with lit.); J.M. May, *Trials of Character* (Chapel Hill and London: University of North Carolina Press, 1988) 31-38. Three other articles focus primarily on the speech: L.A. Thompson, "The Relationship between Provincial Quaestors and their Commanders-in-Chief," *Historia* 11 (1962) 339-55. P. Fabbri, "Q. Cecilio e la Divinatio," *Historia: studi storici per l'antichità classica* 6 (1932) 292-96, deals briefly with the select questions of Caecilius' motives, the order of the speeches, and the mechanics of the proceeding. C.P. Craig, "Dilemma in Cicero's *Divinatio in Caecilium*," *AJP* 106 (1985) 442-446, focuses upon the resonances of the frequent use of dilemma with the description of dilemma at sec. 45.

Of the several commentaries on the speech, see especially K. Halm, Cicero's Ausgewälte Reden,[6] vol.2 (Berlin: Weidmann, 1874), F. Richter, rev. by A. Eberhard (Leipzig: Teubner, 1884), K. Hachtmann (Gotha: Bibliotheca Gothana, 1891), E. Thomas (Paris: Hachette, 1894), and W.E. Heitland and H. Cowie[2] (Cambridge: Cambridge University Press, 1900).

[2] For the ancient evidence, see M. Gelzer, *Cicero, ein biographischer Versuch* (Wiesbaden: Steiner, 1968) 36-38.

senate supreme, in part by mandating that only senators could serve on juries of the *quaestiones perpetuae*, the standing criminal courts. Among these was the *quaestio de rebus repetundis*, the court to try provincial governors for extortion and malfeasance. Since these governors were always senators, there would always be a strong, perhaps insurmountable, bias in favor of the defendant. In 70, the first consulship of Pompeius and Crassus, the last of Sulla's reforms would collapse in the face of popular sentiment and factional politics. Already in 71, Pompeius as consul designate had promised judicial reform (*Ver.* 45.); there was thus reason for provincials to hope that the *quaestio de rebus repetundis* would be less biased towards defendants, since such abuses were clearly jeopardizing senatorial control of the courts. So in 71 Sicilians were already seeking a Roman citizen to serve as prosecutor against their propraetorian governor, C. Verres. Verres' excesses had drawn the attention, if not the action, of the senate even in 72 (*Ver.* 2.96). In his three years as governor of Sicily, 73-71, he had achieved the remarkable record of corruption, thievery, sacrilege and violence that Cicero was to immortalize in the *Verrines*.

Verres was to be defended by Hortensius, the most eloquent pleader at the Roman bar, and a man who would become consul-elect before the case came to trial. Cicero, playing the role of prosecutor for the first, and almost the only, time in his career,[3] would have the opportunity to best Hortensius in court. And there could be political benefits as well.[4]

But before the orator could win his impressive triumph over Verres, and Hortensius, he had to prove his right to prosecute. In January of 70, Cicero and Q. Caecilius Niger, who had been Verres' quaestor, had each asked M'. Acilius Glabrio, the praetor in charge of the *quaestio de rebus repetundis*, for the brief against Verres. Accordingly, a *divinatio* was held; the praetor and his *consilium* listened to the two men, without witnesses or other external evidence, and determined who would be the

---

[3] Cicero's only other known prosecution is that of T. Munatius Plancus Bursa under a charge of *vis* in 52. See J.W. Crawford, *M. Tullius Cicero: The Lost and Unpublished Orations* (Göttingen: Vandenhoeck & Ruprecht, 1984), #79, pp. 230-34.

[4] The precise political component of Cicero's motives and the political significance of the case against Verres are controversial. See esp. T.N. Mitchell, *Cicero, the Ascending Years* (New Haven: Yale University Press, 1979) 107-149 (with lit.). In any case, I believe that Cicero would want to establish his supremacy over Hortensius, that he would not view the case as an impediment to his election as aedile, and that the prosecution itself need not place him with Pompeius as a *popularis* reformer against the interests of the optimate oligarchy.

more suitable prosecutor, and whether the other would-be accuser should be assigned as a *subscriptor* (assisting prosecutor).⁵

Cicero tells us that Caecilius sought the prosecution in collusion with the defense in order to block Cicero from prosecuting (12-13, 23, 29, 58). Although most scholars credit Cicero's charge, Stroh has rightly pointed out that the notion of Caecilius' *praevaricatio* has no demonstrable basis in fact, and is contradicted by Cicero's own later description of the outcome:

> Quod meum factum (viz. accusatio in Verrem) lectissimi viri atque ornatissimi, quo in numero e vobis complures fuerunt, ita probaverunt ut ei qui istius quaestor fuisset, et ab isto laesus inimicitias iustas persequeretur, non modo deferendi nominis, sed ne subscribendi quidem, cum id postularet, facerent potestatem. (*Ver.* 1.15)⁶

> My action (viz., the prosecution against Verrres) was so cordially approved by persons of high character and distinction, including several of yourselves, that they refused to the man who had been Verres' quaestor, and who had a personal quarrel with Verres justified by the harm Verres had done him, not only the opportunity of prosecuting him, but even, though he asked for it, that of supporting the prosecution.

Cicero's triumph over Caecilius is founded on arguments that seem both fair and expeditious for an audience concerned to keep senatorial control of these important juries. The Sicilians want Cicero to prosecute for them (1-5, 11a-22a, 28, 53-54, 73, *et passim*). Further, as the would-be prosecutors' speeches will demonstrate, Cicero is obviously the better speaker, and in that way the more capable *accusator* (esp. 27-47a). Thus to choose Caecilius would be openly to reject the better prosecutor, and so to confirm the popular feeling that the senate abuses, and so should lose, its exclusive control of this court (esp. 6-9, 26, 70-71, 73).

There is nonetheless a rhetorical challenge arising both from the audience's expectations and from the very nature of *divinatio*. The praetor

---

⁵ For the form and name of the procedure, see Pseudo-Asconius, p. 186 Stangl; Gellius, *NA* 2.4.1.

⁶ See Stroh, esp. 177 and n.16; Thomas, 39-40, Fabbri 292-293. Stroh's case against the charge that Caecilius is a *praevaricator* is the fullest and most convincing. His major points are: 1) Cicero relies on *praeteritio* to make the charge, fails to follow through with any proof of it, and does not consistently build his argument on the notion that the charge is substantial. 2) Such a charge will have been a standard *locus* of *divinatio*. 3) in the *actio prima in Verrem*, secs. 16-32, Cicero details the manoeuvres of Verres' camp, but does not mention Caecilius. 4) In the *actio secunda*, *Ver.* 1.15, quoted above, indicates that Caecilius really did have a motive of personal vengeance. (If Hortensius in fact lobbied for Caecilius, as Cicero says in *Div. Caec.* 22-24, it could be purely because Caecilius was the poorer speaker.)

Stroh, 180, suggests that Cicero's statement at *Ver.* 1.15 become an epigraph for analyses of the speech.

and his *consilium* must make a fundamentally deliberative decision based upon the motives, energy, and sincere commitment of the two men. Quintilian, remarking on Cicero's idiosyncratic approach, gives us an outline for the usual ordering of topics in such a case:

> Frequentissimae tamen hae sunt quaestiones, uter maiores causas habeat, uter plus industriae aut virium sit allaturus ad accusandum, uter id fide meliore facturus. (*Inst. Or.* 7.4.34)
>
> Moreover these are the most commonly asked questions: which of the two has a stronger motive, which of the two will bring more diligence or energy to the prosecution, which of the two will do it with a more sincere commitment?[7]

Maiores causae, a stronger motive, should make for greater energy, and will insure a more sincere commitment. Thus the would-be prosecutors' motives will be pivotal for the praetor's decision.

From this perspective, Caecilius, "who had a personal quarrel with Verres justified by the harm Verres had done him," was preferable to Cicero. Romans expected a prosecutor to act from personal animus, and Caecilius has a strong case.[8] Verres has violated the traditional bond of quaestor and praetor through the wrong that he has done to Caecilius. Caecilius therefore has a strong motive for revenge which makes him proof against *praevaricatio*. Further, as Verres' quaestor he has a special knowledge of his praetor's crimes. Finally, he will be a resident of Sicily pleading for fellow Sicilians.[9] Those like Cicero, who did not have a personal motive, were thought to act for profit, and Cicero gives us a clear idea of the low esteem accorded these *quadruplatores* (49-50). The exceptions were young *nobiles* who hoped to make a name for themselves, and to take the defendant's place in the senate, through a successful prosecution. Cicero, of equestrian stock, established in the courts, now in his thirty-seventh year and standing for the aedileship, could hardly be considered such an exception. There was thus something apparently indecorous, even suspicious, in Cicero's asking to be allowed to prosecute (see. esp secs. 69-70).[10] The orator makes clear his need to justify himself from the first sentence of the speech.[11]

---

[7] My translation.
[8] Cf. Stroh, 178-79; Neumeister, 38-39. Also D.F. Epstein, *Personal Enmity in Roman Politics, 218-43 BC* (London: Croom Helm, 1987), esp. 96-126.
[9] Pseudo-Asconius, p. 185 Stangl.
[10] Cf. Sternkopf, 271-272. Stroh, 181-187, has further argued that Caecilius was approached by the Sicilians first and that they later turned to Cicero. Thus the orator's indecorous behavior is compounded by the embarrassing appearance of having pursued his own political gain, luring the Sicilians away from a man who had good

The second part of the rhetorical challenge arises from the nature of the *divinatio* as a demonstration by each competitor that he will be the better speaker. Skill in speaking is after all a vital ability for an *accusator*. But to claim that one is a good speaker is as offensive to ancient as to modern taste; it is the worst act of arrogance that an orator can commit.[12]

In sum, Cicero is in a position in which his very wish to prosecute, based on no personal grievance, will seem mean-spirited and vicious, while the case he makes must involve him in odious self-praise.

The orator will deal with the problem of self-praise by focussing upon the perspectives of others, the Sicilians, Verres and Hortensius. It is simply the fact, in Cicero's version, that these people consider him a

---

qualifications, and good reasons to champion them. Stroh's hypothesis, which makes Cicero's protestations of Sicilian support a mask for the changeover, adds a level of complexity to his interpretation. Unfortunately, his admitted speculation is based on an *argumentum ex silentio*; Cicero never claims that the Sicilians asked him first. But one could reply that there was no need to make the obvious explicit. Stroh further argues that although we do not know how the order of speakers in a *divinatio* is determined, Caecilius does speak last, the position reserved in judicial proceedings for the defense. In a *divinatio*, the analogy might be to one who defends his previously established right to prosecute. Since we have no knowledge of the mechanism for determining the order of speakers in a *divinatio*, this speculation will not carry the weight of Stroh's hypothesis. Stroh freely admits that his hypothesis may not be correct, but argues that, if he can make a case that the Sicilians had chosen Caecilius first, then Caecilius must have made such a case (!): Whether the Sicilians had first chosen Caecilius or not, the assertion that they had done so would offer Caecilius a strong plea, and thus one against which Cicero must defend in the ways that Stroh carefully describes. Here Stroh imputes to Caecilius too much of his own ingenuity.

[11] Si quis vestrum, iudices, aut eorum qui adsunt, forte miratur me, qui tot annos in causis iudiciisque publicis ita sim versatus ut defenderim multos, laeserim neminem, subito nunc mutata voluntate ad accusandum descendere, is, si mei consili causam rationemque cognoverit, una et id quod facio probabit, et in hac causa profecto neminem praeponendum mihi esse actorem putabit.
[It may be, gentlemen, that some of you, or some of the audience, are surprised that I have departed from the line of actions which I have pursued for all these years with regard to criminal proceedings; that having defended many accused persons, and attacked nobody, I have now suddenly changed my policy, and entered the arena as a prosecutor. But anyone whom this surprises has only to understand the motives that govern my action, and he will not only recognize that I am doing right, but will certainly take the view that no one can be held better fitted than myself to conduct the case before us.]

[12] Cf. 36: Intellego quam scopuloso difficilique in loco verser: nam cum omnis adrogatio odiosa est, tum illa ingeni atque eloquentiae multo molestissima. [I am aware that I am here treading on dangerous and difficult ground. Vanity of every kind is disagreeable; but vanity concerning intellectual and rhetorical gifts is far more detestable than any other kind.] Cf. Quintilian 11.1.15; 4.1.56; Neumeister, 39-40; Stroh, 179-80.

promising prosecutor, and despise Caecilius in that role. This allows Cicero to take Caecilius' alleged corruption and incompetence as a fact while leaving implicit, if obvious, his own corresponding virtue and effectiveness. Cicero does not actually claim that he is the better prosecutor as much as he argues, with a powerful show of virtuosity, that Caecilius is wholly unacceptable in any case.

The fact that Caecilius has, and Cicero lacks, a personal motive is harder. The orator overcomes this by using an arrangement that defers until last the question of personal motives.[13] Instead, Cicero structures an argument in which he, however unwilling, is recognized by both Sicilians and the defense as the only prosecutor who can help the court retain its credibility. Through treating the desires of the Sicilians, and of Verres and Hortensius, and through expanding on Caecilius' oratorical shortcomings, the orator creates opportunities to insinuate that Caecilius is a *praevaricator* colluding to insure Verres' acquittal.

As for his actual treatment of Caecilius' argument, Cicero first denies that Caecilius has suffered any wrong. Absent such a wrong, Caecilius is not only deprived of his justification, but made worse than Cicero since he becomes a quaestor violating his relationship with his praetor.

The roles of dilemma and other dilemma structures in implementing this persuasive strategy can best be seen through a close reading of the passages where they occur.

The structure of the speech is *exordium* (1-11a) including an internal *narratio* (2-5) and a *partitio* (10), an *argumentatio* (11b-72) and a *peroratio* (73). The *argumentatio* is divided into three principal sections. The first of these corresponds to the *partitio*, in which Cicero says that the key questions are two, whom the Sicilians want most (11b-22a) and whom Verres wants least (22b-26). The second section (27-47a) first attacks Caecilius under the headings of integrity and sincere commitment (27b-35a), then compares him to Cicero in terms of oratorical skill (35b-47a). Attached to this is a brief treatment of the quality of Caecilius' assisting prosecutors (47b-50 "recipiendus") and a digression arguing that no assisting prosecutor, including Caecilius, should be appointed for Cicero without the orator's approval (50 "quibus ego" - 51). The third section

---

[13] See Stroh 180-181. Cf. Sternkopf, 275.

treats directly the personal motives of Caecilius (52-63a) and the superior motives of Cicero (63b-72). Finally, there is a brief *peroratio* (73).[14]

In the introduction, Cicero immediately and successfully sabotages the structural comparison of the two would-be prosecutors that both the nature of the case and Quintilian's *loci* (above p. 50) lead us to expect. Instead of defending his own desire to prosecute, or dealing with that of Caecilius, the orator is completely absorbed with the task that has been thrust upon him unwilling, and has dragged him from his usual role of defender to that of prosecutor. Of course the Sicilians had their traditional patrons (to whom he carefully defers), but the provincials clamored for Cicero as prosecutor (1-3). This explains why Cicero, against his will, deigns to take the case. There is no hint of Caecilius, much less of the fact that he may have a valid claim.

When this tone has been set, Cicero finally mentions Caecilius, as a potential answer to the orator's dilemma:

> Tuli graviter et acerbe, iudices, in eum me locum adduci ut aut eos homines spes falleret qui opem a me atque auxilium petissent, aut ego, qui me ad defendendos homines ab ineunte adulescentia dedissem, tempore atque officio coactus ad accusandum traducerer. Dicebam habere eos actorem Q. Caecilium, qui praesertim quaestor in eadem provincia post me quaestorem fuisset. (4)
>
> I found myself thrust into a painfully uncomfortable position, gentlemen. Either I must disappoint these people who had come to me for help and succour, or circumstances were forcing upon me the duty of turning prosecutor, after having given myself from my earliest youth to the task of defending the prosecuted. I told them that the could get Caecilius to manage their case, and that he had the advantage having served as quaestor in the province.

We have already seen that Cicero can profess himself in a dilemma in order to give himself a license.[15] And so he does here. Clearly he cannot refuse the case without deceiving the hopes of the Sicilians, however much he abhors the role of prosecutor. By establishing these terms, Cicero shows himself no eager *accusator*, but a victim of his own sense of duty. Thus through this self-inflicted dilemma structure, precipitated by the Sicilians' desires, Cicero can insist on his right to prosecute even as he anticipates the opposition's criticism of his lack of personal animus towards the defendant. The orator can then adduce Caecilius to reflect his own

---

[14] Cf. esp. Sternkopf; Stroh, 175-176 and nn. 10-11, begins a *refutatio* at sec. 47 and ends the *argumentatio* in sec. 71. *Alii alias*. For our purposes, the schema given above is sufficient.

[15] *S. Rosc.* 124. See chapter two, pp. 39-40.

selfless motives, and can cast suspicion on Caecilius' own motives in the process. The total effect is to label Cicero as dutiful, Caecilius as suspect, and, equally important, to maintain that the desire of the Sicilians rather than the personal animus of either would-be prosecutor is the critical factor in deciding this case.[16]

Having insinuated the perspective that will insure his success, the orator even underscores how eager he was to satisfy the Sicilians without undertaking the prosecution himself; he had commended Caecilius to them (!). So Caecilius is first mentioned not as a competitor but as a substitute who would prove unacceptable. Only Caecilius' failings drive Cicero to the "burden of this task" (5).

Now that the praetor and his *consilium* have had their suspicions of Cicero's own motives somewhat mollified, the orator can admit more frankly that he wants this prosecution. In the second part of the *exordium* (6-9), Cicero can seize the role of champion not only of the rights of the provincials, but of the will of the Roman people. Expanding on the general dissatisfaction with the present dispensation, of which senatorial control of the courts is a part, the orator levels his strongest argument (secs. 8-9): Advocates of leaving the courts under senatorial control complain that the prosecutors are as unsuitable as the juries are lacking in rigor. The Roman people is ready to look to another order to serve as jurors. In this dire situation, Cicero has stepped forward as a civic duty, since only suitable and upright prosecutors such as himself can return credibility to the senatorial courts.

This is the decisive argument that Cicero will repeat so emphatically in the *peroratio* (73). It is simply a matter of expediency for the praetor to choose him, despite the question of who has the stronger motive to prosecute.

Having stunned any opposition before he begins his *argumentatio*, Cicero is free to use his own order of argument. Thus his *partitio* can in fact treat "stronger motives," but ignore completely those of Caecilius. The two most appropriate questions, Cicero announces, are what prosecutor the alleged victims want most, and what prosecutor the alleged perpetrator wants least (10).

---

[16] Cf. May, 32. Stroh, 186, argues that the dilemma in which Cicero places himself reflects the dilemma of the praetor and his *consilium*. They must choose either a prosecutor without sufficient personal motive or a prosecutor without sufficient skill.

This *partitio* allows Cicero to start on his firmest ground, the ground prepared in secs. 1-5. It is undeniable that the Sicilians want Cicero.[17] Apparently, Caecilius feels strongly enough about the injury Verres has done him (and perhaps about the rewards of a successful prosecution) that he still wants his revenge, and feels that the Sicilians will be served well in the bargain. From the *loci* that Quintilian gives us, it might not seem unreasonable for Caecilius to make a claim to the prosecution openly on the basis of personal animus and to treat the Sicilians' wishes as secondary. Cicero's defense of the importance of the victims' wishes is thus a real issue. But it is also an easy venue for Cicero's senatorial self-interest argument, and for his oratorical showmanship (17-22a). The fact that Caecilius prefers his own claim, Cicero argues, contravenes the spirit of the law, "cuius legis non modo a populo Romano, sed etiam ab ultimis nationibus iam pridem severi custodes requiruntur." ["a law for which strict guardians have long since been sought not only by the Roman people but even by the most distant nations."] (18)

The mention of the concern of the *populus Romanus* that the spirit of the law be honored of course resonates with the powerful argument for senatorial self-interest that Cicero has already advanced (8-9). In this atmosphere, Cicero can show his eloquence to good effect, performing a prosopopoeia of *Sicilia tota* addressing Verres (19), followed by one of the Sicilians addressing Caecilius (20).[18] The theme that the Sicilians' desire should be honored lends itself nicely to the innuendo, first implied in sec. 4, that Caecilius is not desired because he is a creature of Verres (21-22a).

Remarkable for our purposes is the introductory question, five sections earlier, that leads to this display:

> Adsunt, queruntur Siculi universi: ad meam fidem, quam habent spectatam iam et cognitam, confugiunt: auxilium sibi per me a vobis atque a populi Romani legibus petunt: me defensorem calamitatum suarum, me ultorem iniuriarum, me cognitorem iuris sui, me actorem causae totius esse voluerunt. **Utrum, Q. Caecili, hoc dices, me non Sicilorum rogatu ad causam accedere, an optimorum fidelissimorumque sociorum voluntatem apud hos gravem esse non oportere?** (11-12)
>
> Here before you, with their tale of wrong, stand the whole Sicilian people. I am the man to whose honour, having proved it in the past and not found it wanting, they now fly for refuge. Through me are they

---

[17] With the exception of two cities (sec. 14), which have not sent delegations for reasons that Cicero leaves unclear. The two cities are Syracuse and Messina (*Ver.*2.15 and 114; *Ver.* 4.3 and 140).
[18] May, 33.

seeking help from you and from the laws of Rome. It is I, I and no other, whom they have chosen to protect them in their calamities and avenge their wrongs. **Will you assert, Caecilius, that it is not at the request of the Sicilians that I come forward in this case? Or that this court need pay no serious attention to the wishes of these good and loyal allies of ours?**

The importance of the Sicilians' choice really is at issue. The fact that they have chosen Cicero is not.[19] Through this dilemma, the orator begins his argumentation with an obviously aggressive move, and offers a division of topics that will allow him to begin by maintaining the obvious as if it were disputed. This lengthy argument against a point the opponent has not made (12-16) allows the orator to be impressive and convincing. The treatment of the first prong of the dilemma also provides a vehicle for insinuating that Caecilius is in collusion with Verres (12: "Si id audebis" - 13: "videare"), and for trundling out as supporters the patrons of Sicily, including C. Marcellus, who is a member of the *consilium*, and Cn. Lentulus Marcellinus (13: "Deinde" *ad fin.*). Cicero tells us that these men know of his own dilemma, which he can thus reinforce by repetition:

> Hi sciunt hoc non modo a me petitum esse, sed ita saepe et ita vehementer esse petitum ut aut causa mihi suscipienda fuerit aut officium necessitudinis repudiandum. (14)

> They are aware that this request has not only been made by me, but made so often, and so earnestly, that I had either to take up the case or to disown the obligations of friendship.

The Sicilians want Cicero. Since they do, Cicero need not say why he has been preferred to others, but he modestly assures the audience that more illustrious champions were not available. Cicero would prefer any suitable prosecutor to himself, but would prefer to do it himself rather than have no one prosecute at all (16). Caecilius is obviously "no one."

Thus the dilemma in section 12 forms part of the strategy, initiated in the *exordium* and announced in the *partitio*, of concentrating upon the Sicilians' wishes rather than upon the motives of the prosecutors. The treatment of the two prongs of the dilemma forms a symmetry. The Sicilians want Cicero to accept the case although he does not seek it. The Sicilians do not want Caecilius to get the case even though he seeks it actively.

So the dilemma gives Cicero a framework in which he can ostentatiously and aggressively prove a point that is not contested, can fashion powerful innuendo while doing so, can thus approach the debatable

---

[19] Cf. the different view of Stroh, 184.

issue in the second prong of the dilemma from a position of strength, and can exploit the character of a highly visible argumentative figure to showcase his oratorical skill for an audience who must weigh that skill heavily in their decision.

The second question in Cicero's *partitio*, that of whom the defense wants least (22b-26), then allows the orator to adumbrate his contemptuous treatment of Caecilius' oratorical skill, to depict Hortensius as openly lobbying for Caecilius as an opponent because he is afraid that a real orator might end his own domination of the courts, to warn Hortensius ostentatiously that it will be hard to bribe the jury this time, and finally to illumine again the picture painted in secs. 6-9, that of Cicero the champion both of the Sicilians and of the *populus Romanus*, which has grown intolerant of senatorial *improbitas*.

Thus at the end of the first part of the *argumentatio*, that part announced in the *partitio*, Cicero has depicted himself as effective and his opponent as inept in the eyes of those on both sides of the dispute. By using the perspectives of these two audiences, he has avoided the invidious step of proclaiming directly to the audience the he is the better man. Instead, he has simply characterized the feelings of the Sicilians and of Hortensius towards himself and his opponent. And he has done so with the appropriate expressions of modesty.

Nonetheless, the orator's direct challenge to Hortensius promises the thrill of a world-class competition. From this Olympian height, the orator can spend the next 21 sections (27-47a) lecturing Caecilius in direct address on all the qualities of a prosecutor that he lacks.[20] The two key themes will be charges of Caecilius' criminality and bad faith, and Cicero's expert opinion that Caecilius lacks the oratorical skill to prosecute the case. The orator finds dilemma useful, in very different ways, to reinforce both attacks.

The lesson has four parts: Caecilius' lack of *integritas* and *innocentia* (27b-28), his inability to be a strong and faithful prosecutor (29-35a), his oratorical failings (35b-43), and his certain hopelessness in the face of Hortensius (44-47a).

The first two of these parts are so closely related that their treatment as separate points seems artificial. Their purpose is to undermine, without confronting, the very basis of Caecilius' claims to prosecute, namely that Verres has injured him and has broken the bond of quaestor and praetor.

---

[20] Cf. May 34-36; Sternkopf, 277-282.

Thus Caecilius has a strong personal motive to prosecute, and because of the quaestor/praetor relationship that his praetor has violated, a special knowledge of Verres' crimes. These sections prepare the audience for Cicero's actual attack on Caecilius' claim to a stronger motive (52-63).

Cicero's tactic here is this: Depending upon the recognized fact that the Sicilians prefer him to Caecilius, the orator alleges a reason why they do not want Caecilius. Caecilius, as Verres' quaestor, would not want to gather evidence but to carry it off, since he would otherwise be implicated in his praetor's crimes (28). This explains again the Sicilians' reluctance to use Verres' quaestor (cf. 4, 21-22). Of course this is nonsense. The Sicilians may want Cicero for any number of reasons, most probably because he is a more experienced speaker. Instead, Cicero again uses the Sicilians' preference as grounds for alleging that they suspect the quaestor and praetor were partners in crime.

Since this very bond, broken by Verres, is at the heart of Caecilius' best case, the orator has more work to do. Under cover of changing headings (29 "Deinde accusatorem firmum verumque esse oportet" ["In the next place, a prosecutor must show firmness and honesty."]), the orator inserts a lengthy *praeteritio* (29 "nec ea dico" *ad fin.*) in which he denies that Verres and Caecilius are in fact on bad terms.[21]

Without this root hostility, the quaestor/praetor relationship is instantly transformed from Caecilius' strongest asset into a serious liability. In tandem with the alleged suspicion of the Sicilians, it prepares for the depiction of Caecilius as Verres' fellow criminal in the provincial administration (30-33a).

Once Cicero has gotten to this point through arguments founded in innuendo, he can adduce specific, concrete examples of Verres' misdeeds in which Caecilius is implicated (30-33a). In this context, it is striking that the first and last of Cicero's examples of Verres' misdeeds, on which Caecilius allegedly cannot act without self-incrimination, are underscored with dilemma:

> utrum hoc tantum crimen praetermittes an obicies? Si obicies, idne alteri crimini dabis quod eodem tempore in eadem provincia tu ipse fecisti? audebis ita accusare alterum ut quo minus tute condemnere recusare non possis? Sin praetermittes, qualis erit tua ista accusatio, quae domestici

---

[21] Surely he uses *praeteritio* because he cannot prove this vital contention, and has not yet prepared the audience for the brazen fiction of the alleged wrong Caecilius has suffered (55-58). Cf. Stroh 177 and n.16.

> periculi metu certissimi et maximi criminis non modo sponsionem, verum etiam mentionem ipsam pertimescat? (31)

> Will you pass over a charge of this importance, or bring it up against him? If you bring it up, are you prepared to charge another man with the guilt of doing what you have done yourself at the same time and place? Will you dare to conduct your prosecution of another man in such a way as to leave you no defence against being condemned yourself? If on the other hand you pass this charge over, what can be your value as a prosecutor? Serious and well-grounded as the charge is, the personal risk to yourself will deter you not merely from any suggestion of its truth, but even from any allusion to its existence.

> quid igitur? daturus es huic crimini quod et potuisti prohibere ne fieret et debuisti, an totum id relinques? (33)

> Then, Caecilius, are you likely to include in the charges against him an offense which you could have and should have prevented? Or will you let it pass altogether?

The actual allegations against Verres himself are no doubt factual, the details concrete, and the argument, undergirded by these dilemmas, is ostentatiously a strong conclusion apparently based on facts. And this is all an illusion. Caecilius' duty had been to serve his praetor, and it is exactly his position as quaestor that will now guarantee his special expertise in discovering Verres' crimes. But by his use of innuendo, the orator has turned the tables, asserting that the praetor's criminal behavior must entail the quaestor's criminal behavior. The use of concrete detail, and the aggressive and conspicuous use of dilemma, lend an air of validity to the argument that obscures, and even retroactively legitimizes, this specious assertion. At the same time, the power of the attack underscores Cicero's own virtuosity, reinforcing through his speech the argument that he is the better speaker.

Cicero's exercise of virtuosity becomes more overtly self-conscious in the next line of argument (35b-47a).[22] The orator, ostentatiously aware of the dangers of self-praise,[23] can still advise Caecilius in a friendly way (!) that the case will be far beyond him; it will require all the skills of an orator (37-39). The orator hastens to add that he himself has not attained these skills, despite working towards them since his youth. Cicero in fact knows enough to be afraid of the challenge of prosecuting Verres, while Caecilius is complacent in his ignorance (40-43).[24]

---

[22] Cf. May, 35-37.
[23] See note 12 above.
[24] As Neumeister, 39-40, has pointed out, this treatment allows Cicero to shift the comparison from oratorical talent to diligence, which has much less potential to offend.

The portrayal of Caecilius as an inept speaker culminates in Cicero's second adduction of Hortensius (44-47a). Caecilius could not prosecute effectively even if there were no defense. Cicero, on the other hand, is Hortensius' equal. Although the orator had admitted his apprehension at effectively representing Verres' enormities, facing the greatest pleader of the day holds no terrors for him. Again, the audience is invited to a thrilling duel of champions (44). As for Caecilius, he would not stand a chance. Cicero proceeds to catalogue the tactics of Hortensius that will leave Caecilius befuddled and helpless. If Caecilius can respond to Cicero, then there may be hope for him. But if he is helpless even in this initial sparring, how will he sustain the eloquence of Hortensius himself (45-47a)?

One may feel confident that in this speech Cicero uses as many of the tactics he ascribes to Hortensius as he can. It is certain that he uses two. One is the attack on Caecilius for violating the bond of quaestor and praetor.[25] The other Hortensian tactic Cicero describes in this way:

> Te vero Caecili, quem ad modum sit elusurus, quam omni ratione iactaturus, videre iam videor; quotiens ille tibi potestatem optionemque facturus sit ut eligas utrum velis -- factum esse necne, verum esse an falsum -- utrum dixeris, id contra te futurum. (45)

> But as for you, Caecilius, I can see already, in my mind's eye, how he will outwit you, and make sport of you in a hundred ways; how often he will give you the fullest freedom to choose between two alternatives -- that a thing has or has not happened, that a statement is true or false; and how, whichever you choose, your choice will tell against you.

This is of course the definition of dilemma. This highly recognizable device, which every properly educated senator would have encountered in his youthful studies, is beyond Caecilius. Cicero, and his audience, have a sophistication that Caecilius wholly lacks. Of course Cicero has already confronted Caecilius with three dilemmas in the speech so far (secs. 12, 31, 33). By announcing that this is an Hortensian tactic against which Caecilius is helpless, the orator establishes a resonance; as those memorable dilemmas are recalled, and as Cicero uses the device in

---

[25] 46: Quid? cum commiserari, conqueri, et ex illius invidia deonerare aliquid et in te traicere coeperit, commemorare quaestoris cum praetore necessitudinem constitutam, morem maiorum, sortis religionem, poterisne eius orationis subire invidiam? [Think of it when he begins to bewail his client's unhappy condition: to lighten the load of prejudice against Verres, and shift a portion of it to your own back: to remind us of the close personal tie between a quaestor and his chief, of our national tradition in this matter and the solemn obligation the lot imposes upon them. Can you face the hostility that such arguments will arouse against you?] Cf. 59-63a.

the following arguments, each dilemma will carry not only the weight of its own argument but also the innuendo of Caecilius' oratorical incompetence.[26]

After dispensing with Caecilius' potential assisting prosecutors (47b-50 "recipiendus"), and making clear that he will not have an assisting prosecutor, including the dishonest Caecilius, imposed upon him (50 "Quibus ego" -51), Cicero seems to return to his theme of Caecilius' hopeless incompetence (52). In fact, the orator here begins, at last, his treatment of what is Quintilian's first *locus*, which man has the stronger motives for prosecuting. The orator has already done all he can to render the answer both obvious and unimportant. He has just reminded the audience of his suspicion that Caecilius is in league with the defense (51, cf. 29); it is clear who will act with more sincere commitment (Quintilian's third *locus*). He has also shown who has exercised the greater diligence in preparing to speak, and thus will be the more effective prosecutor (roughly Quintilian's second *locus*). More important, the orator has characterized Caecilius not simply as the poorer speaker, but as absolutely incompetent. Given this, there really is no choice, as the orator points out to his opponent.[27]

As noted above, Cicero structures the speech in this way so that he can effectively demolish his opponent before confronting his own weakest point; Caecilius has a personal motive to prosecute, while Cicero does not. That personal motive is an unspecified wrong done to Caecilius, a wrong that violated the tie of quaestor and praetor. Cicero meanwhile can only advance the motive of wanting to help the Sicilians. He is thus open to charges of greed and political opportunism. But by insisting on Caecilius' incompetence, the orator can make a simple case for the Sicilians' interests. Caecilius' revenge, even if he were competent to exact it, would block the revenge of the province. In short, Cicero answers Quintilian's question "Which of the two has the stronger motive?" by maintaining that the province does (54). Cicero's own motives need not be discussed; he is the agent of the provincial will.

---

[26] Cf. Craig, 442-446.
[27] 53: et hoc te praeterit, non id solum spectari solere, qui debeat, sed etiam illud, qui possit ulcisci; in quo utrumque sit, eum superiorem esse, in quo alterutrum, in eo non quid is velit, sed quid facere possit, quaeri solere. [You forget that it is usual for people to ask not merely who should, but also who can, avenge them. The man who has both qualities is better than any other; but if a man has only one of these things, it is usual to inquire rather what he can do than what he would like to do.]

This argument is certainly strong, but the orator feels that is not sufficient. Caecilius has a personal motive, as Cicero does not, and this fact must be obscured. So, using an habitual tactic, the orator distorts Caecilius' position by perverting the sensible order of his arguments. He first questions whether any injury was done to Caecilius, or rather manufactures a blow that is no injury at all, and vilifies Caecilius in the bargain (55-58). This done, Cicero then treats the bond between quaestor and praetor as an independent ground that Caecilius will advance in favor of his claim to prosecute (59-63a).[28] Here Cicero can dilate, as he had said Hortensius would (46), on the bond between quaestor and praetor, the way of the ancestors, the divine bond of the lot. The orator's argument for his own claim, based on the will of the provincials, the *mos maiorum*, and the self-interest of the senatorial jurors, can then be made decisively (63b ad fin.).

Dilemma plays a capping role in the initial part of this argument (55-58). First, the orator gives his own outrageous version of the wrong that Caecilius had suffered. Whether there is some grain of truth in the details of this version, or whether the entire story is a fabrication, it is clear that the Agonis story cannot provide the justified hostility towards Verres with which the orator will later credit Caecilius. But the distortion is particularly effective, not least since it allows Cicero to showcase his narrative gifts.[29]

The orator then builds on his fiction by claiming that after his version of events Caecilius was on good terms with Verres.

> Hic tu si laesum te a Verre esse dicis, patiar et concedam; si iniuriam tibi factam quereris, defendam et negabo; denique de iniuria quae tibi facta sit neminem nostrum graviorem iudicem esse oportet quam te ipsum, cui facta dicitur. Si tu cum illo postea in gratiam redisti, si domi illius aliquotiens fuisti, si ille apud te postea cenavit, **utrum te perfidiosum an praevaricatorem existimari mavis? Video esse necesse alterutrum, sed ego tecum in eo non pugnabo quo minus utrum velis eligas.** (58)
>
> Now if you maintain that in this matter Verres has injured you, very good; I will allow that. But if you complain that he has done you a wrong, I say no, he has not. And finally, if any wrong has been done you, none of us should resent the matter more gravely than yourself, the alleged sufferer. But if you subsequently made friends with him again, if you visited him several times at his house, if later he dined with you -- **well, which would you have us consider you, a traitor to your friend**

---

[28] Cf. Stroh, 180-181.

[29] Like the Hortensius he depicts in sec. 46, Cicero even casts Verres in a good light, although he soon corrects the impression.

or a traitor to justice? One or the other it is plain to me you must be: but I do not propose to argue the point with you -- you may choose which alternative you will.

The fact that such intimacy can be held as a charge looks to the quaestor/praetor bond and so prepares the way for the next part of the argument. Of course we cannot know if the charges of intimacy in the three "si" clauses are true. Cicero presents them as indubitable by making the dilemma conditional upon them. As in secs. 31 and 33, and at *S. Rosc.* 74, 79, and 93,[30] the very use of dilemma seems to confer legitimacy on the assumptions that inform it.

The dilemma itself is faulty only in its presupposition that Cicero's version of events is true. Otherwise, the argument is quite ironclad, and quite ostentatious. It caps the line of argument, and resonates with section 45. The coda professing Cicero's indifference about the alternative that Caecilius chooses reflects and demonstrates the complete superiority of orators such as Cicero and Hortensius. Caecilius will indeed be unable to answer Cicero (cf. 47). Thus the use of dilemma concurrently advertises Cicero's virtuosity and reinforces the notion of Caecilius' absolute incompetency that renders the question of motives irrelevant.

Having finished this presentation with a flourish, Cicero goes on falsely to impute to his opponent the claim that Caecilius will be a better prosecutor solely because he was Verres' quaestor. This allows the orator to expand upon that bond, and upon the *mos maiorum*, in the manner that he had warned Hortensius would use (56-63. cf. 46). The critical point of Caecilius' position is of course that it was Verres who betrayed the relationship. The orator has already characterized that betrayal as a good deed of Verres, and a deed for which Caecilius had forgiven him. Thus Caecilius' argument is, in Cicero's version, perverse. Again Cicero builds on his distortion with dilemma:

> Qui (sc. Caecilius) si summam iniuriam ab illo accepisti, tamen, quoniam quaestor eius fuisti, non potes eum sine ulla vituperatione accusare; si vero non ulla tibi facta est iniuria, sine scelere eum accusare non potes. Quare cum incertum sit de iniuria, quemquam horum esse putas qui non malit te sine vituperatione quam cum scelere discedere? (60)

> **Even if he has wronged you (sc. Caecilius) deeply, yet, having been his quaestor, your cannot prosecute him without incurring some blame: and if he has not wronged you at all, you cannot prosecute him without incurring criminal guilt. Consequently, the alleged wrong not being proved, can you imagine that there is any member of this court**

---

[30] See above, pp. 34-38.

who would not rather you came out of this affair free from blame than guilty of a crime?

This dilemma is purely moral in its presupposition that it is always wrong for a quaestor to attack his praetor. In fact the figure is a wedding of the dilemma form and a type of Cicero's favored "even if he had..." argument structure.[31] The artificiality of this argument is seen in its amplification, "cum incertum sit de iniuria" ["the alleged wrong not being proved"]. Cicero has stated and will repeat that Verres' did no wrong to Caecilius. This note of doubt is sounded only so that Cicero can reach his conclusion with the nice balance of "sine vituperatione" ["without censure"] with "cum scelere" ["with criminal guilt"].[32] This dilemma again sounds the resonance established in section 45, driving home the point that Cicero and Hortensius are in a higher league than Caecilius, and even enlisting the audience's good will towards Caecilius to keep him from prosecuting.

Cicero's further expansion on the quaestor/praetor bond (61-63a), and his argument for the precedent and positive good of choosing one who is favored by the provincials, and who will not deflate the credibility of the court (63b-73 including the *peroratio*), round out the performance. When the orator has finished, Caecilius has no very good place even to begin his reply.

Admittedly, this speech is very different from that for Roscius of Ameria, both in its genre and in its aims. The choice of a prosecutor looks to the future, and so is fundamentally deliberative. Further, because the speech is basically concerned with a personnel decision, all of the arguments, whether concerned with motive, energy, sincerity, or simply competence, are centered on the two candidates. To some extent, each argument is ethical, and this ethical argument is all directly relevant to the question at issue.

Having conceded these differences, we find in our only extant *divinatio* a substantial replication of the general functions of dilemma forms in *Pro Roscio Amerino*. It is striking that Cicero's profession that he himself is in a dilemma recurs here (4, 14. Cf. *S. Rosc.* 124, above, p. 39). In *Pro Roscio Amerino*, the orator had used the form to alleviate the

---

[31] See C.P. Craig, "The Structural Pedigree of Cicero's Speeches *pro Archia, pro Milone,* and *pro Quinctio,*" *CP* 80 (1985) 136-137.
[32] *Contra* Sternkopf, 288 and n.11, 298.

jury's anxiety that their property would be threatened. Here, the dilemma structure in sec. 4 helps the orator to circumvent the problem of Caecilius' stronger motive for prosecution by claiming that he is being forced to prosecute by duty towards the Sicilians, and thus by the principle that the desire of the victims is paramount. While the specific functions of each of these self-inflicted dilemma structures responds to unique circumstances, both examples give Cicero a license to pursue a line of argument, and a manner of behavior, which would otherwise alienate the audience.

This license is reinforced in our speech by the repetition of the dilemma structure (sec. 14). Through this dilemma form, Cicero both claims that his dilemma is a problem well known to the patrons of Sicily, and that they are sympathetic, and reaffirms the validity of his license to prosecute without any personal grievance against the defendant.

The true dilemmas in the speech likewise reproduce in a general way the functions of the device in *Pro Roscio Amerino*: Cicero uses the presentational value of the device both to give the appearance of invincible argument and concurrently to mask weak assumptions (31, 33, 58). Further, he uses dilemma in a more pronounced way to punctuate the flow of argument (12, 58). In this speech, dilemma is not used to mark a critical parenthesis, as at *S. Rosc.* 128 (above, p. 40), but to create the impression of forceful reasoning at the introduction (12) or conclusion (58) of an entire line of argument.

At the same time, the presentational functions of dilemma in the *Divinatio* are expanded in two important ways: The first of these is the calculated use of the alternative structure and apparent rigor of the device at the beginning of a line of argument to define the debate in a way that allows Cicero to prove impressively, convincingly, and at length a point that is in fact not at issue. Cicero manufactures the dilemma in section 12 in the sense that the first choice he offers, that the Sicilians do not want Cicero, gives the opponent the choice of arguing a point that he has already conceded. This forced molding of material into dilemma form allows the orator to start his argument with conspicuous power, then to prove a point decisively (since the first prong is not really contested), and thus to give the illusion of indomitable strength before dealing with the debatable second prong of the argument. This tactic incidentally organizes an entire section of the argumentation.

The other, more striking feature of the presentational use of dilemma in this speech is the special quality of its resonances. Ordinarily, the content or presuppositions of a dilemma may be called to mind by the repetition of a dilemma of similar content or presuppositions, or perhaps by the simple recurrence of the device itself. But in this speech Cicero explicitly defines dilemma as a Hortensian device against which his opponent will be powerless. Thus each use of the form creates a resonance not only with every other use of the form but with this assertion. Whatever its context, each occurrence of dilemma argues that Cicero is as competent as Hortensius, and that Caecilius is helpless in the face of either. Cicero's explicit and self-conscious treatment of the dilemma form as a token of skill in speaking is a perfect weapon for this contest of oratorical competence; it is as effective as it is unparalleled.

CHAPTER FOUR: *PRO ROSCIO COMOEDO*

The speech for the comedic actor Q. Roscius is the most impenetrable of Cicero's orations. In part because neither the beginning nor the end of the speech has come down to us, there is no scholarly consensus on the facts that give rise to the case. Nor is there consensus on its date. The style itself is idiosyncratic, and has only recently been satisfactorily explained.[1] Among its other peculiarities, the speech shows a remarkable frequency of dilemmas (secs. 9, 16, 25(*bis*), 40, 43, 52, 55), and so demands our attention.

These are the facts: Fifteen years before the present case (37), Q. Roscius, the greatest comedic actor of his time, entered into a partnership with a certain C. Fannius Chaerea to train Fannius' slave Panurgus for the stage. (24-31). The two partners were to split the profits from Panurgus' performances. After Roscius had trained Panurgus, the slave was killed by

---

[1] The following discussion is based upon the text of J. Axer (Leipzig: Teubner, 1976). W. Stroh, *Taxis und Taktik* (Stuttgart: Teubner, 1975) 104-148, includes in his controversial interpretation a clear analysis of the large bibliography on the legal questions concerning the speech. Among the works he cites, these will give a view of the conventional interpretation and its recent variations: F. Wieacker, *Cicero als Advokat* (Berlin: Walter de Gruyter, 1965); V. Arangio-Ruiz, in the introduction to his Italian translation in *Marco Tullio Cicerone, Le Orazioni* (Verona: Mondadori, 1964) 283-309; H.J. Mette, "Der junge Anwalt Cicero," *Gymnasium* 72 (1965) 10-27, esp. 15-19.

On the date, Stroh, 149-156 (with lit.) rejects the mid-seventies in favor of 66. There are real problems with either date, but the evidence seems slightly more favorable to 66. Cf. J. Axer, *The Style and Composition of Cicero's Speech Pro Roscio Comoedo, Origin and Function* (Warsaw: Wydawnictwa Uniwersytetu Warsawskiego, 1980) 54-56. This monograph of Axer is the most convincing treatment of the problem of the style of the speech.

Except for the two books of Axer, These works will hereafter be cited by the authors' last names.

a certain Q. Flavius of Tarquinia (32). Roscius sued for compensation, with Fannius serving as his *cognitor*, or legal agent. But before the court could pronounce a finding against Flavius, Roscius entered into a private agreement with Flavius by which the actor received a farm now worth at least HS 600,000[2] in compensation for the dead slave (32). Fannius was not part of this settlement, and may not have known about it. By accepting the property from Flavius, then neglecting to share it with Fannius, Roscius thus violated the legal principle of the partnership. All income arising from the business of the partnership is the property of all the partners.[3] After twelve years (8 & 37), Fannius pursued a claim against Roscius. The reason for his delay, whether ignorance of Roscius' agreement with Flavius or other circumstances, is unknown.

At this point scholarly consensus on the facts comes to an end. According to the traditional view, Fannius and Roscius went to law before an *arbiter*, C. Calpurnius Piso, to obtain an equitable judgement on Fannius' claim. At the end of this process, through *stipulatio* and *restipulatio*, Roscius promised to pay Fannius HS 100,000 for his earlier work as *cognitor*. Fannius in turn promised to pay Roscius half of any sum he might eventually recover from Flavius (38). Thus Piso orchestrated a settlement that would pay Fannius handsomely, but which would not attach to Roscius the stigma of having cheated his partner.[4] Avoiding this stigma was of great importance; if Fannius had pursued Roscius with an *arbitrium pro socio*, or an *actio furti manifesti*, conviction would have destroyed the great actor's personal and commercial reputation. Accordingly, Roscius paid Fannius a first installment of HS 50,000. But Roscius then neglected to pay the second half (deduced from 4 & 38 and 11 & 22). For his part, Cicero claims that Fannius violated the terms of the arbitral agreement; after the *arbitrium*, but before the present case, Fannius came to his own settlement with Flavius, for which he received HS 100,000. But Fannius neglected to pay half of this sum to Roscius, and so violated the arbitral agreement (38-51). Flavius himself died after the *arbitrium*, but before the present case (42), so he is

---

[2] For all of the numbers in the speech as they appear in Axer's text, see his persuasive rationale in *Style and Composition*, 59-86, with lit.
[3] Cf. Wieacker, 10; Stroh 122-123; Arangio-Ruiz, 293-294; Mette, 18.
[4] Cf. Arangio-Ruiz, 296-297. The *stipulatio*, while not a written obligation, was the source of the debt here at issue. So Wieacker, 12-13, *contra* Arangio-Ruiz, 286-287. Mette, 16, believes that the *stipulatio* had been reinforced by a written contract. For full lit., see Stroh, 106, n.12.

unavailable to give evidence on this matter. Now, three years after the *arbitrium* (8, 32), Fannius brings an *actio certae creditae pecuniae* to recover the remaining HS 50,000 (10-11) owed to him under the arbitral agreement. The same Piso who had served as *arbiter* serves as *iudex* in this suit (12). A certain Saturius speaks for the plaintiff, while Cicero has charge of the defense.

W. Stroh has offered a devastating challenge to this conventional interpretation of Piso's *arbitrium*, and thus to the usual understanding of the factual grounds of the case.[5] He argues that between four and three years previously (8), Fannius had in fact pursued an *actio furti manifesti* against Roscius, and had only relented when Roscius had made a written contract (*pactio*) to pay him HS 100,000 (4).[6] Roscius agreed, so Fannius vacated the suit before the *iudex* could find against Roscius (26). In a completely separate procedure, the two then sought Piso as an *arbiter* only to establish Fannius' compensation for his earlier work as *cognitor* in the suit with Flavius. Piso was thus utterly ignorant of the *pactio*. Stroh argues that the HS 100,000 that Piso then awarded to Fannius (38) must represent an error in the MSS. The actual amount was smaller, and was awarded only on the condition that Fannius first pay to Roscius half of his recoveries from Flavius.[7] Roscius also paid half of his obligation to Fannius under the *pactio*. As for Fannius' suit against Flavius, Stroh believes that it had taken place soon after Roscius' agreement with Flavius, and that Fannius had received nothing from it. Still, he might have received something from Flavius, for reasons unclear, before Flavius' death. In any case, Roscius neglected to pay the second half of the money he had pledged in the *pactio*, and Fannius brought the present suit to recover this sum.

Stroh's interpretation is the most systematic account of the problems in the speech. Granting, as he does, that we can never know the truth, he reconstructs the plaintiff's argument in a way that reveals our piece as perhaps Cicero's most brilliant triumph of arrangement. Further, he makes sense of the troublesome *pactio* mentioned in section 26, and saves the *iudex* Piso from any modern charges of excessive partiality for the defendant. If sections 1-13, denying Roscius' debt, refer to the debt from

---

[5] Stroh, esp. 112-127.
[6] Stroh, 118, believes that the property Roscius had received from Flavius was valued at HS 100,000, not HS 600,000, so he believes that this contract would represent 100% of Roscius' profit from the original transaction.
[7] Stroh, 123-125.

the *arbitrium*, as most scholars assume, then Piso must realize that Cicero is lying. The argument must then be purely a smoke screen to deceive the *corona*. In Stroh's construct, sections 1-13 dispute the existence of a debt from a secret *pactio*, and thus Piso has no information that Cicero's argument is specious. Further, the speech is completely consonant with Stroh's idea of a secret *pactio* until section 38. Only here do we realize that the HS 100,000, the debt first mentioned in section 4, refers to the settlement of Piso's *arbitrium*. If we follow Stroh in believing that the number in section 38 must represent corruption in the MSS, the problem is obviated, and the basis for the traditional view disappears.

Stroh's insistence that 100,000 cannot be the correct reading in section 38 is thus at the heart of his approach. Although his argument for the secret *pactio* conforms nicely with the speech to that point, the huge amount of the award from the *arbitrium* makes no sense in his view, and makes complete sense in the traditional view (which takes section 38 as its starting point). But the MSS clearly read CCCLIII. This same corrupted numeral is used consistently for 100,000 in its fourteen other occurrences in the speech, and nowhere undergoes further corruption.[8] So Stroh's view of the *pactio*, while it makes far better sense than does the traditional interpretation for most of the speech, here collides head on with the MSS.

Given this vexing situation, I propose a compromise that will be at least partially satisfactory. The *pactio* in section 26 does refer to an agreement that Fannius will not pursue Roscius with an action that could disgrace him (an *actio furti manifesti*, for example). Instead, Roscius persuades Fannius to agree to go before an *arbiter* who is sympathetic to Roscius' concern for his reputation, but who will give Fannius what the wronged partner feels he deserves. Fannius, if he feels that this *arbitrium* will not reward him properly, may still pursue the more severe action; Piso is only establishing how much he is owed as *cognitor*. His right to sue for his part of Roscius' settlement with Flavius is not impaired. Piso, concerned both with fairness to Fannius and with Roscius' reputation, is happy to advance these terms. Thus the *pactio* of section 26 is an informal agreement between Fannius and Roscius: Fannius will not pursue an *actio furti manifesti* (or an *arbitrium pro socio*) against Roscius. In return, he will receive HS 100,000 in the arbitral settlement. For cosmetic reasons, he will even make a *repromissio* to pay Roscius half of any recoveries he

---

[8] Thus Axer, *Style and Composition*, 75-79.

may make from Flavius. This *pactio* is not a formal contract at all, but simply an agreement to get an arbitral judgement guaranteeing that Fannius will get his money, and Roscius will preserve his reputation.[9]

But Stroh is nevertheless correct in his observation that Cicero, in sections 1-13 and 26, is denying the existence of a formal *pactio*. This is in fact a typical Ciceronian trick. The formal *pactio* that the orator denies is his own invention, a distortion of the informal *pactio* explained by the plaintiff. Cicero uses this distortion to distract the *corona* from the immediate issue of the debt arising from the *arbitrium*, and to make a show of refuting the opponent by blasting a claim that the plaintiff has in fact never advanced.

This compromise solution is admittedly as speculative as other attempts to understand the speech. Further, it leaves Piso in the position of listening in silence to arguments that he must know are specious. On the other hand, it does account for the presence of the *pactio*, which Stroh has clearly demonstrated, without ignoring the testimony of the MSS.

Accepting this largely conventional view of the facts of the case, we may still agree in general terms with Stroh's reconstruction of the plaintiff's speech.[10] I) Saturius had narrated the background of the partnership in order to demonstrate Roscius' bad behavior in the settlement with Flavius. II) He had then stressed that Roscius' behavior violated the law of partnerships, and that Roscius had effectively, if not legally, deprived him of the opportunity to recover from Flavius.[11] Stroh astutely points out that this accusation, "de tota re decidisti" ["you made a settlement about the whole business"] (34), is a moral censure rather than a legal argument. III) Here Stroh believes that Saturius described the legal *pactio* as the grounds of the present suit. We, on the other hand, must assert that Saturius described the informal *pactio* that led to the arbitral decision. Saturius pointed out that he took this action at Roscius' request,

---

[9] Thus in section 26, "Iudici hic denuntiavit. Absolutus est." ["This man announced this to the judge. He was acquitted."], *Iudici* refers to Piso, who was then the *arbiter*, but who is the *iudex* in the present case.
 Without vitiating the conventional interpretation, one may equally well infer that the mention of this *iudex* argues that Fannius had actually initiated an action against Roscius when he was persuaded to drop it in favor of the *arbitrium*. Thus Stroh, 115-116 & n.46. But it does not necessarily follow from this interpretation that the *pactio* which induced Fannius to abandon the action was a formal contract.
[10] Stroh, 146-148.
[11] Stroh, 131-134. I do not believe Stroh's speculation that Fannius had already tried and failed in such a suit, or that Cluvius had been the judge in that suit.

to save the actor from a decision that would publicly disgrace him. Roscius had in fact already paid HS 50,000 of the money pledged in his *stipulatio*. Given these facts, Fannius' failure to record the debt in his *codex*, his permanent ledger, was completely in the spirit of the *pactio*. So large an arbitral award indicated that Roscius had done wrong despite the language of the *stipulatio*, and Fannius kindly did not post this evidence in his permanent financial record. There seemed to be no need, since the content of the *stipulatio* and *restipulatio* were known, if not publicly, at least to Piso.[12] Further, Roscius had already admitted the debt by paying the first installment.

There are two great problems facing Cicero in this case. The first is that Roscius does in fact owe Fannius the HS 50,000 for which he is being sued. Further, the *iudex* Piso, who has sole responsibility to render legal judgement, knows this. Second, even if Piso might want to show undue favor towards Roscius, he is constrained by public opinion, an opinion for which the *corona* of spectators is both a measure and a conduit. Saturius' recounting of Roscius' original bargain with Flavius has asserted before the *corona*, and thus before the Roman public, that Roscius has cheated his partner. This open attack on Roscius' reputation must prejudice the spectators against the defendant. Finally, because Saturius does publicly attack Roscius' reputation, it would not be enough for Piso to find in favor of the defense. The spectators themselves, although they have no formal role in the case, must be convinced that a judgement for Roscius is equitable. Otherwise, the *arbitrium* becomes a scandal, and Roscius' reputation is practically crippled, or completely destroyed.

Cicero's response to this challenge has three closely linked goals. First, he must convince Piso that a judgement for Roscius would be fair. This he attempts through his argument that Fannius, after the *arbitrium*, had in fact received HS 100,000 from Flavius, but had not given Roscius half, as he had promised to do in his *restipulatio* (39-51). Thus, Cicero argues, Fannius owes Roscius HS 50,000. Since this is the amount of Roscius' debt to Fannius from the *arbitrium*, Piso can feel justified in letting the debts cancel out, and so find for Roscius.

---

[12] There need have been no public knowledge of the terms of the *stipulatio* and *restipulatio*. It is one of the great curiosities of Roman law that a valid oral contract could be struck in the absence of witnesses. So B. Nicholas, *An Introduction to Roman Law*, rev. ed. (Oxford: Clarendon Press, 1975), 193.

Unfortunately, this sensible course is neither legally viable nor publicly acceptable. If Fannius really had recovered HS 100,000 from Flavius, Roscius should still have to pay Fannius what he owes, then pursue his own *actio certae creditae pecuniae* against Fannius to recover his half of the money Fannius had received from Flavius. Further, the public attack on Roscius' behavior in his own settlement with Flavius demands either a rebuttal or an adverse judgement.

Cicero's second goal is to leave Piso the flexibility to accept the surreptitious compromise by demonstrating to the *corona* that Roscius does not owe Fannius the money that he does in fact owe. Third, and closely related, the orator must defend Roscius' reputation before the *corona* by denying that Roscius had cheated Fannius fifteen years before.

Cicero's response to the challenge is completely to misrepresent both the basis of the opponent's case and the thrust of the legal principle that Roscius had originally violated. He does this in five major ways: 1) The orator systematically distorts his opponent's argument about the origin of the present debt (1-13, 25-26); 2) He consistently misrepresents as a legal argument his opponent's complaint that Roscius had left Fannius no opportunity to sue Flavius for himself (32-51); 3) He claims that Fannius had been the one to swindle Roscius (39-51); 4) He argues vigorously against the legal principle that Roscius violated when he settled with Flavius behind Fannius' back (51-56); 5) He interlards these arguments with strong ethical argumentation for Roscius' probity, and for the avarice of Fannius. As part of this campaign, Cicero labels Fannius a Ballio, a Plautine pimp (20). So the orator introduces an amusing and distracting comedic element into this trial of Rome's greatest comic actor.[13]

For an understanding of the roles of dilemma in implementing Cicero's strategy, an overview of the entire *argumentatio* will be useful.

Although the speech as we have it takes up the *argumentatio* in progress, it is clear that the orator uses the specious division between a substantial (1-13) and an *extra causam* (16-56) part of his speech in order to deprive his opponent's arguments of their context, and in order to give the illusion of having shown his client to be legally in the right at the very beginning. This apparent demonstration encourages the audience to relax the rigor of their standards of proof, and to become more receptive to affective arguments. The arguments that Cicero advances under this license are really addressed to the substantial nub of the case.

---

[13] Axer, *Style and Composition*, 25-31 *et passim*.

The "substantial" argument (1-13) is centered upon the formal *pactio*, and thus upon a claim that the plaintiff had never made. The orator deliberately misrepresents Roscius' duty under the *arbitrium*, the obligation to pay Fannius HS 100,000, as a claim of the plaintiff for money that Roscius has contracted to pay under this alleged formal *pactio*. Of course the plaintiff has not alleged any formal contract other than that arising from the *arbitrium*, so this synthetic allegation may be refuted easily and at length. Since Piso is the *iudex*, and Roscius has already paid the first half of the HS 100,000 he owes in accordance with the *arbitrium*, it is clear that this complete misrepresentation of the plaintiff's case will not fool the judge. It is intended to fool the *corona*.

In battering this straw man, Cicero relies on the fact that Fannius had been careless, or kind-hearted, after the *arbitrium*. Because Piso's decision was so transparently an attempt to save Roscius' reputation, Roscius would not want the judgement, or the debt he now had to pay, to be widely publicized. Fannius, content with the prospect of HS 100,000, was accommodating. He did not enter the debt in his formal ledger of accounts (*codex*), although he did make a note of it in his day-book (*adversaria*). A *codex* had much greater evidentiary value than did *adversaria*. Further, the terms of the *stipulatio* and *restipulatio* that ended the *arbitrium* were not, so far as we know, known to any one else except Piso, another attempt to spare Roscius embarrassment.[14] Cicero now pretends that Fannius is using the notice in his *adversaria* to argue that Roscius owes him money under the imaginary *pactio*. This muddies the waters wonderfully.

Thus, after briefly dismissing the possibility that Fannius had loaned Roscius money (inferred from 13), Cicero is arguing, where our text begins, that Roscius had made no *written* contract to pay. The fact that the debt is recorded in Fannius' records *(tabulae)*, but not in Roscius', begins an ascending series of arguments to demonstrate this conclusion -- a conclusion that the plaintiff would not contest. First, Fannius has recorded the debt in his records, but Roscius has not (1-2 "quod debes"). Having made this point, Cicero offers to concede that the account in Fannius' records (in the sense of *codex*) is correct. This allows him to pounce upon the fact that Fannius has not recorded so large a debt in his

---

[14] See n.12 above.

codex. Fannius is thus impossibly brazen to make his claim at all (2 "aeque enim" - 5).

His indignation vented, Cicero admits that Fannius has recorded the debt in his *adversaria*, and this is a further cause of indignation. This bit of fulmination (5-9a) ends with a dilemma that caps the argument based on *codex* and *adversaria*:

> Utrum cetera nomina in codicem accepti et expensi digesta habes an non? Si non, quo modo tabulas conficis? si etiam, quam ob rem, cum cetera nomina in ordinem referebas, hoc nomen triennio amplius, quod erat in primis magnum, in adversariis relinquebas? Nolebas sciri debere tibi Roscium; cur scribebas? Rogatus eras ne referres; cur in adversariis scriptum habebas? (9)

> Have you arranged all the other items of receipts and expenses in the general ledger or not? If you have not, how do you make up your books? if you have, why is it that, when entering all the other items in order, you left this item, which was an extremely large one, for more than three years in your day-book? You did not want it to be known that Roscius was indebted to you. Why then did you put it down? "You had been asked not to enter it." Why then did you put it down in your day-book?

This dilemma is as specious as the whole line of reasoning in sections 1-13. It is quite clear that Fannius does keep financial records, and so to ask whether he does or not, then treat, however dismissively, the idea that he does not is to manufacture an alternative for the sake of the dilemma form. This false dilemma gives the air of invincibility to Cicero's argument, and so fosters the perception of that argument as a legitimate and important unit.

Of course, Fannius' ability to document the debt should not really be decisive in the light of Piso's *arbitrium*, and Saturius had offered good reasons for Fannius' failure to transfer the record the debt from *adversaria* tò *codex*. While he needed some record of the amount to keep his own accounts in order, Fannius had sufficient regard for Roscius' reputation to avoid recording the debt in his permanent records (*codex*). Fannius' kind-hearted action, wrenched from its context, is set within the false context of the issue of an alleged written contract. If the case were about a written contract, then Fannius' behavior would be highly suspicious. In that manufactured setting, sustained in part through the impression created by the dilemma form, Fannius' reasoning is now represented as alternative answers to the question that is the second, substantial prong of the synthetic dilemma.

The perfectly plausible explanation of Fannius' failure to record the debt in his *codices* is thus treated only at the end of this part of the argument, as a pendant to a capping dilemma of which the first choice cannot be seriously considered. Thus the problem of Fannius' failure to transfer the debt from *adversaria* to *codex* for more than three years, a problem upon which Cicero has already expanded, is here posed in such a form that Fannius' sensible explanation is placed in the false context of a debate over a written contract, and so made to appear an unreasonable and transparent falsehood, an impression reinforced by its placement in the dilemma structure.

This tactic is dangerous. Cicero is after all asking questions for which good answers are ready to hand: The case is not about a written contract, but about an obligation from an *arbitrium* arising from an informal *pactio*. Arrangements were made to spare Roscius' reputation. The record was not that important, since Piso knew the content of the *stipulatio*, and Roscius' first payment of HS 50,000 was presumptive proof of the debt.

Before these answers can occur to the *corona*, the orator moves on to the apex of his ascending series of arguments; he will discredit Fannius out of his opponent's own mouth (9b-13a). The transition, "sed haec quamquam firma esse video" ["But although I consider this is sufficiently convincing"], etc., is elegant in that it distracts scrutiny from the previous argument before its weakness can be perceived. It does so by dramatically promising an even stronger argument. This never materializes. Still, the listener is effectively distracted from questioning the forceful impression made by the dilemma.

The dramatically stronger argument (9b-13a) turns out to be simply that Fannius had tried to settle for this same sum through Piso's arbitration three years before the present *iudicium*. Since an *arbitrium* is flexible, but a *iudicium* can only be won if the whole contested sum can be shown to be a valid debt, most people would use an *arbitrium* only if they feared that they would be unable to prove in a *iudicium* that a certain sum of money was owed them. But Fannius went before an *arbiter* first, and thus demonstrated his lack of faith in his case before a *iudicium* such as the present one. This is the grossest nonsense. As we have seen, Fannius is here suing for the half of the arbiter's judgement that Roscius has not yet paid. When Cicero says that the *iudicium* and the *arbitrium* concern the same HS 50,000, he is being truthful only in the loosest sense: The *arbitrium* determined how much Roscius owed Fannius. The *iudicium* is to force Roscius to pay the balance of that sum. But Cicero deceptively implies that Fannius has entered the *arbitrium* hoping to get the HS 50,000 from the written contract that the orator has manufactured. In Cicero's tale, Fannius had first gone to the *arbitrium* hoping to be awarded the sum for which he now sues, but expecting to get less.[15]

Cicero ends this "substantial" part of the argument with an *enumeratio* (13b-14). Fannius does not claim to have made a loan to Roscius, and his records will not support the notion that Roscius made a written commitment to pay him. There remains only the possibility of an oral commitment to pay in the form of a *stipulatio*. Thus is surely the type of commitment that Roscius had made after Piso's *arbitrium*, as Piso will have known. Yet Cicero can dismiss this possibility as well, since the plaintiff can produce no witnesses (!). In short, case closed.

Of course the case is not closed at all. Saturius had surely explained Fannius' misplaced concern for Roscius' reputation, and how this had led to his client's restraint in documenting the debt. This story drew strength from the scandalous tale of Roscius betraying the partnership through his failure to share the profits from his private settlement with Flavius. Fannius, after the judgement in Piso's *arbitrium*, had been magnanimous enough to let Roscius keep his reputation; Fannius was after all being fairly compensated for his share in Flavius' payment to Roscius, even though Piso was sufficiently concerned for Roscius' reputation to want to mask the true reason for the actor's commitment to pay. Thus Cicero has much left to do. He must persuade the public that Roscius' debt to Fannius is not only legally undocumented, but is really not owed. To accomplish this, he must deal, finally, with the private agreement of Roscius with Flavius.

It is a sign of the strength of the plaintiff's case that Cicero does not follow a chronological order in dealing with this problem, but creates and refutes a separate obligation in order to give the appearance of a clear-cut victory. The private agreement of Roscius and Flavius, which is the heart of the matter, he then treats ostensibly *extra causam*, pretending that he is

---

[15] By underscoring, in the midst of this palpable misrepresentation, that Piso has been pressed into service both as *arbiter* and as *iudex*, Cicero demonstrates to us, if not to the *corona*, how patiently Piso will wait for Cicero to convince him to find for Roscius; the *iudex* will be struck more than anyone else by the distortion in Cicero's argument, yet presumably he hears it in silence.

answering an attack on Roscius' reputation -- an attack irrelevant to the substance of the case.[16]

After announcing this pretense in section 15, Cicero puts forth the argument that occupies the rest of our text (16-56). The broad structure of this argument is this: *Ex persona*, Roscius is not the sort of person who would cheat his partner (16-19 *et passim*). Fannius, unlike Roscius, is a Ballio figure, exactly the sort of person who would do anything for profit (20-21). Roscius is so liberal that he has refused payment of many times HS 50,000 for his performances before the Roman people, as Fannius never would have done (22-23 "repudiarit"). Fannius did not use the proper action against one who had cheated a partner (24 "Quid ego" - 25 "indicasti"), and thus indicated that he did not think Roscius guilty. Fannius had no record of a debt. Roscius never sought a friend as *arbiter*, and made no deal with Fannius to settle the question. The *arbiter* did not require Roscius to pay Fannius any of the proceeds from the deal with Flavius because Roscius was innocent of wrongdoing. Fannius even came to Roscius' house to apologize, and to state that Roscius owed nothing from the partnership. But Fannius persists in claiming that he let his claim against Roscius' betrayal of the partnership go because Roscius made a commitment to pay him what he was owed (26).

Only in section 27 does Cicero finally begin to relate the story that leads to Roscius' settlement with Flavius. No sooner does he mention Panurgus than the orator feels he must demonstrate how much more Roscius' training was worth to the partnership than was Fannius' original purchase of the slave. In doing so, the orator offers a characterization of Roscius as the respected master and anxious teacher (27-31). Finally, 16 sections after the *extra causam* argument begins, Cicero mentions the death of Panurgus, and faces the fact of Roscius' private agreement with Flavius. He claims that Roscius settled only for his share of the damages, and left Fannius to sue for his share, so the actor did nothing wrong (32-39 "redemisse"). Further, Cicero argues at length, Fannius has recovered HS 100,000 from Flavius, and so under the terms of the *arbitrium*, owes

---

[16] Section 15: Illa superior fuit oratio necessaria, haec erit voluntaria, illa ad iudicem, haec ad C. Pisonem, illa pro reo, haec pro Roscio, illa victoriae, haec bonae existimationis causa comparata. [What I have said before was necessary; what I am going to say will be voluntary. Then I was addressing myself to a judge, now I address myself to Gaius Piso; then I was pleading for an accused person, now for Roscius; my former speech was prepared to win a cause, the latter to save a good reputation.] Cf. Stroh, 139-140; Wieacker, 14; Arangio-Ruiz, 289; Mette, 18.

Roscius HS 50,000 that he has failed to pay (39 "Quid si" - 51 "Roscium petisse"). Finally, Cicero represents as the plaintiff's last desperate claim what is really his strong legal basis -- that anything Roscius recovered for himself in a suit arising from the property of the partnership does belong to the partnership. Our text breaks off during Cicero's attempt to refute this position (51 "Iam intellegis" - 56).

The entire ostensibly *extra causam* section of the *argumentatio* begins with a dilemma:

> Pecuniam petis, Fanni, a Roscio. quam? dic audacter et aperte. **utrum <quae> tibi ex societate debeatur, an quae ex liberalitate huius promissa sit et ostentata?** (16)[17]
>
> You, Fannius, demand money from Roscius. What money? Speak boldly and frankly. **Was it owing to you from the partnership, or money which had been promised and offered to you by my client's generosity?**

As Stroh has correctly pointed out, this dilemma presents two choices, neither of which corresponds to Fannius' real course of action. He is not seeking money owed him from the partnership, but money pledged in the *arbitrium* before Piso. The second choice Cicero offers, meant to reflect Roscius' pledge of payment resulting from the *arbitrium*, asserts that Roscius, under no pressure because of any earlier misdealings, pledged money to Fannius out of the goodness of his heart. Since the second choice, in this distorted form, is obviously unacceptable, Cicero does not consider it further.[18] Rather he goes on to treat Fannius' alleged contention that money is owed him from the partnership. Again, while the plaintiff's case had the debt from Roscius' settlement with Flavius at its root, that is not the legal issue in the present case. Thus the dilemma presents as its viable alternative an option that is deceptively vague, if not completely false.

So, without actually rushing *in medias res*, this dilemma announces that serious arguments are in store, and that Cicero will attack directly the very heart of Fannius' story that Roscius cheated him in the partnership. Once the tone of vigorous argument is set, Cicero can then proceed not to his treatment of the facts (for which we must wait until section 32), but to a carefully constructed ethical argument. This ethical argument is a comparison of defendant and plaintiff in terms of the first two broad topics

---

[17] Cf. Stroh, 114.

[18] Stroh, 145-146, plausibly speculates that Cicero did in fact take up this theme again, in the lost portion of the *argumentatio*, as an explanation of Roscius' earlier payment of HS 50,000.

of the *constitutio coniecturalis* or stasis of fact, namely character and motive.[19] It is necessary to insure that the *corona* is already biased, and prejudiced, when the facts are discussed. By using the dilemma form, Cicero sustains an appearance of rigor that makes for a better transition from the apparently rigorous argument that precedes, and in turn lends a greater aura of substance to the ethical arguments that follow.

In Cicero's lengthy comparison of grasping plaintiff and munificent defendant (17-23 "repudiarit"), his attack on Fannius as a Ballio lends a comic air to the proceeding that the orator fully exploits.[20] Cicero, moving from general ethical concerns to a truly relevant act, then uses as his decisive proof of Roscius' good conduct in the partnership the fact that Fannius did not pursue him with an *arbitrium pro socio* (24 "Quid ego" - 25 " indicasti").[21] The fact that Fannius opted for the gentler form of *arbitrium* is the closest thing that Cicero has to a substantial, rather than purely ethical, argument that Roscius had not acted improperly in the partnership. Accordingly, the orator punctuates this tendentious line of argument with a dilemma form:

> quem per arbitrium (sc. pro socio) circumvenire non posses, cuius de ea re proprium non erat iudicium, nunc per iudicem condemnabis, cuius de re nullum est arbitrium? **quin tu hoc crimen aut obice ubi licet agere, aut iacere noli ubi non oportet.** Tametsi iam hoc tuo testimonio crimen sublatum est. Namque quo tu tempore illa formula uti noluisti, nihil hunc in societatem fraudis fecisse iudi<casti.> (25)

> Will you secure the condemnation by a judge, who has none of the powers of an arbitrator in a matter like this, of the man whom you could not get the bettter of before an arbitrator, whose proper function it was to pronounce a decision upon it? **Then either launch this charge where it is lawful to start an action or do not launch it where it ought not to be brought.** However, your own evidence has already refuted it. For at the time when you refused to employ that formula, you rendered your judgement that Roscius had not been guilty of fraud against the partnership.

Again, the line of argument assumes that the present case is Fannius' direct attempt to recover money Roscius owes him from the settlement with Flavius. Cicero clearly implies that the *arbitrium* under Piso concerned such a claim, and that, unsatisfied in that *arbitrium*, Fannius is pressing that claim in the present case. This is simply not true.

---

[19] Cf. *Inv.* 2.17-39.
[20] Axer, *Style and Composition*, 25-31 *et passim*.
[21] For Fannius' motives in declining to pursue an *arbitrium pro socio*, see esp. Wieacker, 10-12.

The dilemma itself orders Fannius to choose a different procedure or to desist. Since the choice is already made, and Fannius obviously will not desist, the form of the device is here being used purely to give an impression of strong argument, and to end a passage (starting at 17) largely dominated by ethical proofs.

Having synthesized this crescendo, Cicero now seems to recap three of the plaintiff's contentions one by one: that Roscius had pledged to pay Fannius, that Roscius asked Fannius to agree upon an *arbiter* sympathetic to Roscius, and that Roscius came to a deal with Fannius in order to end the *arbitrium* (25 <con>dicionis - 26). It is striking that Cicero has in our text so far only mentioned the first of these three contentions, and that he now recaps this one in dilemma form:

> <con>dicionis tabulas habet an non? si non habet, quem ad modum pactio est? si habet, cur non nominas. (25)
>
> Does he have records of the arrangement or not? If he does not, how is there a contract? If he does, why do you not cite them?[22]

The dilemma at the end of section 25 underscores the refutation of the *pactio* already offered in sections 1-13. Playing on the double meaning of *pactio*, as informal agreement or formal contract, Cicero can discredit Saturius' entire story. There was no contract for Roscius to pay Fannius, and so Roscius was acquitted in the *arbitrium* because of his complete innocence. The more probable interpretation, that this innocence amounts to an orchestrated judgement that did not label Roscius a betrayer of his partner, is submerged, as is the fact that Roscius had obtained that judgement by agreeing to pay Fannius HS 100,000, half of which he has already paid, and half of which he is being sued for in the present case.

It is noteworthy that this dilemma form, following hard on the last, is likewise specious. It is already clear that Fannius cannot document the *pactio* (since there is no *pactio* in the legal sense). It is also clear that Fannius' record of the debt he is owed through the judgement in the *arbitrium* is insufficient; he had relied on Piso, and had kindly avoided making records that could potentially embarrass Roscius by strongly implying the true situation. Cicero has claimed that Fannius' sole record of his judgement in the *arbitrium*, a record in his *adversaria*, is in fact the evidence that Fannius would use to prove that there had been a legal *pactio*. The evidence is understandably inadequate. Fannius, after all, had never maintained any such thing. Thus Cicero's initial question, "Does he

---

[22] My translation. Cf. Stroh, 114.

have the records or not?" is one that has already been answered. There is no real choice.

The dilemma thus serves to invoke the entire edifice of misrepresentation of sections 1-13 at the moment when the vital facts that it distorts are finally treated explicitly.

We have already noted the course of Cicero's argument from this point; finally, he reviews the facts, inserting an encomium of Roscius' liberality and expertise (27-34a), and brings his argument to bear on one claim of the plaintiff:

> "de tota re" inquit "decidisti."
> Ergo huc universa causa deducitur, utrum Roscius cum Flavio de sua parte an de tota societate fecerit pactionem. (34)
>
> "It was about the whole business," he says, "that you made a settlement." The whole cause then comes to this: did Roscius make an agreement with Flavius only for his own share or for the partnership as a whole?

Stroh rightly points out that Saturius' claim that Roscius had settled *de tota re* is a moral censure rather than a legal contention.[23] Saturius' actual claim was that although Roscius settled with Flavius on his own account, whatever he recovered was still the property of the partnership. And this is a valid point in Roman law. Cicero takes Saturius' complaint that Roscius had gotten all that was to be had from Flavius, and treats it as a legal contention that Roscius had not settled under his own name. This distortion underpins the argument of sections 34-51.

That argument is divided into three contentions: 1) Flavius had not demanded from Roscius a guarantee against further litigation, which would have been normal had Roscius been acting for the partnership (35 "quid ita" - 37a). 2) Fannius' *repromissio* in the *arbitrium*, to give Roscius half of any amount he might eventually recover from Flavius, is proof that Fannius still believed the he retained the right to sue Flavius (37a-39 "redemisse"). Finally 3) Fannius had in fact already sued Flavius and recovered HS 100,000. Incidentally, he had neglected to pay Roscius the half of this sum specified in his *repromissio* (39 "quid si" - 51 "petisse").

This third point, treated at far the greatest length, is the *antikategoria*: Fannius, it turns out, has been withholding what *he* owes to Roscius. The contention that this argument supposedly refutes, namely that Roscius had vitiated Fannius' *legal* ability to sue Flavius ("de tota re decidisti") is of course a contention that the plaintiff has never made; it is

---

[23] Stroh, 130. I am not convinced by Stroh's contention that Fannius had already sued Flavius.

a pure Ciceronian distortion. Further, Cicero's proof that Fannius actually received this money from Flavius is based on a second-hand report by two senators who have deposed that they heard the story from one Cluvius, the man who had been *iudex* in that suit.   At the time of this reputed conversation, the quondam *iudex* was admittedly not under oath.

In short, Cicero's tale here is ludicrously weak. This is all the more awkward because the claim that Fannius has withheld HS 50,000 from Roscius is the only argument that refutes "de tota re decidisti" ["you have settled the whole business"] in the plaintiff's sense -- that Roscius had effectively made it impossible to recover from Flavius. This is Cicero's basis for persuading Piso to put good sense before legalism, to allow the debts to cancel out, and so to see his way clear to save Roscius' reputation by finding for the defendant.[24] Obviously, a veneer of invincible rational argument is needed. Thus the first of the two dilemmas in his treatment of this topic:

> quam ob rem, cum de tota re decidisset cum Roscio, HS CCCIƆƆ separatim Fannium dissolvit? hoc loco, Saturi, quid pares respondere scire cupio; **utrum omnino Fannium <a> Flavio HS CCCIƆƆ non abstulisse an alio nomine et alia de causa abstulisse?** (40)

> On this point, Saturius, I should like to know what answer you propose to make; **that Fannius never got 100,000 sesterces at all from Flavius or that he got them on some other claim or for some other reason?**

The orator's trick here is to muddy the critical question, viz. whether Fannius received HS 100,000 from Flavius or not. Cicero rather asks whether he did not receive the money or received it for some other purpose. The first alternative momentarily imputes an argument to the opponent only to dismiss it. The second choice, while not strictly impossible, is nothing the plaintiff would even assert. Yet Cicero uses it to impute to the plaintiff, if only for a moment, the attempt to explain away the payment from Flavius; thus the synthesized dilemma helps Cicero extra-rationally to further the notion that there was such a payment.

Less subtle, and less effective, is Cicero's use of the device in treating the hearsay evidence in the depositions of the two senators, T. Manilius and a certain C. Luscius Ocrea. This evidence is no sooner read than defended by an elaborately developed dilemma (43 "utrum dicis" - 45), of which the root statement is "utrum dicis Luscio et Manilio, an et

---

[24] One may well speculate that Cicero's *exordium* had contained a promise to Piso to show that fairness would demand that he rule for Roscius. The *iudex* has certainly been patient in waiting for this demonstration.

Cluvio non esse credendum?" ["Do you say that we ought not to believe Luscius and Manilius or Cluvius?"] (43)

Since this dilemma is directed at the credibility of witnesses, it is an ethical argument with substantial consequences. Nonetheless, the argument is fundamentally about persons and the proper reaction to them. As one would expect, the development praises each of these parties, and challenges Fannius to insult them by labelling them perjurers. Luscius and Manilius are apparently known to Piso, and Cluvius, Cicero says, is one whom Fannius had trusted as *iudex*, so surely he must trust him as a witness. Thus the opponent, already a characterized as a Plautine pimp, is left with the choice of which good people he is determined to vilify unjustly.

Of course Fannius might reply that he does not know this Cluvius, and that in any case the man was not even under oath. Cicero cannot admit the first objection, since it undercuts his entire contention that there was a *iudicium* between Fannius and Flavius. To the second objection, he protests too much, contending that Cluvius' testimony is more reliable exactly because he is not under oath (46-47)! We are left with the impression that a dilemma form has been used forcefully to present an ethical argument which is to provide Piso and the *corona* with grounds of judgement unsupported by the facts.

After further ethical arguments, Cicero finally introduces the plaintiff's valid legal claim that, although Roscius had settled with Flavius in his own name, Flavius' payment is the property of the partnership. The orator of course treats this compelling claim as though it were the last desperate assertion of a plaintiff doomed to lose (51 "hoc cum sentit" - 52 "dici").[25]

> **quaero enim potueritne Roscius ex societate suam partem petere necne. si non potuit, quem ad modum abstulit? si potuit, quem ad modum non sibi exegit?** nam quod sibi petitur, certe alteri non exigitur. (52)
> **I ask: could Roscius have been able or not to claim his share in accordance with the partnership? if he could not, how did he get the money? if he could, how was it that he did not demand and get it for himself,** for what is claimed for oneself is certainly not demanded for another?

This dilemma, like the others, is specious. Roscius may certainly settle with Flavius in his own name in a matter pertaining to the partnership, and he did so. Thus Cicero is again molding into dilemma

---

[25] Cf. Stroh, 145.

form material that could be more simply expressed. But there is another trick here: the trumped-up question "Could Roscius settle in his own name for his share of the partnership?" requires a positive answer. But this simple answer obscures the fact that whatever resources he recovers under his own name from the affairs of the partnership must still be divided among the partners. Thus the argument that is the second question of the dilemma, and for which the dilemma is a springboard, is in this case simply not valid. The stark, either-or structure of the device allows Cicero to give the appearance of strong argument while omitting to acknowledge the critical proviso that would vitiate his argument.

Finally, Cicero tries to make the case that what a man recovers in a suit he undertakes in his name is properly his. He will support this with four arguments: 1) Fannius had been Roscius' *cognitor*, and there would have been no need for him to be if Roscius' settlement automatically went to the partnership (53-54). 2) Fannius had recovered HS 100,000 from Flavius himself, so Roscius' settlement had left Fannius an action against Flavius. Thus Roscius' settlement was not on behalf of the partnership. This is a reprise of the specious argument based upon Cicero's misrepresentation as a legal contention Fannius' complaint that Roscius had left him nothing to recover from Flavius (55 through "petere debes?"). 3) Cicero makes the false analogy that partners are like heirs. Each looks to his own share (55 "simillima" ad fin.). 4) If the settlement of each partner were the property of the partnership, Fannius' *restipulatio* to pay Roscius half of anything he might recover would be unnecessary. This last argument is easily answered, since the *restipulatio* was purely cosmetic.

Here our text breaks off. In this last flurry of specious, twisted argumentation anchored by the false dilemma in section 52, there is yet one final use of the device, in the reprise of the argument that Fannius' recovery of HS 100,000 from Flavius showed that Roscius' settlement had been only for himself, since he had left Fannius an action.

> cum de sua parte Roscius transegit cum Flavio, actionem tibi tuam reliquit an non? si non reliquit, quem ad modum HS CCCIƆƆ ab eo postea exegisti? si reliquit, quid ab hoc petis quod per te persequi et petere debes? (55)
>
> When Roscius made an arrangement with Flavius for his own share, did he leave you your right of action or not? If not, how did you afterwards get 100,000 sesterces from Flavius? If he did, why do you claim from Roscius what your ought to claim and try to obtain yourself?

Again, Cicero's assumption is that, if Fannius is left an action after Roscius' settlement, then Roscius' settlement is completely on his own behalf, and thus all his to keep. By making this assumption the basis of a dilemma, Cicero asserts it without having to defend it. In doing so, he connects this argument with his previous misrepresentation as a legal contention Fannius' complaint that Roscius had left him nothing to recover from Fannius, and reasserts the key claim that Fannius *has* recovered from Flavius. This claim both labels Fannius a swindler who has broken his *restipulatio*, and shows to Piso a calculus of financial fairness that will not compromise Roscius' reputation.

This final dilemma, like the preceding one, is specious. The first choice, that Fannius does have an action, is legally possible, but actually unfeasible. There is apparently nothing left to recover. That had been the thrust of Saturius' complaint "de tota re decidisti" ["you have settled the whole business"]. For the same reason, the second choice, that Fannius has no action against Flavius, is legally incorrect but practically accurate. Fannius would have no action against Flavius simply because such an action would result in a judgement that Flavius could not pay in any case, even if Flavius were still alive. Cicero of course offers his own unproven but potent reason that Fannius has no action against Flavius, viz. that he has already successfully sued Flavius once. In fact, the dilemma form is largely a mere vehicle for Cicero's reassertion of Flavius' alleged payment of HS 100,000 to Fannius. It is this allegation, after all, that is at the heart of the orator's appeal to the *iudex*.

In summary, the dilemmas in this speech find a variety of familiar uses and forms in the individual sections and subsections of the *argumentatio*. At the same time, the presentational functions of the device in this speech expand the repertoire we have seen in *pro Roscio Amerino* and the *Divinatio in Caecilium*. As in the earlier speeches, dilemmas are used to cap a line of argument (9, 25(i); Cf. *Div. Caec.* 58, above pp. 62-63), or to introduce a new argument with the appearance of rational invincibility (16, 40, 52; Cf. *Div. Caec.* 12, above pp. 55-56). They further provide resonance with the content of previous argument (25(ii) with secs. 1-13; 55 with secs. 39-51), and with both form and content of other occurrences of the device (9 and 25(ii)).[26]

Still, there are three elements of Cicero's use of dilemma that emerge for the first time in our speech. To begin, the first dilemma in

---

[26] Cf. *Div in Caec.* 14 and 4 (above pp. 55-56, 53), *et passim*.

section 25 underscores the principal non-ethically based substantial argument that Cicero has advanced in a passage (starting at 17) dominated by ethical argumentation. In order to integrate this protracted passage characterizing client and opponent into his demonstration, the orator finishes that section with an apparent show of invincible proof not founded on ethical assumptions. This dilemma does not so much punctuate the argument as form a bridge that helps Cicero to incorporate his overtly ethical arguments into his central demonstration.[27]

Second, we may note that the most common combination of form and content of the device is the expression in an alternative question of the two choices, the second of which cannot be taken seriously in light of Cicero's previous arguments. The choices are then dispensed with in reverse order in "if" clauses. (9, 25(ii), 52, 55. cf. 40). Cicero had previously used this chiastic form only at *Div. Caec.* 31 (above p. 59) and at *Tul.* 38 (below, p. 185). What is new and striking here is both its frequency and the fact that the second choice is never to be taken seriously. Perhaps Cicero so favors this remarkably elaborate chiastic form precisely to present a stronger show of rigor since the dilemmas do not contain two serious choices.

Finally, the lack of serious choices is a broader characteristic of the device in this speech. Of the remaining three dilemmas, one offers a second choice that vitiates the opponent's case, and so is hardly a real choice (16), and one is a virtual word-play that does not really offer two alternatives (25(i)). In short, seven of the eight dilemmas in the speech are arguably specious manipulation of language. They follow the dilemma form while really offering the opponent only one option. This is not to say that they fail of the technical requirements to be called dilemmas, or that we have not seen such a form before (Cf. *Div. Caec.* 12, above, pp. 55-56). Still, it is clear that in this speech Cicero has deliberately forced ill-suited material into dilemma form with remarkable frequency. Finally, he has manufactured so many dilemmas that only one other Ciceronian speech, *pro Caelio*, contains more examples of the device.

Why? While it is impossible to give a certain explanation of Cicero's enthusiasm for these forced dilemmas in this speech, we may offer this observation: The style and ethical argumentation of the speech are integral to Cicero's persuasive strategy, as Axer has shown. By playing Roscius against a Ballio of an opponent, the orator brings the stuff

---

[27] Cf. esp. *Planc.* 35 (below, p. 134).

of comedy to his defense of a celebrated comic actor. And this definition of dramatic roles both delights the *corona* and distracts them from the weaknesses of Cicero's legal arguments.[28] But the *corona* expects more from a lawyer than simply to be amused. When the orator exercises his license in making Fannius a Plautine pimp, he must be doubly sure to give the impression of rigorous argument as well. It is thus no coincidence that this speech, with *pro Caelio* the most self-consciously comedic of Cicero's orations, contains the most plentiful examples of this ostentatious presentational form of aggressive, substantial argument.

---

[28] Axer, *Style and Composition*, 47.

CHAPTER FIVE: *PRO SULLA*

Cicero's speech in defense of the accused Catilinarian P. Sulla in 62 is also a defense of the orator himself, both for his actions during his consulship and for the very fact that he has undertaken the defense.[1] In a judicial oration so involved with personal and political justification of the *patronus*, ethical argument is supreme. Cicero's reliance on dilemma forms (secs. 10, 21, 25 (*bis*), 39, 81) should thus reflect the roles of form as argument in an overtly ethical persuasive arena.

These are the facts: P. Sulla, nephew of the dictator, a leader of the colony at Pompeii, and a brother-in-law of Pompeius, had been elected along with P. Autronius Paetus in the consular elections for 65. Both men were charged with *ambitus*, convicted, and deprived of their offices, which were then filled by L. Manlius Torquatus senior and L. Aurelius Cotta.[2] Torquatus' son and namesake had prosecuted Sulla in the *ambitus* trial (50). The young Torquatus may have believed that Sulla had plotted with Autronius and Catiline to murder his father during the year 65. In any case, in the wave of criminal cases that followed Catiline's defeat and death at Pistoia in 62, the young Torquatus prosecuted P. Sulla under the

---

[1] See the introduction to the *Budé* edition of A. Boulanger, *Cicéron, Discours*, tome 11 (Paris: Société d'Édition "Les Belles Lettres", 1946) 89-108; the introduction to the *Loeb* translation of C. MacDonald, *Cicero*, vol. 10 (Cambridge, MA: Harvard University Press, 1977) 302-312; J.S. Reid's commentary (Cambridge: Cambridge University Press, 1882); James M. May, *Trials of Character* (Chapel Hill and London: University of North Carolina Press, 1988) 69-79; Erich S. Gruen, *The Last Generation of the Roman Republic* (Berkeley: University of California Press, 1974) 283-285.
[2] Primary sources in T. R. S. Broughton, *Magistrates of the Roman Republic*, revised ed., 3 vols. (Chico, CA: Scholars Press, 1984-1986), vol. 2, p.157.

lex Plautia de vi.³ He charged Sulla both with his role in the plot against Torquatus senior and with participating in the conspiracy of 63 (11). Torquatus' assisting prosecutor was a certain Cornelius, son of another conspirator (51). Sulla was defended by Hortensius and Cicero. Hortensius handled allegations concerning the plot against the consuls of 65 (12-14, 51),⁴ while Cicero treated charges relating to the conspiracy that he had thwarted (12-14 *et passim*). As was his custom (*Brutus* 190; *Orator* 130), Cicero spoke last. Sulla would continue active in political life (*Att.* 4.18.3), so we can be sure that he was acquitted.

In our speech, Cicero's primary goal is to persuade the jury of Sulla's innocence of any complicity in the Catilinarian conspiracy. Since Cicero himself is the most authoritative witness on that score,⁵ this should be straightforward. If there were any conclusive evidence of Sulla's guilt, it would have been raised by the prosecution, and answered in our speech.⁶ The defendant is further buoyed by an immensely influential group of supporters in Rome, and surely by his position as Pompeius' brother-in-law.

Cicero has a second goal which is purely political, and for which his defense of Sulla provides a convenient vehicle. The orator's action in executing the Catilinarians without trial on 5 December of 63 had already

---

[3] See MacDonald (above n.1), 305 and note d.

[4] This plot, the so-called first Catilinarian conspiracy, cannot have happened in the manner represented in the sources. See T.N. Mitchell, *Cicero: The Ascending Years* (New Haven: Yale University Press, 1979) 223-225 and n.94, with lit. Of the works he cites, see esp. H. Frisch, "The First Catilinarian Conspiracy: A Study in Historical Conjecture," *Class. et Med.* 9 (1948) 10-36; R. Seager, "The First Catilinarian Conspiracy," *Historia* 13 (1964) 338-347; R. Syme, *Sallust* (Berkeley: University of California Press, 1964) 87-102. Also J.T. Ramsey, "Cicero *pro Sulla* 68 and Catiline's Candidacy in 66 BC," *HSCP* 86 (1982) 121-131.

[5] Cf. 13: Atque haec inter nos partitio defensionis non est fortuito, iudices, nec temere facta; sed cum videremus eorum criminum nos patronos adhiberi quorum testes esse possemus, uterque nostrum id sibi suscipiendum putavit de quo aliquid scire ipse atque existimare potuisset. [Moreover, gentlemen, this division of the defence between us has not been made at random or recklessly; but when we saw that we were being retained as advocates to rebut charges upon which we could give evidence, each of us thought that he should deal with the events about which he had been able to acquire some personal knowledge and form a personal opinion.]

[6] There is still good reason to believe that Sulla was not completely ignorant of the conspiracy of 63, merely too prudent to commit himself. So MacDonald (above n.1), 312. Cf. Boulanger (above n.1), 94-95. Per contra, E. Ciaceri, *Cicerone e i suoi tempi*² (Genova, Roma, Napoli, Città di Castello: Società Anonima Editrice Dante Alighieri, 1941) 7-13, finds the orator's refutation of the charges the honorable defense of an innocent man.

provoked protest. Already in that same month, the tribune Metellus Nepos had not allowed Cicero to make the traditional address on leaving the consulship. In the present trial, Torquatus could level the charge that Cicero had acted cruelly in conducting these executions (30-31). The negative reaction that Clodius would finally employ to drive Cicero into exile was already apparent in July of 62. The orator needed to justify his actions. By defending an accused Catilinarian who was not obviously guilty, he could show his moderation, build bridges to Sulla and his powerful friends, and use the occasion explicitly to paint a favorable picture of his own character and motives.[7]

The answer to the challenge of making an apologia out of the case arises naturally from the tactics of the young Torquatus. Faced with a *patronus* who was himself the strongest witness for the defense,[8] it fell to Torquatus to discredit this witness as best he could. The prosecutor could attempt this with real enthusiasm, since he was convinced of Sulla's guilt and may well have believed that Sulla had conspired to kill the elder Torquatus. Thus Cicero's defense of Sulla seemed intolerable, the more so in that Cicero was a personal friend of both Torquati and no friend of Sulla.[9] Young Torquatus could further accuse Cicero of *regnum*, of behaving like a tyrant by abusing his enormous prestige, heretofore used to convict conspirators, in order to save a conspirator who happened to be wealthy and well connected (3-35, 80-87).

Cicero's answer to the charge of violated friendship is straightforward -- immediate counter-complaint (2), followed by remonstrances, and ostentatious forbearance (esp. 30, 46-47, 50). Cicero makes clear that his decision among conflicting duties is quite normal, and should not affect his relationship with the Torquati (49).[10]

Torquatus' other personal attacks on Cicero are so far from challenging that they reinforce Cicero's purpose in undertaking the defense. These attacks, probably sincere and certainly necessary to counteract Cicero's enormous prestige, largely shift the focus of the trial from Sulla to Cicero. The speech thus naturally becomes not only a

---

[7] Gellius, *NA* 12.12.2, preserves the story that Sulla had also loaned Cicero two million sesterces to buy the house on the Palatine.
[8] Cicero will even manufacture an elaborate witness's oath for himself at sections 86-87.
[9] On Cicero's later opinion of P. Sulla, see *Off.* 2.26; *Fam.* 9.10.3; 15.17.2
[10] Cf. P.A. Brunt, "'Amicitia' in the Late Roman Republic," *Proceedings of the Cambridge Philological Society* 11 (1965) 1-20, esp. 13-16.

defense and endorsement of Sulla's behavior, but a convenient forum for Cicero to justify his actions against the Catilinarians.

The speech may be broadly divided into an *exordium* (1-2), a defense of Cicero's undertaking to defend Sulla (3-35), refutation of the charges (36-68), a delayed *locus de vita ac moribus*, or treatment of the defendant's life and morals (69-79), a final statement of Cicero's special position and of his testimony for Sulla (80-87), and a peroration (88-93).

As usual, Cicero establishes principal themes at the outset. Sulla, a victim of laudable ambition, and of the hatred felt for his colleague Autronius, is being hounded in his misery. But fortunately this presents Cicero with the opportunity to display his leniency and compassion (1). Since Torquatus, the orator's intimate friend,(*"familiaris ac necessarius"*), has wronged him personally, Cicero's duty to his client, as well as to himself, compels him to reply (2).

Cicero's first move is thus to answer Torquatus' charge that he has been inconsistent, regularly testifying against the other Catilinarians, but choosing to defend this one (3-11). Cicero can point to Hortensius and the other noteworthy supporters of Sulla, and imply that Torquatus' charge impugns the integrity of all of them (3-5. cf. 81-82). Neither Cicero nor these illustrious men supported the other accused Catilinarians when they came to trial (6 - 7 "deberet"). But where this case is concerned, to separate Cicero from the supporters of Sulla would be to single him out, to deny him his inherent compassion and kindness (7 "Quam ob rem" - 8). No, for all good men, duty is one. As consul Cicero had only led his fellows for the common cause, doing what all good men wanted done. Now, as a private citizen, he continues to support the common cause. While he accepts responsibility for his deeds, he shares the glory with all good citizens. (9)

Only when Cicero has completely submerged within the community of all good men his responsibility both for undertaking the defense of Sulla and for the acts of his consulship, does he address Torquatus' formulation of the charge against him:

> 'In Autronium testimonium dixisti,' inquit; 'Sullam defendis.' **Hoc totum eius modi est, iudices, ut, si ego sum inconstans ac levis, nec testimonio fidem tribui convenerit nec defensioni auctoritatem; sin est in me ratio rei publicae, religio privati offici, studium retinendae voluntatis bonorum, nihil minus accusator debet dicere quam a me defendi Sullam, testimonio laesum esse Autronium.** (10)

> "You gave evidence against Autronius," he says, "and yet you are defending Sulla." **The long and the short of it, gentlemen, is that if I**

PRO SULLA 93

am inconsistent and unstable, no credence should have been given to my evidence then nor weight to my defence now. But if I do show regard for the public interest, respect for personal obligation and a desire to retain the good-will of loyal men, the last thing that the prosecutor should say is that I gave damaging evidence against Autronius but am defending Sulla.

After taking seven sections to characterize himself as simply part of the community of all good men, it is easy enough to meet Torquatus' criticism that Cicero is defending Sulla capriciously, or self-servingly, or because of Sulla's ties with Pompeius. Since these charges impugn the orator's character, Cicero offers the jury two extreme choices with no middle ground: Either he is completely untrustworthy, whether in accusing a Catilinarian or in defending Sulla, or he is trustworthy in both roles. In this dilemma form, artificial because the first choice is impossible in this context, the second choice provides an opportunity for Cicero to celebrate the version of his motives already argued in sections 3-9. More interestingly, Cicero uses the apparently exhaustive character of the device as a way of neutralizing any ambivalence the jury may feel about the range of motives that the orator may have for defending a man as wealthy and well connected as Sulla. Given only the two choices, the wellspring of Cicero's action must be his sterling character.[11] Any more discerning examination of the orator's motives is simply excluded from consideration. By thus asserting Cicero's monolithic integrity, this dilemma form may serve to summarize, amplify, and conclude this section of his self-defense.

Cicero, in a completely disingenuous explanation of his division of topics with Hortensius (11-14a), leaves the treatment of the first conspiracy to his colleague since the orator was not sufficiently involved in public affairs in 66 to know of it (!). Even here, the criminal Autronius is made the foil for the blameless Sulla (13 "Qui vobis ... deterritos esse"). This contrast will now carry the weight of the next seven sections (14b-20).

By framing the contrast between a guilty Autronius and an innocent Sulla as a way of defending himself from Torquatus' charge of high-handedness, Cicero is able, under cover of self-defense, to make strong ethical arguments for his client, and to adduce in an inoffensive manner his claim to special knowledge that Sulla was no conspirator. Equally

---

[11] Cf. Scholia Bobiensia, p. 77 Stangl: "Et hic iam se animis iudicum latenter insinuat, ut praesens defensio in testimonii vicem cedat." ["And here already he covertly insinuates himself into the minds of the jurors, so that the present defense may serve in place of testimony."]

important for the orator's larger political agenda, he is able to sound again the theme of his leniency and compassion begun in section 1. Cicero can depict himself as one torn by the interests of the state from the natural compassion that would have had him defend Autronius, despite the fact that Autronius had sent the assistant prosecutor's father to kill him (18-19). Since there is no evidence of Sulla's guilt, it has been a joy to Cicero to oblige Sulla's prominent supporters by undertaking the defense (20).

Only after this elaborate self-depiction, in which Cicero emerges as a paragon of compassion tempered by patriotism, does he counter the most hurtful of Torquatus' barbs, that Cicero has established an intolerable *regnum*, a tyranny of personal prestige (21). In this context the next dilemma form occurs.

> An tum in tanto imperio, tanta potestate (sc. consulatus) non dicis me fuisse regem, num privatum regnare dicis? quo tandem nomine? 'Quod in quos testimonia dixisti,' inquit, 'damnati sunt; quem defendis, sperat se absolutum iri.' **Hic tibi ego de testimoniis meis hoc respondeo, si falsum dixerim, te in eosdem dixisse; sin verum, non esse hoc regnare, cum verum iuratus dicas, probare.** De huius spe tantum dico, nullas a me opes P. Sullam, nullam potentiam, nihil denique praeter fidem defensionis exspectare. (21)
>
> Or do you mean that I was not a tyrant when I wielded an all-embracing power but that I am a tyrant as a private citizen. On what account? "Because," he says, "those against whom you gave evidence were condemned and the man whom you defend hopes to be acquitted." **My reply to you concerning the evidence I gave is this: if I lied, you too gave evidence against those defendants; but if I spoke the truth, it is not tyranny, when one tells the truth on oath, to make good one's case.** Of Sulla's hopes I have only this to say: Publius Sulla expects from me no limitless resources, no misuse of my power, nothing but the conscientious discharge of the duties of a counsel for the defense.

Torquatus' has argued simply that Cicero has testified against others guilty of conspiracy, and they have all been convicted. Now, he is defending an individual guilty of conspiracy, and the guilty party, Sulla, may well hope to be acquitted. Cicero wildly distorts this argument, pretending that the prosecution has accused him of tyranny for testifying against the guilty conspirators as well as for defending Sulla. Thus this dilemma is manufactured as an ostentatious, powerful answer to a charge that Torquatus has not made at all. So Cicero's demonstration that Torquatus' attack would backfire upon him ("you too gave evidence against those defendants"), and his further implication that Torquatus would criticize him for testifying truly, are the purest hokum.[12] In fact, there would be no loss of continuity if this dilemma form were omitted. It serves here only to make a specious show of strong argument at the beginning of Cicero's defense against a telling attack.

The remainder of Cicero's refutation of the notion that he is a *rex*, a tyrant (22-29), and his explicit counter-attack on Torquatus (30-35), are devoted to the principal tasks of 1) making Torquatus seem offensive, unreasonably petulant, and silly, and 2) showing Cicero, as part of a group of all good men that includes Torquatus, as the savior of the state through his execution of the Catilinarians.[13]

Torquatus, a patrician, had played into Cicero's hands by calling him, after Tarquinius Priscus and Numa, Rome's third *peregrinus rex* (22). Cicero can concentrate on the charge of foreignness, and point out that many illustrious Romans have come from the *municipia* of Italy (23), as do many competitors for office, and voters whose support is necessary to advance in public life (24). In short, Cicero warns Torquatus that his attitude is politically unwise,[14] and does so in such a way that his opponent's offensiveness is given the greatest possible emphasis.

As a pendant and complement to this argument, Cicero springs one of his favorite tactics, underscored by a dilemma form.

> Ac si, iudices, ceteris patriciis me et vos peregrinos videri oporteret, a Torquato tamen hoc vitium sileretur; est enim ipse a materno genere municipalis, honestissimi et nobilissimi generis, sed tamen Asculani. **Aut igitur doceat Picentis solos non esse peregrinos aut gaudeat suo generi me meum non anteponere.** (25)

> Even, gentlemen, if it had been right for the other patricians to think the two of us foreigners, Torquatus at any rate should have kept quiet about this defect; for he is himself the citizen of an Italian borough on his mother's side, a very honourable and distinguisehd family, but still one from Asculum. **Let him then either show that only the people of Picenum are not foreigners or be glad that I do not rate my family more highly than his.**

In terms of ethical argument, this is the equivalent of *antikategoria*, capped with a dilemma at the end of Cicero's consideration of the "peregrinus" slander. It is noteworthy that the matter of the municipal

---

[12] Contrast Scholia Bobiensia, pp. 79-80 Stangl, which takes no note of Cicero's distortion here.
[13] See May (above n.1), 71-73; C.P. Craig, "The *Accusator* as *Amicus*: A uniquely Roman Tactic of Ethical Argumentation," *TAPA* 111 (1981) 31-38, 33-34.
[14] Cf. Cicero's friendly advice to the prosecutor about the political dangers of vilifying the defendant's origins in *ambitus* trials: *Mur.* 15-17; *Planc.* 19-23. In those cases, *patronus* and defendant are linked. Here the charge concerns the *patronus* alone.

origin of Torquatus' maternal ancestors can only come at this point in Cicero's argument, and that it cannot be raised at all without threatening the orator with a difficulty. The mention of Torquatus' maternal lineage must be deferred until this point because the orator's strategy has been to identify himself with a large group whom the patrician Torquatus disparages; Torquatus must be outside that group for the strategy to work. Once Cicero mentions his opponent's municipal roots, he cannot amplify his point at any length lest he seem to be attacking Torquatus (or Torquatus' mother!) for the very fault that he has just shown to be no fault. Here the dilemma form, addressed to the jury, gives a memorable emphasis without the need for a more lengthy, and potentially self-defeating, *amplificatio*.

Very different is the false dilemma form at the end of this same section:[15]

> Qua re neque tu me peregrinum posthac dixeris, ne gravius refutere, neque regem, ne derideare. Nisi forte regium tibi videtur ita vivere ut non modo homini nemini sed ne cupiditati quidem ulli servias, contemnere omnes libidines, non auri, non argenti, non ceterarum rerum indigere, in senatu sentire libere, populi utilitati magis consulere quam voluntati, nemini cedere, multis obsistere. **Si hoc putas esse regium, regem me esse confiteor; sin te potentia mea, si dominatio, si denique aliquod dictum adrogans aut superbum movet, quin tu id potius profers quam verbi invidiam contumeliamque maledicti?** (25)

> Do not, then repeat the reproach that I am a foreigner, if you do not want to be refuted more conclusively; nor that I am a tyrant, if you do not want to make yourself more ridiculous. You may of course think it tyrannical to live in such a way that you are in bondage to no man nor even to any passion; to make light of all excesses; to need neither gold, nor silver, nor any other possession; to give your opinion freely in the Senate; to consult the people's interests more than their wishes; to yield to no man; to resist many. **If you think that this is tyrannical, then I admit that I am a tyrant; but if my despotic power, my tyranny, if some overbearing or arrogant utterance angers you, why do you not produce this rather than a prejudicial phrase and abusive slander?**

In the phrase "peregrinus rex," or "foreign tyrant," Cicero had originally focussed upon the aspect of foreignness. Thus this further refutation of the notion that he is a tyrant is to be expected for balance. In this context, we see a special dilemma form appropriated as a tactic for defense against name-calling. As we have seen elsewhere, the dilemma form is used for emphasis at the crescendo of a section of argument. As

---

[15] But not at the end of the treatment of the *rex* theme, which Cicero will use as a foil for his self-sacrificing and courageous behavior through section 29.

we have also seen elsewhere, there are not really two choices; the first choice is quite impossible, and is only offered sarcastically. The form is noteworthy in that this first synthetic, impossible choice is directed against Cicero himself. It is in fact a device to showcase the orator standing on his dignity. The second choice, surprisingly mild, then shows Cicero's forbearance towards his good friend Torquatus, and so underscores again the politically useful theme of the leniency of Cicero's nature. So the argumentative form becomes a vehicle for Cicero's positive self-portrait.

The mechanisms of the remainder of Cicero's apologia are straightforward; his heroic posture (26-29), his attack on Torquatus' speaking ability (31), and his extensive use of the *accusator*-as-*amicus* tactic, lead him finally to close his self-defense. At this point, Cicero has already praised Sulla's blameless character, exalted his own compassion and leniency, extolled his own heroism, and has shown the prosecution to be hasty and offensive. Further, the orator has used his special position as *patronus*/witness to assure the jury of Sulla's innocence of the conspiracy. In the absence of telling evidence against his client, Cicero has won before he begins to deal with the charges.

And this is probably just as well for his client. While we cannot be sure of the extent of Sulla's complicity in the conspiracy, and while it is clear that Torquatus could not demonstrate his guilt conclusively, Cicero's treatment of the charges leads one to think that they were substantial.[16] While a detailed treatment of the charges will not aid our present purpose, we must note one striking sign that Torquatus' case was well founded. This is the order of Cicero's refutation of two of the charges he attributes primarily to Torquatus: 1) that the testimony of the Allobroges implicates Sulla (36-39), and 2) that Cicero had tampered with the testimony, to Sulla's advantage, before it was officially recorded (40-44). It seems unlikely that Torquatus would argue from evidence that he felt had already been adjusted to favor Sulla, and would only later point out that that evidence had been skewed. It would be much simpler, and more effective, for the prosecutor to argue that Cicero had caused adjustments to be made in the Allobroges' testimony before it was published, and that even so one could still glimpse proof of Sulla's guilt from the sanitized version of the testimony that was made public.[17]

---

[16] See n.6 above.
[17] E. Gabba, "Cicerone e la Falsificazione dei Senatoconsulti," *Studi classici e orientali* 10 (1961) 89-96, 91-92, argues that Cicero could have made such changes.

Thus Cicero's treatment of the content of the public record prior to, and independent of, his treatment of the allegation that he tampered with that record, is a distortion that must rob Torquatus' argument of some of its power. Cicero sustains this burlesque at length, and makes his refutation a show of careful argument. If Cassius, trying to woo the Allobroges into the conspiracy, had mentioned Sulla as a participant, the testimony would be worthless, since it would be clear that Cassius was simply dropping names in an attempt to win over the Gauls. But Cassius had not volunteered Sulla's name. Because of the public linkage of Sulla with Autronius, whom Cassius had mentioned, the Allobroges had asked if Sulla were involved as well. Cassius had replied that he did not know. By declining to name Sulla as a conspirator, Cassius was either protecting him or truthfully admitting that he did not know. But Cassius protected no one else, and it was to his advantage to use Sulla's name as well. Thus he really did not know whether Sulla was involved. But Cassius knew every detail of the conspiracy. Therefore his ignorance of Sulla's involvement proves Sulla's innocence. In any case, it cannot be used to argue Sulla's guilt. There is no other passage in the speeches more closely reasoned than this demonstration. And this demonstration hinges upon a *divisio* that is a dilemma form. Of the two choices, the first is argued to be impossible, and the second taken to prove that Sulla is innocent:

> Etenim cum se negat scire Cassius, utrum sublevat Sullam an satis probat se nescire? (39)

> When Cassius says that he does not know, is he trying to clear Sulla or does he convince us that he really does not know?

This dilemma is noteworthy because the choice argued to be impossible really seems more probable. Given that Cassius is a conspirator, one might expect him to be unscrupulous in pursuing the plot. It would be useful for him, as Cicero concedes, to use Sulla's name to persuade the Allobroges, whether Sulla was really a conspirator or not. It is more likely that Cassius was restrained from mentioning Sulla by a specific consideration (e.g., assenting to a request of Sulla), rather than by an uncharacteristic paroxysm of honesty in this one case. Cicero finesses this problem by allowing only one possible motive for Cassius to withhold Sulla's name, his fear that the Allobroges would tell all. This is a gross oversimplification of the range of Cassius' possible motives, and the simple phrases that Cicero manufactures for his interlocutor ("Sublevat apud Gallos." Quid ita? "Ne indicent." ["He is trying to clear him with the Gauls." Why? "To stop them including him in their information."]) lend credibility to the trick. Thus the orator refutes, simply by omitting the possibility, a plausible and most damning interpretation of the facts, viz., that Cassius did not implicate Sulla before the Allobroges because Sulla had specifically requested that he not do so. By finessing this problem, Cicero obscures the only indication of Sulla's possible guilt that we know came into the public record of the Allobroges' testimony.

The final dilemma form comes in that part of the speech between the delayed treatment of Sulla's life and character (69-79) and the *peroratio* proper (88-93). These sections (80-87) finally assert to the fullest Cicero's status as the savior of the state from the conspiracy, and thus as a decisive witness that Sulla was not involved (cf. 13-14). This argument culminates in Cicero's equivalent of the witness's oath (86-87). Cicero begins this section by returning to the charge that he is abusing his *auctoritas* and expecting special consideration for his client. Without the mention of *regnum*, "tyranny," this is the theme of sections 3-35 all over again. The notions of Cicero's special status, and of his right to act in Sulla's defense, bracket the traditional elements of the *argumentatio*, the treatment of the charges (36-68) and the argument concerning the defendant's life and character (69-79).[18]

Within this second bracketing passage (80-87), Cicero again asserts as part of his special status that all good men supported him against Catiline (81-82). He is helped by the fact that Torquatus had apparently criticized several of Sulla's consular *advocati* (supporters and character witnesses) by pointing out that these men had also been *advocati* of Catiline during his trial in 64. Torquatus may have alleged that these men had then abandoned the other conspirators, but were now supporting Sulla because of his wealth and connections. This argument, an attack on the *auctoritas* of prestigious public figures supporting their friend, was part of Torquatus' bold and necessary attempt to undermine the overwhelming influence of the opposition; these great men had, after all, served as character witnesses for Catiline.

This fact is obviously embarrassing. Cicero defuses it with an ingenious use of the prosecutor's own family. Torquatus' father had defended Catiline *de repetundis* (i.e., on a charge of provincial misgovernment) in 65.[19] Cicero will even use the word *advocatus*, rather

---

[18] Cf. May (above n.1), 77-78.
[19] Cicero himself had contemplated serving as Catiline's *patronus*. *Att.* 1.2.

than *patronus*, to describe this role.[20] Then the fact that Torquatus was not among Catiline's *advocati* in 64 can be taken to be irrelevant. At one time or another the elder Torquatus and Sulla's present consular supporters were all *advocati* of Catiline. But Cicero uses a dilemma form to sculpt this point into an even more decisive argument:

> Quin etiam parens tuus, Torquate, consul reo de pecuniis repetundis Catilinae fuit advocatus, improbo homini, at supplici, fortasse audaci, at aliquando amico. Cui cum adfuit post delatam ad eum primam illam coniurationem, indicavit se audisse aliquid, non credidisse. 'At idem non adfuit alio in iudicio, cum adessent ceteri.' **Si postea, cognorat ipse aliquid quod in consulatu ignorasset, ignoscendum est eis qui postea nihil audierunt; sin illa res prima valuit, num inveterata quam recens debuit esse gravior?** Sed si tuus parens etiam in ipsa suspicione periculi sui tamen humanitate adductus advocationem hominis improbissimi sella curuli atque ornamentis et suis et consulatus honestavit, quid est quam ob rem consulares qui Catilinae adfuerunt reprendantur? (81)
>
> Furthermore, in his consulship your father, Torquatus, was counsel for Catiline when he was answering a charge of provincial misgovernment. Rogue he may have been, but he was a suppliant; reckless perhaps, but he had once been a friend. Inasmuch as he appeared for him after that first conspiracy had been reported to him, he indicated that he had heard something, but did not believe it. "But he did not support him in court in another trial, although others did." **If he had subsequently discovered something which he did not know when he was consul, then we must excuse those who heard nothing later. But if that first piece of information had any substance, ought it to have carried more weight when it was old than when it was fresh?** If, moreover, your father, even when suspecting danger to himself, was still induced by his kindly nature to giev respectability to the body which supported that unscrupulous wretch by appearing with the curule chair and both his personal and consular insignia, is there any reason why the consulars who supported Catiline should be blamed?

The first prong of this dilemma is straightforward and reasonable. If Torquatus was ignorant of Catiline's plans when he defended him, others who were ignorant of Catiline's plans (as Cicero insists that Catiline's consular *advocati* in 64 were ignorant) likewise cannot be blamed for supporting him. The second prong, on the other hand, is perverse and fascinating: If the evidence against Catiline had convinced the elder Torquatus before he defended Catiline in 65, why should he have defended

---

[20] *advocatus* as "pleader" is common only in later usage. See *OLD* s.v. "advocatus" 1 a and b, and Pseudo-Asconius p.190 Stangl: Qui defendit alterum in iudicio aut patronus dicitur, si orator est; aut advocatus, si aut ius suggerit aut praesentiam suam commodat amico. [He who defends another in a legal case is either called *patronus*, if he is a pleader, or *advocatus*, if he either gives legal advice or supports his friend by his presence.]

him, then refused to support him in the later trial? This second alternative is nonsense. The elder Torquatus cannot be accused of believing the reports of Catiline's nefarious designs (which probably did not yet exist in any case). Cicero would not dare to make such a statement. But the hypothetical syntax of the form allows him to raise the possibility that Torquatus senior did believe the information against Catiline but defended him anyway. This notion, advanced only hypothetically, and thus requiring no support, is then simply presumed in what follows. The elder Torquatus is depicted as so given over to *humanitas* that he defended Catiline despite his suspicion that Catiline was plotting against him. *A fortiori*, the consulars who served as character witnesses for Catiline in 64 cannot be censured for letting their kindness overpower their judgment. Cicero thus implies something closely akin to what he has already denied, namely that although the consulars might know that Catiline was pernicious, it was still acceptable for them to serve as *advocati* for him. They were only following, in a more modest way, the example of Torquatus senior.

While several of the presentational functions of dilemma have now become predictable, the special environment of this speech, dominated by ethical arguments regarding *patronus*/witness rather than defendant, is underscored by the expanded uses of five of the six dilemma forms to make ethical arguments.

Certainly we see the usual presentational functions of making a show of vigorous reasoning at the beginning of a line of argument (21).[21] Further, Cicero takes full advantage of the presentational effect that arises from the apparent invincibility of the device. Part of that apparent invincibility is the impression that a dilemma is exhaustive. The dilemma seems to cover every possibility, so the possibilities that it does not treat seem to disappear (10, 39).

But the ethical grounding of these arguments employing dilemma leads to new effects. The dilemma at section 10 is noteworthy because it is actually about Cicero, and is addressed directly to the jury rather than to the opponent. It is their judgement of him, after all, that has become the central issue. We have already noted that Cicero here uses the dilemma structure to exclude from consideration harmful interpretations. But those

---

[21] Cf. *Div. Caec.* 12 (above pp. 55-56), 58 (pp. 62-63); *Q. Rosc.* 16, 40, 52 (pp. 79, 83-84), or at its end (10, 25(i)). Cf. *Q. Rosc.* 9, 25(i) (pp. 75, 80).

interpretations here concern his own motives; Cicero advances the simplistic ethical argument that he is either a man of integrity or not, and that there can be no gray areas. Because of the apparently exhaustive nature of the device, any question of the compelling political grounds for his defense of Sulla simply disappears.

The use of the device at section 21 is, presentationally, simply an ostentatious show of reasoning at the beginning of a new line of argument. It is also a synthesized dilemma based on a radical distortion of the opponent's position.[22] This example differs from those in the earlier speeches in that it is about Cicero and contains a purely ethical counterattack. It is then a completely misleading token of powerful argument in the ethical sphere.

The first occurrence of the device in section 25, again addressed to the jury, is also a synthetic dilemma in which the first choice is impossible and the second, a virtual *praeteritio*, seems editorial rather than argumentative. In an argument dealing now offensively with ethical concerns, viz. the lineage of his opponent, Cicero forces his material into this form to emphasize a point of view that he cannot amplify further without obviously contradicting himself.

The dilemma form at the end of section 25 is not a true dilemma, so we must be cautious about gauging its presentational value. Still, it is clear that the form becomes a vehicle for Cicero's positive self-portrait. The form is not a true dilemma both because the first choice is impossible in the context and because it attacks Cicero rather than his opponent. Unlike earlier dilemmas addressed to Cicero, this one is not aimed at the orator in both its parts. Further, the prong aimed at Cicero is purely sarcastic.[23] The second prong, rather than refuting his opponent, chides his *amicus*, and so by its very moderation reinforces the image that Cicero wants to project politically.

The dilemma in section 81 is also part of an ethical argument, but one not directly concerned with Cicero. Torquatus has attacked the consulars who are Sulla's supporters and character witnesses, since they had performed the same office for Catiline. Cicero's solution, a comparison of these *advocati* with the prosecutor's own father, employs the dilemma not only to posit a proposition that would be both offensive to

---

[22] Cf. *Div. Caec.* 12 (above pp. 55-56); *Rosc. Com.* 16 (p. 79), 25(i) (p. 80), 25(ii) (p. 81), 40 (p. 83), 52 (p.84), 55 (p. 86).
[23] Contrast *S. Rosc.* 124 (above, p. 39); *Div. Caec.* 4, 14 (pp. 53, 56).

state and impossible to prove, but then to use this proposition as a basis for further argument.

To sum up, dilemma forms, while remarkably plentiful in *Pro Sulla*, are not integral to the persuasive strategy in a unitary sense; the special qualities of the device and of its repetition do not function together to make a single definable contribution to the persuasive strategy as they do in the *Divinatio in Caecilium* or *Pro Roscio Comoedo*. Instead, Cicero shows the range of uses of a presentational argument form, and its variants, in an arena dominated by ethical argumentation. Under the pretense of forceful reasoning, he masks the question of his own self-interested motives (10), completely distorts his opponent's criticisms (21), finishes with vigor an argument that he cannot afford to amplify (25(i)), vents his own sarcasm (25(ii)), and insinuates false premises that seem to co-opt even the opponent's father for his cause (81). Because Cicero is himself the most important witness for his client, ethical attacks upon him undermine his reliability, and so are directly relevant to the question at issue. So the dilemma forms with which he defends himself (10, 25(ii)) while obviously part of his political agenda, are not simply vehicles for *obiter dicta*. Since his opponent has defined the ethical arena as the battleground, the orator's counterattacks in that arena (21, 25(i), 81) also seem completely appropriate. Thus Cicero demonstrates with decisive force the ways in which the special qualities of the dilemma form are applicable within a dominantly ethical context.

CHAPTER SIX: *PRO CAELIO*

In the speech for Caelius, Cicero constructs an argumentation that is both demonstrably specious and almost mysteriously powerful.[1] Scholars have noted the orator's patent inconsistencies, odd repetitions, reliance on comedic characterization to carry weak points, and his misleading displays of apparent vigorous argument.[2] Nevertheless, initial readers of the

---

[1] An earlier version of this chapter appeared as "Reason, Resonance, and Dilemma in Cicero's Speech for Caelius," *Rhetorica* 7 (1989) 313-328. Parts of that article are reprinted by permission of the University of California Press. For full bibliography on the speech, see C.J. Classen, "Ciceros Rede für Caelius," *ANRW* I.3 (1973) 60-93; W. Stroh, *Taxis und Taktik* (Stuttgart: Teubner, 1975), 243-303, 312-313. To their collections add T.P. Wiseman, *Catullus and his World: A Reappraisal* (Cambridge: Cambridge University Press, 1985) 54-91; M.R. Salzman, "Cicero, the *Megalenses* and the defense of Caelius," *AJP* 103 (1982) 299- 304; H.C. Gotoff, "Cicero's Analysis of the Prosecution Speeches in the *Pro Caelio*: An Exercise in Practical Criticism," *CP* 81 (1986) 122-132; J.M May, *Trials of Character* (Chapel Hill and London: University of North Carolina Press, 1988) 105-116. Other basic works for this study are E. Norden, "Aus Ciceros Werkstatt," *Sitz. Preuss. Ak. Wiss. phil.-hist. Kl.*, (Berlin, 1913) 12- 32 = *Kleine Schriften zum Klassischen Altertum*, (Berlin: de Gruyter, 1966) 144-164; R. Heinze's classic "Ciceros Rede *Pro Caelio*," *Hermes* 60 (1925) 193-258; R. Reitzenstein, "Ciceros Rede für Caelius," *NAWG* (1925) 25-3; E. Ciaceri, "Il Processo di M. Celio Rufo e l'arringa di Cicerone," *RAAN* (11) 1929-30, 1-24; idem, *Cicerone e i suoi tempi*, 2 vols. (Genova, Roma, Napoli: Società Anonima Editrice Dante Alighieri, 1939-1941) 2.86-96; F. Lovera, "Questioni riguardanti il processo de vi di M. Celio Rufo e l'orazione di Cicerone," *Il Mondo Classico* 6 (1936) 167-178; H. Drexler, "Zu Ciceros Rede *pro Caelio*," *NAWG* 1944, 1-32; G. Pacitti, "Cicerone al processo di M. Celio Rufo" in *Atti I Congresso Internazionale di Studi Ciceroniani* 2 vols. (Roma: Centro di Studi Ciceroniani, 1961), 2. 67- 79; K. Geffcken, *Comedy in the Pro Caelio (with an appendix on the in Clodium et Curionem)* (Leiden: Brill, 1973). The best commentary is R. G. Austin, *M. Tulli Ciceronis "Pro M. Caelio Oratio"* (Oxford: Clarendon Press, 1960).
These works will hereafter be referenced by the authors' last names.

[2] Among the striking inconsistencies is Cicero's use of the *locus de testibus* arguing that witnesses are useless (21-22), followed by the claim at section 55 that he needs no

speech, and certainly initial hearers, must feel themselves persuaded, or at least hard pressed to form coherent objections to Cicero's presentation. A great part of Cicero's persuasive power inheres in his ability to argue extra-rationally in a way that seems superficially to be rationally compelling. I will argue that the presentational aspect of dilemma, which occurs nine times in the speech for Caelius (secs. 35, 50, 52, 53 (*ter*), 58, 61, 62), is integral to Cicero's persuasive strategy, and to the remarkable effectiveness of the speech.

These are the circumstances of the case: Caelius was tried before the *quaestio de vi*, the standing court for cases of seditious violence, in early April of 56. The prosecutor, the young Atratinus, used the case to forestall Caelius' threatened renewal of a prosecution against his father for *ambitus* (illegal electioneering practices). He chose this venue because the *quaestio de vi*, alone of the standing courts, met during festal days, and so offered the fastest means of neutralizing Caelius' attack. Atratinus' assisting prosecutors were L. Herennius Balbus and a certain P. Clodius, not the brother of Clodia. The charges directly pertinent to seditious violence were apparently those concerning a riot at Naples, an assault on Alexandrians at Puteoli, and the property of Palla (23). It is likely that all of these charges concerned the ill-fated Alexandrian embassy, led by the philosopher Dio, who came to Italy to lobby against the reinstatement of Ptolemy Auletes on the Egyptian throne (Cassius Dio, 39.13-14). Thus the allegation that Caelius had been involved in Dio's murder (23-24), if more than an innuendo, could also have been a charge proper to the court. The allegation that Caelius had earlier attempted to murder Dio (51-55), although apparently not substantiable, allowed the prosecution to import ancillary charges unrelated to *vis*, namely the taking of Clodia's gold under false pretenses (53) and the attempt to poison her (56-69). Finally, there were the predictable allegations concerning the defendant's past life (3-20, 26)[3] and the treatment of Caelius' morals (25-29) that indicated that Caelius

---

arguments because he has a witness. The apparent repetition of section 28 in sections 41-43, and of section 38 in sections 48-50, led Norden to his famous, if unpersuasive, theory of Ciceronian improvisation. (Classen, 85-86, properly refutes Norden's thesis. Cf. Austin, pp. 159-161, for a survey of other views.) Geffcken's seminal monograph demonstrated Cicero's use of comedic stereotypes. Classen, esp. 87-88 and n.111, demonstrated the orator's pattern of obfuscation through the appearance of vigorous argument.

[3] Cf. esp. *Inv.* 2.32-37.

should be convicted whether guilty or innocent of the present charge, a procedure for which there were precedents (71).[4]

Caelius spoke first in his own defense. He was followed by no less a personage than M. Licinius Crassus, the richest man in Rome and a partner of Pompeius in the sometimes strained alliance of the so-called first triumvirate. Finally Cicero, following his custom (*Brutus* 190; *Orator* 130), gives the last speech before witnesses are called.[5] In this final speech, the orator has two principal tasks: 1) to counter the prosecution's scathing attack on Caelius' past life and his morals, 2) to discredit the allegations of Clodia, the famous charges of gold taken and attempted poisoning (30, 51). Cicero's task is especially challenging, since he must avoid reference to any possible political motive for Clodia's testimony, and in fact must de-emphasize the entire political dimension of the case. All of the charges connected with the embassy derived extra force from the public indignation at the treatment of the Alexandrians and the consequent hostility towards Pompeius, who championed the cause of Ptolemy against them. Neither Crassus nor Cicero (nor, probably, Caelius) wishes to dissociate himself from Pompeius at this time, yet the defense must

---

[4] For the circumstances and the charges, see Stroh, 243-249, with lit.. I differ from him only in that I agree with Heinze, 220, that the actual murder of Dio was not a substantial charge directly supported by Clodia's story of an earlier murder attempt. Rather the prosecution used the charge of attempted murder of Dio to allow them to adduce the charges of gold and poison in this court. The charge of attempted murder was in turn buttressed by reference to the actual murder of Dio, which would further help direct towards the defense the popular hostility towards Pompeius resulting from the crime. If the murder of Dio really were a substantial charge, it would be the most important as well as the most inflammatory charge of *vis*. Not even Cicero could have dismissed it as briefly as he does in sections 23-24.

For the strategy of obtaining a conviction on general principles, see Reitzenstein, 26-27; Lovera, 173. Since we know nothing of the case of M. Camurtius and C. Caesernius mentioned in section 71, it is quite possible that Heinze, 203, is also correct that the prosecution was here arguing for a conviction based upon a broader interpretation of the law.

[5] Stroh, 299-303, arguing that Cicero spoke last, gives a remarkably clear statement of the evidence for the opposing position that Caelius spoke last. He then attempts to refute these arguments. Stroh errs in following the other camp's notion that Quintilian 4.2.27 says that Caelius spoke after Cicero. Thus he feels obliged to discredit Quintilian's testimony. But Quintilian simply says no such thing. Rather he gives an ideal order of arguments in a case such as the *Caeliana*, then indicates which arguments were spoken by Cicero, which by Caelius. He nowhere says that the actual proceeding followed the order of arguments he gives. I must thank Professor Robert Kaster for valuable help on this point.

maintain that Caelius is not guilty of treating Dio and the embassy as Pompeius would have liked.[6]

The key to Cicero's success is the depiction of the love affair between Caelius and Clodia, an affair which, Cicero makes clear, Caelius terminated. This love affair, together with its unhappy end, has powerful results: 1) It attributes to Clodia a motive for lying without discussing her family's political hostility towards Pompeius. Thus Cicero can avoid the controversial issue of Pompeius' behavior towards Dio and the embassy, behavior that the orator and his client have no wish to censure but cannot endorse without goading the jury to indignation. 2) Concurrently the affair allows Cicero to portray Clodia as the very type of a *meretrix*, a prostitute,[7] and thus untrustworthy on general grounds. 3) Finally, it allows the orator to relate the entire attack on Caelius' manner of life to this one episode. And this episode, if the idea that Clodia behaves like a *meretrix* is accepted, is relatively defensible by Roman standards.[8]

But only relatively defensible. Indeed, the use of the love affair, which potentially reinforces the prosecution's negative portrayal of Caelius' character, is a central problem for understanding the rhetorical challenge. Heinze explained it by contending that the love affair and its termination were general knowledge in the City, but that the prosecution had avoided specific mention of it lest in pursuing Caelius they also hurt Clodia's credibility as a witness. Rather, the prosecutors had inveighed against Caelius' lifestyle in the most general terms. Cicero then took the bull by the horns, successfully basing his defense upon the knowledge that all shared and that none would mention.[9]

In fact, the use of the love affair is so successful that Stroh, author of the most ingenious thorough analysis of the speech, takes the opposite view, arguing that Cicero himself invents the love affair. Of course Stroh

---

[6] For the private origin and subsequent political dimension of the case, see Heinze, 195-197; so also Stroh, 245-246; cf. Classen, 93-94. Wiseman offers the fullest speculation on the political issues attached to the prosecution. The political dimension is also strongly emphasized by Lovera, Ciaceri, "Processo di Celio," esp. 17-18, and Pacitti.
[7] For the use of the *meretrix* stereotype here, see Geffcken, 27-47. See also M.B. Skinner, "Clodia Metelli," *TAPA* 113 (1983) 273-287, esp. 275-6; more exotically (Clodia as Cybele to Caelius' Attis), Salzman, 302.
[8] Cf. Stroh, 274. Heinze, 247, notes the impossibility of disgrace with a *meretrix* and the misapplication of the word to Clodia. Pacitti, esp. 72-73, stresses the focus upon Clodia's personal motives as a distraction from the political dimension.
[9] Heinze, 228; 245-248.

does not deny the possibility that there was a real love affair. Rather he argues that there is no reason to assume that such an affair, and its ending, were known to the whole city, as Heinze had supposed. According to Stroh, the jury's actual perception of the affair is controlled by Cicero's presentation of it in his speech.[10]

To understand the role of dilemma in the speech, indeed to understand the entire rhetorical challenge, we must take account of these two conflicting views. To embrace either, a leap of faith is required. I believe that the love affair took place, that Caelius spurned Clodia, and that there was some general knowledge of these facts. Given this, I believe that Heinze and Stroh are both right, but right for different segments of the audience. It is a fair assumption that all of the jurors do not have exactly the same knowledge or belief about the affair. For those jurors who believe that there has been an affair and that Caelius terminated it, Heinze shows masterfully how the speech works. For the jurors who would be ignorant of the affair, or even have heard a different version, Stroh's demonstration of the way in which Cicero molds the audience's perceptions is largely persuasive. At least initially, Cicero must concurrently reinforce the views of one group and shape the perception of the other group.

There is one final element of the rhetorical challenge that remains the same for either group: Cicero must present Caelius as Clodia's lover, but he must present him in the best light. So, while the affair is obvious to any reader of the speech, Cicero will not be put in the position of explicitly conceding Caelius' involvement. He will make no declarations that may remain, undefended by context, in the jury's minds, or that may be quoted by the prosecution later in the proceeding.[11] We see this principle most clearly in Cicero's denial, in sections 44-47, that Caelius has ever strayed from the straight and narrow. The denial is of course set in the midst of Cicero's defense of leniency for young men who stray from the path of virtue, a defense obviously offered with Caelius in mind. Here, and generally, Cicero will offer no admissions, or even statements that can be

---

[10] Stroh, esp. 269-273. He also argues convincingly, at 296-298, for the uselessness of the Catullan corpus as evidence on this point.

The strongest opposition to both Heinze and Stroh is the apparently sensible view of Austin (on section 29), that Cicero would not have mentioned a fact as damaging as the love affair if the prosecution had not mentioned it first. Cf. Reitzenstein, 32. We cannot know who is right. Still, given the demonstrable usefulness of the love affair in the speech, the positions of Heinze and Stroh seem more plausible than does Austin's.
[11] Cf. Heinze, 246-247.

easily twisted by those tactics which he himself regularly uses against his opponents.[12] Cicero does not explicitly admit the love affair until the *peroratio*. Even there, the orator gives the prosecution no quotable quote that may later be used against him.[13]

The love affair is then necessary to Cicero's persuasive strategy. Yet he is constrained, as a matter of self-defense, from making explicit factual declarations about it. The very structure of dilemma as alternate possibilities which allow one to build an argument on a statement without admitting that it is a fact is thus the perfect vehicle for Cicero's purpose. It allows him to posit the affair without admitting in any quotable form his client's misconduct.

The speech is divided into an *exordium* (1-2), a *praemunitio* (3-50) addressing the prejudices against Caelius and defending his character, a much shorter *argumentatio* (51-69), and a *peroratio* (70-80)[14] in which Cicero finally inserts the traditional chronological treatment of the defendant's life and character (72-77a). Because the speech has been so thoroughly analyzed by others, it will be necessary here only to note the argumentative context for each dilemma form.

---

[12] Cicero's apparent distortion of his opponent's intent is found in almost every judicial speech. In the *Caeliana*, see, e.g., the treatment of Caelius' father in section 3 (with Austin's note). Gotoff even argues that Cicero in this speech does more than twist the opponent's words, that he actually imputes to them ideas and attitudes which are not grounded, however perversely, on anything the prosecution has said.

[13] Section 75: In hoc flexu aetatis -- nihil enim occultabo fretus humanitate ac sapientia vestra -- fama adulescentis paululum haesit ad r.ietas notitia nova eius mulieris et infelici vicinitate et insolentia voluptatum, quae, cum inclusae diutius et prima aetate compressae et constrictae fuerunt, subito se non numquam profundunt atque eiciunt universae. Quae ex vita vel dicam quo ex sermone -- nequaquam enim tantum erat quantum homines loquebantur -- verum ex eo quicquid erat emersit totumque se eiecit atque extulit, tantumque abest ab illius familiaritatis infamia ut eiusdem nunc ab sese inimicitias odiumque propulset. [At what may be called the turning point of his age (for I will hide nothing from you, gentlemen, relying upon your sympathy and good sense) his youthful reputation came for a while to grief through his recent acquaintance with this lady, his unfortunate proximity to her and his inexperience of the pleasures which, after they have been under somewhat long restraint and during early youth curbed and controlled, quite often suddenly break loose and burst out in a flood. But from such a life, or shall I say from such gossip (for the reality was by no means so bad as people maligned) -- from this, whatever it was, he emerged and completely broke loose and escaped, and he is so far from the disgrace of being intimate with that woman, that he now has to defend himself against her enmity and hatred.] Cf. Heinze, 247.

[14] This broad structure follows the divisions in Austin's commentary.

PRO CAELIO   111

It is striking that the first dilemma in the speech occurs in the much-discussed section 35, the bridge passage between the prosopopoeia of Appius Claudius Caecus and that of Clodius. Through these prosopopoeiae, Cicero will establish, for the uninformed jurors, his version of the relationship between Clodia and Caelius. By doing so through these imported characters, he will avoid confessing the validity of any untoward admissions. Still, it is necessary for the force of Cicero's argument that he articulate in his own persona the problem with Clodia's testimony, and this is the function of section 35.[15]

> Tu vero, mulier -- iam enim ipse tecum nulla persona introducta loquor -- si ea quae facis, quae dicis, quae insimulas, quae moliris, quae arguis, probare cogitas, rationem tantae familiaritatis, tantae consuetudinis, tantae coniunctionis reddas atque exponas necesse est. Accusatores quidem libidines, amores, adulteria, Baias, actas, convivia, comissationes, cantus, symphonias, navigia iactant, idemque significant nihil te invita dicere. **Quae tu quoniam nescio qua mente effrenata atque praecipiti in forum deferri iudiciumque voluisti, aut diluas oportet ac falsa esse doceas aut nihil neque crimini tuo neque testimonio credendum esse fateare.**
>
> But as for you, woman (for now it is myself alone and not an imaginary person who addresses you), if you have any intention of proving your deeds, your words, your assertions, your intrigues, your allegations, you will have to render an account of and explain such intimacy, such familiarity, such a close connexion. The accusers are dinning into our ears the words debauchery, amours, misconduct, trips to Baiae, beach-parties, feasts, revels, concerts, musical parties, pleasure-boats; they also inform us that they say nothing of which you do not approve. **And since in some mad and reckless frame of mind you have desired that these matters should be brought into the Forum and into court, you must either disprove them, and show that they are false, or else you must confess that neither your accusation nor your evidence is to be believed.**]

Cicero treats the love affair as part of the constellation of charges against Caelius' lifestyle. Thus Clodia's involvement in such an affair allows the orator to presume that she enjoys the same lifestyle that the prosecution had imputed to Caelius. In the dilemma itself, Cicero does not present to her the option of denying the love affair. Rather he presents to her the choices of denying a whole lifestyle or of admitting that her testimony is worthless.[16] This is a slight but important shift of emphasis.

---

[15] So Reitzenstein, 28-29, 31, arguing convincingly that Norden, 155-156, is wrong to consider section 35 an improvisation. Cf. Heinze, 233-235; Drexler, 31; Stroh, 282-283; Austin, *ad loc.* and p. 161.
[16] Stroh, 283, astutely notes this change, but offers a very different view of its importance.

The lifestyle cannot easily be denied.[17] Further, the dilemma by its nature apparently considers all the possibilities (there is no third choice), and thus gives the illusion of completeness. Within this context, the assumption that there has been a love affair is not questioned but presumed to be true. So the ostensibly exhaustive character of dilemma helps Cicero to establish the love affair in the uninformed jurors' minds without having to substantiate it.[18] For those jurors already in the know, this dilemma seems simply to assert the facts, again without making a quotable admission about Caelius.

But the fuller impact of this dilemma is felt only in conjunction with the next one, in section 50. The task of making Clodia a *meretrix* without sullying Caelius, has been largely effected at this point,[19] and the distinction between jurors who are in the know and those who are not has disappeared. Both groups will now be certain that Caelius has been involved with a virtual *meretrix*, and that this is the source both of the charges concerning gold and poison and of Caelius' exaggerated reputation for moral laxity. The effect is nicely summarized in the dilemma in section 50:

> Si quae mulier sit eius modi qualem ego paulo ante descripsi, tui dissimilis, vita institutoque meretricio, cum hac aliquid adulescentem hominem habuisse rationis num tibi perturpe aut perflagitiosum esse videatur? **Ea si tu non es, sicut ego malo, quid est quod obiciant Caelio? Sin eam te volunt esse, quid est cur nos crimen hoc, si tu contemnis, pertimescamus? Qua re nobis da viam rationemque defensionis. Aut enim pudor tuus defendet nihil a M. Caelio petulantius esse factum, aut impudentia et huic et ceteris magnam ad se defendendum facultatem dabit.**
>
> ...if there existed a woman such as I painted a short while ago, one unlike you, with the life and manners of a courtesan -- would you think it very shameful or disgraceful that a young man should have had some dealings with such a woman? **If you are not this woman, as I prefer to think, for what have the accusers to reproach Caelius? But if they will have it that *you* are such a person, why should we be afraid of this accusation, if you despise it? Then it is for you to show us our way and method of defense; for either your sense of propriety will disprove any vicious behaviour by Caelius, or your utter impropriety will afford both him and the rest a fine opportunity for self-defense.**

---

[17] Whether this lifestyle is justly imputed is of course another question. See esp. Skinner (above, n.7), with lit..
[18] Stroh, 283.
[19] On 31-50, see esp. Stroh, 279-291; Classen, 78-83. Both follow Reitzenstein, 32, in rejecting the idea of Heinze 244, 257-8, that sections 39-50 were added later for publication.

The double standard has been thoroughly ensconced. Again, the basic focus is on Clodia's reprehensible lifestyle. At the same time, the notion that Clodia's testimony is worthless if *she* is the sort of person the prosecution wants *her* to be underscores Cicero's linkage of the prosecution's entire attack on Caelius' past life and character to this single affair.[20] Finally, because dilemma is an obvious and memorable device, there is a resonance of the dilemma in 50 with that in 35, a resonance which reemphasizes the vivid picture of Clodia's lifestyle; it thus stresses the love affair without admitting it, and makes the inference that she is an unreliable witness seem even more patent. The emphasis is the more forceful because this final dilemma is repeated in a different form; the double protasis with questions in apodosis is amplified by the following "either...or" statement. By the end of section 50, then, not only is there a uniform understanding of Cicero's version of the relationship, but there is a complex of ideas which have been put forth explicitly or implicitly in dilemma form: Clodia's lifestyle, the affair, its end, her consequent unreliability as a witness. These themes will be evoked whenever the dilemma form is used in the speech hereafter.

Only when this groundwork has been laid does Cicero finally discuss the charges of the gold taken and the attempted poisoning of Clodia.[21] Cicero begins with the issue of the gold, since, unlike the exchange of poison before witnesses, it depends upon Clodia's testimony alone. Since this is purely a matter of Caelius' word against Clodia's, it affords Cicero greater scope for amplifying his major themes before he treats the poisoning charge, which is obviously thornier. Thus the orator will maintain that Clodia, given the disgraceful lifestyle shown so vividly in the love affair, and given the fact that she was jilted, has both the character and the motive to lie.

The dilemma, by its very use, evokes this complex of assumptions. And dilemma is used three times in sections 52-53a, the most frequent occurrence of the device in so brief a span in the entire Ciceronian corpus:

---

[20] This linkage seems the most satisfactory explanation of Cicero's transparent pretense, here and in section 38, of not wishing to speak of Clodia as a *meretrix*, a pretense abandoned in section 57. Also attractive is the explanation of Reitzenstein, 32, that Herennius had hesitated to mention Clodia, and that Cicero, with a full measure of irony, is showing himself even more discreet than the prosecutors. Cf. also Stroh, 291-292.

[21] The earlier treatment of the gold and the poison (30b-32) had considered them as allegations of moral impropriety rather than as substantial charges. See Reitzenstein, 28; Heinze, 230-231.

Duo enim sunt crimina una in muliere summorum facinorum, auri quod sumptum a Clodia dicitur, et veneni quod eiusdem Clodiae necandae causa parasse Caelium criminantur. Aurum sumpsit, ut dicitis, quod L. Luccei servis daret, per quos Alexandrinus Dio qui tum apud Lucceium habitabat necaretur. Magnum crimen vel in legatis insidiandis vel in servis ad hospitem domini necandum sollicitandis, plenum sceleris consilium, plenum audaciae! (52) **Quo quidem in crimine primum illud requiro, dixeritne Clodiae quam ob rem aurum sumeret, an non dixerit. Si non dixit, cur dedit? Si dixit, eodem se conscientiae devinxit.** Tune aurum ex armario tuo promere ausus es, tune Venerem illam tuam spoliare ornamentis, spoliatricem ceterorum, cum scires quantum ad facinus aurum hoc quaereretur, ad necem legati, ad L. Luccei, sanctissimi hominis atque integerrimi, labem sceleris sempiternam? Huic facinori tanto tua mens liberalis conscia, tua domus popularis ministra, tua denique hospitalis illa Venus adiutrix esse non debuit. (53) Vidit hoc Balbus; celatam esse Clodiam dixit, atque ita Caelium ad illam attulisse, se ad ornatum ludorum aurum quaerere. **Si tam familiaris erat Clodiae quam tu esse vis cum de libidine eius tam multa dicis, dixit profecto quo vellet aurum; si tam familiaris non erat, non dedit. ita si verum tibi Caelius dixit, o immoderata mulier, sciens tu aurum ad facinus dedisti; si non est ausus dicere, non dedisti.**

Two indictments, for the gravest crimes, are brought against Caelius, and in both the name of one woman appears: he is charged with having taken some gold from Clodia, and with having prepared poison to murder this same Clodia. The gold, according to you, he took to give to the slaves of Lucius Lucceius, to procure the assassination of Dio of Alexandria, who at the time was living with Lucceius. It is a grave charge against a man, the he either plotted against the life of an ambassador, or incited slaves to murder their master's guest -- it is a plot rich in villainy, rich in daring! (52) **And in regard to this charge, I first ask, whether he told Clodia for what purpose he took the gold, or whether he did not. If he did not tell her, why did she hand it over? If he did tell her, she made herself his accomplice in this crime.** Did you venture to fetch this gold from your chest, to despoil of her ornaments that Venus of yours, despoiler of your other lovers, when you knew for how great a crime this gold was wanted -- to assassinate an ambassador, to bring on a most virtuous and upright man, Lucius Lucceius, an everlasting stain of guilt? To an outrage so great your generous heart should never have been privy, that open house of yours should never have lent its aid, that hospitable Venus of yours should never have been an accomplice. (53) Balbus had this point in mind; he said that Clodia was not in the secret, and that Caelius told her another story -- that he wanted the gold for the expenses of some games. **But if he was as intimate with Clodia as you claim that he was, since you harp so much on his profligacy, he would certainly have told her why he wanted the gold; if he was not so intimate, she never gave it. Thus, if Caelius told you the truth, you abandoned woman!, you knowingly gave him the gold to commit a crime; if he did not venture to tell you, you did not give it.**

In this passage Cicero presumes that Caelius did in fact take the gold to effect Dio's murder.[22] Cicero can afford this implicit concession for the sake of argument, since every one of the three dilemmas also presupposes the love affair. Thus each underscores both Clodia's lack of integrity and her motive for fabricating the whole business, and so argues Caelius' innocence. Cicero, addressing Clodia directly, wisely amplifies the point of the dilemma addressed to the prosecution in section 52; Clodia is making a charge that, if taken seriously, implicates her in an attempted murder. This prepares the move to the unavoidable discussion of the prosecution's response -- that Caelius had received this gold from Clodia under false pretenses. The orator addresses this perfectly sensible explanation in the second dilemma of the group, turning from Clodia to address Herennius Balbus, the most effective detractor of Caelius' character. "Si tam familiaris erat Clodiae quam tu esse vis cum de libidine eius tam multa dicis" ["But if he was as intimate with Clodia as you claim that he was, since you harp so much on his profligacy"] is arch. Like the dilemma addressed to Clodia in section 50, this one simply assumes that the love affair creates a link through which the prosecution's entire attack on Caelius' character is an attack on Clodia's as well. Again, the dilemma structure allows Cicero to make this defensive counter-move without explicitly admitting that the relationship ever happened. At the same time, the fact of the intimacy is no longer in doubt. Thus the second horn of the dilemma, "si tam familiaris non erat, non dedit" ["if he was not so intimate, she never gave it"] will not receive serious consideration. This leaves the orator free to presume that there is no middle ground--either the two were intimate or they were not close enough for Clodia to give Caelius the gold even on a pretext. The notion that there might be no relationship, and thus that Clodia would have no grounds for knowing or suffering from Caelius' activities, also reflects the dilemma in section 50. Again the dilemma form allows Cicero to explore the fictive consequences of the absence of the relationship without making the harmful and (at this point) quite incredible assertion that Caelius and Clodia were not lovers. The final dilemma of the sequence harnesses the same presuppositions. Addressed to Clodia, it returns Cicero from his direct foray against Herennius to the personage in whom are focused the resonant themes of whorish behavior, a motive for false testimony, and the single misadventure in the defendant's talented, spirited youth. The very form of

---

[22] Cf. Classen, 88.

the device helps to keep these resonances in the jurymen's minds. Concurrently, the dilemma form presents the appearance of exhaustive and invincible reasoning.

By reemphasizing, through the dilemma form, both Clodia's putative character and her motive for lying, Cicero firmly establishes her as a foil for the virtuous Lucius Lucceius, whose deposition apparently indicated that he knew of no such attempt on the life of Dio, who was then a guest in his home. Cicero's placing of the entire argument in the hands of a witness (contrast sections 22, 66), and of a witness who will not testify in person, is weak.[23] The argument works, to the extent that it does, because of the contrast between Lucius Lucceius, "a most virtuous man and a most honorable witness," and the picture of Clodia asserted earlier in the speech and reemphasized, in part through the recurring dilemmas, in the immediately preceding sections.

Once these dilemmas have done their damage, Cicero boldly treats them as conventional, convincing, but unnecessary argument (53: "Quid ego nunc argumentis huic crimini, quae sunt innumerabilia, resistam?" ["Why should I now counter this charge with arguments, which are numerous?"]). The orator's expressed intent to rely on Lucceius' testimony rather than the usual arguments of the practiced speaker allows him an elaborate *praeteritio*. He rehearses the arguments which he need not use to refute the charge of Caelius' complicity in the murder attempt on Dio (53b-54 "relinquo omnia"). it is not surprising that this self-conscious mustering of expected arguments is introduced by the dilemmas in section 53a, and includes yet another dilemma form:

> Possum etiam alia et ceterorum patronorum et mea consuetudine ab accusatore perquirere, ubi sit congressus cum servis Luccei Caelius, qui ei fuerit aditus; **si per se, qua temeritate! si per alium, per quem?** (53b)
>
> I can also ask the prosecutor other things, in accordance both with my own custom and with that of other pleaders: Where did Caelius meet the slaves of Lucceius? What approach did he have? **If he did it himself, how recklessly! If he did it through someone else, through whom?**

This example neither shares the presuppositions nor participates in the resonances of the earlier uses of the device in the speech. Rather it resembles the form at *S. Rosc.* 74 (above, p. 34), in which the second alternative is a question leading to a further chain of diaeretical reasoning. Here, however, there is no further argument, and the form simply illustrates the type of argument that Cicero is not going to use. Still, it has

---

[23] Cf. Austin, *ad loc.*

its effect as part of the refutation in passing of the charge that Caelius had been involved in the attempt on Dio's life. Also, like the dilemmas in the *Divinatio in Caecilium*, it stands as one symbol of the tactics of the experienced pleader.

Sections 56-69 deal, finally, with the charge that Caelius attempted to have Clodia poisoned with the aid of a go-between, one Licinius, and the help of some of her slaves whom he had corrupted. The attempted corruption of Clodia's slaves could be a troublesome allegation. Instead, Cicero makes it a wonderful opportunity. Wouldn't Caelius know that, for a woman who lives like a prostitute, slaves are in fact their mistress' intimates?

> Si enim tam familiaris erat mulieris quam vos voltis, istos quoque servos familiaris dominae esse sciebat. Sin ei tanta consuetudo quanta a vobis inducitur non erat, quae cum servis eius potuit familiaritas esse tanta? (58)
> For if he was so intimate with the woman as you will have it, he knew that those slaves also were on intimate terms with their mistress. But if an association as close as you allege did not exist between the two, how could there have been such close intimacy between him and the slaves?

This dilemma, addressed to the prosecution, uses the same underlying assumptions as do the dilemma in section 50 and the first dilemma in section 53; the entire argument depends upon the jury's acceptance of the intimacy between Clodia and Caelius. Like those dilemmas, this one is also a vehicle for trundling out the entire complex of feelings about Clodia, and for tying the attack on Caelius' character to this single, unadmitted affair. The attempted corruption of the slaves is linked to the dilemma form, tied to the implicit assumption of Caelius' intimacy with Clodia, and thus transmogrified from a serious allegation into another tool for vilifying Clodia's character.

Also noteworthy is the interrogative structure. The dilemma, itself a highly recognizable argumentative device, is employed as part of a barrage of questions which Cicero uses to give the illusion of refuting the accusation without doing so in any substantive way. As Classen points out, this specious refutation flows into the digression on Metellus Celer, at the end of which Cicero leaves the topic of Caelius' approach to Clodia's slaves, and creates the illusion that it has been sufficiently answered.[24]

---

[24] Classen, 89. For a general discussion of Cicero's use of this tactic, with parallels, see Classen's "Ciceros Kunst der Überredung," in W. Ludwig, ed., *Éloquence et Rhétorique chez Cicéron*, Fondation Hardt Entretiens, vol. 28 (Fondation Hardt: Vandoeuvres-Genève, 1982), 149-184, esp. 168-171.

The treatment of the handing over of the poison in the Senian baths (61-69) is complex and mysterious enough that Cicero must be obfuscating a substantial allegation.[25] The dilemma in section 61, used to call into question the need for Licinius as a go-between, harnesses startling presuppositions in the service of this deception:

> Hic primum illud requiro, quid attinuerit ferri in eum locum constitutum, cur illi servi non ad Caelium domum venerint. **Si manebat tanta illa consuetudo Caeli, tanta familiaritas cum Clodia, quid suspicionis esset si apud Caelium mulieris servus visus esset? Sin autem iam suberat simultas, exstincta erat consuetudo, discidium exstiterat, hinc illae lacrimae nimirum et haec causa est omnium horum scelerum atque criminum.** (61)

> At this point I first ask what was the good of arranging for the poison to be brought to that place? Why did not those slaves go to Caelius at his house? **If there still existed between Caelius and Clodia such intimacy and such close association, what suspicion could arise if one of the lady's slaves had appeared at Caelius' house? But if some disagreement now lurked between them, if their association had been broken off, if a rupture had taken place, "the cat," assuredly, "is out if the bag," and we have the reason for all these crimes and accusations.**

This dilemma, resonating with the slave-mistress intimacy theme of the dilemma in section 58, not only assumes the affair, but, for the first time, assumes it for either horn of the dilemma. Logically, this seems a critical point: Cicero is finally basing his argument on the fact, rather than the possibility, that the affair took place. He is presupposing, as an absolute, a situation which he has heretofore avoided admitting in any absolute way.

Rhetorically, this move is less startling. The point of positing that there was no affair has been double. It has kept Cicero from making any explicit admission of Caelius' misbehavior, and it has allowed Cicero to posit Clodia's ignorance of the charges for which she is a witness. The first function is served here, since Cicero's admission of the affair, while logically implicit, is certainly not quotable. The very fact that Cicero uses the dilemma form resonates with the preceding three dilemmas, all of which, like this one, have posited the relationship as the first alternative, and all of which impugn the witness and so undermine the credibility of the charges. On the other hand, the second function of positing that there was no affair, to deny Clodia's knowledge of any misdeeds, is less useful here. In fact, the second alternative of the preceding three dilemmas, that there

---

[25] Cf. Austin, *ad loc.*

PRO CAELIO   119

was no relationship, would be self-destructive in this context. Something had happened in the Senian baths. There were witnesses, and slaves who had been manumitted for their good services. Cicero's argument is that the choice of public baths for the handing over of the poison to Clodia's corrupted slaves makes no sense. Given the intimacy between Clodia and Caelius, Caelius might, without suspicion, have dealt with Clodia's slaves directly in his own home. The prosecution would of course have denied so great an intimacy, and so have shown that the rendez-vous in the Senian baths, which did take place, showed a certain criminal prudence. Thus Cicero cannot here posit the absence of the relationship without reenforcing the prosecution's argument. The resonance of this dilemma form with the content of the dilemmas that have come before allows the orator to glide over the critical concession of the love affair by emphasizing again the entire thematic complex, most especially the general notion of the unreliability of the critical witness. Further, it sustains the mood of doubt that Cicero will need in order to deal with apparently more substantial allegations.

The final dilemma, in section 62, differs from seven of the eight earlier dilemmas in that it does use the existence of the love affair as a premise:

> Cur enim potissimum balneas publicas constituerat? in quibus non invenio quae latebra togatis hominibus esse posset. **Nam si essent in vestibulo balnearum, non laterent; sin se in intimum conicere vellent, nec satis commode calceati et vestiti id facere possent et fortasse non reciperentur, nisi forte mulier potens quadrantaria illa permutatione familiaris facta erat balneatori.** (62)

> For why had she specially fixed on the public baths, where I do not see that there could be any hiding-place for men in their togas? **For if they were in the forecourt they would not be hidden: but if they wanted to pack themselves away inside, they could not conveniently do so in their shoes and outdoor dress, and perhaps would not be admitted -- unless possibly that lady of influence had bought the favour of the bathman by her usual two-bit deal.**

In this dilemma, addressed neither to Clodia nor to the prosecutors, but to the jury, Cicero again draws on the resonances created by his previous uses of the device. By this point, the very dilemma form, as well as *quadrantaria illa permutatione*,[26] keeps in the jury's minds how worthless the slighted vamp's entire story must be.

---

[26] This of course implies that Clodia charged a *quadrans*, the amount of the entry fee to the baths, for her sexual favors. Cf. Caelius' phrase, "quadrantariam Clytemnestram" (quoted by Quintilian, 8.6.52).

In summary, eight of the nine dilemmas in the *Caeliana* are concerned to undermine the reliability of a witness. Thus they are ethical in their assumptions, or conclusions, or both, and are at the same time strictly relevant to the question of fact that the jury must decide. All nine dilemmas share in the most general way some functions of the device that we have noted in earlier speeches. But within this speech those functions play a remarkably direct and unitary role in Cicero's overarching persuasive strategy.

Thus the dilemma in section 35 makes the presuppositions upon which it is founded seem valid, even though these presuppositions have not been proven.[27] We also see the presentational aspect of the device that gives the illusion of exhaustiveness, and so simply excludes from consideration the possibilities that it does not admit.[28] Finally, in a manner akin to earlier synthetic forms, this dilemma redefines an issue in a way that is more useful to Cicero.[29]

The dilemma in section 50 caps an extended section of argument.[30] More important, it recapitulates themes established in the earlier use of the device.[31]

The three dilemmas that cluster together in sections 52-53a, aside from their resonances, stand as examples of the type of argument that the orator then tells us he is not going to use. So they share with the dilemma in section 53b[32] the symbolic status of tools of the practical speaker, although not in the unitary way that we have seen in the *Divinatio in Caecilium*.

The dilemma in section 58 forms with the barrage of questions a "smoke screen" for obscuring the inadequacy of Cicero's treatment of a topic.[33]

The dilemma in section 62, unlike that in section 61, finds a comparandum in an earlier speech. It combines the functions of effective argument and vehicle for innuendo in direct address to the audience. This

---

[27] Cf. very generally *S. Rosc.* 93 (above pp. 37-38); *Div. Caec.* 31, 33, 58 (pp. 59, 62-63).
[28] Cf. esp. *Sul.* 10 and 39 (above, pp. 94-95, 100)
[29] Cf. *Div. Caec.* 12 (above, pp. 55-56); *Q. Rosc.* 16, 25(bis), 43, 52, 55 (pp. 81, 82-83, 85-86, 88); *Sul.* 21 (p. 96).
[30] Cf. *Q. Rosc.* 9, 25(i) (above pp. 77, 82); *Sul.* 10 (pp. 94-95).
[31] Cf. *Div. Caec.* 14 and 4 (above, pp. 56, 53); *Q. Rosc.* 25(ii) and 9 (pp. 83, 77).
[32] Cf. also *S. Rosc.* 74 (above, p. 34).
[33] See n.24 above.

dilemma form addressed to the audience is a powerful way of dismissing an opponent's claims to be taken seriously (cf. *Har. Resp.* 5, below p. 199).

More generally, we noted in conjunction with the discussion of *Pro Roscio Comoedo* that the sheer number of dilemmas may add an illusion of invincible, coherent argumentation that can balance an array of comic elements in a speech. The audience is happy to be amused, and the famous comic elements in the *Caeliana* would delight Cicero's hearers. But a jury must still respect its oath. Amidst the comic touches there must still be the appearance of a case convincingly argued. And so dilemma may occur so frequently in this speech exactly because it is, along with *Pro Roscio Comoedo*, the most overtly comical of Cicero's orations.

But these disparate observations miss the most important reason for the remarkable frequency of dilemma in the speech. Cicero's whole argument hinges on the jury's acceptance of his version of Caelius' relationship with Clodia, since the relationship gives Clodia a motive for lying without adducing external political considerations. At the same time, the relationship reduces the scathing attack on Caelius' character to an attack on this one relatively defensible episode. But Cicero must depict this relationship without making any quotable admissions of Caelius' misbehavior. The dilemma is the ideal vehicle for Cicero's argument since it 1) allows him to posit the affair without admitting it, 2) gives the illusion of exhaustive, invincible argument, and 3) contributes a unique persuasive resonance; the repetition of the dilemma form, like the incantatory repetition of a phrase, endows with a specious validity the ideas it evokes. Thus dilemma allows Cicero to keep his version of the relationship always before the jury, to conjure with it, and to do so without ever admitting in any quotable form that Caelius was actually involved in an unsavory situation. The fact that dilemma occurs with such extraordinary frequency in the *Caeliana* is thus essential to the success of the persuasive strategy, and to the remarkable power of the speech.

CHAPTER SEVEN: *PRO PLANCIO*

Cicero's oration defending Cn. Plancius on a charge of *ambitus* (corrupt electioneering practices) in 54 is one of two Ciceronian *ambitus* defense speeches that have come down to us virtually complete.[1] But in contrast with the earlier speech for Murena, the oration for Plancius is remarkable for its frequent use of dilemma and other dilemma structures; while the orator only uses this device once in *Pro Murena* (sec. 57), dilemma occurs five times in *Pro Plancio* (secs. 35, 44, 46, 54, 84). Further, other dilemma structures occur another seven times in the speech for Plancius (secs. 4, 6, 79, 83, 88, 89(*bis*)).[2] An analysis of Cicero's persuasive strategy will lead us to an understanding of the special role of the dilemma form in this speech, both in its mechanical and in its

---

[1] Basic works for this study are W. Kroll, "Ciceros Rede fuer Plancius," *RhM* 86 (1937) 127-139; L.R. Taylor, "Magistrates of 55 B.C. in Cicero's *Pro Plancio* and Catullus 52," *Athenaeum* (new series) 42 (1968) 12-28; J. Adamietz, "Ciceros Verfahren in den Ambitus-Prozessen gegen Murena und Plancius," *Gymnasium* 93 (1986) 102-117; James M. May, *Trials of Character*, (Chapel Hill and London: University of North Carolina Press, 1988) 116-126; C.P. Craig, "Cicero's Strategy of Embarrassment in the Speech for Plancius," *AJP* 111 (1990) 75-81, parts of which are here reprinted by permission of Johns Hopkins University Press. See also the introduction to the *Budé* edition of Pierre Grimal, *Cicéron, Discours*, tome 16, pte. 2, (Paris: Société d'Edition "les belles lettres," 1976); G.A. Kennedy, *The Art of Rhetoric in the Roman World* (Princeton: Princeton University Press, 1972), 204-205. With the exception of the article by the present author, these works will hereafter be referenced by the authors' last names alone.

Of the several commentaries, the most useful for this study are the monumental edition of E. Wunder (Leipzig: C.H.F. Hartmann, 1830); E. Koepke[3], rev. G. Landgraf (Leipzig: Teubner, 1887); H.W. Auden (London: MacMillan, 1897); G.B. Bonino (Torino: Giovanni Chiantore, 1923).

[2] The different frequencies of the device in the two speeches are certainly tied to the difference in the two rhetorical challenges. See Craig (above, n.1).

presentational aspects. Further, this oration, like the speech for Sulla, will exemplify the uses of dilemma forms in what is dominantly ethical argumentation.

The circumstances of the case are these: Cn. Plancius was the son of a leading equestrian tax farmer. As quaestor in Macedonia in 58, he had guaranteed the safety of Cicero during the terrible time of the orator's exile. Plancius and M. Iuventius Laterensis, a *nobilis* of strong political convictions, both stood for the curule aedileship for 55.³ Elections were finally held in 55, and Plancius was elected ahead of Laterensis, but the election was declared invalid. A second election was duly held and here Plancius gained one of the two curule aedileships. Laterensis lost. The next year, Laterensis initiated a prosecution against Plancius for election bribery under the *lex Licinia de sodaliciis* of 55. His assisting prosecutor was L. Cassius Longinus. Plancius was defended by Cicero, perhaps preceded by Hortensius.⁴ We do not know with certainty whether Plancius was acquitted.

There are five principal difficulties that Cicero must face in his speech:⁵ 1) Plancius may be guilty of the charges. He is prosecuted under the *lex Licinia de sodaliciis*, which embraced organized, systematic bribery (45 "Decuriatio tribulium, discriptio populi, suffragia largitione devincta" ["the systematic organization of the tribes and the electorate into sections and allotments, and the restriction of the freedom of the poll by bribery"]) through the action of associations, *sodalicia*.⁶ It could also include *coitio*, in the sense of the combined action of two candidates to pool votes obtained by such bribery to shut out a competitor (53b-54).⁷

---

³ I adopt the chronology of Taylor. Cf. T. R. S. Broughton, *Magistrates of the Roman Republic. American Philological Association Monographs*. revised ed. 3 vols. (Chico, CA: Scholars Press, 1984-1986), vol. 3, p.158.
⁴ Although it is generally assumed, on the basis of section 37, that Hortensius was involved in the defense as well, there is no conclusive evidence of this. See Taylor, p. 25 and n.41.
⁵ The analysis that follows reproduces in slightly abridged form that in Craig (above, n.1).
⁶ For a discussion, with thorough bibliography, of the issues surrounding the *lex Licinia*, see most recently C. Venturini, "L'Orazione pro Cn. Plancio e la Lex Licinia de Sodaliciis," *Studi in Honore di Cesare San Filippo*, vol. 5 (Milan: Guiffrè, 1984) 787-804. Of the works he cites, see esp. J. Linderski, "Ciceros Rede Pro Caelio und die Ambitus- und Vereinsgezetsgebung der ausgehenden Republik," *Hermes* 89 (1961) 106-119.
⁷ Cicero treats this *coitio* as a charge proper to a *communis ambitus causa* (47). Such a combination was illegal only if the votes which one candidate promised to another

Laterensis offered to adduce from Plancius' own Voltinian tribe witnesses that there had been systematic bribery (54). The prosecutor could even assert, although he apparently could not prove, that one of Plancius' bribery agents had already been caught with money in hand (55); 2) The *lex Licinia de sodaliciis* enjoins a procedure that places the defense at a disadvantage. The prosecution proposes four tribes from which the jury is to be selected. The defense has the right to reject only one tribe, rather than to challenge the prospective jurors individually. So the prosecution should be able to get a favorable jury (36-41); 3) The comparison of the prosecutor's birth and accomplishments with those of the accused would favor Laterensis. This comparison, or *contentio dignitatis*, is apparently a standard and important type of argument in *ambitus* trials.[8]

Two other elements of the challenge are much more personally concerned with Cicero, and are most important for the orator's strategy. 4) The prosecutor has personal claims on Cicero almost as great as those of the defendant. Plancius, as quaestor in Macedonia, had protected Cicero assiduously during his exile. Meanwhile, Laterensis was helping the orator's family in Italy and working for Cicero's return, as the orator explicitly acknowledges (73). 5) A closely related difficulty is that this bond between Cicero and Laterensis had included a shared opposition to the first triumvirate. Laterensis had withdrawn his candidacy for the tribunate in 59, since those elected would be constrained to swear to uphold Caesar's legislation (cf. 13). Also in 59, Cicero's public remarks on the triumvirs had stirred them to allow Clodius' transfer to the plebs, and so to start the chain of events that would lead to Cicero's exile.[9] In 54, however, only Laterensis remained constant. Cicero had sung his palinode (*Att.* 4.5). At the bidding of the triumvirs, he was now defending

---

were obtained through bribery. It would properly fall under the *lex Licinia* only if that bribery were done through associations. Thus the Scholia Bobiensia (p.152 Stangl) describes the *lex Licinia* as attacking those who enlisted associations "ea potissimum de causa, ut per illos pecuniam tribulibus dispertirent ac sibi mutuo eadem suffragationis emptae praesidia communicarent." ["especially for this reason, so that through them they might distribute money to the tribes and share among themselves the same security of a bought vote."] If *coitio* were simply a pledge of support between two candidates, then Laterensis would have incriminated himself by complaining that Plancius and Plotius had not been true to their earlier pledge to deliver the Aniensis and Teretina to him. This hardly seems likely, *pace* Venturini (above, n.6) 795-6.

[8] Cf. R. Preiswerk, *De Inventione Orationum Ciceronianarum*, (Basel, 1905) 42-43; Adamietz, 116-117.

[9] For a complete collection of ancient sources on this episode, see M. Gelzer, *Cicero: ein biographischer Versuch* (Wiesbaden: Steiner, 1968) 124-25 and nn. 165, 167-69.

the likes of Vatinius, whose hideous appearance and mendacity he had immortalized in the *in Vatinium*.[10] Thus Laterensis characterized Cicero as a man untrue to his friends and untrue to himself, as a creature of the triumvirs, twisting the truth to aid the son of a wealthy supporter and beneficiary of Caesar's legislation.[11] Laterensis had further explicitly argued that Cicero was dishonestly exaggerating his debt of gratitude to Plancius, and that, even if the orator were in Plancius' debt, that should not sway the jury from deciding on the basis of the facts.[12]

The attack on Cicero for failing his friends and for being inconsistent is irrelevant to the legal issue. So it differs from the attack upon Cicero in the trial of Sulla, in which Cicero's role as witness demanded an attempt to discredit him. Nevertheless, Laterensis' onslaught comprises a devastating argument, so much so that the ethical argument focussed upon Cicero seems to have occupied the prosecution at least as much as did the actual charges. The fact that Cicero's speech is dominated by ethical argument is thus dictated by the prosecution's strategy.[13]

At the same time, Cicero's response to these attacks in the *Planciana* is both ingenious and unique. Only in this speech does he claim to be embarrassed, even grieved, by the conflicting claims of his friend the prosecutor and those of his client.[14] And only in this speech does this embarrassment lead him to a systematic and ostentatious forbearance. In the exordium (1-5), he defines a community of his supporters that includes the jury and all supporters of Plancius, and that should include his former

---

[10] Later in the year, he would even defend Gabinius, the consul who had abetted his exile, and whom he had earlier (*Pis.* 25) labelled an over-perfumed and over-rouged dancing girl.

[11] Sections 91 and 31-35. For the connection of Plancius' father to the triumvirs, especially Crassus, see Taylor, p. 22 & n.28; Grimal, 16-18.

[12] Section 4. For the political climate of the speech, see especially Taylor, 24-27.

We should not let Cicero's disposition of his arguments obscure the real possibility that Laterensis' comments on Cicero's vassalage to the triumvirs (91), and his comments upon the apparently offensive anti-optimate (and pro-triumvirate) attitude of Plancius' father (31-35), are parts of the same argument in the prosecutor's speech. This argument would link both Cicero and Plancius, through Plancius senior, to Laterensis' three *bêtes noires*.

[13] So Kroll, 132-133; Kennedy, 204; May, 120-121. Adamietz, 102-103, points out that the actual treatment of the charges, in sections 53b-57, comprises only one twentieth of the speech.

[14] This is in strong contrast to the orator's response to the equally awkward necessity of opposing Sulpicius and Cato in the speech for Murena. See Craig (above, n.1), esp. 79-80 and n.16.

supporter Laterensis.¹⁵ The orator is astonished that Laterensis, "hominem studiosissimum et dignitatis et salutis meae" ["a person most supportive both of my prestige and of my safety"] (2), should prosecute the man responsible for Cicero's very survival. Cicero confesses himself at a loss when one friend and supporter attacks another. Thus, throughout the speech, he assumes a posture of determined friendship in the face of hurtful action. He refuses to engage in the *contentio dignitatis*, lest he have to level a *contumeliosa oratio* against his friend the prosecutor (6).¹⁶ He has the Roman people tell Laterensis that he was not elected aedile because the electorate wants him to have the greater office of the tribunate (13). He rebukes Laterensis' assisting prosecutor for praising Laterensis insufficiently (63). He explicitly refuses to match the force of Laterensis' attacks on his character. However he has been insulted, he will answer no less considerately or amicably (72). He asserts his debt of gratitude to Laterensis in the strongest terms (73, 78). Finally, the orator freely admits that he is in anguish, torn between honoring Laterensis and the necessity of doing his duty towards Plancius (79).¹⁷

---

¹⁵ Cf. C.P. Craig, "The *Accusator* as *Amicus*: a uniquely Roman tactic of ethical argumentation," *TAPA* 111 (1981) 31-37.
¹⁶ As Adamietz, 116-117, observes, this does not mean that the arguments proper to a *contentio dignitatis* are omitted. Most are raised later (58-67), in Cicero's response to the speech of Cassius.
¹⁷ 6: Ita, si cedo illius ornamentis, quae multa et magna sunt, non solum huius dignitatis iactura facienda est sed etiam largitionis recipienda suspicio est; sin hunc illi antepono, contumeliosa habenda est oratio, et dicendum est id quod ille me flagitat, Laterensem a Plancio dignitate esse superatum. [Consequently, if I yield the palm to my opponent's endowments (and they are beyond question many and great), I must not merely jettison my client's honour, but I must lay myself open to the suspicion of corrupt collusion; if, on the other hand, I put the claims of my client before those of my friend, my speech must be devoted to vituperation, and I must state, since he importunes me for an answer, that the merits of Laterensis are surpassed by those of Plancius.];
13: '...Pete igitur eum magistratum in quo mihi magnae utilitati esse possis; aediles quicumque erunt, idem mihi sunt ludi parati; tribuni pl. permagni interest qui sint.' ['...Seek, then, an office wherein your services maybe of great value to me; whoever may be the aediles, the games organized for me are the same; but the personality of the tribunes of the plebs is a matter of paramount importance to me.'];
63: Atqui non modo confiteor summa in Laterense ornamenta esse sed te etiam reprehendo quod ea non enumeres, alia quaedam inania et levia conquiras. [Yet not merely do I grant that the highest endowments are to be found in Laterensis, but I would even find fault with you for being at pains to gather instances of specious and trivial qualities, instead of enumerating the solid endowments he possesses];
72: Respondebo tibi nunc, Laterensis, minus fortasse vehementer quam abs te sum provocatus, sed profecto nec considerate minus nec minus amice. [I now proceed to

The rhetorical reason for this embarrassment is not far to seek. Cicero's credibility has been impaired by the prosecution's embarrassing, even devastating, characterization of his toadying submission to the triumvirs. The orator's only hope is to distract from this negative picture by offering an alternate and coherent portrait of himself. For this goal, Cicero's embarrassment is doubly useful. First, because it is linked to the orator's ordeal, it presupposes, and thus helps both to emphasize and to validate, the heroic tableau of Cicero sacrificing himself for the fatherland (esp. 96-100).[18] Second, it allows Cicero to maintain his central focus upon *gratia*, in the sense of "gratitude." Because of Cicero's embarrassment, he treats Laterensis with the model forbearance and consideration that a friend and benefactor can properly expect. He further reinforces this model behavior with two separate encomia of *gratia* (68-69, 80-81). Used to counter Laterensis' and Cassius' arguments that Cicero exaggerates his obligation to Plancius, these commonplaces also allow the orator to underscore how vital the feeling of gratitude is, not just in his relations with Plancius or Laterensis, but in the jury's relations with him. *Gratia* is, after all, the mother of all the other virtues (80). Thus, through

---

reply to you, Laterensis, using less vehemence, perhaps, than you prompt me to use, but in a spirit, I dare avow, of no less consideration and friendship.];
73: qui (sc. Laterensis) cum mihi esses amicissimus, cum vel periculum vitae tuae mecum sociare voluisses, cum me in illo tristi et acerbo luctu atque discessu non lacrimis solum tuis sed animo, corpore, copiis prosecutus esses, cum meos liberos et uxorem me absente tuis opibus auxilioque defendisses, sic mecum semper egisti, te mihi remittere atque concedere ut omne studium meum in Cn. Planci honore consumerem, quod eius in me meritum tibi etiam ipsi gratum esse dicebas. [When you (sc. Laterensis) were on terms of close friendship with me, when you were ready even to risk your life at my side, when in the bitter heartrending hour of my departure you had put, not merely your tears, but your powers, mental, bodily, and material, at my service, when you had protected my wife and children in my absence with your succour and your substance, in all your dealings with me you gave me to believe that you readily granted me full permission to devote all my efforts to promoting Plancius' advancement, because, as you alleged, you yourself viewed with gratitude his services to me.];
78: Atque haec cum vides, quo me tandem in te animo putas esse, Laterensis? ullum esse tantum periculum, tantum laborem, tantam contentionem quam ego non modo pro salute tua sed etiam pro dignitate defugerim? [Bearing all this in mind, Laterensis, what feelings do you think I cherish towards you? Do you think that there is any perip, any hardship, any struggle so great that I should shring from meeting it, if I could so further, not your welfare only, but even your mere wordly position?];
79: Distineor tamen et divellor dolore et in causa dispari offendi te a me doleo. [But I am torn by a painful dilemma, and in such a disparity of interests it goes to my heart to offer you an affront.]
[18] Cf. May, 123-125.

his consistent forbearance toward Laterensis, complemented by the encomia of gratitude, Cicero provides the jury with both example and praise of the attitude which those under an obligation should assume. In the course of doing so, he makes a point of reminding them, often and at length, of his heroic suffering for them, and thus of their own obligation to him (*passim*, esp. 25-6, 68-74, 86-90, 95-100).

The orator's embarrassment, and studied forbearance towards his opponent, are thus as essential as they are unique. They are bound up with, and so assert, an heroic portrait of the orator that neutralizes Laterensis' devastating picture of Cicero as a vassal of the triumvirs. Equally important, the orator's ostentatious embarrassment leads him to treat Laterensis in a way that exemplifies the consideration that Cicero himself, and of course Cicero's client, can properly expect from every decent member of the jury.

Discussion of the role of dilemma forms in this strategy requires an understanding of the movement of Cicero's argument in the speech. The gross structure of the speech, *exordium* (1-6a), *argumentatio* (6b-100), *peroratio* (101-104) is not at all helpful in this. Further, the literature on all rhetorical aspects of the *Planciana*, not just the structure of the argument, is surprisingly sparse. So an exceptionally full treatment of some parts of the argumentation will be necessary to provide a sufficiently broad context for our understanding of Cicero's uses of our chosen argument form in this oration.

Our analysis may conveniently begin in section 4, where the first dilemma form occurs as part of Cicero's rationale for his later trundling out of the pathetic details of his exile.

> Equidem ad reliquos labores, quos in hac causa maiores suscipio quam in ceteris, etiam hanc molestiam adsumo, quod mihi non solum pro Cn. Plancio dicendum est, cuius ego salutem non secus ac meam tueri debeo, sed etiam pro me ipso, de quo accusatores plura paene quam de re reoque dixerunt. Quamquam, iudices, si quid est in me ipso ita reprehensum ut id ab hoc seiunctum sit, non me id magno opere conturbat; non enim timeo ne quia perraro grati homines reperiantur, idcirco, cum me nimium gratum illi esse dicant, id mihi criminosum esse possit. **Quae vero ita sunt agitata ab illis ut aut merita Cn. Planci erga me minora esse dicerent quam a me ipso praedicarentur, aut, si essent summa, negarent ea tamen ita magni ut ego putarem ponderis apud vos esse debere,** haec mihi sunt tractanda, iudices, et modice, ne quid ipse offendam, et tum denique cum respondero criminibus, ne non tam innocentia reus sua quam recordatione meorum temporum defensus esse videatur. (3-4)

The labours involved in my present advocacy are already greater than those of the general run of cases; but I must go beyond these, and take upon myself the further burden of speaking, not only on behalf of Gnaeus Plancius, whose safety I am in duty bound to protect no less carefully than my own, but also on behalf of myself, for our opponents have said almost more about me than about my client and his case. But, gentlemen, if any criticism has been passed upon myself in which he is not involved, that does not greatly trouble me. Gratitude is the rarest of human qualities, and I have no fear, therefore, lest the imputation of excessive gratitude to my client should be converted into a damaging charge against me. **But these matters have been so vigorously argued by the other side that they have either said that the services of Cn. Plancius towards me were less than I myself expected them to be, or they have said that, even if those services were the greatest, nevertheless they were not so great that I might think that they ought to carry some weight with you.** So I must treat these matters, gentlemen of the jury, moderately, lest I myself somehow offend, and only at that point when I have answered the charges, lest the accused seem to have been defended not so much by his own innocence as by the recollection of my crisis.[19] (3-4)

Cicero claims that the prosecution has confronted him with a dilemma: either he was exaggerating his debt to Plancius or, if the debt existed, it should not be an important factor in the jury's eyes.[20] We have come to expect that Cicero's acknowledgement that he is in a dilemma is a tactic to grant him a license to do something that the jury would find objectionable.[21] Here, conveniently, the dilemma has been leveled by the opponent; it is thus Laterensis' doing that compels the orator to discuss the circumstances of his own exile. That discussion, as we have seen, will be integral to his persuasive strategy.

The next section (5-6) establishes another key element in the persuasive strategy, Cicero's determination to honor his duty toward the prosecutor. The orator here confesses himself vexed at the prospect of speaking against his friend Laterensis, and the more vexed because Laterensis has insisted upon a *contentio dignitatis*:

> (5) Mihi autem non id est in hac re molestissimum, contra illum dicere, sed multo magis quod in ea causa contra dicendum est in qua quaedam hominum ipsorum videtur facienda esse contentio. (6) Quaerit enim Laterensis atque hoc uno maxime urget qua se virtute, qua laude Plancius, qua dignitate superavit. **Ita, si cedo illius ornamentis, quae multa et magna sunt, non solum huius dignitatis iactura facienda est sed etiam largitionis recipienda suspicio est; sin hunc illi antepono, contumeliosa habenda est oratio, et dicendum est id quod ille me flagitat,**

---

[19] My translation of dilemma and following sentence.
[20] For the form of the argument, see C.P. Craig, "The Structural Pedigree of Cicero's Speeches *Pro Quinctio*, *Pro Archia* and *Pro Milone*, " *CP* 80 (1985) 136-37.
[21] cf. *S. Rosc.* 124 (above, p. 39); *Div. Caec.* 4 (p. 53).

Laterensem a Plancio dignitate esse superatum. Ita aut amicissimi hominis existimatio offendenda est, si illam accusationis condicionem sequar, aut optime de me meriti salus deserenda.

But although it is painful to me to choose the course of attacking my friend, it is still more painful that the case in which I am called upon to do so is one in which a comparison of individual qualities seems to be inevitable. For there is one question which Laterensis propounds, and for an answer to which he presses with peculiar urgency; it is the question by what moral qualities, by what superiority in distinction and reputation, Plancius surpasses himself.. Consequently, if I yield the palm to my opponent's endowments (and they are beyond question many and great), I must not merely jettison my client's honour, but I must lay myself open to the suspicion of corrupt collusion; if, on the other hand, I put the claims of my client before those of my friend, my speech must be devoted to vituperation, and I must state, since he importunes me for an answer, that the merits of Laterensis are surpassed by those of Plancius. So I am faced with the alternative of either damaging the reputation of a dear friend, if I pursue the line to which his speech has prompted me, or of betraying the cause of one to whom I am under a deep obligation.

Again, Cicero finds himself in a dilemma, this one born of his ostensible loyalty to both men. "sin hunc illi antepono, contumeliosa habenda est oratio" ["if, on the other hand, I put the claims of my client before those of my friend, my speech must be devoted to vituperation"] is especially telling. Laterensis had mounted a *contumeliosa oratio*, both against Plancius and against Cicero himself. Cicero's statement amounts to an assertion of his right to respond in kind. Laterensis has put the orator in a position where attack on his friend the prosecutor is unavoidable. We, and the jury, expect it.

This is, in the broadest terms, another example of Cicero professing himself in a dilemma in order to gain license for tactics that would otherwise alienate his audience. But this example is unique in that Cicero gains that license, then ostentatiously refuses to use it; the expectation that Cicero must now attack Laterensis is largely disappointed.[22] Cicero escapes his dilemma by refusing to become involved in a *contentio dignitatis* proper. Using exemplary forbearance, he will discuss only those relatively mechanical issues that determined Laterensis' failure at the polls (6b-26). Among those issues not really related to *dignitas*, Cicero counts the influence which his own support of Plancius will have had with the voters (24b-26). Plancius saved Cicero as the people of Minturnae had saved Marius (Cicero's fellow townsman and fellow savior of Rome).

---

[22] Contrast *Mur.* 21, where Cicero creates an expectation that he must attack Sulpicius, then proceeds to do so humorously and at length.

Thus the voters respected Cicero's motives for campaigning on Plancius' behalf. This heavy-handed obtrusion of Cicero's debt to Plancius, and implicitly of the citizens' debt to Cicero, rounds out a passage in which the orator undermines Laterensis' contention that he should have been elected. But Cicero does so without resorting, in his own persona, to the traditional *contentio dignitatis* and the inevitable *contumeliosa oratio*.[23] So the dilemma structure in section 6 serves as a springboard for an argument that denies the opponent's position that, absent bribery, Laterensis would have been elected, and does so in a way that showcases Cicero's dutiful forbearance while reminding the jury of their own duty to the *patronus*.

In the next section (27-35), the orator deftly merges *contentio*, or rather non-*contentio*, with the standard Hellenistic and Roman *locus* of the defendant's past life (*Inv.* 2.32-37 and 1.34-36; cf. *Mur.* 11-13). This merging is convenient indeed, since it allows Cicero to rehearse Plancius' career simply in the manner of a review of the defendant's life, and thus not in comparison with Laterensis. Having pointed to Plancius' virtues, both public and domestic, and having used this as the wedge for a recapitulation with pathetic overtones (29), Cicero returns to the *contentio* aspect unambiguously only in section 30a, and finally makes the forceful point that Plancius' life shows him as Laterensis' equal in qualifications for the aedileship.

Only after this crescendo does Cicero deal in lightning fashion with the prosecution's various charges of immorality (30b-31a). Immediately he moves on to the large problem, and grand distraction, of Plancius' father (31b-35). It is obvious that Laterensis had attacked Plancius senior effectively, and that Cicero is constrained to answer.[24] Further, since Plancius' father had strong ties to the triumvirs, as does Cicero, the attack on the father serves to bring odium on *patronus* and defendant concurrently. The danger of this argument for Laterensis, as Cicero demonstrates, is that it offers an opportunity to defend the entire equestrian order, and the average businessman, against a putative senatorial arrogance. Since equites and *tribuni aerarii* make up two thirds of the jury, senators only one third, Laterensis is giving an advantage to the defense.

---

[23] This is not to say that Cicero avoids a *contentio*. He will simply take this up with Cassius later (58-67) rather than addressing Laterensis directly.
[24] Less obvious is the manner in which this lengthy treatment leaves the morals charges in relative obscurity.

But the situation is, of course, more complex. We cannot usefully view the jury simply as three voting blocks, with senators opposed to Plancius senior and to Caesar's law, and equites and *tribuni aerarii* in the other camp. No doubt there were a few in the senatorial portion of the jury who were more securely in the orbit of their fellow senators Crassus, Pompeius, and Caesar than in the orbit of Cato and Laterensis. Laterensis' attack invites Cicero to define a simple opposition of equites vs. senators. For Cicero to do so is to concede, and thus to create an expectation, that there is greater solidarity among senatorial jurors than they may really feel. Equally dangerous, such a simple opposition runs contrary to Cicero's strategy. It makes him a part of factional squabbling, and so diminishes his ethos as the friend of all good men, who has suffered for all Romans, been supported by all present, and has a claim on all members of the jury.

The issue of Plancius' father is then an important ethical argument that bears no logical relation to the charges proper. Still, Cicero must answer it, and so he introduces that answer with the usual alacrity. He tells Laterensis that this attack is unworthy of Laterensis' integrity (31: "O vocem duram atque indignam tua probitate, Laterensis!"). The orator then proceeds to speak as the defender of the value of fatherly love (31: "Pater ut" *ad fin.*). Finally, he extolls Plancius senior as the very model, by birth and accomplishments, of a prominent *eques* (32). Only after this distracting prologue does Cicero touch upon what must have been the heart of Laterensis' remarks. In the course of the struggle that finally led to Caesar's remission of the tax contract in Asia, Plancius senior had apparently made some unforgivable remarks about some senators, perhaps about the senate itself. Cicero is exquisitely vague on what was actually said, even as he justifies the utterances (33-34). The orator makes clear that Plancius was not provoked by the senate, but by a small group within it.[25] Finally, having justified the elder Plancius' remarks without repeating them, the orator raises the possibility that the offensive words were falsely attributed to Plancius in any case (34 through "conferuntur").

---

[25] (34) Cum senatus *impediretur* quo minus, id quod hostibus semper erat tributum, responsum equitibus Romanis redderetur, omnibus illa iniuria dolori fuit publicanis, sed eum ipsum dolorem hic tulit paulo asperius. [When the senate *was prevented* from replying to a petition of the Roman knights, a privilege which had never been refused even to our enemies, the injustice was resented by all the tax-farmers, but Plancius made rather less efforts to conceal this resentment than did the others.] (emphasis mine)

The whole passage to this point is a masterpiece of composure under fire. Nevertheless, it is quite obviously defensive; we see Cicero dealing as best he can with a profound embarrassment. As he brings his treatment of Plancius' father to an end, Cicero works to dispel this impression of defensiveness by incorporating dilemma, as an aggressive argumentative tactic, into his last words on the subject:

> Nam quod primus scivit legem de publicanis tum cum vir amplissimus consul id illi ordini per populum dedit quod per senatum, si licuisset, dedisset, **si in eo crimen est quia suffragium tulit, quis non tulit publicanus? si quia primus scivit, utrum id sortis esse vis, an eius qui illam legem ferebat? Si sortis, nullum crimen est in casu; si consulis, *statuis*[26] etiam hunc a summo viro principem esse ordinis iudicatum.**
> (35)
> As regards the fact that he was the first to vote for the law that dealt with the tax-farmers, on an occasion when a consul of supreme distinction accorded to that body through the medium of the popular assembly a privilege which he would have accorded them through the medium of the senate had he been permitted to do so, **if you say that his giving his vote is a chargeable offense, who was there among the tax-farmers who did not give his vote? If the offense lies in the fact that he was the first to vote, do you impute this fact to chance, or to the proposer of the law? If you impute it to chance, then you have nothing to charge *him* with; if to the consul, then you admit that our highest accounted Plancius to be the leading man of his order.**

This dilemma, like the entire passage, is devoted completely to ethical argumentation. The structure is that of "Either A OR B_1 or B_2". If it had been wrong for the elder Plancius to vote for the law, then what tax farmer did not do the same thing? The first choice is for Laterensis to admit that Plancius' action was not unique, and thus to see the obloquy he has heaped on the elder Plancius also spatter a powerful group who are well represented on the jury (A). If Laterensis does not wish to offend an important part of his audience, his other choice is either to admit that Plancius cast the first vote for the law by chance, and thus to trivialize his objection to Plancius' action (B_1), or to admit that Caesar, the consul, held Plancius in highest esteem (B_2). Laterensis would of course embrace B_2 immediately, and use it as proof of Plancius' sordid leanings. That is probably exactly what the prosecutor had done. In fact, Laterensis' course of action is represented as one alternative favorable to the elder Plancius -- this as the last choice in an elaborate dilemma structure. Thus, by virtue of the presentational value of the dilemma, as well as the framing of the

---

[26] "statuis," Clark's emendation of the senseless MSS readings "splendor" and "splendor Cn. Planci" surely gives the proper sense of the passage.

alternative ("si consulis, *statuis* etiam hunc a summo viro principem esse ordinis iudicatum" ["if to the consul, then you admit that our highest accounted Plancius to be the leading man of his order"]), Cicero can make a show of aggressive refutation at the end of this section, while offering his opponent a choice that the opponent would in fact happily take. But this choice is couched in terms of praise for Caesar that the opponent would reject. The dilemma here serves 1) presentationally, to finish a tendentious and defensive section of ethical proof with an argument that is based upon broader premises rather than upon specific ethical assumptions about the elder Plancius. Those premises are: All individuals bear equal responsibility for the unanimous action of a group to which they belong (A). A man is not blameworthy for being first of a group to take an action if he is thrust into that position by chance (B_1) or by a higher authority (B_2). In part because of the form itself, in part because this argument is not based upon specific ethical assumptions about Plancius, the dilemma helps to bestow upon the treatment of the defendant's father an impression of aggressive and decisive argument. 2) Within that aggressive argumentative structure, the form allows Cicero to impose a positive interpretation on an action which the opponent would use in an ethical attack, and to do so in a context that leaves no venue for dispute of that positive interpretation.

The following sections (36-55), in which Cicero deals with the actual charges,[27] include a conventional passage in which Laterensis' accusations are taken as attacks upon the established Roman custom of gaining and exercising *gratia*[28] (44-47a). It is in this context that the next dilemmas occur:

(44) Etenim quis te tum audiret illorum (sc. senatorum), aut quid diceres? **Sequestremne Plancium? Respuerent aures, nemo agnosceret, repudiarent. An gratiosum? Illi libenter audirent, nos non timide** confiteremur. Noli enim putare, Laterensis, legibus istis quas senatus de ambitu sanciri voluerit id esse actum ut suffragatio, ut observantia, ut gratia tolleretur.... (46) Ego Plancium, Laterensis, et ipsum gratiosum esse dico et habuisse in petitione multos cupidos sui gratiosos, **quos tu si sodalis vocas, officiosam amicitiam nomine inquinas criminoso; sin,**

---

[27] In fact, much of his argument (36-47a) is devoted to asserting that no plausible charge against Plancius falls under the *lex Licinia de sodaliciis*, and that Laterensis has used this law only because it allows him to stack the jury.

[28] Cf. *Mur.* 67-77, and *De Orat.* 2.105: "...de ambitu raro illud datur, ut possis liberalitatem atque benignitatem ab ambitu atque largitione seiungere." ["...on a charge of corrupt election practices, lavish generosity can seldom be distinguished from profuse bribery."]

quia gratiosi sint, accusandos putas, noli mirari te id quod tua dignitas postularit repudiandis gratiosorum amicitiis non esse adsecutum.

For then who of the those men (sc. senators) would listen to you, or what would you say? That Plancius was a bribery agent? Their ears would shun this. No one would acknowledge it. They would reject it. Or that he was popular? They would gladly hear this. We would admit it without hesitation. For you must not think, Laterensis, that the measures dealing with corrupt practices which the senate has submitted to the will of the people had for their object the abolition of electoral rivalry, interest, and popularity;...I tell you, Laterensis, that not only is Plancius himself popular, but that the host of ardent supporters who backed his candidature were also popular. **If you apply to these the name of "cronies," you are sullying disinterested friendship with a name that is a stain; but if you think that their popularity renders them amenable to prosecution, cease to wonder that by your refusal to cultivate the friendship of popular persons you should have failed to win that distinction which your merits demanded as their due.**

Each of these dilemmas in based, in both its parts, on the assumption of Plancius' innocence.[29] As usual, the use of the device seems to confer validity (however irrationally) on the assumption on which it is based. The dilemma in section 44 puts Laterensis in a hypothetical position, and limits his options in that position to either making a specific charge that he cannot prove or making a charge ("Or that he was popular?") that is really a virtual concession of Plancius' innocence. Further, this second charge that Cicero puts in Laterensis' mouth is one that sets the prosecutor at odds with Roman tradition. The dilemma in section 46 further allows Cicero to offer two completely ludicrous interpretations of Laterensis' behavior as though they were sensible hypotheses. If Laterensis calls influential men "sodales," associates in the sense of the *lex Licinia de sodaliciis*, he defames them. If, on the other hand, he thinks that men must be prosecuted simply because they are influential, then he is manifesting a hostility to the customs and common sense of the Roman people, and that hostility insured his defeat at the polls. As with the dilemma in section 44, both prongs are founded upon the assumption of Plancius' innocence, so it is obvious that Laterensis is following neither hypothetical course that Cicero presents. Still, as in section 44, the very use of the device reinforces that assumption of innocence. Equally important, both the

---

[29] The grounds for this assumption have come in Cicero's invitation to Laterensis to prove any impropriety under the *lex Licinia*, an invitation juxtaposed with yet another comment upon Laterensis' disregard of the spirit of the law in his selection of a jury who would not be acquainted with the facts (45: "Decuriatio tribulium - 46:"qui scirent iudicare").

choices offered to Laterensis set him at odds with the *gratiosi*, those who possess influence and popularity. And the support of the *gratiosi*, as Cicero has recently emphasized (45), is a traditional and vital part of political success. The dilemma thus moves forward a double argument. Not only is Plancius implicitly innocent, but Laterensis is the sort of person who could lose the election on his own; there is no need to postulate any wrongdoing at all.

The defense culminates in those brief sections (53b-55a) in which Cicero actually addresses Laterensis' charges. As the commentators point out, Cicero deflects, rather than refutes, the charge of *coitio*.[30] The fact that Laterensis has necessarily attacked both the alleged members of this *coitio*, Plancius and A. Plotius, but has only prosecuted Plancius, is also held up as inconsistent (54: "Sed tamen ... sis interrogatus").[31]

In the midst of these counterattacks comes the dilemma in section 54:

> nam quod questus es pluris te testis habere de Voltinia quam quot in ea tribu puncta tuleris, indicas aut eos testis te producere qui, quia nummos acciperent, te praeterierint, aut te ne gratuita quidem eorum suffragia tulisse.

> I say this, because by complaining that you have more witnesses from the Voltinian tribe than the number of votes you got in that tribe, you show, either that those whom you are producing as witnesses are men who were bribed to withhold their vote from you, or even that you made it worth their while to vote for you.

In other words, either Laterensis' witnesses accepted bribes to prefer another to him in the polls, in which case they are corrupt and thus not credible, OR they did not vote for Laterensis simply because he was not sufficiently popular. The second choice again reinforces the notion that Laterensis lost the election solely through his own fault.[32] The prongs of the dilemma attack the prosecution in two different spheres. The first

---

[30] See n.7 above on Laterensis' apparent *coitio*.

[31] 54: "Sed tamen tu A. Plotium, virum ornatissimum, in idem crimen vocando indicas eum te adripuisse a quo non sis interrogatus." ["Moreover, by involving the accomplished Aulus Plotius in the same charge with my client, you betray the fact that you have haled before the tribunal of justice the man who did not, like the other, intercede with you in his own behalf."] Cf. Taylor, p. 24, n.35. Note that in "in idem crimen vocando". *vocare in* is here used in the sense of "call into," so , roughly, "involve". cf. *OLD*, s.v. *voco*, 8a. It does not mean "summon into court" as do "vocare in ius" and "vocare in iudicium". Cf. *OLD*, s.v. *voco*, 4c.

[32] The implication that people who did not vote for Laterensis will not oblige him as witnesses, and that Cicero is thus implying that the witnesses will not do as Laterensis expects, may also be present, but is hardly necessary.

undermines the credibility of the witnesses, the second asserts directly that the very allegation of wrongdoing is groundless.

Here the dilemma is not used to round off a section of argument with the impression of indomitable reasoning. Rather it is simply part of a catalogue of refutations, introduced by the loose connective "nam quod." In form, it provides relief from the interrogatory method of Cicero's earlier treatment of the charge of *coitio*, and of the impending treatment of the alleged, but uncharged, *divisor*.

Cicero rounds off his treatment of the criminal charges with *loci* concerning witnesses (55b - 56 "debeatis") and rumors (57) in which his forbearance can resurface.[33] These *loci* form the bridge to the treatment of L. Cassius (58-71), in which the orator approaches more closely (esp. in sections 58-67) the comparison of the candidates that he had renounced in addressing Laterensis (5).

It is clear that Cassius' argument had followed two lines: Laterensis came from a more august family than did Plancius, and regularly these noble families are elected over those of more common origin. Further, any exceptions have regularly been those of common origin who distinguished themselves extraordinarily. But Plancius has accomplished nothing in any of the three principal fields where such distinction is gained: He is neither a remarkable soldier, nor an effective orator, nor a respected jurisconsult.[34] Laterensis, on the other hand, pairs illustrious birth with outstanding service in the provinces. Plancius therefore could have been preferred to Laterensis only through bribery.

Cicero had already conceded Laterensis' superior pedigree, and had managed to cast it as a potential political disadvantage (18). His answer to Cassius is fuller, and more devious. Having challenged the reliability of his opponent's examples, and having praised Cassius' speech as one worthy of reply, especially for its treatment of Cicero himself, the orator counterattacks on three fronts: 1) He argues, speciously, that more illustrious lineage does not facilitate election to public office (59-62); 2) He diminishes Laterensis' personal achievements (62-67, including the famous story of Cicero's return from his quaestorship); and 3) He defends

---

[33] esp. 56: "...et quod ita de me meriti sunt illi ipsi quos ego testis video paratos ut eorum reprehensionem vos vestrae prudentiae adsumere, meae modestiae remittere debeatis." ["...and also because the persons whom I see ready to give evidence have done such a good service to myself that the task of criticizing them is one which you must impose on your own good judgement, and permit me diffidently to forego."]
[34] Cf. *Mur*.21-30, esp. 24.

his earlier assertion of the magnitude of his debt to Plancius (68-90, 100-104, after section 70, again addressing Laterensis rather than Cassius).

By claiming initially that he must respond to the statements made about himself (58), Cicero asserts his license to speak of himself in every section of this argumentation. In fact, those words which Cicero has promised "pro me ipso" (3), and had justified through the dilemma form in section 4, will comprise most of the rest of the speech (68-99). Here the orator will respond to the argument that he is exaggerating his debt to Plancius, and that, even if he were not, Cicero's favor is not sufficient reason to acquit the defendant (4). After preliminaries, including a *locus* on gratitude (68), Cicero meets the charges that 1) Plancius did not do so much, and that 2) in any case, Cicero was not really in mortal danger. It is this latter assertion, also made by Laterensis, that will provide a focus for the orator's grand counterattacks. Already, he emphasizes at length the danger he has undergone at the hands of the seditious (71). Since Laterensis had claimed that this danger was insignificant, the topic of the propriety of Cicero's gratitude allows him to move smoothly from his treatment of Cassius back to the *accusator*. Here the orator plays with great effect the wronged friend exercising forbearance,[35] building to the "problem" that really is the basis of Cicero's strategy, the conflicting claims of Laterensis and Plancius:

> Sed ego haec meis ponderibus examinabo, non solum quid cuique debeam sed etiam quid cuiusque intersit, et quid a me cuiusque tempus poscat. Agitur studium tuum vel etiam, si vis, existimatio, laus aedilitatis; at Cn. Planci salus, patria, fortunae. **Salvum tu me esse cupisti; hic fecit etiam ut esse possem. Distineor tamen et divellor dolore et in causa dispari offendi te a me doleo; sed me dius fidius multo citius meam salutem pro te abiecero quam Cn. Planci salutem tradidero contentioni tuae.** (79)

> I shall, however, proceed to weigh in the scales of my own discretion not merely my obligation to each individual, but also the interests that each has at stake, and the demands which the emergency of each makes upon me. *Your* stake lies in the achievement of your ambitions, or, if you prefer to put it on higher ground, your reputation, and the credit you gain by becoming aedile; my client, on the other hand, stakes his citizenship, his country, his fortunes. *Your* wish was for my safety; *he* put into my hands the power of gaining that safety. **But I am torn by a painful dilemma, and in such a disparity of interests it goes to my heart to offer you an affront; but, upon my honour, I will far more readily**

---

[35] Esp. 72: "Respondebo tibi nunc, Laterensis, minus fortasse vehementer quam abs te sum provocatus, sed profecto nec considerate minus nec minus amice."["I now proceed to reply to you, Laterensis, using less vehemence, perhaps, that you prompt me to use, but in a spirit, I dare avow, of no less consideration and friendship."]

sacrifice my existence as a citizen in your behalf, than surrender that of Plancius to your claims. (79)

Like most dilemmas in which Cicero professes to find himself, this one leads him to take the action that he needs to take for the good of his case. At the same time, his virtuous anguish, followed by the second *locus* on gratitude (80-81), provides a clear model of dutiful behavior. Thus his admission of being caught in this dilemma is at the heart of his persuasive strategy.

Having consolidated his position of moral superiority, the orator deals piecemeal with several remarks of his opponent in a way that makes the *accusator* seem mean-spirited by comparison. Among these remarks was the statement of Laterensis that he had not wanted the trial to fall too near the *ludi Romani*, lest Cicero use references to the ceremonial cars carrying the procession of statues of the gods in order to gain pity for his client. Cicero answers smirk for smirk, ironically professing that Laterensis has placed him in a dilemma:

> Deridebor, si mentionem tensarum fecero, cum tu id praedixeris; sine tensis autem quid potero dicere? (83)

> Now that you have predicted my use of the sacred cars, I shall have but to breathe a word of them to arouse a smile; and if I cannot mention the sacred cars, how shall I be able to make a speech at all?

Here Cicero's claim to be caught in a dilemma engineered by Laterensis simply adds to the sarcasm.

In the next section (84), Cicero uses a dilemma differently to answer Laterensis' observation that while he had served honorably in Bithynia, Cicero had studied rhetoric on Rhodes.

> 'Rhodi enim,' inquit, 'ego non fui' -- me volt fuisse -- 'sed fui,' inquit -- putabam in Vaccaeis dicturum -- 'bis in Bithynia.' **Si locus habet reprehensionis ansam aliquam, nescio cur severiorem Nicaeam putes quam Rhodum; si spectanda causa est, et tu in Bithynia summa cum dignitate fuisti et ego Rhodi non minore.** (84)

> "For I," he says, "never went to Rhodes," implying that I did. "But," he adds, "I have been" -- I thought he was going to say "among the Vaccaei" -- "twice in Bithynia." **If localities give any handle for censure, I cannot understand why you should think that Nicaea is a place of stricter morals than Rhodes; if we are to consider our respective motives, the business that took me to Rhodes was just as highly respectable as the business that took you to Bithynia.**

Here the joke ("among the Vaccaei"[36]) does all the work. The dilemma itself presents Cicero at his mildest and most forbearing. The

---

[36] An Iberian people whose harsh and uncultivated manner of living would leave no opportunity either for sensual indulgence or for oratorical practice.

orator gives the impression of patiently talking good sense to a prosecutor whose own hostility has led him into silliness.

This piecemeal approach, carried through section 85,[37] shows Laterensis' spite, as opposed to Cicero's dutiful forbearance, and so prepares the way for the answer to an assertion of the prosecution that will prove very useful to the defense. Laterensis and Cassius had claimed that Cicero had shown a lack of courage by going into exile without offering resistance (86-90).[38] Cicero argues that his action was one of self-sacrifice for the good of all, that he had, implicitly, done an even greater deed than had the celebrated Q. Metellus Numidicus. For Cicero to have resisted would have meant terrible bloodshed with virtually no hope of success. The orator underscores this point, essential for his argument, by framing the situation in early 58 as a dilemma.

> Nihil dico amplius nisi illud: **victoriae nostrae gravis adversarios paratos, interitus nullos esse ultores videbam.** (88)
>
> I will say but one thing more on this matter: **I realized that, if we won, formidable adversaries would be set in array against us; but that, if we fell, there would be none to avenge us.**
>
> Hisce ego auxiliis salutis meae si idcirco defui quia nolui dimicare, fatebor id quod vis, non mihi auxilium, sed me auxilio defuisse; sin autem, quo maiora studia in me bonorum fuerunt, hoc eis magis consulendum et parcendum putavi, tu id in me reprehendis quod Q. Metello laudi datum est hodieque est et semper erit maximae gloriae? (89)
>
> If I say that my motive in refusing to avail myself of the help of those who were ready to strike for my safety was a reluctance to fight, I shall make the confession you desire, that it was not my helpers who failed me, but I my helpers. But if I say that the more earnest good patriots showed themselves in my cause, the more careful of their interests and sparing of their efforts I thought it my duty to be, can you impute blame to me for that which in the case of Quintus Metellus has been counted to his credit, and today is, and ever will be, the fairest jewel in his reputation?
>
> ...ego tantis periculis propositis cum, **si victus essem, interitus rei publicae, si vicissem, infinita dimicatio pararetur,** committerem ut idem perditor rei publicae nominarer qui servator fuissem? (89)
>
> ...and in face of such grave peril, **and the prospect of the downfall of the state should I fall, and an endless series of struggles should I**

---

[37] The disposition of the argument in section (85) is noteworthy. Laterensis had taken the opportunity to refer to Cicero's embarrassing dispatch to Pompeius about the suppression of the Catilinarian conspiracy. Cicero apparently cannot let this remark pass unanswered, and does not want to deal with it in the course of his later defense of his relationship with the triumvirs (91-94), so he incorporates it here.

[38] Cicero, in a more candid and self-indulgent mode, might once have agreed with Laterensis. Cf. *Att.* 3.15.7.

prevail, was I, who had once been the saviour of the republic, now to gain for myself the name of its destroyer?

I stress that none of these three dilemma structures is a true dilemma. The first and third narrate a past circumstance in which Cicero, by choosing one course of action, would have been placed in an inescapable dilemma. Thus Cicero justifies, even ennobles, the other course of action. The middle dilemma form simply amplifies the first, anchoring the narrative to the present argument by focussing upon Laterensis.

The mechanism of this narrative dilemma confronting Cicero in the past is very different from that of dilemmas with which he claims to be confronted in the present. Here Cicero was not forced to choose between the two undesirable alternatives, but made a choice that avoided the dilemma entirely. In the present, on the other hand, he regularly must endure one of the choices in the dilemmas that he claims confront him. (The self-professed dilemma in section 6 from which he escapes is the exception rather than the rule.) Still, self-professed dilemmas in the present and in the past have similar results. They justify an action that is open to criticism.

Only after Cicero has established that leaving Rome without a fight was an act of self-sacrifice for which all good citizens should be grateful does he attempt to answer the most damaging attack on his character, Laterensis' branding of him as a creature of the triumvirs (91-94). This defense is strengthened, extra-rationally, by its disposition between the story of Cicero's self-sacrifice and the tale of all that he suffered in his exile, when his very survival depended upon Plancius (95-100). This is the last, most elaborate answer to the charge that Cicero has exaggerated his debt to his client. It blends seamlessly into the tearful peroration, where Cicero finally makes explicit his insistence that Plancius and the jurors are all his supporters, and that Plancius' outstanding service to Cicero should merit his acquittal by Cicero's other supporters (101-104).[39]

The dominance of ethical argument focussed both by the prosecution and by the defense on one of the *patroni* is remarkable in this speech. Unlike *Pro Sulla*, in which the ethical arguments concerning Cicero at least related to his role as witness, the speech for Plancius is unabashedly viewed by both sides primarily as a contest concerned with the rhetoric of advocacy; one feels that Cicero's determination to make the *Planciana* a

---

[39] Esp. section 101 'Memini... simul audiebam'.

speech about himself merely uses a playing field marked out by the prosecution. On that field, the orator's every utterance must be calculated with an eye to his role as the benefactor of all, and to Plancius' role as that benefactor's savior. The orator turns to advantage the embarrassment of Laterensis' past kindnesses and support exactly by being embarrassed, by announcing a determination to do nothing to hurt one in whose debt he stands. This forbearance is in fact an extended bit of teaching by example; it shows the jury, all in Cicero's debt, that such debtors must be as accommodating as possible.

The true dilemmas in the speech contribute to individual lines of argument, while the other dilemma structures are vital for the general strategy. The dilemma in section 35, as we have noted, serves 1) presentationally, to finish a tendentious and defensive section of ethical proof with an argument that is based upon broader premises rather than specific ethical assumptions. The combination of the dilemma form and this use of broader premises allows the argument to give, and to confer upon the preceding ethical argument, the impression of being both aggressive and decisive.[40] 2) Within that aggressive argumentative structure, the form allows Cicero to impose a positive interpretation on an action which the opponent would use in an ethical attack, and to do so in a context that leaves no venue for dispute of that positive interpretation. We may also note that this is the only use of a dilemma form in the speech to punctuate the beginning or end of a line of argument.[41]

The dilemmas in sections 44 and 46 use the appearance of convincing reasoning, founded on the implicit premise that Plancius is completely innocent, to impute to the opponent two choices either of which offends the jury. The dilemma form here has a double function. Because of its exhaustive nature, it helps mask the fact that these choices do not really describe the opponent's range of actions or intentions.[42] Second, and equally important, the construction of a dilemma based upon an

---

[40] Cf. *Q. Rosc.* 25(i) (above, p. 80).
[41] The dilemma form in section 6a does come at the end of the *exordium*, but it does not serve to mark the transition to the *argumentatio*. That transition occurs without any clearly marked break.
[42] Cf. *Sul.* 10, 39 (above, pp. 92-93, 98); *Cael.* 35, 50, 52, 53a(*bis*) (pp. 111-112, 114).

implicit and unproven assumption appears, completely irrationally, to make that assumption seem more acceptable.[43]

In section 54, the dilemma actually has to do with the strength of the prosecution's case under the *lex Licinia*. Like seven of the dilemmas in the *Caeliana*, this one is concerned with discrediting witnesses. And like two of those in the *Caeliana*,[44] its prongs attack the prosecution in two different spheres. One prong impugns the credibility of the witnesses, the other asserts directly that the very allegation of wrongdoing is groundless. Also like a dilemma in the *Caeliana* (58, above p. 117) this use of the device is simply part of a catalogue of refutations. In form, it provides relief from the interrogatory method of the arguments that precede and follow it.[45]

The dilemma in section 84 is self-consciously instructional. The orator gives the impression that he is harnessing its demonstrative power to make the obvious explicit to a respected opponent whose emotions have made him a bit dense.

The other dilemma structures have a more strategic use. It is interesting that in this speech Cicero makes his most abundant use of the dilemma form directed at himself.[46] With the exception of the rather trivial sarcastic usage in section 83, these dilemmas in which he finds himself serve 1) to give him license to make himself such a central topic (4), 2) most important, to define his strategically essential embarrassment as one caught between the claims of two supporters (6, 79), and 3) referring to the situation in 58, to ennoble the flight into exile that placed everyone so firmly in his debt (*ter* in 88-89). The first and third of this cluster of three dilemma structures reflect a new usage in that they do not justify the speaker's accepting one of two unpalatable choices,[47] but justify his actions because they avoided a dilemma.

This wide variety of uses of the device contrasts vividly with the series of dilemmas in the speeches for Caelius and for Q. Roscius, where

---

[43] Cf. *S. Rosc.* 74-79, 93 (above, pp. 34-36, 37-38); *Div Caec.* 31, 33, 58 (pp. 59, 62-63); *Cael. passim.*

[44] *Cael.* 35, 50 (above, pp. 111-112).

[45] Cf. C.J. Classen, ""Ciceros Kunst der Überredung," in W. Ludwig ed., *Éloquence et Rhétorique chez Cicéron*, Entretiens sur l'Antiquité Classique 28 (Vandoeuvres-Genève: Fondation Hardt, 1982), 149-184. 168-170.

[46] Besides the seven examples of this form at *Planc.* 4, 6, 79, 83, 88, and 89 (*bis*), there are only seven other examples in the speeches, at *S. Rosc.* 124 (above, p. 39); *Div. Caec.* 4, 14 (above, pp. 53, 56); *Dom.* 91 (below, p. 197); *Sest.* 44 (below, p. 199); *Phil.* 2.32 (below pp. 157-158); 11.19(i) (below, p. 209).

[47] Cf. *Div. Caec.* 4 and 14 (above pp. 53-54, 56).

almost every dilemma is bent towards the larger persuasive end. It also contrasts with the usage of dilemma forms in the speech for Sulla, where there is no unitary undergirding of the dominant themes of the ethical argumentation either with dilemma or with other dilemma structures. In the speech for Plancius, the presentational uses of dilemma are unsurprising, the mechanical uses as diverse as the parts of the argument are disparate. On the other hand, the role of half of the dilemma structures in the speech, all directed toward the orator, is to facilitate a larger strategy of ethical argument focussed upon Cicero himself. In turn, it is this strategy that gives the *Planciana* both its unity and its power.

CHAPTER EIGHT: *THE SECOND PHILIPPIC*

Readers both ancient and modern have recognized Cicero's *second Philippic* as a masterpiece of invective.¹ Cicero's self-defense, and blasting of Antonius, use every resource of the mature orator. Among his

---

¹ For bibliography, see the edition of W.K. Lacey, *Cicero: Second Philippic* (Warminster: Aris & Phillips, 1986). Add George Kennedy, *The Art of Rhetoric in the Roman World* (Princeton: Princeton University Press, 1972), 270-272. Lacey's is the most sensitive commentary on style. See more generally W.R. Johnson, *Luxuriance and Economy: Cicero and the Alien Style* (Berkeley: University of California Press, 1971). For historical matters, see esp. J.D. Denniston's commentary, *M. Tulli Ciceronis in M. Antonium Orationes Philippicae Prima et Secunda* (Oxford: Clarendon Press, 1926). For text and translation, D.R. Shackleton Bailey, *Cicero, Philippics* (Chapel Hill and London: University of North Carolina Press, 1986) in conjunction with the apparatus of P. Fedeli's Teubner text (Leipzig: Teubner, 1982). Also see the Budé edition of A. Boulanger and P. Weilleumier, *Cicéron, Discours*, tome 19 (Paris: Société d'Edition "les belles lettres," 1972), and the Loeb of edition of W.C.A. Ker (New York: Putnam, 1926). For historical background, see the works in English cited by Bailey, p. xi, esp. R. Syme, *The Roman Revolution* (Oxford, Clarendon Press, 1939), 95-148; H. Frisch, *Cicero's Fight for the Republic: The Historical Background of Cicero's Philippics* (Copenhagen: Glydendal, 1946), 42-143. To Bailey's list, add E.G. Huzar, *Marc Antony, A Biography* (Minneapolis: University of Minnesota Press, 1978). Except for the essay by Stroh, the works mentioned above will hereafter be referenced by the authors' last names.

For the question of the relationship of this and Cicero's other *Philippics* to the speeches of Demosthenes, see M. Delaunois, "Statistiques des Idées dans le cadre du plan oratoire des *Philippiques* de Cicéron," *LEC* 34 (1966) 3-34; D.J. Taddeo, Jr., *Signs of Demosthenes in Cicero's Philippics*, (Stanford University diss., 1971); A. Weische, *Ciceros Nachahmung den Attischen Redner* (Heidelberg: Carl Winter, Universitätsverlag, 1972), 100-104, 166-194, esp. 193-194; W. Stroh, "Die Nachahmung des Demosthenes in Ciceros Philippiken," in W. Ludwig, ed., *Éloquence et Rhétorique chez Cicéron*, Fondation Hardt Entretiens, tome 28 (Vandoeuvres-Genève: Fondation Hardt, 1982), 1-31; C.W. Wooten, *Cicero's Philippics and their Demosthenic Model* (Chapel Hill and London: University of North Carolina Press, 1983).

weapons, Cicero uses dilemma forms no less than nine times in the speech (true dilemma at secs. 16, 54, 56, 84, 100, 110 (*bis*); other dilemma structures at secs. 32, 75). This use of the device is the more remarkable since dilemma forms occur only six times in all the other *orationes Philippicae*, and only once in Cicero's pure invective against Piso.[2] We must discover what Cicero's use of the device can teach us about the argumentative tactics of this oration, and about the orator's general range of effects employing dilemma.

The circumstances surrounding Cicero's fictive speech are too well known to require detailed rehearsal:[3] Antonius, Caesar's colleague in the consulship in 44, had consolidated his power after the Ides of March. Cicero had left Rome on 7 April (*Att.* 14.1.1), and only returned at the end of August, lured by mistaken information that the senate was asserting itself against Antonius' excesses (*Phil*.1. 7-9; *Att*.16.7.1). During the orator's absence, Antonius' early attempts to use civility and accommodation to help him become the unchallengeable head of the government had failed. Bold in his moves to consolidate power, and forced by Octavian's competition to play the partisan leader at the expense of a statesmanlike pose, Antonius could now depend only on intimidation to insure that the anti-Caesarians and even some of the Caesarians in the senate would not defy him. That defiance could reveal that he was no leader of the state, but merely an embattled head of a faction. When Antonius called a meeting of the senate for 1 September in order to vote divine honors for Caesar, Cicero sent the consul his apologies, pleading that he was still tired from his journey (*Phil*. 1.12). At the meeting of the senate, Antonius vented his anger upon the absent orator (*Phil*. 1.12). The next day, on 2 September, the senate again met, but this time Cicero attended while Antonius was absent. In reply to Antonius' attack of the previous day, the orator delivered the *first Philippic*. This speech, despite its relative restraint, had confirmed as a political reality the lack of senatorial consensus in support of Antonius.[4] And it had done more.

---

[2] *Phil*. 3.21; 5.5; 9.6; 11.5; 11.19 (*bis*); *Pis*. 39.
[3] Because of Cicero's copious correspondence (more than two hundred letters between the death of Caesar and August of 43), and because of the ancients' interest in Octavian's beginnings, this period is the best documented in ancient history. For a full narrative of events from the Ides of March through November of 44, see Frisch, 42-155; Syme, 95-148; Huzar, 81-103.
[4] Piso's speech on 1 August had already signaled this dissent. *Att*. 16.7.5; *Phil*. 1.10; *Fam*. 12.2.1.

Cicero had criticized the consul not only for fabricating, but for contravening plans of Caesar (*Phil.* 1.16-24). Thus the orator undermined as well Antonius' role as leader of the adherents of Caesar. Antonius then took seventeen days to polish a scathing reply, which he delivered in the senate on 19 September (*Phil.* 5.19; *Fam.* 12.2.1). Cicero, who was absent that day, composed the *second Philippic* as though it were his answer to Antonius on this occasion. Although Cicero had finished a draft of the speech by 25 October (*Att.* 15.13.1), and had received Atticus' criticisms by 5 November (*Att.* 16.11.1-3), he will only have published it after Antonius had turned north towards Mutina on 29 November.[5]

Given that the speech was never delivered, we may well question the possibility of reading it as a realistic representation of an attempt to persuade the senate in the specific circumstances of 19 September. There is a sense in which we simply cannot accept the speech as such a representation. If Cicero could have faced Antonius in the senate on that day, he would have attended the meeting. If that climate had obtained, the senate might have heard the oration with greater sympathy than hostility or fear. But that climate had not obtained. Thus Cicero's representation of what he would have said had he attended unrealistically presupposes several conditions: Cicero is courageous enough to launch an *ad hominem* attack on the consul, despite the surrounding guard of Antonius' Ituraeans. Those in the audience who are not rigorous adherents of Antonius have the courage to listen. And this collective show of fortitude demonstrates so forcefully that Antonius commands no consensus in the Senate that it renders impossible any of the consul's plans for violent retaliation.

This courageous display of speaker and hearers, and its restraining effect on the power and potential violence of Antonius, is of course an enormous fiction. Still, it is the only element of the speech that is not congruent with the circumstances of 19 September. Nowhere in the speech does Cicero explicitly borrow data, or direction, from later events. In that sense, the speech does depict an oral attempt to persuade a certain audience on a given date. To the extent that we can accept Cicero's fiction, it is then meaningful to speak of the rhetorical challenge.[6]

---

[5] See J.N. Settle, *The Publication of Cicero's Speeches* (University of North Carolina dissertation, 1962), 274-280.

[6] *Per contra*, R.G.M. Nisbet, "The Speeches" in T.A. Dorey, ed., *Cicero* (London: Routledge and Kegan Paul, 1965), 47-79, p. 75, "The second speech has been considered the best of the series (sc. Cicero's *Philippics*), both in ancient and in modern times. Yet it was never delivered, and even if we had not been told, we could

150   FORM AS ARGUMENT

The nature of the challenge is defined by Antonius' invective against Cicero in the senate on 19 September, as well as by the circumstances that brought about that attack. Antonius' speech on 19 September was necessarily an attempt to discredit Cicero with both pro- and anti-Caesarian constituencies, and incidentally to reassert his own role as leader both of the republic and of the adherents of Caesar.

From Cicero's speech, we can reconstruct the panoply of charges that Antonius had levelled. While it is true that the consul blames the consular for every political disaster of the last twenty years,[7] clear themes do emerge: Cicero acted illegally and ruthlessly in having the Catilinarian conspirators executed (11-19). Further, Cicero's poetic composition about his consulship was painfully bad (20). Cicero had planned the murder of Clodius (21-22). He had caused the civil war by alienating Pompeius from Caesar (23-24). The orator had then shown cowardice in his slowness to join Pompeius in Greece; through his timidity, he had become detestable to the leader of his cause (37-39). He had masked his fear with an annoying flippancy in the optimate camp (39-40a).[8]   Cicero was an ingrate. He had betrayed his friendship with Antonius despite the fact that Antonius had saved his life (3-10); the orator had further shown treachery to a benefactor by participating in the plot to assassinate Caesar (25-36). Cicero had again shown cowardice by his recent protracted absence from Rome, and by avoiding the senate on his return (76).[9] His behavior on 2

---

have guessed that it was not a speech at all but a pamphlet." Cf. Stroh, "Nachamung des Demosthenes," (above, n.1) 28.

But the fact that the *second Philippic* is a pamphlet need not debar us from appreciating the work as if it were the speech it pretends to be. I would extend to this pamphlet the conclusions for the judicial speeches advanced by W. Stroh, *Taxis und Taktik*, Stuttgart: Teubner, 1975, 51-54; any published Ciceronian speech is meant to be read as a representation of an oral act of persuasion unless there is compelling evidence to the contrary in the text itself.

At the same time, the *second Philippic* is really an anti-Antonian pamphlet, and may certainly be read as such; the two functions of representation of a persuasive process and of tract vilifying Antonius are not mutually exclusive. For our present purpose, we will simply find it more useful to concentrate upon the former aspect.

[7] Cf. E. Rawson, *Cicero: A Portrait*, rev. ed. (Ithaca: Cornell University Press, 1983), 271.

[8] The fact that Cicero does not treat these charges concerning Pompeius in chronological order, but groups them as a lesser attack at the end of his apologia may be evidence that they are especially telling.

[9] The separation of Cicero's response to the charge from the body of his apologia may result from that fact that he had already answered it in the *first Philippic* (4-10). Or it may result from the fact that that answer was not very strong, and it seems prudent to

September had shown his ingratitude further, and stood in stark contrast to the sentiments expressed in a letter (*Att.* 14.13B) that Antonius read to the audience (8b-10a). There was also a point of which we know nothing, the claim that the orator received no legacies (40b-42a). In any case, we may imagine Antonius' speech proceeding chronologically,[10] moving through the orator's actions since the outbreak of the civil war to a crescendo celebrating Cicero's ingratitude, betrayal and cowardice. A unifying element in that crescendo, the common flaw behind these faults, is the orator's vicious lack of constancy.

Antonius presented this condemnation so forcefully and so personally that no reconciliation was possible. Cicero's goal is thus to answer Antonius' attack in such a way that he galvanizes the opposition to the consul. So the *second Philippic*, like the speech it answers, is a personal invective with a political end.

In theory, Cicero's invective is a deliberative speech in that he is ostensibly attempting to persuade his opponent to reform and obviously attempting to persuade the senate to withdraw their support from Antonius. In fact, his invective will operate on different parts of the audience in different ways. The devout republicans will be affirmed in their hostility to Antonius. This affirmation is an important part of Cicero's task, but is not persuasion in the usual sense.[11] Another group, Antonius and those loyal to him, can only be incensed. The possibility of persuasion, and thus of the rhetorical challenge, inheres in only one part of the audience, those Caesarians already disillusioned with Antonius. These may be persuaded to act. There is after all a young contender for the Caesarian leadership. Still, in order completely to separate these Caesarians from Antonius, Cicero must do more than demonstrate that his opponent is a bad man. That demonstration, necessary for the anti-Caesarian faithful and for his own dignity, is only to be expected. In the course of his invective, the orator must further show that Antonius is a bad Caesarian. But Cicero is

---

treat Antonius' point as briefly as possible, and remove it from the context of the treatment of Cicero's failings.
[10] Similarly chronological is Cicero's treatment of Antonius in sections 43ff., as well as the orator's procedure in the *in Pisonem*. The chronological narrative conforms well with the directions offered in *Rhet. Her.* 3.13-15.
[11] Rather than being persuasive, such affirmation is epideictic in the sense that it increases the intensity of adherence to certain shared values. See Ch. Perelman and L. Olbrechts-Tyteca, *The New Rhetoric: A Treatise on Argumentation*, (tr. J. Wilkinson and P. Weaver) (Notre Dame and London: University of Notre Dame Press, 1969), 47-51.

of course avowedly anti-Caesarian, and must be true to that constituency even to the point of glorying in Caesar's assassination (25-36). Thus the orator is constrained explicitly to undermine his credibility with the very group of Caesarians whom he hopes to persuade. Here is the rhetorical challenge.

Cicero's double task, to affirm and persuade, calls forth all of the tools of invective,[12] and some important additions. The orator's structural and thematic debt to Demosthenes in this has been well explored.[13] Cicero will defend himself and attack Antonius by identifying his own actions with the good of the Roman state, and by systematically portraying Antonius as an underminer of Rome's safety and Rome's values. Besides the Demosthenic influence, we also note most of the usual *loci* of invective common in Greek practice, and seen earlier in the *in Pisonem*.[14] Further, Cicero's opponent possesses the standard, and Greek-derived, vices of the stereotypical tyrant.[15] We also find Antonius' drinking, and propensity for

---

[12] That the invective form is useful in speeches concerned with more than simple praise and blame was recognized in ancient theory as well as practice. Thus *Rhet. Her.* 3.15: "et si separatim haec causa minus saepe tractatur, at in iudicialibus et in deliberativis causis saepe magnae partes versantur laudis aut vituperationis." ["...and if epideictic is only seldom employed by itself independently, still in judicial and deliberative causes extensive sections are often devoted to praise or censure."] At *De Orat.* 2.43-50, Cicero had had Antonius' grandfather go so far as to maintain that praise and blame, while among the tactics of the orator, do not properly constitute a separate genus coequal with the deliberative and the judicial.

[13] Of the works cited in note 1 above, see esp. Delaunois, 9-12; Taddeo, 32-66; Weische, 193-194; Stroh, "Nachahmung des Demosthenes," 1-5, 27-29; Wooten, 53-57.

[14] W. Suess, *Ethos*, Leipzig, 1910 (reprint Aalen: Scientia Verlag, 1975), 247-267, extracts ten invective *topoi* from the Greek tradition, and shows how nine apply in *in Pisonem*. R.G.M. Nisbet adopts this treatment in his commentary on *in Pisonem* (Oxford: Clarendon Press, 1961, esp. appendix VI.). These are the corrlelations of these ten categories with the *second Philippic*. The first three, relating to family origins, are: 1) father a slave; 2) barbarian origin; 3) ancestor's menial occupation. None of these can effectively be leveled against Antonius, but note the remarks on members of his family at 18, 42 and 44, 3 and 90. Other topics are: 4) thievery, etc., cf. 41, 43, 50, 62, 93, 97, 103-104; 5) sexual misconduct, including homosexual prostitution, cf. 3, 6, 15, 20, 24, 44-46, 48, 50, 57, 59, 69, 99, 105; 6) hostility to family (*misophilia*), cf. 14, 56, 98-99; 7) sullen appearance, not attributed to Antonius; 8) dress, manner and appearance, cf. 57, 63, 76, 86, 111, 105-107; 9) cowardice in war, cf. 70b, 74b-75, 78b; 10) squandering of one's patrimony (more generally, prodigality), cf. 24, 35, 65-67.

[15] See J.R. Dunkle, "The Greek Tyrant and Roman Political Invective of the Late Republic," *TAPA* 98 (1967) 151-171, esp. 164; also, the same author's "The Rhetorical Tyrant in Roman Historiography: Sallust, Livy and Tacitus," *CW* 65.1 12-20. These standard vices are *vis* (violence), *superbia* (arrogance), *libido* (individual

vomiting in public, put to use in conjunction with the standard Ciceronian *loci* of penury, sacrilegious defiance of public religion and indecorous behavior in public office.[16] Finally, the speech also conforms with Hellenistic theory of praise and blame in its topics and in the chronological treatment of Antonius (cf. *Inv.* 2.177-178, *Rhet. Her.* 3.10-15). Although the Hellenistic *loci* of praise and blame are so broad as to be unavoidable, one could argue that Cicero does in fact follow the rhetorical prescription of constructing a speech that reveals in its object the opposites of the four cardinal virtues; we are certainly left with a strong sense of Antonius' foolishness, injustice, intemperance, and even, to a lesser extent, of his cowardice.

But congruences with the earlier practice and theory of invective do not properly emphasize a central principle of Cicero's strategy. That principle, seen in Demosthenes and borrowed more immediately from judicial oratory, is *antikategoria*, the turning back of the same charge upon one's accuser.[17] Again and again, Cicero accuses Antonius of attempting the very deed of which he is accused: the mustering of armed men in the City (19), the murder of Clodius (21 and 49), the start of the civil war itself (70b-72, cf. 23-24), even the assassination of Caesar (34b-36a and 74a).

This strategy of *antikategoria* informs a central theme of Cicero's entire attack, Antonius' inconsistency. As we have seen, the common element behind Antonius' crescendo of charges against the orator has been a vicious lack of constancy. The orator responds in kind, but with greater

---

capriciousness as opposed to the rule of law, and including acts of sexual aggression), *crudelitas* or *saevitia* (cruelty), and *avaritia* (greed).

[16] Lacey, 247, offers a helpful index including references to Antonius' drunkenness (30, 42, 62f., 67, 81, 84, 87, 104) and vomiting (63, 76, 84, 104). For general classifications and collections of the standard Ciceronian *loci* of invective, see J.B. Game, *An Introduction to the Philippics of Cicero and to the Study of his Invective*, (Yale University diss., 1909); I. Opelt, *Die lateinischen Schimpfwörter und werwandte sprachliche Erscheinungen: Eine Typologie* (Heidelberg: Carl Winter, 1965); N.W. Merrill, *Cicero and Early Roman Invective*, (U. of Cincinnati diss., 1975), 98-198.

[17] The device is not discussed in ancient rhetoric before Quintilian's mention of *antikategoria* at *Inst. Or.* 3.10.4. It occurs in *De Corona* 17-52, in which Demosthenes claims that Aeschines, not he, must bear the blame for the disgraceful Peace of Philocrates (cf. also 136). Cicero's fondness for the strategy in judicial contexts spans his career. It is central in speeches as diverse in time and subject as *pro Roscio Comoedo*, *pro Cluentio* and *pro Ligario*. In our speech, the orator makes much greater use of it than does Demosthenes in *De Corona*.

force. He will demonstrate that Antonius himself is not only inconstant, but so inconsistent in his behavior that he is self-contradictory.

Cicero sets the tone for the entire speech by focussing immediately on an area where intellectual coherence is an essential and highly visible qualification -- that of oratory itself. The orator raises the notion that Antonius has challenged him to an oratorical duel.[18] Although Cicero immediately dismisses the idea, he acts accordingly. As the acknowledged master of eloquence in the senate, Cicero thus defines a situation in which he is sure to win. In fact, he can treat his opponent as a hopeless student. Now effective speaking is a tribute to one's education and talent. Cicero's refutations of Antonius' attacks and criticisms of his behavior are filled with expressions of scorn and amazement at the quality of his opponent's reasoning. Thus the orator constantly impugns Antonius' intelligence, impaired alike by nature, wine and flashes of madness. Much of this can be attributed to the Hellenistic *locus* of the opponent's stupidity and to the Ciceronian *locus* of "*oratio inepta.*"[19] But there is more; Antonius is inconsistent on the most basic level of rational coherence.[20]

This portrait, well established in Cicero's critique of Antonius' speech (through 43), creates a focus of resonance. The orator's subsequent treatment of Antonius' own actions, before and after the Ides of March, need only stress his inconsistency to conjure up the picture of the incoherent Philistine intellectually hobbled by stupidity, wine, and frenzy. The devastating portrait evoked by charges of Antonius' inconsistent behavior is useful for the persuasive as well as epideictic purposes of the speech. Within Cicero's catalogue of Antonius' cupidity, cowardice, stupidity, avarice and arrogance are abundant examples of Antonius' actions that have been clearly at odds with Caesar's interests and wishes;[21] the leader of the Caesarian faction is in fact a bad Caesarian. Cicero can

---

[18] Section 2: an decertare mecum voluit contentione dicendi? hoc quidem est beneficium. quid enim plenius, quid uberius mihi quam et pro me et contra Antonium dicere? [Perhaps he wished to meet me in an oratorical duel. That is kind of him. Could I find any richer or more rewarding theme than in defending myself and attacking Antonius?]

[19] See Merrill, above n.16, 183-194.

[20] Esp. 18, 19, 31-32. Also 9, 10, 16, 25, 28, 29, 30, 42-43, 54, 65, 80-81, 97. Delaunois, above n.1, 10, finds only five examples of this theme. Unfortunately, he spares the reader the actual citations (p.7, n.12), so that it is impossible to ascertain where our disagreement lies.

[21] See 34b, 43, 71-74a, 74b-75, 80 and 88, 91, 94-95, 97, 98, 100, 103-104, 109, 110-111, and the comparison of Caesar with Antonius at 116-117.

THE SECOND PHILIPPIC 155

argue this central deliberative point before his pro-Caesarian hearers without defending Caesar's actions, a defense which would alienate his anti-Caesarian hearers. The orator can do so because his discussion of Antonius and Caesar is merely a part of his ostensible invective on the faults and vices that are revealed by Antonius' lack of self-consistency.

In the introduction, we noted that one traditional use of dilemma is to underscore the inconsistency of the target's thought or action.[22] Thus we might expect Cicero to have recourse to dilemma in this special circumstance, in which Antonius' extreme inconsistency is the common ground supporting the epideictic and deliberative functions of the speech.

In order to understand precisely the presentational and mechanical roles of dilemma in both the invective and persuasive functions of the speech, and to account in a detailed way for the high frequency of its use, it will be necessary to examine each occurrence in its context, but not to rehearse the work section by section.

The speech is divided into an *exordium* (1-10), a defense of Cicero (11-43), an attack on Antonius (44-114) and a *peroratio* exhorting Antonius to reform, and declaring that the orator does not fear him (115-119). Every part of the oration is permeated with the treatment of Antonius' faults of character and action.

The first dilemma, at section 16, comes in the midst of Cicero's defense of his consulship, and shortly before the orator's first elaboration of Antonius' incoherence in section 18. Antonius, Cicero tells us, had dared to charge that Cicero had had armed slaves on the *clivus Capitolinus* during the Catilinarian crisis. This charge, which will be the basis of an *antikategoria* (19), is easily denied. Cicero denies it in such a way that Antonius is labelled as either ignorant (thus implicitly stupid) or unbearable, for his remarks insult the free men who occupied the *clivus Capitolinus* that day.

> O miser, sive illa tibi nota non sunt -- nihil enim boni nosti -- sive sunt, qui apud talis viros tam impudenter loquare. (16)
>
> Miserable wretch, whether you don't know what happened (wholesome knowledge does not come your way) or whether you do! Such shameless talk before an audience!

---

[22] E.g., Aristotle, *Rhet.* 2.23.1400b5-8 (above, p. 11); Demosthenes 26.14; C. Gracchus, *ORF*[4], p.184, no. 32 (= Gellius, *NA* 11.13.1) (p. 24); Cicero, *Inv.* 1.45 (pp. 9-10);, *Rhet. Her.* 2.38 (pp. 14-15).

156   FORM AS ARGUMENT

The form "sive...sive" ["whether...or"], which states alternatives without really offering choices is rare,[23] and does not correspond with most of the examples in the rhetorical literature. This dilemma does not invest an argument with the appearance of invincible reasoning; it has no substantial presentational use. Rather it is a form peculiarly suited to the needs of invective. As Cicero frames it, Antonius' behavior is clearly offensive. The only open question concerns his awareness of his own offensiveness. Thus both choices concern the opponent's self-awareness, an arena that Cicero explores only to suggest that his target is stupid without precluding the alternative that he is instead insufferably brazen. This dilemma, purely concerned with ethos, is grounded in the arena of Antonius' self-awareness in such a way that either alternative makes him contemptible and pathetic. Only here and at section 54, a parallel usage, is the opponent simply "miser," a miserable wretch, whichever alternative applies.

The next dilemma form occurs in Cicero's treatment of the allegation that he had been part of the conspiracy to assassinate Caesar (25-36). The allegation itself, which Antonius will have used to demonstrate and amplify Cicero's ingratitude towards Caesar, was a rhetorical master stroke. If Cicero were to admit the charge, it would be unsafe for him, as it was for the conspirators, even to be in the City. If he were to deny his part in the murder, he would seem to distance himself from the men whom he had publicly supported, and so would demonstrate his own inconstancy again. Yet Cicero answers at the greatest possible length. He does so both because of the severity of the charge[24] and because of the advantages it can be made to offer for the principal themes of his own patriotism, of the tyranny which Caesar began and Antonius is trying to continue, and of the colossal stupidity revealed by his opponent's inconsistency.

Cicero must deny his part in the conspiracy since that truth is generally known, and since any claim to have been part of the conspiracy

---

[23] Cf. the "*eite...eite*" construction in Pseudo-Hermogenes, *Inv.* 4.6. for *sive...sive*, cf. 110(i) and *Tull.* 32 (below, p. 185); *Dom.* 22(ii) (p. 197); *Sest.* 32 (p. 199).
[24] Here the fiction of the speech sustains the greatest strain. The threat of the veterans is enough to keep the conspirators out of the capital, and is part of the threat that kept Cicero away from the senate on 19 September (*Fam.* 12.2.1). Only in the fiction of the speech, then, is that threat not severe. Still, Cicero's strong anti-Caesarian posture is perfectly in accord with what he would have said on 19 September, if we may judge from the remarks he had made about Caesar in the Senate in the *first Philippic* (esp. 32, 35).

would be dangerous. This does not stop the orator from adopting the brave pose of wishing that he could be included, and of considering the assassination a source of the highest glory (25-27, 29, 32b-34), even as he sarcastically refutes Antonius' evidence that he was involved (28). The very ingratitude of Trebonius and Cimber is explicitly made to redound to their glory (27). This posture, which allows no middle ground, shows Cicero already entrenched in the rhetoric of crisis.[25]

It is the essence of the rhetoric of crisis that it reflects a situation in which values are clearly defined and compromise is impossible. From this vantage point, every major figure in Roman politics has, since 17 March, been behaving inconsistently. On that day, Antonius and Lepidus agreed with the conspirators to accept the compromise that Cicero himself had advocated: Caesar would be held to have died of natural causes, so that the conspirators would not be treated as criminals. On the other hand, all of Caesar's *acta* would be enforced. By supporting this compromise, Cicero put himself in the ridiculous position of denouncing Caesar as a tyrant, yet insisting that the dead tyrant's wishes be honored. Antonius was in the equally nonsensical position of having to treat Caesar's murderers as fellow magistrates and respected members of the senate even as he pursued (and augmented) the wishes of their victim.

This inconsistency of Antonius, arising from the compromise of 17 March, gives the orator an easy target (30-32a). Cicero can demonstrate at length that Antonius has not treated the conspirators as criminals. But they are either criminals or liberators; there is no middle ground. Therefore, in Antonius' view, they are liberators. This rare bit of formal syllogistic argument with a disjunctive major premise serves to reinforce Cicero's claim that Antonius is an idiot incapable of coherent reasoning.[26]

---

[25] Wooten (above, n.1), 168-175.
[26] Sections 31-32: atqui haec acta per te. non igitur homicidas. sequitur ut liberatores tuo iudicio, quando quidem tertium nihil potest esse. quid est? num conturbo te? non enim fortasse satis quae diiunctius dicuntur intellegis. [And yet all this was done by you. Therefore you do not take them for murderers. It follows that in your judgment they are liberators, since there is no third possibility. Ah, I fear I am confusing you. Perhaps you don't quite understand a logical dilemma.] Note that, despite Bailey's turning of "diiunctius dicuntur," this passage is itself not a dilemma; Antonius is not given two mutually exclusive choices, either of which hurts him. But it is still a demonstration that Antonius has taken a position that is logically inconsistent with his behavior.

In this context, Cicero invokes his most sarcastic use of the dilemma form:[27]

> Itaque iam retexo orationem meam, scribam ad illos ut, si qui forte, quod a te mihi obiectum est, quaerent sitne verum, ne cui negent. **etenim vereor ne aut celatum me illis ipsis non honestum aut invitatum refugisse mihi sit turpissimum.** (32)
>
> So I now take back what I just said. I shall write to them and tell them, if anyone should inquire whether your charge against me is true, not to deny it. **Frankly I am afraid that they may be criticized themselves for keeping me in the dark, or else that the refusal of an invitation to join may be highly discreditable to me.**

There is more here than the heavy sarcasm that underscores Antonius' inadequacy as a speaker. The very charge that Antonius has advanced is one that Cicero wishes that he could admit, lest his friends the conspirators be criticized for excluding him, or he himself be criticized for refusing to be included in the glory of the deed with which Antonius charges him. This compromise embodied in the dilemma form effectively expresses Cicero's membership in the group who support the liberators without actually claiming for him the position of liberator. He thus neatly escapes the trap that Antonius has laid for him.

Having gone on to tease Antonius with the *antikategoria* that he also had tried to kill Caesar (34b-36a), Cicero hurls at his opponent yet another of the charges that Antonius had leveled at him (51-55a, cf. 23-24), that of starting the civil war. The orator rehearses the ground in sections 51-53: The motion to order Caesar to lay down his arms, the tribune Antonius' veto, the judgment of the senate against him, his flight, Caesar's use of the episode to justify his cause. There follows a section of *amplificatio* introduced by a vigorous invective dilemma:

> O miserum te, si haec intellegis, miseriorem, si non intellegis hoc litteris mandari, hoc memoriae prodi, huius rei ne posteritatem quidem omnium saeculorum umquam immemorem fore, <propter unum te> consules ex Italia expulsos, cumque eis Cn. Pompeium, quod imperi populi Romani decus ac lumen fuit, omnis consularis qui per valetudinem exsequi cladem illam fugamque potuissent, praetores, praetorios, tribunos plebis, magnam partem senatus, omnem subolem iuventutis, uno[que] verbo rem publicam expulsam atque exterminatam suis sedibus! (54)
>
> What a miserable creature you are if you realize this! More miserable still, if you do not realize what is being recorded by historians, handed down to memory so that in all ages to come it will never pass out of men's minds: namely, that on your sole account the consuls were driven from Italy, and with them Gnaeus Pompeius, the pride and ornament of the Roman empire, as well as all consulars whose health allowed them to

---

[27] Cf. *Planc.* 83, above, p. 140.

follow that disastrous exodus, the praetors, the praetorians, the tribunes of the plebs, a large part of the Senate, all our rising youth -- that in a word the Commonwealth was driven out, banished from its home.

This dilemma, like that in section 16, has no presentational value as apparent invincible argument. Rather it is noteworthy because the two choices offered the opponent both regard his self-awareness, and both make him pathetic. Antonius is either wretched because he knows that his actions will brand him forever, or even more wretched because he is too stupid to realize that this is so. Both prongs assume that his behavior has caused the civil war, so both assume what Cicero is trying to prove. Again, this use of a dilemma to concentrate on aspects of the opponent's psychological state (viz., he is either crushed with guilt or extremely obtuse) is an adaptation to the needs of invective. Dilemma allows Cicero to stress the themes of Antonius' depravity and stupidity in a form that emphasizes his own rhetorical skill, and so further underscores Antonius' inadequacy.

Very different, and more conventional, is the dilemma in Cicero's next attack (55b-56). During the year of Antonius' tribunate, he "restored" many, but neglected to restore his own uncle, C. Antonius Hybrida.

> restituebat multos calamitosos: in eis patrui nulla mentio. **si severus, cur non in omnis? si misericors, cur non in suos?** (56)
>
> He brought many banished men back home, but among them there was no mention of his uncle. If he is severe, why not to all? **If compassionate, why not to his own kith and kin?**

Yet Antonius had restored a certain Licinius Lenticula who had been convicted of gambling. Cicero makes clear that the restoration of any such individuals is an evil, and that the omission of Antonius Hybrida is a crime within a crime (55b).

We are hindered from understanding fully Cicero's tactics by our ignorance of Licinius Lenticula and of the nature of Antonius' aid to him. Still, it is clear that he was "de alea condemnatum," convicted for gambling.[28] Antonius Hybrida, on the other hand, was actually in exile, convicted in 59 before the *quaestio de repetundis*, the standing court for cases of provincial misgovernment, despite the best efforts of Cicero, with whom he had shared the consulship in 63. Now, those restored from exile in 49 were only men who had been sentenced under the *lex Pompeia de ambitu* of 52.[29] "si misericors, cur non in suos?" ["If compassionate, why not to his own kith and kin?"], is thus based on the false assumption that

---

[28] See Denniston *ad loc.*
[29] See Denniston *ad loc.*; Lacey *ad loc.*

Antonius had the power to restore his uncle at this time. Cicero simply ignores the fundamental distinction between the two cases. And this makes for a useful ligature. The orator's purpose in section 56 is to label Antonius a gambler who has subverted the laws for a disreputable fellow gambler, a relatively trivial charge in the wake of his argument that Antonius had started the civil war "ut Helena Troianis." By leveling the distinction and using the dilemma, Cicero introduces the charge as part of the amplification upon the "scelus in scelere" that Antonius has disregarded members of his own family. Thus the transition from enormity to relative triviality is much less abrupt, and much more damning.

But Cicero has most of the civil war left to treat. The orator admits that this is slippery ground, and pointedly avoids fighting again the battle of Pharsalia explicitly to avoid offending Caesar's veterans (59). Further, he even tries to distinguish between the motives of Caesar's veterans and the motives of Antonius ("illi secuti sunt, tu quaesisti ducem." ["they followed their general, you sought him out"]). Steering well clear of the problem of the veterans, the orator concentrates more upon Antonius' domestic and civic behavior than upon his military successes (61-70a). He uses the fact that Antonius had acquired Pompeius' property, and had then been unable to pay for it, as a device for contrasting Antonius with Pompeius. (The contrast of Caesar with Pompeius is not directly explored.) More important, the orator stresses Antonius' differences with Caesar. Not only his relative blood lust (71), but Antonius' inability to pay for Pompeius' estate, and his resultant fall from grace with Caesar, is treated in loving detail (71-74a). This theme, adumbrated in the charge that Antonius had tried to kill Caesar (34b-36a), is the key to the purely persuasive component of the speech. It will be emphasized repeatedly in what follows.

Dilemma will play a substantial role in creating this emphasis. As part of this stress upon the differences between the characters of Antonius and Caesar, and their resultant disagreements, Cicero finds fault with Antonius' failure to fight by Caesar's side in Africa or Spain. Dolabella, after all, had fought in both campaigns. The orator emphasizes his criticism with a dilemma form:

> aut non suscipienda fuit ista causa, Antoni, aut, cum suscepisses, defendenda usque ad extremum. (75)

> You should either not have enlisted under that banner, Antonius, or having done so you should have fought for it to the end.

The dilemma form obviously is a tool to drive a wedge between Antonius and every good Caesarian, for whom Dolabella here stands.[30] Thus Cicero avails himself of two different (but not conflicting) ethical standards. Caesar's side was in the wrong, but disloyalty to a bad cause is still disloyalty, and grounds for censure.[31] Thus Dolabella can be praised for his *constantia* at least. The Caesarians in the senate who have grown disenchanted with Antonius must hate Cicero's support of the liberators. Still, even among enemies, there is a community of values. Antonius' cowardice excludes him from this community and unifies the orator with the Caesarians in their moral superiority over Antonius. Further, Antonius' lack of consistency in this area does form a resonance with his self-contradictory behavior elsewhere, even though Cicero makes clear that his opponent's inconsistent behavior is motivated simply by cowardice, not by rational incoherence born of stupidity, wine or madness.

The dilemma that accomplishes this is another rare form well designed for invective. With alternate past contrary to fact apodoses it condemns the ethical decisions Antonius has already made. Since these are criticisms of past failings of character, there is no real choice.

Cicero's next discussion of the variances between Antonius and Caesar is his protracted treatment of the question of Dolabella's consulship (79-84a). The facts seem to be these: Caesar had decided that Dolabella and Antonius should be consuls for 44. Then, perhaps at Antonius' instigation, he decided that he would hold himself the consulship he had offered to Dolabella. In compensation, Caesar wished Dolabella to become suffect consul in his place when he left for the Parthian campaign. Dolabella, his pride wounded, lambasted Antonius in the senate on 1 January of 44. Antonius replied that, as an augur, he was sure that he would find evil omens that would preclude Dolabella's election. Accordingly, the election was held, presided over by Caesar. Only after the voting was finished did Antonius pronounce the election invalid because he had noticed an evil omen. He was obviously lying, but his pronouncement was still obeyed.[32] Caesar will have been furious. But

---

[30] This contrast, as well as a wicked sense of *ironia*, caused Cicero to praise Dolabella so highly that Atticus had to suggest restraint (*Att.* 16.11.2). See also Lacey *ad loc.*
[31] Another bit of *antikategoria*: Lacey notes that this criticism of Antonius anticipates Antonius' claim that Cicero was inconsistent. It also looks forward to Cicero's description of the quarrel over Dolabella's consulship for 44 (79-84a).
[32] That the election was held invalid is clear from section 88, where we also learn that this issue was on the agenda for the meeting of the senate on the Ides of March.

Antonius was flexible; after Caesar's assassination, he treated Dolabella as a properly elected consul, despite the problem which his augural pronouncement had raised.[33] This passage thus underscores Antonius' hostility to Dolabella and differences with Caesar. At the same time, it celebrates his stupidity, mendacity and impiety. Antonius is virtually the anti-augur.

> The entire section is punctuated with a synthetic dilemma:
> sed adrogantiam hominis insolentiamque cognoscite. quam diu tu voles, vitiosus consul Dolabella; rursus, cum voles, salvis auspiciis creatus. **si nihil est cum augur eis verbis nuntiat quibus tu nuntiasti, confitere te, cum "alio die" dixeris, sobrium non fuisse; sin est aliqua vis in istis verbis, ea quae sit augur a collega requiro.** (84)
>
> But look at the arrogance, the insolence of him! So long as *you* wish, Dolabella's consulship is flawed; the moment your wishes change, the auspices were in order. **If it means nothing when an augur makes an announcement in the terms in which you made yours, admit that when you said "Meeting adjourned" you were not sober. On the other hand, if those terms have any force, as one augur to another I ask you to tell me what it is.**

Now, in September, it is clear that Antonius' pronouncement that the meeting was adjourned is being ignored by all, and that Dolabella is functioning as consul (although Cicero says in section 87 that the augural college will have to consider this matter). There is then no force to Antonius' words, and the second alternative, supposing that there is such a force, is a dummy constructed in order to create a dilemma form.

Obviously the dilemma does not directly emphasize the differences between Antonius and Caesar. Rather it provides a memorable emphasis at the end of a lengthy discussion of circumstances arising from the disagreement of Antonius and Caesar. Further, concurrently with this deliberatively effective emphasis, the device adds the useful invective theme of Antonius drunkenness, the resonant theme of Antonius as sacrilegious, and the closely related theme of his stupidity. Cicero has after all argued that Antonius falsified the auspices, but that he did not do so in the easier and more effective way open to him (81 through "postulanda prudentia"). The orator contrives this use of the dilemma both to play on these themes and, of course, to underscore again Antonius' inconsistency in a context in which he is known to have disagreed with Caesar.

---

[33] See T. R. S. Broughton, *Magistrates of the Roman Republic. American Philological Association Monographs*. revised ed. 3 vols. (Chico, CA: Scholars Press, 1984-1986), vol. 2, p. 319 for a full collection of the sources.

Cicero, having emphasized again in his chronological treatment both Antonius' vicious character and his forgery of *acta Caesaris* that in fact disregarded Caesar's wishes (esp. 92-97), then raises the issue of the senatorial commission to hold inquiry about Caesar's *acta* (100). Carefully noting that the senate had agreed to Caesar's *acta* only for the sake of peace, the orator points out that the senate's good will does not extend to Antonius' forgeries.

> Sed ad chirographa redeamus. quae tua fuit cognitio? acta enim Caesaris pacis causa confirmata sunt a senatu: quae quidem Caesar egisset, non ea quae egisse Caesarem dixisset Antonius. unde ista erumpunt, quo auctore proferuntur? **si sunt falsa, cur probantur? si vera, cur veneunt?** (100)
>
> But to get back to the holographs: what inquiry did you make? Caesar's acts were confirmed by the Senate for the sake of peace -- that is, what Caesar did, not what Antonius might say Caesar had done. Where do these holographs spring from, on whose authority are they produced? **If they are forgeries, why are they approved? If genuine, why are they for sale.**

The effect is of course to underscore the inconsistency of Antonius' action, both as a public official and as a Caesarian. He has been true to neither trust, and so Cicero adds to the cumulative effect of both his invective and deliberative arguments.

Cicero then implies (falsely)[34] that the commission to investigate the *acta* never met. This leads to the Kalends of June, Antonius' arms, and a bridge to the discussion of Antonius' visit to Campania in April and May (100b-107). Cicero's description of Antonius' actions after his return to Rome in May is calculated to drive deeper the wedge between Caesarians and Antonius (108-110a). He had disregarded Caesar's laws, and even his will (109).

The last dilemmas in the speech occur in section 110, in Cicero's further demonstration of Antonius' violation of Caesar's wishes. Again, Cicero uses the curious strategy of attacking Antonius both for supporting Caesar and for failing to support him consistently. He holds up as an embarrassment the fact that Antonius has been appointed as *flamen divo Iulio*, a special priest of the deified Caesar. Further, the fact that Antonius has not entered on this office is taken as his acknowledgement that he should be embarrassed. Cicero even offers to preside at the inauguration. The entire double edged attack ends with an exclamatory dilemma in uncommon form:

---

[34] See Denniston *ad loc.*

et tu in Caesaris memoria diligens, tu illum amas mortuum? Quem is honorem maiorem consecutus erat quam ut haberet pulvinar, simulacrum, fastigium, flaminem? est ergo flamen, ut Iovi, ut Marti, ut Quirino, sic divo Iulio M. Antonius. quid igitur cessas? cur non inauguraris? sume diem, vide qui te inauguret: collegae sumus: nemo negabit. **o detestabilem hominem, sive quod tyranni sacerdos es sive quod mortui!** (110)

And are you concerned for Caesar's memory, do you love him in his grave?
    What greater honor had Caesar attained than to have a sacred couch, an image, a gable, a special priest? Just as Jupiter and Quirinus have their priests, so the divine Julius has Marcus Antonius. Why delay then? Why are you not inaugurated? Choose a date, chooses someone to inaugurate you. We are your colleagues, nobody will refuse. **Detestable man--whether because you are the priest of a tyrant or because you are the priest of a dead man!**[35]

    The dilemma itself does not crystallize the inconsistency of Antonius' behavior. Still it does serve both to criticize Caesar and to emphasize Antonius' role as *flamen divi Iulii*, and his hesitancy to assert it. That hesitancy, which makes the attack possible, is obviously inconsistent with Antonius' alleged devotion to Caesar. The syntax is like that of the form in section 16, the general mechanism like that of the dilemma in section 54. Here the two alternatives need not even be mutually exclusive.

    The final dilemma in the speech, at the end of section 110, further attacks Antonius both for his support of Caesar and for his inconsistency in that support. Antonius had added a day to public *supplicationes*, or thanksgivings to the gods, to pray to Caesar. The fictive day of Cicero's speech would fall on the day after the *ludi Romani*, at which there had been a *lectisternium*, a banquet for the gods, with attendant *supplicatio*. Yet Antonius has not extended the *ludi Romani* an extra day to honor Caesar.

quaero deinceps num hodiernus dies qui sit ignores, nescis heri quartum in circo diem ludorum Romanorum fuisse, te autem ipsum ad populum tulisse ut quintus praeterea dies Caesari tribueretur? cur non sumus praetextati? cur honorem Caesaris tua lege datum deseri patimur? an supplicationes addendo diem contaminari passus es, pulvinaria contaminari noluisti? **aut undique religionem tolle aut usque quaeque conserva.** quaeris placeatne mihi pulvinar esse, fastigium, flaminem, mihi vero nihil istorum placet: sed tu, qui acta Caesaris defendis, quid potes dicere cur alia defendas, alia non cures? nisi forte vis fateri tu omnia quaestu tuo, non illius dignitate metiri. (110-111)

Next let me ask whether you are unaware what day it is. Don't you know that yesterday was the fourth day of the Roman games in the circus. And don't you know that you yourself put a law through the assembly of the

---

[35] My translation of last sentence only.

people providing that a fifth day be added for Caesar? Why are we not in our holiday clothes? Why do we let the honor granted Caesar by your law be omitted? Perhaps you allowed Thanksgivings to be polluted by adding a day, but did not want the same to happen to the sacred couches? **Either abolish religion altogether or preserve it at every point.** You ask whether I approve of the sacred couch, the gable, the special priest. Certainly not, none of it has my approval. But you are the defender of Caesar's acts; how can you reconcile defense of some with indifference to others? Unless you choose to admit that you measure everything by your own profit, not Caesar's honor.

Here again we see the tactic that the anti-Caesarian Cicero uses to attack Antonius as a bad Caesarian. The orator makes abundantly clear in section 111 that he does not approve of the addition of this day for Caesar. Nonetheless, he can attack Antonius' failure to observe it. Again consistency is the issue, and Antonius fails to measure up.

The strategy that these last five dilemmas support, that of damning Antonius as a bad Caesarian without approving of Caesar, will be emphasized again in the peroration.[36] And it should be. For in the midst of Cicero's most sustained invective, this is the argument at the heart of his deliberative speech.

As we have seen, the *second Philippic* shows a wide variety of dilemma forms, and a variety of uses that range from the familiar to rare functions well suited to the unique circumstances of this speech. Since the speech is an invective with a deliberative goal, and not simply a deliberative speech, it is unsurprising that all of the dilemmas are concerned to censure Antonius' character on the basis of past actions rather

---

[36] 116-117: fuit in illo ingenium, ratio, memoria, litterae, cura, cogitatio, diligentia; res bello gesserat, quamvis rei publicae calamitosas, at tamen magnas; multos annos regnare meditatus, magno labore, magnis periculis quod cogitarat effecerat; muneribus, monumentis, congiariis, epulis multitudinem imperitam delenierat; suos praemiis, adversarios clementiae specie devinxerat. quid multa? attulerat iam liberae civitati partim metu partim patientia consuetudinem serviendi. cum illo ego te dominandi cupiditate conferre possum, ceteris vero rebus nullo modo comparandus es. [Caesar had intellect, calculation, memory, culture, concentration, reflection, industry. His military achievements, even though disastrous to the Commonwealth, had been great. Aiming at monarchy for many years, he worked hard and ran great risks; and so he had accomplished his dream. He had cajoled the ignorant populace with shows and buildings and largesses and feasts. He had bound his own followers by rewards, his adversaries by a show of clemency. In short, he had succeeded in habituating a free community to servitude, partly through its fears, partly through its long-suffering. In your lust for despotic power I can compare you with him, but in all other respects there is no comparison.]

Finally, Cicero's determination to make a strong contrast leads him into generosity towards Caesar, but no devout republican will mistake that generosity for approval.

than to clarify future choices; all of the arguments are fundamentally ethical.

The uses of dilemma at sections 56, 100 and 110(*bis*), based on actions of Antonius, underscore the inconsistency of his behavior. In doing so, they reflect a conventional use of the form.[37] Presentationally, they resonate with the contrast that Cicero has drawn between himself and Antonius as speakers.

Conventional also is the occurrence of the device in section 84. The dilemma is synthetic, the result of forcing the material into the dilemma mold. Aside from the resonance that it contributes to the topic of comparative skill in speaking, the form has a double function. It provides a platform for innuendos of Antonius' stupidity, sacrilegious behavior, and drunkenness, and it marks the end of the treatment of a topic,[38] in this case the discussion of Antonius' abuse of augural power.

The dilemma form directed at Cicero (32) initially seems familiar, a simple bit of sarcasm (cf. *Planc.* 83, above p. 140). Nevertheless, it helps the orator forcefully to claim the only position that allows escape from Antonius' trap. In essence, it gives Cicero a license to praise the tyrannicides while denying the potentially dangerous assertion that he was directly involved in Caesar's death. In the broadest sense, it is then also akin to the other dilemmas that give Cicero a license to act in a manner which the audience might find offensive.[39] We have not seen before this blending of the two functions of Cicero's profession that he is in a dilemma.

Likewise new, despite its conventional mechanism, is the compositional function of the dilemma in section 56. While we have seen that dilemma can be used to punctuate arguments, especially by marking the breaks where they begin or end, the dilemma in section 56 has exactly the opposite effect. It helps to create a seamless transition that imposes continuity between topics of jarringly disparate importance.

More striking still is the occurrence of two "sive...sive" ["whether...or"] types (16, 110(i)), almost as many as in all the other

---

[37] E.g., Aristotle, *Rhet.* 2.23.1400b5-8 (above, pp. 11-12); Demosthenes 26.14 (p. xx); C. Gracchus, *ORF*[4], p.184, no. 32 (= Gellius, *NA* 11.13.1) (p. 24); Cicero, *Inv.* 1.45 (pp. 9-10);, *Rhet. Her.* 2.38 (pp. 14-15).
[38] Cf. *Q. Rosc.*, 9, 25(i) (above, pp. 75, 80); *Sul.* 10 (pp. 92-93); *Cael.* 50 (p. 112); *Planc.* 35 (p. 134).
[39] Cf. *S. Rosc.* 124 (above p. 39); *Div. Caec.* 4, 14 (pp. 53, 55-56); *Planc.* 4, 6, 79, 88-89(*ter*) (pp. 129-131, 139-140, 141-142).

orations together. This form, while considered a true dilemma by pseudo-Hermogenes (*Inv.* 4.6, above pp. 19-20), here has no discernible presentational value as invincible argument. Nevertheless, it is especially well suited for invective, since it can allow a damning apodosis to stand, e.g. that the opponent is "miser" or "detestabilis," irrespective of the innuendo-laden protasis one may choose, whether Antonius is obtuse or brazen, whether he is the priest of a tyrant or of a dead man. The best parallel is *pro Sestio* 32, where Piso is cruel in either case.[40] Compare also the use of this form to amplify another dilemma, directed against Clodius, at *De Domo Sua* 22.[41] In section 54 of our speech, the alternate apodoses, that Antonius is *miser* or *miserior*, depending upon his ignorance or indifference to the bad repute he has earned, uses the more familiar syntax[42] to argue in the same way.

The dilemma form in section 75 is also tailor-made for invective. It is unique in that it poses alternate past contrary-to-fact apodoses in the ethical sphere. While the protases allow no real choice, this form differs from narrative dilemma in that each alternative stands as a present censure. This unparalleled usage embodies Cicero's strategy of criticizing Caesar, yet criticizing Antonius for his inconsistent behavior as a Caesarian. Here then is the complete adaptation of the argument form to the particular requirements of a unique rhetorical challenge.

Why is dilemma so frequent in this speech? There is no unitary answer. Rather each occurrence is best understood in terms of the specific line of argument which contains it. Still we may draw these generalizations: Every use of the device asserts or amplifies at least one of the invective *loci* of the opponent's stupidity, drunkenness, familial disloyalty, thievery, cowardice, and impiety. Dilemma can be simply a vehicle for these themes (esp. 84), and some of the forms (16,54,75,110(i)) seem especially suited to invective. At the same time, the simple goal of vilifying an opponent, of affirming an audience in its hostility and contempt, does not require repeated use of dilemma. The fact that there is only one example of the device in the *In Pisonem* demonstrates that.[43] But our speech differs from the invective against Piso in at least two important

---

[40] Quoted in appendix I below, p. 199.
[41] Quoted in appendix I below, p. 197.
[42] Cf. *Har. Resp.* 5, quoted in appendix I below, p. 199, against an adherent of Clodius who is either a complete wretch or stupid.
[43] *Pis.* 39, quoted in appendix I below, p. 203.

ways. First, Cicero makes skill in speaking a substantial theme. We have already seen in the *Divinatio in Caecilium* how this fact can promote the presentational use of such an easily recognizable and ostentatious device of the trained speaker. Second, this speech is more than an invective; Cicero hopes not only to vilify his target, but to persuade a portion of the audience to act. He wants to move Caesarians to abandon Antonius. As we have seen, five of the dilemma forms either specifically underscore Antonius' inconsistency in his divergence from Caesar's plans (75, 100, 110(ii)) or emphasize other arguments that do so (84, 110(i)). This inconsistent behavior is the key theme that allows the orator to criticize Antonius as a bad Caesarian without approving of Caesar. The orator prepares for his exposition of Antonius' inconstancy towards Caesar by constructing a portrait of Antonius as unprincipled, indeed as incapable even of coherent thinking. Once this portrait is established, dilemma has value as a device that underscores an opponent's inconsistencies (esp. 56, 110(ii); cf. 75). Further, its use creates resonances that reinforce this portrait of Antonius as incoherent (56, 75, 84, 100, 110(*bis*)). These resonances both strengthen the general invective attack upon Antonius and draw strength from that depiction to underscore Antonius' lack of fidelity to Caesar and his plans.[44] This strategy, arising from the circumstances of 19 September, from the fact of Antonius' own attack upon Cicero's viciously inconsistent behavior, and from the orator's predilection for *antikategoria*, give dilemma a special utility in the *second Philippic*.

---

[44] By the time that Cicero delivered the *third Philippic* on 20 December, the split between Antonius and Caesar's son was complete, and Antonius' leadership of the Caesarian faction was over. Arguments about his inconsistency underscored with dilemma forms are not common in the rest of the *Philippics* because they are no longer needed.

CHAPTER NINE: SOME GENERALIZATIONS

At the end of each of the seven preceding chapters, I have summarized the ways in which dilemma forms are integrated into the argumentation of individual speeches. These chapters, with their summaries, provide a detailed and context-specific account of the ways in which the formal, stylistic quality of dilemma, that of an emphatic, highly recognizable, educationally sanctioned token of irrefutable argument, interacts with the content of individual arguments to create persuasive effects. They also provide a specific description of the ways in which the stylistic quality of dilemma helps the orator to delimit the internal structure of his argumentation, and to create resonances that undergird an entire speech. The analysis of the argumentative role of each dilemma form has further shown the ways in which Cicero develops established functions of the device as aggressive, *ad hominem* argument, and the ways in which the orator extends the uses of dilemma forms through applying them to targets other than the opponent. From this treatment there has emerged a picture of the persuasive mechanisms that Cicero uses in employing this one form both in argument and as argument.

Now, it will be useful to offer some general statements about these persuasive mechanisms. Such generalizations have the advantage of conciseness, and the great disadvantage that they must be divorced from the individual contexts that make each example meaningful. Thus this final chapter will not contain the most satisfying observations in this study, only those that can be most briefly stated.

Most of our observations have concerned the role of dilemma forms in specific arguments and lines of argument. At the end of each chapter, we have tried to gauge the effect of dilemma on each speech as a whole.

Since every use of the device affects both the line of argument and the entire speech in which it occurs, the same example may be used to illustrate functions at both levels. Further, the various possible effects of dilemma in specific lines of argument are not mutually exclusive. So, to take an extreme example, the dilemma at *pro Caelio* 50 (above, pp. 112-113, 120-121) is important at the broader level for the pattern of resonance that we have noted in the speech. On the narrower level of individual arguments and lines of argument, this same form concurrently gives an illusion of rigor, makes viable premises disappear, asserts a hypothetical which can then be used as an established premise, and serves as a forceful marker at the end of a section of argument.

To provide a scheme for organizing our typology of uses, we may first view dilemma in terms of the mechanisms of its presentational effects. Next, it will be useful to catalogue the different types of aggressive *ad hominem* attack that Cicero can advance in dilemma form. Finally, we may summarize the most salient uses of dilemma form that are not aimed directly at an opponent, and so are most innovative in light of the expectations of the classical rhetorical tradition.

Before presenting these results, it is important to note again the limitations of the data upon which they are based. Since the analyses that lead to an empirically derived typology must be founded in an understanding of broader argumentative contexts, and even of entire speeches, an exhaustive discussion would involve treating each of one hundred twenty-six examples of dilemma form within the context of one of the twenty-nine Ciceronian speeches in which dilemma forms occur. So, for example, there are textbook instances of dilemma at *pro Quinctio* 81 and at *second Verrine* 2.150 that cannot responsibly be included in a typology of presentational uses in the absence of a detailed study of their broader argumentative contexts. Without claiming to have made such an exhaustive study, I believe that the following schema, based upon fifty-six examples from our seven speeches, along with forty-seven obvious parallel uses and twelve other comparanda from the remaining speeches, is sufficiently comprehensive to offer valid generalizations.[1]

---

[1] In the notes to the following typology, each citation of a dilemma previously discussed is followed in parentheses by **bold-face** page numbers referring to that discussion. Citations of all dilemmas, whether previously discussed or not, are followed in parentheses by the page numbers where they are quoted in the first appendix below.

General Presentational Effects

A) In individual arguments:

A.1) The most common and fundamental presentational use of dilemma is to give the illusion of rigor. Dilemma distracts from the weak assumptions of an argument, or even legitimizes those assumptions, through the simple appearance of strong argumentation. The fact that dilemma, as a perceived invincible argument form, premises certain assumptions, leads one to perceive the assumptions themselves as valid. Often, the assumptions that are legitimized in this way are grounded in Cicero's characterization of the principals involved. Whether ethical or not, this mechanism obtains for all dilemmas of which the content advances weak or specious arguments.[2]

Of the 126 occurrences of dilemma forms in Cicero's orations, 89 conform to Quintilian's definition of dilemma, if we include four examples cast in "sive...sive" ["whether...or"] form (see n. 16 below). Of these 89, there are 9 that cannot responsibly be assigned to the classifications that follow: *Quinct.* 81 (183); *Ver.* 2.150 (188), 177 (188); 3.84 (188-189), 106 (189); *Clu.* 175 (193); *Flac.* 84 (197); *Vat.* 10 (200); *Planc.* 84 (**140**, 206). There are two other dilemma structures, at *Ver.* 2.144 (188) and *Font.* 3 (190, fragmentary) that have no place in this scheme. Finally, the twelve examples labelled with "cf." in the following notes have important similarities with the uses I identify, but also have important differences.

In the previous seven chapters, I have labelled eleven occurrences of dilemma as synthetic: *Q. Rosc.* 9 (**75**, 191), 16 (**79**, 191), 25(i) (**80**, 192), 25(ii) (**81**, 192), 40 (**83**, 192), 52 (**84**, 192), 55 (**86**, 192); *Sul.* 21 (**94**, 195), 25(i) (**95**, 195), 25(ii) (**96**, 195); *Phil.2.* 84 (**162**, 208). To these add *Quinct.* 81 (183); *Tul.* 38 (185); *Prov.* 46(i) (202). Cf. the dilemma form at *Quinct.* 64-65 (182). This classification indicates a necessarily subjective judgment that ill-suited material has been forced into a dilemma form to answer either a point that the opponent has in fact already conceded or a point that he would not argue at all. These synthetic dilemmas, which occur most frequently in civil pleadings, have the same range of uses as their less strained counterparts. In order to help the reader identify the most prevalent uses of these synthetic dilemmas, in what follows I italicize the citation number of each synthetic form.

[2] In our speeches, the examples are: *S. Rosc.* 74 (**34**, 183), 79 (**35-36**, 184), 93 (**37-38**, 184); *Div. Caec.* 31 (**59**, 186), 33 (**59**, 186), 58 (**62-63**, 186); *Q. Rosc.* *9* (**75**, 191), *16* (**79**, 191), *25(i)* (**80**, 192), *25(ii)* (**81**, 192), *40* (**83**, 192), *52* (**84**, 192), *55* (**86**, 192); *Sul.* 39 (**98**, 195). *Cael.* 35 (**111**, 200), 50 (**112**, 200), 52 (**114**, 200), 53(i) (**114**, 201), 53(ii) (**114**, 201), 58 (**117**, 201), 61 (**118**, 201), 62 (**119**, 201); *Planc.* 44 (**135**, 205), 46 (**135-136**, 205); *Phil.2.* 56 (**159**, 207). All of these examples except those in *Q. Rosc.* include assumptions based on characterization. While examples of this class can regularly come only from analysis of the specific argumentative context, two obvious comparanda are *Quinct.* 41 (182; based on ethical assumptions as last element in an *enumeratio*) and 73 (182; with Kinsey's note on *iudicium accipere* ad sec. 62.)

A.2) A dilemma may serve to make opposing arguments disappear; it may dismiss valid assumptions, including valid assumptions about character, simply through excluding them from its apparently exhaustive structure.³ This exclusion of valid premises is fundamentally mechanical. The dilemma structure can only offer two possibilities. But it is also presentational. The structure allowing only two possibilities is also a structure giving the appearance of invincible argument. If the argument is not exhaustive, and thus fails to represent the range of pertinent possibilities, it is not really invincible. Thus the perception that the dilemma does embody invincible argument entails the assumption that it does not exclude those pertinent possibilities. The effectiveness of the device to dismiss valid assumptions without a hearing is thus dependent both upon its mechanical structure and upon the audience's recognition of that structure as a form of invincible argument, i.e., upon the audience's acceptance of its presentational effect.

A.3) The form may establish useful but insubstantiable assumptions by introducing them as mere alternatives rather than as facts.⁴ Once introduced, these assumptions may nonetheless be used as the foundation for further argument. This process is certainly extra-rational, but does not seem to depend as do the first two uses on the illusion of rigor that the form provides.

A.4) The device may serve to lend variety to a barrage of refutations meant to give the illusion that Cicero is adequately treating topics which he is in fact skirting.⁵

---

³ Thus esp. *Q. Rosc.* 40 (**83**, 192), 52 (**84**, 192), 55 (**86**, 192); *Sul.* 10 (**92-93**, 195; technically directed to the audience), 39 (**98**, 195); *Cael.* 35 (**111**, 200), 50 (**112**, 200), 52 (**114**, 201), 53(i) (**114**, 201), 53(ii) (**114**, 201), 61 (**118**, 201); *Planc.* 44 (**135**, 205), 46 (**135-136**, 205). With the exception of the examples in *Q. Rosc.*, each instance excludes at least one assumption concerning the character of one of the principals that could benefit Cicero's opponent.
This use of dilemma is one species of a general Ciceronian tactic of posing alternatives that seem exhaustive, but fail to cover viable possibilities. Cf. the catalogue in C.J. Classen, "Ciceros Kunst der Überredung," in W. Ludwig, ed., *Éloquence et Rhétorique chez Cicéron*, Entretiens sur l'Antiquité Classique, Vol. 28 (Vandoeuvres-Genève: Fondation Hardt, 1962), 149-84, 168 and n.4.
⁴ *Sul.* 81 (**100**, 196); *Cael.* 35 (**111**, 200), 50 (**112**, 200), 52 (**114**, 200), 53(i) (**114**, 201), 53(ii) (**114**, 201), 61 (**118**, 201); *Planc.* 44 and 46 (**131-133**, 205).
⁵ *Cael.* 58 (**117**, 201); *Planc.* 54 (**137**, 205). See C.J. Classen (above, n.3) 168-170. The deception works because a barrage of questions combined with dilemma can be an

SOME GENERALIZATIONS

A.5) A dilemma founded upon non-ethical assumptions, coming at the end of an extended passage devoted to characterization, can help to integrate such a protracted passage of ethical argument into the larger argumentative structure.[6]

B) To punctuate sections of argument:

Often in conjunction with these uses of the device, the presentational power and memorable quality of dilemma render it especially useful for three types of demarcation:

B.1) Dilemma can serve to begin a line of argument with the appearance of invincible reasoning.[7] It is noteworthy that in every example of this usage that we have seen the material has been forced into dilemma form, presumably for just this purpose. This is especially striking at *Div. Caec. 12*, where the dilemma also provides the organizing principle for the following ten sections of the argument.

B.2) On the other hand, the form can serve to cap a line of argument with that same appearance of rigor. In one interesting instance, we have seen that the form does not supplement, but actually replaces, the usual amplification at the end of an argument.[8]

B.3) The earliest usage that we noted, at *S. Rosc.* 128 (**40**, 185), has a slightly different function. Here the dilemma serves as a memorable marker of Cicero's principal argument, and so marks a break while the orator inserts an important parenthesis.

B.4) As another reminder that stylistic forms are proof against ironclad generalizations, we must note again the one use of dilemma that is diametrically opposed to all of these functions of demarcation. At

---

effective way to underscore legitimate argument. Cf. the pointed questions and the diaeretical reasoning of *S. Rosc.* 74 (**34**, 183). With *S. Rosc.* 74, cf. *Ver.* 3.118 (189); *Cael.* 53(iii) (**116**, 201).

[6] *Q. Rosc.* 25(i) (**80**, 192); *Planc.* 35 (**134**, 204).

[7] *Div. Caec.* 12 (**55-56**, 186); *Q. Rosc.* 16 (**79**, 191), 40 (**83**, 192), 52 (**84**, 192); *Sul.* 21 (**94**, 195). Also *Tul.* 38 (185); *Flac.* 59 (196).

[8] *Div. Caec.* 58 (**62-63**, 186); *Q. Rosc.* 9 (**75**, 191), 25(i) (**80**, 192); *Sul.* 10 (**92-93**, 195), 25(i) (**95**, 195); *Cael.* 50 (**112**, 200); *Planc.* 35 (**134**, 204); *Phil.2. 84* (**162**, 208). As substitute for an imprudent amplification, *Sul.* 25(i) (**95**, 195), and cf. *Clu.* 135 (193) and *Mur.* 57 (195), in which Cicero makes a sharp point with dilemma rather than elaborating an argument that would undermine or distract from his principal thrust. Other uses of dilemma forms forcefully to conclude the discussion of a topic or a line of argument are *Quinct.* 41 and 64-65 (182); *Ver.* 2.191 (188), 3.169 (189), 5.135 (190); *Clu.* 114 (193); *Sul.* 25(ii) (**96**, 195); *Flac.* 53 and 58 (196); *Vat.* 20 (200); *Phil.* 3.21 (208).

Phil.2.56 (**159**, 207), the orator uses a dilemma not to mark a division between topics, but to bind together in the same set of accusations arguments of widely disparate importance.

C) To create resonances throughout entire speeches:

Regarding entire speeches, the roles of the dilemma form as argument all depend upon the resonance born of repetition. This resonance has three sources. It may result from the recapitulation in dilemma form of the thrust of a previous argument.[9] More commonly, it may result from repetition that recapitulates both the form and the content of earlier argument. So seven of the first eight dilemmas in the *Caeliana* argue that Clodia is not a reliable witness. Finally, the resonance may be that of a repeated form that reinforces, purely through that repetition, the conclusions of previous arguments (e.g., *Cael*. 62 (**119**, 201).). The noteworthy functions of dilemma in an entire speech, which are not mutually exclusive, flow from the second and third of these types of resonance.

C.1) Irrespective of the content expressed in dilemma form, repetition of the device plays upon the audience's knowledge of the place of dilemma in rhetorical theory and oratorical practice to argue for the oratorical superiority of the speaker who uses it.[10]

C.2) Because the device has a structure that is both hypothetical and memorable, its repetition allows Cicero to establish for the audience themes that are useful for his case, but that cannot be represented as facts.[11]

C.3) Because one function of the form is to underscore lack of self-consistency, repetition of dilemma can help to foster the impression that an opponent lacks such self-consistency, or is even irrational.[12]

C.4) The repeated use of dilemma directed at the orator can aid both in defining and in sustaining an ethically based persuasive strategy.[13]

---

[9] E.g., *Q. Rosc*. 25*(ii)* (**81**, 192) with secs. 1-13,, and 55 (**86**, 192) with secs. 39-51)
[10] In *Div. Caec*, this superiority is a factor vital to the audience's final judgment. Above, chapter three, pp. 58-59 *et passim*. Cf. also *Phil*.2, above, chapter eight, p. 154 *et passim*.
[11] *Cael*. Above, chapter six, p. 121 *et passim*.
[12] Cf. *Phil*.2. Above, chapter eight, pp. 154-155, 168, *et passim*. In this speech, the content of arguments is at least as important as the dilemma form in creating this effect. See D.4 below.
[13] *Planc*. See chapter seven above.

C.5) In speeches especially rich in comedic elements, the value of the form as a token of irrefutable argument provides a counterpoise by giving a decorous appearance of rigor. This role of counterpoise partially accounts for the plethora of dilemmas in *Pro Caelio* and *Pro Roscio Comoedo*. In the earlier speech Cicero achieves this effect by consistently forcing arguments into dilemma form.[14]

Other Noteworthy Uses

D) Invincible argument as ethical attack against opponent:

D.1) Ethical arguments are part of the effect of an entire section of argument, or of an entire speech. They are sustained by assumptions, innuendos, and themes repeated in the course of making arguments towards the orator's putative aim. So it is no surprise that dilemma, like any form of substantial argument, may serve as a scaffold on which to hang ethical themes that are not central to its ostensible conclusion.[15]

D.2) The most direct use of dilemma in ethical argument is to attack in a general way the deficient character or mental state of an opponent. The regular pattern is to prove, or assume as fact, that the opponent's behavior has been wrongful or deficient, and then to propose in dilemma form alternate unflattering explanations for the opponent's action. This is the sort of ethical attack we might properly expect from a political opponent, and it is this type of opponent whom Cicero regularly singles out with this form, whether in an ostensibly judicial context or not.[16]

---

[14] *Q. Rosc.*, above, chapter four, esp. pp. 87-88. *Cael.*, above, chapter six, esp. p. 121. In *Q. Rosc.*, seven of the eight forms, those at secs. 9 (**75**, 191), 16 (**79**, 191), 25(i) (**80**, 192), 25(ii) (**81**, 192), 40 (**83**, 192), 52 (**84**, 192), 55 (**86**, 192), are synthetic.

[15] *Cael.* 62 (**119**, 201); *Phil.2.* 84 (**162**, 208). Cf. *Div. Caec.* 12 (**55-56**, 186) and the praise of Caesar at *Planc.* 35 (**134**, 204). Also *Agr.* 1.11 (193).

[16] *Phil.2.* 16 (**155**, 207), 54(**158**, 207), 110(i) (**164**, 208). Also *Har. Resp.* 5 (199); *Sest.* 32 (199); the complex formulation at *Pis.* 39 (203), and the narrative dilemma at *Ver.* 1.144 (187; the only use in which Cicero is formally the prosecutor, and his juridical goal is thus directly served). Cf. the form directed at an unspecified opponent at *Phil.* 5.5 (208), and that directed at Clodius' relation at *Dom.* 134 (199). In the introduction, we noted that dilemma in ethical attack based upon alternate explanations of a wrong action ("My opponent is either a charlatan or a fool.") occurs already in the Attic orators. Thus Andocides 2.2-3 (**22**); Demosthenes 20.102; 22.40-41; 23.133-134; 24.122.

D.3) Closely linked to the previous type is the form that we have labelled the narrative dilemma. The orator may narrate in dilemma form a past circumstance in which his opponent was in the wrong, and so was confronted with two choices, either of which emphasizes his opponent's worthlessness.[17] This form is especially pointed when Cicero explains that the opponents extricated themselves only by the disreputable action of opposing his side in the present judicial proceeding.[18]

D.4) The device may serve to underscore the target's lack of self-consistency. We have said that dilemma can be a vehicle to emphasize inconsistencies. In fact one could find at the basis of any argument the premise that the opponent's words, assumptions or actions are inconsistent with perceived facts or generally held views. Self-consistency is much narrower. The target lacks self-consistency if his words, assumptions or actions seem to contradict each other in a given situation, or if he responds in widely disparate ways to fundamentally similar situations. Cicero consistently uses this tactic not to demonstrate the flaw in an argument, but to assert the flaw in an individual.[19]

This type of dilemma is the principal use for the "sive...sive" ["whether...or"] form with one apodosis. Thus *Phil.2.* 16 (**155**, 207), 110(i) (**164**, 208); *Sest.* 32 (199). (The only other "sive...sive" forms in the speeches are those at *Tul.* 32 (185) and *Dom.* 22(ii) (197)). Since this "sive...sive" form is not treated as a dilemma before pseudo-Hermogenes (above, pp. 19-20), it is unclear how emphatic a presentational value it can have for Cicero's audience.

[17] *S. Rosc.* 120 (**38**, 184); *Phil.2.* 75 (**160**, 208). Also *Ver.*2.74 (187) and 3.135 (189); *Caec.*4 (191); *Flac.* 39 (196; against witnesses). Cf. *Clu.* 69 (192; against Staienus). Most elaborate, and quite unique, is *Vat.* 20 (200), where Cicero confronts his target with a past dilemma in the protasis of a past contrary-to-fact condition.

Since no present choice is offered in any of these instances, these examples are technically not true dilemmas. With the uses noted at E.1, E.4 and E.5, they form a subclass of "narrative dilemmas." Cf. Isocrates 17.27-28 (**23**).

[18] *Caec.* 4 (191); *Flac.* 39 (196).

[19] *Phil.2.* 56 (**159**, 207), 75 (**160**, 208), 100 (**163**, 208), 110(ii) (**164-165**, 208) and *Phil.* 3.21 (208); *Sul. 25(i)* (**95**, 195); also *Dom.* 125(i) and 125(ii) (198-199) and cf. 124 (197); *Sul. 21* (**94**, 195); *Lig.* 29 (207). *Cael.* 35 (**111**, 200), against the witness Clodia, is the only attack on the self-consistency of a witness, and thus is the best parallel to *Inv.* 1.45 (**9-10**).

In the Attic orators, dilemma based on inconsistency is used for dominantly ethical attack at Demosthenes 26.14 and 51.16. Cf. 18.217 (**20-21**); 22.40-41; 58.12; Isaeus 6.58.

SOME GENERALIZATIONS

D.5) A final way in which the ubiquitous and polymorphous nature of Cicero's ethical arguments co-opt the dilemma form is in the construction of dilemmas with alternatives that do not refute the opponent's arguments in a strict sense. Rather they offer two choices, either of which makes the opponent offensive to the audience.[20]

E. **Dilemma forms *not* directed at the opponent:**
Dilemma forms directed at individuals other than the opponent and his supporters have little in common with the rhetorically prescribed functions of the device. Still, one of two characteristics of dilemma is at the base of each of these expanded uses. The first is that dilemma assumes the inflexible necessity of the circumstances that give rise to the choices that it offers. The second is that the use of dilemma, whether in proof or in refutation, is fundamentally, aggressively adversarial.

E.1) When Cicero explains that his client is caught in a dilemma, with the harsh necessity of circumstances weighing upon him, he may expect the audience to feel compassion. If the opponent is responsible for the client's discomfort, the audience's anger against Cicero's adversary can be stoked at the same time.[21]

In Cicero, the only examples of dilemma that function primarily to underscore the opponent's lack of self-consistent reasoning with little emphasis on ethical argument are those at *Clu.* 114 (193) and 135 (193). Cf. also *Agr.* 2.57 (194).

[20] *Q. Rosc.* 43 (**83-84**, 192); *Planc.* 46 (**135-136**, 205). The choices need not hurt the opponent's case, and thus need not be true dilemmas in a narrow sense. They are not less effective for that. Arguably the most powerful example of this device is the only dilemma in the *Catilinarians*. At the end of the first prosopopoeia of *patria* at *Cat.* 1.18 (195), the fatherland makes a devastating emotional appeal to Catiline (and the senate) for Catiline to leave the City and free the fatherland from dread: "...si est verus, ne opprimar, sin falsus, ut tandem aliquando timere desinam." ["...if it is well founded, that I may not be destroyed: if groundless, that I may at long last cease to feel afraid."]

Other good examples are at *Ver.* 2.142 (187; whether Verres is convicted or not, the money he stole will not be recovered) and at *Balb.* 13-14 (202-203; either choice demeans Pompeius and so inflames the audience). Also *Agr.* 2.43, 46, and 61 (194). Cf. *Ver.* 3.182 (190); *Dom.* 22(i) (197); *Flac.* 58 (196), in which the first prong offends the audience. The oddest example is at *Lig.* 23 (206-207), in which both of Tubero's choices are shown to be offensive to Caesar, but the whole argument is cast as contrary-to-fact. See also E.2 below.

In the Attic orators, there are two clear examples of this general use of dilemma: Lysias 27.6; Demosthenes 25.64-66.

[21] *S. Rosc.* 30 (**33**, 183). Narrative dilemma forms are also used to elicit pity for those whom Cicero represents, and anger against his opponents, at *Quinct.* 32 (182),

E.2) The audience itself may become the object of attack. There are three disparate instances in which the audience is made the target. The first is closely in keeping with a tactic that we have already seen. At *Phil.* 11.19(ii) (209), Cicero claims that his opponent has placed the audience in a dilemma. Since being forced to make either choice alienates the audience from the opponent, this has much the same offensive impact on the audience as do the forms noted at D.5 above. On the other hand, at *Caec.* 8 (191) Cicero himself places the audience in a dilemma. He hypothesizes an objection of a *iudex recuperatorve* in an "if" clause, then refutes the hypothetical with a dilemma. This conditional attack on those who are to be persuaded is unique, perhaps because it is simply imprudent. Very different is *Prov.* 46 (202) in which the senators are given the choice of putting themselves in an impossible situation or of agreeing with Cicero.[22]

E.3) Dilemma forms directed at Cicero himself may allow him sarcastically to dismiss the force of an opponent's attack.[23]

E.4) Cicero's narration of past dilemmas that confronted him can work both to excite compassion and to justify his past actions.[24]

E.5) But the most interesting and common function of dilemma forms aimed at Cicero is to give the orator a license for behavior that the

---

Ver. 3.37 (188; the equites), *Phil.* 11.5 (209; Trebonius). and cf. *Phil.* 9.6 (208-209; Ser. Sulpicius Rufus).

[22] The dilemma which C. Gracchus had put to the plebs (above. p. 24), while an antecedent example of placing the audience in a dilemma, does not compare closely with any of these three instances. The most similar is *Caec.* 8, which also poses alternate consequences of a hypothetical in "aut...aut" ["either...or"] form.

[23] *Planc.* 83 (**140**, 205); *Phil.* 2.32 (**158**, 207).

[24] Cicero finds himself in a narrative dilemma at *Div. Caec.* 4 (**53**, 185) and 14 (**56**, 186); *Planc.* 4 (**129-130**, 204), 88, 89(ii) (**141-142**, 206). Also *Dom.* 91 (197); *Sest.* 44 (199), and the dilemma of Metellus Numidicus at *Sest.* 37 (199), which is merely a way to amplify Cicero's own predicament. These last five examples deal with the motive for Cicero's departure into exile, and cast that motive as the avoidance of a dilemma.

Cf. also *Caec.* 3(i) (190), in which Cicero proclaims that he has labored to escape a dilemma, and *Caec.* 3(ii) (190-191), in which the orator offers the textbook refutation of that dilemma by *conversio*, as explained in *Inv.* 1.83-84 (above, pp. 12-13); *Rhet. Her.* 2.38-39 (above, pp. 14-15).

In the introduction, we noted that self-professed narrative dilemmas occur already in the Attic orators, where they also justify the speaker's past actions: Andocides 2.7-8; Antiphon, *Tetralogies* 1.beta.3; Isocrates 17.6 & 10.

SOME GENERALIZATIONS

audience would otherwise find unattractive, or downright offensive.[25]

Given the limited scope of this investigation, this typology is not certainly exhaustive. Nonetheless, the results here offered do define and enumerate the principal uses of dilemma that depend, in whole or in part, upon the ease of recognition, memorable quality, and accepted rhetorical role of the form to underscore invincible argument. It is in these uses that the stylistic value of the argument form is defined. Further, these results show the strong interrelationships between the use of this aggressive argument form and tactics of ethical argument in Cicero's speeches. If these conclusions, and the readings on which they are based, can focus attention upon the value of form as argument, provide a broader understanding of Cicero's range of tactics, and foster a deeper appreciation of the orator's response to unique rhetorical situations, this work will have achieved its aim.

---

[25] This technique of licensing through the speaker's profession that he is in a dilemma appears in the rhetorical tradition at *Rhet. Her.* 4.52 (above, p. 16). In the Attic orators, the most famous example must be *De Corona*, 4. (Demosthenes 18.4). Add Antiphon 1.1, Isocrates 6.70; Demosthenes 27.53. Cf. the purely pathetic example at Isocrates 14.46-47. Cicero provides examples from each phase of his career: *S. Rosc.* 124 (**39**, 185); *Div. Caec.* 4 (**53**, 185) and 14 (**56**, 186); *Planc.* 4 (**129-130**, 204), 6 (**130-131**, 204), 79 (**139-140**, 205); *Phil.2.* 32 (**157-158**, 207), and the passages cited in the previous note. Cf. also *Sul.* 25(ii) (**96**, 195) and *Planc.* 89(i) (**141**, 206). Add *Phil.*11.19(i) (209), in which Cicero professes that he is in a dilemma, identifies his situation with the concerns of his audience, and so immediately claims that his opponent has placed the entire senate in that dilemma. Here the usage goes beyond license to criticism of the opponent for constructing the situation in the first place.

APPENDIX ONE: DILEMMA FORMS IN CICERO'S ORATIONS

In this list, I regularly use the Oxford Classical Texts of Cicero's Orations edited by Clark and Peterson. The exceptions are *Pro Roscio Comoedo*, for which I use the text of Axer (Leipzig: Teubner, 1976), and the *Philippics*, for which I use the text of D.R. Shackleton Bailey (U. of North Carolina Press, 1986). Dilemma structures that do not fully meet Quintilian's definition of dilemma are marked with an asterisk ("*"). Citation numbers are italicized for those arguments in which both choices are not really considered, and thus the use of the dilemma form is synthetic. In citations where extra context is given, the actual text of the dilemma form is set off between double slashes ("//"). After each entry, the general syntactical form of the device is given within square brackets. Finally, the ways in which each form has been categorized in the typology above (pp. 171-179) are also listed within square brackets.

Unless otherwise indicated, the translations are taken from the editions in the *Loeb Classical Library* cited in the bibliography, except for the translations of examples in the *Philippics*, which are those of Shackleton Bailey's University of North Carolina Press edition. Occasionally, minor corrections in the *Loeb* translations have been necessary as an aid to clarity. Despite the presence of good translations, it has in rare cases been necessary to translate passages anew in order to emphasize properly the presence of a dilemma structure. These new translations are marked "(CPC)".

The examples are given in the chronological order of Schanz. An alphabetized list of the examples, with their locations in this appendix, will be found on pp. 211-212.

Quinct. 32: Conturbatus sane discedit Quinctius; neque mirum, cui haec optio tam misera tamque iniqua daretur //ut aut ipse se capitis damnaret, si satis dedisset, aut causam capitis, si sponsionem fecisset, priore loco diceret.// [conditional + aut...aut] [E.1]

Quinctius withdrew quite distracted; and no wonder, since a wretched and unfair alternative was offered him -- //either to condemn himself to lose his civil rights if he gave security, or to plead first in an action in which they were at stake, if he entered into an "engagement."//

Quinct. 41: //Restat ut aut summa neglegentia tibi obstiterit aut unica liberalitas. Si neglegentiam dices, mirabimur, si bonitatem, ridebimus;// neque praeterea quid possis dicere invenio.   [conditional + aut...aut] [A.1, B.2]

//The only alternative is that extreme negligence or unparalleled generosity prevented you from demanding the money. If you plead negligence, we shall be astonished, if you plead generosity, we shall laugh;// and I do not know what other excuse you can find.

Quinct. 64-65: //(64) Aut haec facta non sint necesse est aut C. Aquilius, talis vir, iuratus hoc ius in civitate constituat: cuius procurator non omnia iudicia *acceperit* quae quisque in verba postularit, cuius procurator a praetore tribunos appellare ausus sit, eum non defendi, eius bona recte possideri posse, ei misero, absenti, ignaro fortunarum suarum omnia vitae ornamenta per summum dedecus et ignominiam deripi convenire.. (65) Quod si probari nemini potest, illud certe probari omnibus necesse est, defensum esse iudicio absentem Quinctium.// Quod cum ita sit, ex edicto bona possessa non sunt.   [aut...aut] [B.2]

//It is necessary, then, either that these things have not taken place or that such a man as Gaius Aquilius should on his oath lay down as law in this state: that one whose agent has not consented to stand trial on any issue, whatever the terms in which the claim may have been drawn up, one whose agent has ventured to appeal from the praetor to the tribunes, is not defended; that his goods may be legally possessed; that it may be thought fit that the unhappy man, during his absence, ignorant of what is happening to him, may be stripped with the greatest disgrace and ignomy of all that makes life honourable. But if such an interpretation of the law cannot be admitted by anyone, certainly everyone must admit that Quinctius during his absence was legally defended.// This being so, his goods were not possessed in accordance with the edict.

Quinct. 73: Qua re aut doceas oportet Alfenum negasse se procuratorem esse, non deiecisse libellos, iudicium accipere noluisse, aut, cum haec ita facta sint, ex edicto te bona P. Quincti non possedisse concedas.   [aut...aut] [A.1]

Wherefore you must either prove that Alfenus denied that he was my client's agent, that he did not tear down the placards, that he refused to stand trial; or, since these facts are established, you must admit that you did not take possession of Quinctius's good in accordance with the edict.

APPENDIX I: DILEMMA FORMS IN CICERO'S ORATIONS

Quinct. 81: An, ante quam postulasti ut bona possideres, misisti qui curaret ut dominus de suo fundo a sua familia vi deiceretur? //Utrumlibet elige; alterum incredibile est, alterum nefarium, et ante hoc tempus utrumque inauditum. DCC milia passuum vis esse decursa biduo? dic. Negas? ante igitur misisti. Malo; si enim illud diceres, improbe mentiri viderere; cum hoc confiteris, id te admisisse concedis quod ne mendacio quidem tegere possis.// [alternate questions]

Now, before applying for authority to take possession of the goods, did you send an agent to see that the owner was expelled from his own estate by force and by his own slaves? //Take your choice; the one is incredible, the other is atrocious; both are unprecedented. Do you maintain that seven hundred miles were covered in two days? Tell me. You answer no? Then you sent your agent beforehand. I like this better; for if you said the former, you would show yourself a bare-faced liar; in admitting the latter, you allow that you have been guilty of a crime which you cannot cover up even by a lie.//

*S. Rosc. 30: hanc condicionem misero ferunt ut optet utrum malit cervices *T. Roscio* dare an insutus in culleum per summum dedecus vitam amittere. [alternate questions] [E.1]

They reduce the wretched man to the position of choosing whether he prefers to offer his throat to Titus Roscius or to be sewn up in a sack and lose his life in a most disgraceful way. (CPC)

S. Rosc. 74: Quo modo occidit? //ipse percussit an aliis occidendum dedit? Si ipsum arguis, Romae non fuit; si per alios fecisse dicis, quaero quos? Servosne an liberos? *Si liberos*, quos homines? indidemne Ameria an hosce ex urbe sicarios? Si Ameria, qui sunt ei? cur non nominantur? si Roma, unde eos noverat Roscius qui Romam multis annis non venit neque umquam plus triduo fuit? ubi eos convenit? qui conlocutus est? quo modo persuasit? 'Pretium dedit'; cui dedit? per quem dedit? unde aut quantum dedit? Nonne his vestigiis ad caput malefici perveniri solet?// [conditional and alternate questions] [A.1]

How did he kill him? //Did he strike the blow himself, or entrust the task to others? If you maintain that he did it himself, I answer that he was not in Rome; if you say that he did it by the hands of others, I ask you, who were they? Slaves or free men? If free men, who are they? from the same place Ameria, or some of these assassins from Rome? If from Ameria, who are they, why are their names not given? if from Rome, how did Roscius, who for several years did not come to Rome and never stayed there more than three days, make their acquaintance? Where did he meet them? how did he get an interview with them? how did he persuade them? He gave them a bribe. To whom, and through whom, did he give it? where did the money come from, and how much was it? Is it not by following up all such traces that the starting point of the crime is usually reached?//

184   FORM AS ARGUMENT

S. Rosc. 79: Conveniat mihi tecum necesse est, si ad hunc maleficium istud pertinet, aut ipsum sua manu fecisse, id quod negas, aut per aliquos liberos aut servos. Liberosne? quos neque ut convenire potuerit neque qua ratione inducere neque ubi neque per quos neque qua spe aut quo pretio potes ostendere. Ego contra ostendo non modo nihil eorum fecisse Sex. Roscium sed ne potuisse quidem facere, quod neque Romae multis annis fuerit neque de praediis umquam temere discesserit. Restare tibi videbatur servorum nomen, quo quasi in portum reiectus a ceteris suspicionibus confugere posses; ubi scopulum offendis eius modi ut non modo ab hoc crimen resilire videas verum omnem suspicionem in vosmet ipsos recidere intellegas. [aut...aut] [A.1]

We must needs agree that, if my client is connected with this crime, he either committed it with his own hand, which you are unable to prove, or by the agency of others, free men or slaves. Free men? You are unable to show how he was able to meet them, by what means he persuaded them, by whose agency, what expectations he raised, what bribe he offered. I, on the contrary, prove that Sextus Roscius not only did not do, but could not have done, any of these things, seeing that for several years he had neither been in Rome nor had ever left his farm without good reason. It seems that the only thing left to you was to name the slaves; this appeared a kind of harbour where you might take refuge when driven from your other false allegations, instead of which you have struck upon such a sort of rock that you not only see the charge rebound from Sextus Roscius, but also understand that every suspicion recoils upon yourselves.

S. Rosc. 93: Erat tum multitudo sicariorum, id quod commemoravit Erucius, et homines impune occidebantur. Quid? ea multitudo quae erat? //Opinor, aut eorum qui in bonis erant occupati, aut eorum qui ab eis conducebantur ut aliquem occiderent. Si eos putas qui alienum appetebant, tu es in eo numero qui nostra pecunia dives es; sin eos quos qui leviore nomine appellant percussores vocant, quaere in cuius fide sint et clientela; mihi crede, aliquem de societate tua reperies;...// [conditional + aut...aut] [A.1]

As Erucius has told us, at that time there was a crowd of assassins, and men were killed with impunity. Well, of whom was this crowd composed? //I imagine either of those who were occupied in buying properties, or of those who were hired by them to murder somebody. If you think the criminals were those who coveted the property of others, you are one of the number, you who are enriched by our wealth; but if you think they were those who are called by the milder name of bandits, inquire under whose protection, whose dependants they are, and believe me, you will find one of your associates.//

*S. Rosc. 120 : //Res porro abs te eius modi postulabatur ut nihil interesset, utrum eam rem recusares an de maleficio confiterere.// Quae cum ita sint, quaero abs te quam ob causam recusaris. [alternate questions] [D.3]

//Further, the request made to you was of such a kind that it made no difference whether you refused it or confessed the crime.// This being so, I ask you why you refused it.

APPENDIX I: DILEMMA FORMS IN CICERO'S ORATIONS 185

S. Rosc. 124: Venio nunc ad illud nomen aureum Chrysogoni sub quo nomine tota societas latuit; de quo, iudices, neque quo modo dicam neque quo modo taceam reperire possum. //Si enim taceo, vel maximam partem relinquo; sin autem dico, vereor ne non ille solus, id quod ad me nihil attinet, sed alii quoque plures laesos se putent.// [conditional] [E.5]

"I come now to that golden name of Chrysogonus, under which the whole association is concealed. I am at a loss gentlemen, how to speak of this name, or how to remain silent about it. If I remain silent, I omit a most important part of my argument; if I mention it, I am afraid that not Chrysogonus alone -- that is a matter of indifference to me -- but several others may consider themselves insulted. Nevertheless, the case is of such a nature that it does not seem that I need say much against "brokers" generally: for this case is assuredly of a novel and remarkable character.

S. Rosc. 128: Profecto aut haec bona in tabulas publicas nulla redierunt nosque ab isto nebulone facetius eludimur quam putamus, aut, si redierunt, tabulae publicae corruptae aliqua ratione sunt; nam lege quidem bona venire non potuisse constat. [aut...aut] [B.3]

In any case, either this sale was not entered on the public registers, and we are being cheated by this rascal more cleverly than we think, or, if it was, the registers have been tampered with in some way, for it is evident that the property could not have been sold by virtue of the law.

Tul. 32: Nunc, sive illa defensione uti voluisses sive hac qua uteris, condemneres necesse est; [sive...sive] [cf. D.2, n.16]

Now, whether you had wanted to use that defense or this one which you are using, you must lose. (CPC)

Tul. 38: Dicis oportere quaeri, homines M. Tulli iniuria occisi sint necne. //De quo hoc primum quaero, venerit ea res in hoc iudicium necne. Si non venit, quid attinet aut nos dicere aut hos quaerere? Si autem venit, quid attinuit te tam multis verbis a praetore postulare ut adderet in iudicium 'INIURIA,' et, quia non impetrasses, tribunos pl. appellare et hic in iudicio queri praetoris iniquitatem, quod de iniuria non addidisset?// [conditional and alternate questions] [B.1]

You say that it ought to be investigated whether the people of M. Tullius were killed wrongfully or not. Concerning this first I ask whether this matter has come before this court or not. If it has not, what need is there either for us to speak or for these people to inquire? However if it has come before this court, what need is there for you to ask the praetor at such great length to add the word "wrongfully" to the court's instructions, and, because you had not obtained this, to call the tribunes of the plebs and to complain here in court about the unfairness of the praetor, because he had not added language about wrongful action? (CPC)

Div. Caec. 4: Tuli graviter et acerbe, iudices, in eum me locum adduci ut aut eos homines spes falleret qui opem a me atque auxilium petissent, aut ego, qui me ad defendendos homines ab ineunte adulescentia dedissem, tempore atque officio coactus ad accusandum traducerer. [aut...aut] [C.1, E.4, E.5]

I found myself thrust into a painfully uncomfortable position, gentlemen. Either I must disappoint these people who had come to me for help and succour, or circumstances were forcing upon me the duty of turning prosecutor, after having given myself from my earliest youth to the task of defending the prosecuted.

Div. Caec. 12: Utrum Q. Caecili, hoc dices, me non Siculorum rogatu ad causam accedere, an optimorum fidelissimorumque sociorum voluntatem apud hos gravem esse non oportere? [alternate questions] [B.1, C.1, C.5, D.1]
Will you assert, Caecilius, that it is not at the request of the Sicilians that I come forward in this case? Or that this court need pay no serious attention to the wishes of these good and loyal allies of ours?

**Div. Caec.* 14: Hi sciunt hoc non modo a me petitum esse, sed ita saepe et ita vehementer esse petitum ut aut causa mihi suscipienda fuerit aut officium necessitudinis repudiandum. [aut...aut] [C.1, C.5, E.4, E.5]
They are aware that this request has not only been made by me, but made so often, and so earnestly, that I had either to take up the case or to disown the obligations of friendship.

Div. Caec. 31: utrum hoc tantum crimen praetermittes an obicies? Si obicies, idne alteri crimini dabis quod eodem tempore in eadem provincia tu ipse fecisti? audebis ita accusare alterum ut quo minus tute condemnere recusare non possis? Sin praetermittes, qualis erit tua ista accusatio, quae domestici periculi metu certissimi et maximi criminis non modo spo*ns*ionem, verum etiam mentionem ipsam pertimescat? [conditional and alternate questions] [A.1, C.1, C.5]
Will you pass over a charge of this importance, or bring it up against him? If you bring it up, are you prepared to charge another man with the guilt of doing what you have done yourself at the same time and place? Will you dare to conduct your prosecution of another man in such a way as to leave you no defence against being condemned yourself? If on the other hand you pass this charge over, what can be your value as a prosecutor? Serious and well-grounded as the charge is, the personal risk to yourself will deter you not merely from any suggestion of its truth, but even from any allusion to its existence.

Div. Caec. 33: Quid igitur? daturus es huic crimini quod potuisti prohibere ne fieret et debuisti, an totum id relinques? [alternate questions] [A.1, C.1, C.5]
Then, Caecilius, are you likely to include in the charges against him an offense which you could have and should have prevented? Or will you let it pass altogether?

Div. Caec. 58: Si tu cum illo postea in gratiam redisti, si domi illius aliquotiens fuisti, si ille apud te postea cenavit, //utrum te perfidiosum an praevaricatorem exisitmari mavis? Video esse necesse alterutrum, sed ego tecum in eo non pugnabo quo minus utrum velis eligas.// [alternate questions] [A.1, B.2, C.1, C.5]
But if you subsequently made friends with him again, if you visited him several times at his house, if later he dined with you -- //well, which would you have us consider you, a traitor to your friend or a traitor to justice? One or the other it is plain to me you must be: but I do not propose to argue the point with you -- you may choose which alternative you will.//

APPENDIX I: DILEMMA FORMS IN CICERO'S ORATIONS

Div. Caec. 60: Qui (sc. Caecilius) si summam iniuriam ab illo accepisti, tamen, quoniam quaestor eius fuisti, non potes eum sine ulla vituperatione accusare; si vero non ulla tibi facta est iniuria, sine scelere eum accusare non potes. [conditional] [C.1, C.5]

Even if he has wronged you (sc. Caecilius) deeply, yet, having been his quaestor, you cannot prosecute him without incurring some blame: and if he has not wronged you at all, you cannot prosecute him without incurring criminal guilt.

*Ver.*1.144: Hic te si res ipsa, si indignitas iniuriae tuae non commovebat, si pupilli calamitas, si propinquorum lacrimae, si D. Bruti, cuius praedia suberant, periculum, si M. Marcelli tutoris auctoritas apud te ponderis nihil habebat, //ne illud quidem animadvertebas, eius modi fore hoc peccatum tuum quod tu neque negare posses, -- in tabulas enim legem rettulisti,-- neque cum defensione aliqua confiteri?// [neque...neque = aut...aut] [D.2]

Even if the actual facts, the shamefulness of the wrong you were doing, left you unmoved; if the ruin of that boy, and the tears of his kinsmen, and the risk to Decimus Brutus whose land was involved, and the personal authority of the boy's guardian Marcus Marcellus -- if all this counted for nothing to you: yet did it not even occur to you that this piece of your misconduct was of a kind that you would be able neither to deny (having entered the contract on your books) nor , admitting it, to justify in any sort of way?

Ver. 2.74: "Si dimisisset eo tempore quaestionem, post, illis adhibitis in consilium quos ablegarat, absolutum iri Sopatrum videbat; sin autem hominem miserum atque innocentem ita condemnasset, cum ipse praetor sine consilio, reus autem sine patrono atque advocatis fuisset, iudiciumque C. Sacerdotis rescidisset, invidiam se sustinere tantum non posse arbritrabatur." [conditional] [D.3]

If he were to adjourn the trial now, he saw that when the court met later, with those members present whom he had got rid of, Sopater would be acquitted; if on the other hand he now condemned this unfortunate and guiltless man, having himself presided without a council and having left the accused without advocate or supporters, and reversing thereby the decision of Sacerdos, he felt that he would be unable to face the hatred that such an action would entail.

*Ver.*2.142: Si condemnatus eris, non, opinor, id ages ut ista pecunia in quinquennio consumatur in statuis; sin absolutus eris, quis erit tam amens qui te ex tot tantisque criminibus elapsum post quinquennium statuarum nomine arcessat? [conditional] [D.5]

If you are found guilty, it will not, I imagine, be your object to have this money spent on statues within the next five years; and if you are acquitted, no one will be such a fool, after your escape from all these grave charges, as to arraign you five years later for your behaviour about the statues.

*Ver.*2.144: Nam si per eos statuae fiebant a quibus tibi iste honos habebatur, audio; sin Timarchidi pecunia numerabatur, desine quaeso, simulare te, cum in manifestissimo furto teneare, gloriae studiosum ac monumentorum fuisse. [conditional]

For if the making of the statues was carried out by the persons who paid you that honour, well and good; but if the fact is that the money for them was paid in cash to Timarchides, kindly drop this pretence of a thirst for monumental fame, now that you stand plainly convicted of being a thief.

Ver. 2.150: Si honoris causa statuam dederunt, inimici non sunt; credamus testibus; tum enim honori tuo, nunc religioni suae consulunt. Sin autem metu coacti dederunt, confiteare necesse est te in provincia pecunias statuarum nomine per vim ac metum coegisse. Utrum tibi commodum est elige. [conditional]

If they gave this statue to do you honor, they are not your enemies; let us, then, believe their evidence; they were thinking of your honour then, they are thinking of their consciences now. If on the other hand, they were frightened into giving it, you have to admit that you, as governor, extorted the money, nominally for statues, by violence and intimidation. Choose the alternative that suits you!

Ver. 2.177: Aut hoc contendat numquam esse factum, aut omnia tela excipiat necesse est. Negas esse factum? Placet ista mihi defensio, descendo; aequa enim contentio, aequum certamen proponitur. Producam testis, et producam pluris eodem tempore; quoniam tum cum actum est una fuerunt, nunc quoque una sint; cum interrogabuntur, obligentur non solum iuris iurandi atque existimationis periculo, sed etiam communi inter se conscientia. etc. [aut...aut]

Either he must contend that this never happened, or he must be ready to face every such assault. Do you say that it did not happen? Good, that is the line to take; I am ready for you; here is a fair field for us, and no favour. I will now bring forward my witnesses; and I will bring forward a number of them together; they were with one another when the thing was done, let them be so now. When they are examined, they will be bound to speak truth, not only by the risk of perjury and infamy, but by their partnership in knowledge of the facts. Etc.

*Ver.*2.191: Nam aut exhibeas nobis Verrucium necesse est aut te Verrucium esse fateare. [aut...aut] [B.2]

Either you must show us Verrucius, you know, or you must confess that Verrucius is you.

*Ver.*3.37: His hoc opponitur, 'Deportatum habeas ante Kalendas Sextilis.' Deportabo igitur. 'Nisi pactus eris, non commovebis.' [other] [E.1]

Such men are met with the order, "Deliver your corn before the first of August." Very good: then I will. "No, unless you have come to terms, you shall not move it."

*Ver.*3.84: Per deos immortalis, utrum tibi sumes ad defensionem, tantone minoris te decumas vendidisse ut ad medimna DC HS $\overline{XXX}$ lucri statim sua voluntate civitas adderet, hoc est tritici medimnum II, an, cum magno decumas vendidisses, te expressisse ab invitis Liparensibus hanc pecuniam? [alternate questions]

In God's name, what line of defense do you take here? That you sold those tithes so much too cheap that the place promptly added, of its own accord, a bonus of 30, 000

APPENDIX I: DILEMMA FORMS IN CICERO'S ORATIONS 189

sesterces, the equivalent of 2000 bushels of wheat? Or that you sold those tithes dear, and then wrung this sum of money from the reluctant inhabitants?

*Ver.*3.106: Tantone minoris decumae venierunt quam fuerunt, an, cum satis magno venissent, hic tantus tamen frumenti pecuniaeque numerus ab aratoribus per vim ablatus est? Utrum enim horum dixeris, in eo culpa et crimen haerebit. [alternate questions]
Were those tithes sold for all that amount below their value? Or were they sold dear enough, and all this corn and all this money then torn forcibly from the farmers? Make which reply you will: be it this or that, the charge against you is unanswerable.

Ver. 3.118: Iam id porro utrum libentes an inviti dabant? Libentes? amabant, credo, Apronium. Inviti? qua re nisi vi et malo cogebantur? [alternate questions] [cf. A.4, n.5]
And what is more, did they pay that willingly or reluctantly? Willingly? Well -- of course they were fond of Apronius. Reluctantly? Then what, unless it were brutal violence, made them pay it?

*Ver. 3.135: Satisne vobis praetori improbo circumdati cancelli videntur in sua provincia, immo vero in sella ac tribunali, ut aut de suo capite iudicium fieri patiatur praesens ac sedens, aut confiteatur se omnibus iudiciis convinci necesse esse? [aut...aut] [D.3]
A tolerably close net, you will agree, to be woven round a dishonest governor -- that he should be compelled, in his own province, nay, on his own seat of judgement, either to sit there and allow an issue that might mean his own ruin to be tried in his own presence, or to confess that no court could try him and not find him guilty.

*Ver.*3.169: //utrum factum negabis an tibi hoc licitum esse defendes? Negare qui potes? an ut tanta auctoritate litterarum, tot testibus publicanis convincare? Licuisse vero qui? Si hercule te tuam pecuniam praetorem in provincia faeneratum docerem, tamen effugere non posses; sed publicam, sed ob frumentum decretam, sed a publicanis faenore acceptam, hoc licuisse cuiquam probabis?// [alternate questions] [B.2]
Will you deny the truth, or will you plead that your action was lawful? Deny its truth -- how can you? will you attempt it, only to be refuted by all these convincing documents and the evidence of these tax-farmers? And how can you plead that your action was lawful? Why, good heavens, were I to prove that you, while governor of a province, had been lending out your own money there, even that would be enough to convict you. But it was public money, money voted for corn purchase, money received from the tax-farmers plus the interest already due; and how will you make anyone believe that your lending out that money was lawful?

Ver. 3.182: Nam si potest ista pecunia sine aratorum iniuria detrahi, populus Romanus habeat, in tantis praesertim aerari angustiis; sin autem et populus Romanus voluit, et aequum est ita soli aratoribus, tuus apparitor parva mercede populi conductus de aratorum bonis praedabitur? [conditional] [cf. D.5]

If that amount can be deducted without injustice to the farmers, let the nation have it, especially with the treasury depleted as it now is; if the nation has willed that it should be paid to the farmers, and if it is just that it should be so paid, shall a fellow whom the nation pays a few shillings a week to work in your office go preying upon the farmers' property?

*Ver.*5.135: Quae si dices, tenebere; sin alia dices, ea quae a me dicta sunt non refutabis. [conditional] [B.2]

And if you say this, you will be proved a liar; whereas if you say anything else my charges against you will be unanswerable.

Font. 3: Acceptas populo Romano pecunias omnis isti rettulerunt; //si protinus aliis aeque magnas aut solverunt aut dederunt, ut, quod acceptum populo Romano est, id expensum cuipiam sit, certe nihil potest esse detractum. Sin aliquid domum tulerunt, ex eorum arca, e ra...// [conditional][1]

All those persons entered duly monies that they had received on account of the people of Rome; if they forthwith paid out or advanced to others equally large sums, so that what was received on account of the people of Rome was expended upon some person or other, then it is clear that nothing can have been embezzled. But if some of them took money home with them, from their cash in hand and from their...

Caec. 3(i): Itaque longe alia ratione, recuperatores, ad agendam causam hac actione venio atque initio veneram. Tum enim nostrae causae spes erat posita in defensione mea, nunc in confessione adversarii, tum in nostris, nunc vero in illorum testibus; de quibus ego antea laborabam ne, //si improbi essent, falsi aliquid dicerent, si probi existimarentur, quod dixissent probarent//; [conditional] [cf. E.4, n.23]

And so, gentlemen, my plans for the conduct of my case in these proceedings are very far different from what they were originally; for then the success of our case rested upon my powers of defense, now it rests on the admissions of my adversary: then I was relying upon our witnesses, but now upon theirs. These witnesses of theirs at one time caused me anxiety: //if they were dishonest, they might lie; if they succeeded in passing for honest, what they said might be believed.//

Caec. 3(ii): nunc sum animo aequissimo. //Si enim sunt viri boni, me adiuvant, cum id iurati dicunt quod ego iniuratus insimulo; sin autem minus idonei, me non laedunt, cum eis sive creditur, *creditur* hoc ipsum quod nos arguimus, sive fides non habetur, de adversarii testium fide derogatur.// [conditional] [See above, p. 178, n.23]

Now I am completely happy about them: //if they are good men, they help my case by saying on their oath what I, not on my oath, merely suggest; and if they are not so satisfactory, they do my case no harm: for if the court believes them, it believes the

---

[1] This seems to be a dilemma, but the lacuna makes it impossible to be sure, much less to classify it further.

APPENDIX I: DILEMMA FORMS IN CICERO'S ORATIONS   191

very point we seek to prove; and if it does not credit them, then my opponent's witnesses are discredited.//

Caec. 4: Nam, si negassent vim hominibus armatis esse factam, facile honestissimis testibus in re perspicua tenerentur; sin confessi essent et id quod nullo tempore iure fieri potest tum ab se iure factum esse defenderent, spernarunt, id quod adsecuti sunt, se iniecturos vobis causam deliberandi et iudicandi iustam moram ac religionem. [conditional] [D.3]

For had they denied the employment of force thorugh armed men, they would have been easily and incontrovertibly met by unimpeachable evidence: but should they admit the fact and then put forward the defence that what can never be done lawfully was on that occasion lawfully done by themselves, they hoped -- and their hopes were realized -- that they would give you ground for deliberation and make you feel a legitimate scruple about deciding the case at once.

Caec. 8: Ac si qui mihi hoc iudex recuperatorve dicat: 'potuisti enim leviore actione confligere, potuisti ad tuum ius faciliore et commodiore iudicio pervenire; qua re aut muta actionem aut noli mihi instare ut iudicem tamen,' //is aut timidior videatur quam fortem, aut cupidior quam sapientem iudicem esse aequum est, si aut mihi praescribat quem ad modum meum ius persequar, aut ipse id quod ad se delatum sit non audeat iudicare.// [conditional + aut...aut] [E.2]

and if any judge or assessor were to say to me: "But you might have brought your action by a less stringent process: you might have secured your rights by an easier and more convenient form of trial; so either adopt a different process or do not press me to pronounce judgement," //he would none the less seem either more nervous than a resolute judge ought to be or more presumptuous than a wise one; for either he is lacking in the courage to try the case himself or he is seeking to prescribe the method which I am to employ in pursuing my rights.//

Q. Rosc. 9: utrum cetera nomina in codicem accepti et expensi digesta habes an non? si non, quo modo tabulas conficis? si etiam, quam ob rem, cum cetera nomina in ordinem referebas, hoc nomen triennio amplius, quod erat in primis magnum, in adversariis relinquebas? [conditional and alternate questions] [A.1, B.2]

Have you arranged all the other items of receipts and expenses in the general ledger or not? If you have not, how do you make up your books? if you have, why is it that, when entering all the other items in order, you left this item, which was an extremely large one, for more than three years in your day-book?

Q. Rosc. 16: Pecuniam petis, Fanni, a Roscio. quam? dic audacter et aperte. //utrum <quae> tibi ex societate debeatur, an quae ex liberalitate huius promissa sit et ostentata?// [alternate questions] [A.1, B.1]

You, Fannius, demand money from Roscius. What money? Speak boldly and frankly. //Was it owing to you from the partnership, or money which had been promised and offered to you by my client's generosity?//

Q. Rosc. 25(i): quin tu hoc crimen aut obice ubi licet agere, aut iacere noli ubi non oportet. [aut...aut] [A.1, A.5, B.2]

Then either launch this charge where it is lawful to start an action or do not launch it where it ought not to be brought.

Q. Rosc. 25(ii): <con>dicionis tabulas habet an non? si non habet, quem ad modum pactio est? si habet, cur non nominas? [conditional and alternate questions] [A.1]

Does he have records of the agreement or not? If he does not, how is there a contract? If he does, why do you not cite them? (CPC)

Q. Rosc. 40: Hoc loco, Saturi, quid pares respondere scire cupio; //utrum omnino Fannium <a> Flavio HS CCCIƆƆ non abstulisse an alio nomine et alia de causa abstulisse.// [alternate questions] [A.1, A.2, B.1]

On this point, Saturius, I should like to know what answer you propose to make; //that Fannius never got 100,000 sesterces at all from Flavius or that he got them on some other claim or for some other reason?//

Q. Rosc. 43: utrum dicis Luscio et Manilio, an etiam Cluvio non esse credendum? [alternate questions] [D.5]

Do you say that we ought not to believe Luscius and Manilius or Cluvius?

Q. Rosc. 52: //quaero enim potueritne Roscius ex societate suam partem petere necne? si non potuit, quem ad modum abstulit? si potuit, quem ad modum non sibi exegit?// nam quod sibi petitur, certe alteri non exigitur. [conditional and alternate questions] [A.1, A.2, B.1]

//I ask: could Roscius have been able or not to claim his share in accordance with the partnership? if he could not, how did ne get the money? if he could, how was it that he did not demand and get it for himself,// for what is claimed for oneself is certainly not demanded for another?

Q. Rosc. 55: cum de sua parte Roscius transegit cum Flavio, actionem tibi tuam reliquit an non? si non reliquit, quem ad modum HS CCCIƆƆ ab eo postea exegisti? si reliquit, quid ab hoc petis quod per te persequi et petere debes? [conditional and alternate questions] [A.1, A.2]

When Roscius made an arrangement with Flavius for his own share, did he leave you your right of action or not? If not, how did you afterwards get 100,000 sesterces from Flavius? If he did, why do you claim from Roscius what you ought to claim and try to obtain yourself?

Clu. 69: Quae pecunia simul atque ad eum delata est, homo impurissimus statim coepit in eius modi mente et cogitatione versari, nihil esse suis rationibus utilius quam Oppianicum condemnari; //illo absoluto pecuniam illam aut iudicibus dispertiendam aut ipsi esse reddendam//; damnato repetiturum esse neminem. [aut...aut] [cf. D.3]

As soon as the money was brought to him, the foul fellow began to turn things over in his mind and say to himself: "Nothing will suit my book better than the conviction of Oppianicus: //if he is acquitted, I shall either have to distribute the money among the judges, or pay it to him;// but if he is convicted there will be no one to ask for the money back."

APPENDIX I: DILEMMA FORMS IN CICERO'S ORATIONS

Clu. 114: Aut hoc iudicium reprehendas tu cuius accusatio rebus iudicatis nitebatur necesse est aut, si hoc verum esse concedis, Oppianicum gratiis condemnatum esse fateare.   [conditional + aut...aut]   [B.2, D.4 n.19]

You, then, who rested the case for the prosecution on judicial decisions, are bound either to find fault with their decsion in this case or, if you will allow that it was a right one, to admit that the conviction of Oppianicus was not due to bribery.

Clu. 135: Sed tu, Atti, consideres censeo diligenter utrum censorium iudicium grave velis esse an Egnati. Si Egnati, leve est quod censores de ceteris subscripserunt; ipsum enim Cn. Egnatium quem tu gravem esse vis ex senatu eiecerunt; sin autem censorium, hunc Egnatium quem pater censoria subscriptione exheredavit censores in senatu, cum patrem eicerent, retinuerunt.   [conditional and alternate questions]   [D.4 n.19; cf. B.2]

But as for you, Attius, I advise you to consider carefully whether you wish the judgement of the censors or that of Egnatius to carry weight. If that of Egnatius, then no weight can be attached to the censors' endorsements in other cases; for this very Gn. Egnatius, whose judgement you wish to carry weight, the censors expelled from the senate. But if that of the censors, Egnatius the younger, whose father disinherited him in the style of a censor's endorsement, was retained in the senate by the very censors who expelled his father!

Clu. 175: Mortis ratio, iudices, eius modi est ut aut nihil habeat suspicionis aut, si quid habet, id intra parietes in domestico scelere versetur.   [conditional + aut...aut]

The circumstances of his death, gentlemen, are such as to admit of no suspicion; or, if any be admissible, to confine it to the four walls of his house, and to incriminate his own people.

Agr. 1.11: Hic quaero, si Hiempsali satis est cautum foedere et Recentoricus ager privatus est, quid attinuerit excipi; sin et foedus illud habet aliquam dubitationem et ager Recentoricus dicitur non numquam esse publicus, quem putet existimaturum duas causas in orbe terrarum repertas quibus gratis parceret.   [conditional]   [D.1]

Here I ask, if Hiempsal is sufficiently safeguarded by the treaty and the Recentoric territory is private property, what was the use of the exeption being made? But if there is any uncertainty in the treaty, and the Recentoric land is sometimes said to be public property, who does he suppose will imagine that only two things have been found in the whole world such that he spared them for nothing?

*Agr.*2.43: //Hac tanta de re P. Rullus cum ceteris xviris conlegis suis iudicabit, et utrum iudicabit? Nam utrumque ita magnum est ut nullo modo neque concedendum neque ferendum sit. Volet esse popularis; populo Romano adiudicabit. Ergo idem ex sua lege vendet Alexandream, vendet Aegyptum, urbis copiosissimae pulcherrimorumque agrorum iudex, arbiter, dominus, rex denique opulentissimi regni reperietur. Non sumet sibi tantum, non appetet; iudicabit Alexandream regis esse, a populo Romano abiudicabit.// [other] [D.5]

Shall this important affair be decided by Rullus with his colleagues the decemvirs, and which way will he decide? For each alternative is of such importance that you must by no means give way to him nor put up with his decision. If Rullus desires to be a friend of the people, he will award the kingdom to the Roman people. And so too, by virtue of this law, he will sell Alexandria, he will sell Egypt, and we shall discover that he is the judge, the arbiter, the owner of a most wealthy city and of the most beautiful country -- in fine, the king of a most flourishing kingdom. O but he will not take so much for himself, he will not be greedy: he will decide that Alexandria is the king's, he will decide that it is not the Roman people's.

Agr. 2.46: At quanta calamitas populi, si dixerit, quantus ipsi quaestus, si negarit! [conditional] [D.5]

What a calamity for the people if he says so! What a great gain for him if he does not say so!

Agr. 2.57: Ac, si est privatus ager Recentoricus, quid eum excipis? sin autem publicus, quae est ista aequitas ceteros, etiam si privati sint, permittere ut publici iudicentur, hunc excipere nominatim qui publicum se esse fateatur? [conditional] [cf. D.4 n.19]

And if the Recentoric district is private, why do you except it? but if it is public, what kind of equity is it to allow other lands, even if private, to be adjudged public, and to except particularly by name one which is acknowledged to be public property?

Agr. 2.61: nam si est aequum praedam ac manubias suas imperatores non in monumenta deorum immortalium neque in urbis ornamenta conferre, sed ad xviros tamquam ad dominos reportare, nihil sibi appetit praecipui Pompeius, nihil; volt se in communi atque in eodem quo ceteri iure versari. Sin est iniquum, Quirites, si turpe, si intolerandum hos xviros portitores omnibus omnium pecuniis constitui, qui non modo reges atque exterarum nationum homines sed etiam imperatores vestros excutiant, non mihi videntur honoris causa excipere Pompeium, sed metuere ne ille eandem contumeliam quam ceteri ferre non possit. [conditional] [D.5]

For if it is just that our generals should not employ their booty and spoils on monuments to the immortal gods nor for the embellishment of Rome, but should have to carry them away to the decemvirs as it were to their masters, then Pompeius wants nothing for himself in particular, nothing; he only wishes to live under the common law, under the same law as the rest. But if it is unjust, O Romans, if it is disgraceful, if it is intolerable that these decemvirs should be appointed tollmen over all the moneys of everybody, men to examine not only kings and men of foreign nations, but even your generals, it seems to me that Pompeius is not excepted to do him honour, but that his enemies are afraid that he may not be able to submit to the same insult as the rest.

APPENDIX I: DILEMMA FORMS IN CICERO'S ORATIONS

Cat.1.18: Quam ob rem discede atque hunc mihi timorem eripe; //si est verus, ne opprimar, sin falsus, ut tandem aliquando timere desinam.'// [conditional] [D.5]
Depart then, and free me from this dread; //if it is well founded, that I may not be destroyed: if groundless, that I may at long last cease to feel afraid.//

Mur. 57: Cuius competitores si nihil deliquerunt, dignitati eorum concessit, cum petere destitit; sin autem eorum aliquis largitus est, expetendus amicus est qui alienam potius iniuriam quam suam persequatur. . [conditional] [cf. B.2]
If his fellow candidates observed the law, he conceded their superior claims when he ceased to run, but if one of them was guilty of bribery, then he really is a friend to be cultivated since his is prosecuting an injury done to someone else and not that done to himself.

Sul. 10: Hoc totum eius modi est, iudices, ut, si ego sum inconstans ac levis, nec testimonio fidem tribui convenerit nec defensioni auctoritatem; sin est in me ratio rei publicae, religio privati offici, studium retinendae voluntatis bonorum, nihil minus accusator debet dicere quam a me defendi Sullam, testimonio laesum esse Autronium. [conditional] [A.2, B.2]
The long and the short of it, gentlemen, is that if I am inconsistent and unstable, no credence should have been given to my evidence then nor weight to my defence now. But if I do show regard for the public interest, respect for personal obligation and a desire to retain the good-will of loyal men, the last thing that the prosecutor should say is that I gave damaging evidence against Autronius but am defending Sulla.

Sul. 21: Hic tibi ego de testimoniis meis hoc respondebo, si falsum dixerim, te in eosdem dixisse; sin verum, non esse hoc regnare, cum verum iuratus dicas, probare. [conditional] [B.1, D.4]
My reply to you concerning the evidence I gave is this: if I lied, you too gave evidence against those defendants; but if I spoke the truth, it is not tyranny, when one tells the truth on oath, to make good one's case.

Sul. 25(i): Aut igitur doceat Picentis solos non esse peregrinos aut gaudeat suo generi me meum non anteponere. [aut...aut] [B.2, D.4]
Let him then either show that only the people of Picenum are not foreigners or be glad that I do not rate my family more highly than his.

*Sul. 25(ii): Si hoc putas esse regium, regem me esse confiteor; sin te potentia mea, si dominatio, si denique aliquod dictum adrogans aut superbum movet, quin tu id potius profers quam verbi invidiam contumeliamque maledicti. [conditional] [B.2; cf. E.5]
If you think that this is tyrannical, then I admit that I am a tyrant; but if my despotic power, my tyranny, if some overbearing or arrogant utterance angers you, why do you not produce this rather than a prejudicial phrase and abusive slander?

Sul. 39: Etenim cum se negat scire Cassius, utrum sublevat Sullam an satis probat se nescire? [alternate questions] [A.1, A.2]
When Cassius says that he does not know, is he trying to clear Sulla or does he convince us that he really does not know?

Sul. 81: Si postea cognorat ipse aliquid quod in consulatu ignorasset, ignoscendum est eis qui postea nihil audierunt; sin illa res prima valuit, num inveterata quam recens debuit esse gravior? [conditional] [A.3]

If he had subsequently discovered something which he did not know when he was consul, then we must excuse those who heard nothing later. But if that first piece of information had any substance, ought it to have carried more weight when it was old than when it was fresh?

*Flac. 39: Si veras protulissent, criminis nihil erat, si falsas, erat poena. [conditional] [D.3]

If they had produced the genuine records, there was nothing with which to accuse Flaccus; if the forged, there was the penalty awaiting them.

Flac. 53: Qua re, si hunc habent auctorem Tralliani doloris sui, si hunc custodem litterarum, si hunc testem iniuriae, si hunc actorem querelarum, remittant spiritus, comprimant animos suos, sedent adrogantiam, fateantur in Maeandri persona esse expressam speciem civitatis. Sin istum semper illi ipsi domi proterendum et conculcandum putaverunt, desinant putare auctoritatem esse in eo testimonio cuius auctor inventus est nemo. [conditional] [B.2]

If, then, the people of Tralles have this man to vouch for their afflictions, to guard their records, to bear witness to their wrongs, to voice their complaints, let them calm their airs, curb their pride and check their arrogance, let them admit that in the character of Maeandrius is reproduced the nature of his city. If, however, they have themselves always thought that he should be trampled upon and trodden underfoot at home, let them stop thinking that there is any value in evidence which no one has been found to authenticate.

Flac. 58: Vobis autem est confitendum, si consiliis principum vestrae civitates reguntur, non multitudinis temeritate, sed optimatium consilio bellum ab istis civitatibus cum populo Romano esse susceptum; sin ille tum motus est temeritate imperitorum excitatus, patimini me delicta volgi a publica causa separare. [conditional] [B.2; cf. D.5]

And you must admit, if your cities are ruled by the councils of their leading men, that those cities declared war upon the Roman people not as a result of the impetuosity of the mob, but upon the decision of their best men. If, on the other hand, that rising was provoked by the rashness of ignorance, then allow me to distinguish between the crimes of the mob and the position of the city.

Flac. 59: At enim istam pecuniam huic capere non licuit.//Utrum voltis patri Flacco licuisse necne? Si licuit *uti*, sicuti certe licuit, ad eius honores conlata, ex quibus nihil ipse capiebat, patris pecuniam recte abstulit filius; si non licuit, tamen illo mortuo non modo filius sed quivis heres rectissime potuit auferre.// [conditional and alternate questions] [B.1]

But Flaccus had no right to take the money. //Do you maintain that Flaccus' father had a right or not? If he had a right, as was certainly the case, to use money collected for the celebrations in his honour from which he got no personal benefit, then the son was justified in taking his father's money. If, however, he did not have the right, after the father's death not only the son but any heir could take it quite legitimately.//

APPENDIX I: DILEMMA FORMS IN CICERO'S ORATIONS 197

Flac. 84: sed quaero, usu an coemptione? Usu non potuit; nihil enim est de tutela legitima nisi omnium tutorum auctoritate deminui. Coemptione? Omnibus ergo auctoribus; in quibus certe Flaccum fuisse non dices. [alternate questions]

...but I ask whether the marriage was by cohabitation or by sale? If it was a common-law marriage, that was not possible because no alienation in the status of a legal ward can be made without the consent of the guardians. If it was a marriage by sale? Then it was with the approval of all the guardians; but surely you are not going to say that Flaccus was one of them.

Dom. 22(i): //Quas aut numquam tibi ille (sc. Caesar) litteras misit, aut, si misit, in contione recitari noluit.// At, sive ille misit sive tu finxisti, certe consilium tuum de Catonis honore illarum litterarum recitatione patefactum est. [conditional + aut...aut] [cf. D.5]

//Either Caesar never sent you this letter, or if he did send it, he did not wish it to be recited at a mass meeting.// But whether he sent it or whether it is a mere fiction of your own, the fact remains that your recitation of it was a revelation of your motive in so distinguishing Cato.

Dom. 22(ii): Quas aut numquam tibi ille litteras misit, aut, si misit, in contione recitari noluit. // At, sive ille misit sive tu finxisti, certe consilium tuum de Catonis honore illarum litterarum recitatione patefactum est.// [sive...sive] [cf. D.2, n.16]

Either Caesar never sent you this letter, or if he did send it, he did not wish it to be recited at a mass meeting. //But whether he sent it or whether it is a mere fiction of your own, the fact remains that your recitation of it was a revelation of your motive in so distinguishing Cato.//

Dom. 91: mihi aut te interfecto cum consulibus, aut te vivo et tecum et cum illis armis decertandum fuit. [aut...aut] [E.4]

...but in my case I had the prospect of an armed struggle with the consuls had you been slain, or, had you survived, with you and them combined.

Dom. 124: Quod si tum nihil est actum, quid in meis bonis agi potuit? sin est ratum, cur ille gurges, helluatus tecum simul rei publicae sanguine, ad caelum tamen exstruit villam in Tusculano visceribus aerari, mihi meas ruinas, quarum ego similem totam urbem esse passus non sum, aspicere licuit? [conditional] [cf. D.4]

If none of your actions was valid in that case, what validity could there have been in your actions with regard to *my* property? And if your actions in his case still hold good, why is it that, in spite of all, that prodigal, having glutted his appetite along with you upon the blood of the republic, rears a villa in Tusculum up to the skies out of the bowels of the treasury, while I, who refused to allow the entire city to share a like fate, have not been permittted even to look upon the ruins of mine?

198   FORM AS ARGUMENT

Dom. 125(i): Omitto Gabinium; quid? exemplo tuo bona tua nonne L. Ninnius, vir omnium fortissimus atque optimus, consecravit? //Quod si, quia ad te pertinet, ratum esse negas oportere, ea iura constituisti in praeclaro tribunatu tuo quibus in te conversis recusares, alios everteres; sin ista consecratio legitima est, quid est quod profanum in tuis bonis esse possit?// An consecratio nullum habet ius, dedicatio est religiosa? Quid ergo illa tua tum obtestatio tibicinis, quid foculus, quid preces, quid *verba* prisca valuerunt? ementiri, fallere, abuti deorum immortalium numine ad hominum timorem quid voluisti? Nam si est illud ratum--mitto Gabinium--tua domus certe et quicquid habes aliud Cereri est consecratum: sin ille ludus fuit, quid te impurius, qui religiones omnis pollueris aut ementiundo aut stuprando? [conditional] [D.4]

I leave Gabinius and pass to another question. Did not Lucius Ninnius, the bravest and best of men, take his cue from you when he consecrated your property? //If you assert that his proceedings, so nearly affecting you as they do, should be held to be ineffective, you created in your memorable tribunate a precedent, to which you take exception when it is applied against you, but which you apply against others to their undoing. If your consecration possesses legal validity, what of your own property can be held to be unconsecrated?// Or are we to consider that, while a consecration has no binding force, a dedication is inviolably sacred? What then was the efficacy of your employment of a flute-player as witness on that occasion, of your brazier, of your prayers, and your time-honoured formula? Why did you desire to lie, to deceive, and to misapply the majesty of the immortal gods to the intimidation of men? If that act holds good, -- I waive your proceedings against Gabinius, -- there can be no doubt that your house and anything else that you possess has been devoted to Ceres; but if it as a mere farce, what can be more loathsome than your defilement of all sanctities either by falsehood or by immorality?

Dom. 125(ii): Omitto Gabinium; quid? exemplo tuo bona tua nonne L. Ninnius, vir omnium fortissimus atque optimus, consecravit? Quod si, quia ad te pertinet, ratum esse negas oportere, ea iura constituisti in praeclaro tribunatu tuo quibus in te conversis recusares, alios everteres; sin ista consecratio legitima est, quid est quod profanum in tuis bonis esse possit? An consecratio nullum habet ius, dedicatio est religiosa? Quid ergo illa tua tum obtestatio tibicinis, quid foculus, quid preces, quid *verba* prisca valuerunt? ementiri, fallere, abuti deorum immortalium numine ad hominum timorem quidvoluisti? //Nam si est illud ratum--mitto Gabinium--tua domus certe et quicquid habes aliud Cereri est consecratum: sin ille ludus fuit,quid te impurius, qui religiones omnis pollueris aut ementiundo aut stuprando?// [conditional] [D.4]

I leave Gabinius and pass to another question. Did not Lucius Ninnius, the bravest and best of men, take his cue from you when he consecrated your property? If you assert that his proceedings, so nearly affecting you as they do, should be held to be ineffective, you created in your memorable tribunate a precedent, to which you take exception when it is applied against you, but which you apply against others to their undoing. If your consecration possesses legal validity, what of your own property can be held to be unconsecrated? Or are we to consider that, while a consecration has no binding force, a dedication is inviolably sacred? What then was the efficacy of your employment of a flute-player as witness on that occasion, of your brazier, of your prayers, and your time-honoured formula? Why did you desire to lie, to deceive, and to misapply the majesty of the immortal gods to the intimidation of men? //If that act holds good, -- I waive your proceedings against Gabinius, -- there can be no doubt that

APPENDIX I: DILEMMA FORMS IN CICERO'S ORATIONS 199

your house and anything else that you possess has been devoted to Ceres; but if it as a mere farce, what can be more loathsome than your defilement of all sanctities either by falsehood or by immorality?//

Dom. 134: qui aut nihil dixit nec fecit omnino, poenamque hanc maternae temeritatis tulit ut mutam in delicto personam nomenque praeberet, aut, si dixit aliquid verbis haesitantibus postemque tremebunda manu tetigit, certe nihil rite, nihil caste, nihil more institutoque perfecit. [conditional + aut...aut] [cf. D.2]

No, but either he said and did nothing whatsoever, and suffered retribution for his mother's indiscretion by playing a dumb part and merely lending his name to the crime that was being committed, or, supposing that he did stammer out a few words, and did lay a quaking hand upon the door-post, we may be quite sure that nothing was done properly or correctly or according to the prescribed tradition.

Har. Resp. 5: qui si sensit quo se scelere devinxerit, non dubito quin sit miserrimus; sin autem id non videt, periculum est ne se stuporis excusatione defendat. [conditional] [D.2]

If he has realized the nature of the sin that has enthralled him, I cannot doubt that he is the most wretched of men; but if he is blind to this, he may attempt to defend himself by pleading congenital dulness of wit.

Sest. 32: Sive illa vestis mutatio ad luctum ipsorum sive ad deprecandum valebat, quis umquam tam crudelis fuit qui prohiberet quemquam aut sibi maerere aut ceteris supplicare? [sive...sive] [D.2]

Whether that change of dress was intended to show their own grief, or as a sign of entreaty, who ever was so cruel as to prevent anyone either from mourning for himself or from intercession on behalf of others.

**Sest.* 37: Cessit (sc. Metellus Numidicus), //ne aut victus a fortibus viris cum dedecore caderet, aut victor multis et fortibus viris rem publicam orbaret.// [aut...aut] [E.4]

He (sc. Metellus Numidicus) yielded, either for fear that if defeated by brave men he might fall with disgrace, or, if victorious, he might bereave the State of many brave citizens.

**Sest.* 44: Ego vero, vel si pereundum fuisset ac non accipienda plaga mihi sanabilis, illi mortifera qui imposuisset, semel perire tamen, iudices, maluissem quam bis vincere; erat enim illa altera eius modi contentio ut neque victi neque victores rem publicam tenere possemus. [neque...neque = aut...aut] [E.4]

But even if I had been doomed to perish, instead of receivng a wound which for me was curable but fatal to the man who had inflcited it, I would still have preferred, gentlemen, to perish once rather than to conquer twice. For the nature of that second struggle was such that, whether vanquished or victors, we should not have been able to preserve the constitution.

Vat. 10: //Cum mihi hoc responderis, aut ita impudenter ut manus a te homines vix abstinere possint, aut ita dolenter ut aliquando ista quae sunt inflata rumpantur//, tum memoriter respondeto ad ea quae de te ipso rogaro. [alternate questions + aut...aut]

//When you have answered this, either so impudently that people can hardly keep their hands off you, or so painfully that all these swellings of yours at last burst,// then answer, sir, with careful recollection, the questions I shall put to you concerning yourself.

Vat. 20 sed quaero, si ad cetera vulnera, quibus rem publicam putasti deleri, hanc quoque mortiferam plagam inflixisses auguratus tui, utrum decreturus fueris, id quod augures omnes usque ab Romulo decreverunt, Iove fulgente cum populi agi nefas esse, an, quia tu semper sic egisses, auspicia fueris augur dissoluturus. [alternate questions] [B.2, D.3]

-- but I ask you, after all those other wounds, by which you thought the State was being destroyed, if you had inflicted this mortal blow also by your augurate, did you propose to decree, as all augurs since Romulus have decreed, that when Juppiter lightens it is sacrilege to transact business with the People, or, because you had always so transacted it, did you propose as augur to make a complete end of the auspices?

Cael. 35: Quae quoniam tu mente nescio qua effrenata atque praecipiti in forum deferri iudiciumque voluisti, aut diluas oportet ac falsa esse doceas aut nihil neque crimini tuo neque testimonio credendum esse fateare. [aut...aut] [A.1, A.2, A.3, C.2, C.5]

And since in some mad and reckless frame of mind you have desired that these matters should be brought into the Forum and into court, you must either disprove them, and show that they are false, or else you must confess that neither your accusation nor your evidence is to be believed.

Cael. 50: Ea si tu non es, sicut ego malo, quid est quod obiciant Caelio? Sin eam te volunt esse, quid est cur non crimen hoc, si tu contemnis,pertimescamus? Qua re nobis da viam rationemque defensionis. Aut enim pudor tuus defendet nihil a M. Caelio petulantius esse factum, aut impudentia et huic et ceteris magnam ad se defendendum facultatem dabit. [conditional + aut...aut] [A.1, A.2, A.3, B.2, C.2, C.5]

If you are not this woman, as I prefer to think, for what have the accusers to reproach Caelius? But if they will have it that you are such a person, why should we be afraid of this accusation, if you despise it? Then it is for you to show us our way and method of defense; for either your sense of propriety will disprove any vicious behaviour by Caelius, or your utter impropriety will afford both him and the rest a fine opportunity for self-defense.

Cael. 52: Quo quidem in crimine primum illud requiro, dixeritne Clodiae quam ob rem aurum sumeret, annon dixerit. Si non dixit, cur dedit? Si dixit, eodem se conscientiae scelere devinxit. [conditional and alternate questions] [A.1, A.2, A.3, C.2, C.5]

And in regard to this charge, I first ask, whether he told Clodia for what purpose he took the gold, or whether he did not. If he did not tell her, why did she hand it over? If he did tell her, she made herself his accomplice in this crime.

Cael. 53(i): Si tam familiaris erat Clodiae quam tu esse vis cum de libidine eius tam multa dicis, dixit profecto quo vellet aurum; si tam familiaris non erat, non dedit. [conditional] [A.1, A.2, A.3, C.2, C.5]
But if he was as intimate with Clodia as you claim that he was, since you harp so much on his profligacy, he would certainly have told her why he wanted the gold; if he was not so intimate, she never gave it.

Cael. 53(ii): Ita si verum tibi Caelius dicit, o immoderata mulier, sciens tu aurum ad facinus dedisti; si non est ausus dicere, non dedisti. [conditional] [A.1, A.2, A.3, C.2, C.5]
Thus, if Caelius told you the truth, you abandoned woman!, you knowingly gave him the gold to commit a crime; if he did not venture to tell you, you did not give it.]

Cael. 53(iii): si per se, qua temeritate!, si per alium, per quem? [conditional] [C.2, C.5; cf. A.4, n.5]]
...if in person, how rash he was; if by proxy, who was it?

Cael. 58: Si enim tam familiaris erat mulieris quam vos voltis, istos quoque servos familiaris dominae esse sciebat. Sin ei tanta consuetudo quanta a vobis inducitur non erat, quae cum servis eius potuit familiaritas esse tanta? [conditional] [A.1. A.4, C.2, C.5]
For if he was so intimate with the woman as you will have it, he knew that those slaves also were on intimate terms with their mistress. But if an association as close as you allege did not exist between the two, how could there have been such close intimacy between him and the slaves?

Cael. 61: Si manebat tanta illa consuetudo Caeli, tanta familiaritas cum Clodia, quid suspicionis esset si apud Caelium mulieris servus visus esset? Sin autem iam suberat simultas, exstincta erat consuetudo, discidium exstiterat, hinc illae lacrimae nimirum et haec causa est omnium horum scelerum atque criminum. [conditional] [A.1, A.2, A.3, C.2, C.5]
If there still existed between Caelius and Clodia such intimacy and such close association, what suspicion could arise if one of the lady's slaves had appeared at Caelius' house? But if some disagreement now lurked between them, if their association had been broken off, if a rupture had taken place, "the cat," assuredly, "is out if the bag," and we have the reason for all these crimes and accusations.

Cael. 62: nam si essent in vestibulo balnearum, non laterent; sin se in intimum conicere vellent, ne satis commode calceati et vestiti id facere possent et fortasse non reciperentur, nisi forte mulier potens quadrantaria illa permutatione familiaris facta erat balneatori. [conditional] [A.1, C.2, C.5, D.1]
For if they were in the forecourt they would not be hidden: but if they wanted to pack themselves away inside, they could not conveniently do so in their shoes and outdoor dress, and perhaps would not be admitted -- unless possibly that lady of influence had bought the favour of the bathman by her usual farthing deal.

Prov. 46(i): Qua re aut vobis statuendum est legem Aeliam manere, legem Fufiam non esse abrogatam, non omnibus fastis legem ferri licere; cum lex feratur, de caelo servari, obnuntiari, intercedi licere; censorium iudicium ac notionem et illud morum severissimum magisterium non esse nefariis legibus de civitate sublatum; si patricius tribunus plebis fuerit, contra leges sacratas, si plebeius, contra auspicia fuisse; aut mihi concedant homines oportet in rebus bonis non exquirere ea iura quae ipsi in perditis non exquirant, praesertim cum ab illis aliquotiens condicio C. Caesari lata sit ut easdem res alio modo ferret, qua condicione auspicia requirebant, leges comprobabant, in Clodio auspiciorum ratio sit eadem, leges omnes sint eversae ac perditae civitatis. [aut...aut] [E.2]

You must, therefore, either decide that the Aelian Law holds good and that the Fufian Law has not been repealed; that a law cannot be passed on all days whereon public business is lawful; that when a law is being proposed, the sky can still be watched, that announcement of evil omens and veto by intervention are still permissible; that the censors' verdict and power of investigation and their most strict supervision of morals have not been removed from the State by pernicious laws; that if Clodius was a patrician when he held the tribunate of the commons, the *leges sacratae* were defied, while, if he was a plebeian, the auspices were disregarded. Or, if not, then my opponents must allow me, when measures are good, not to examine too closely those points of law which they themselves do not examine when measures are bad, especially since they more than once proposed to Gaius Caesar that he should put forward his same proposals in another way, thus showing that they approved his measures but insisted on the observance of the auspices; and since all Clodius' laws, implying the overthrow and ruin of the State, stand in the same relation (as Caesar's) to the auspices.

Prov. 46(ii) [nested within 46(i)]: si patricius tribunus plebis fuerit, contra leges sacratas, si plebeius, contra auspicia fuisse; [conditional] [E.2]
that if Clodius was a patrician when he held the tribunate of the commons, the *leges sacratae* were defied, while, if he was a plebeian, the auspices were disregarded.

Balb. 13-14: (13) utrum enim inscientem vultis contra foedera fecisse an scientem? Si scientem, -- O nomen nostri imperi! O populi Romani excellens dignitas! O Cn. Pompei sic late longeque diffusa laus ut eius gloriae domicilium communis imperi finibus terminetur! O nationes, urbes, populi,reges, tetrarchae, tyranni, -- testes Cn. Pompei non solum virtutis in bello sed etiam religionis in pace! Vos denique, mutae regiones, imploro, et sola terrarum ultimarum; vos, maria, portus, insulae, litora! Quae est enim ora, quae sedes, qui locus in quo non exstent huius fortitudinis tum vero humanitatis, cum animi tum consili impressa vestigia? Hunc quisquam, incredibili quadam atque inaudita gravitate virtute constantia praeditum, foedera scientem neglexisse violasse rupisse dicere audebit? (14) Gratificatur mihi gestu accusator: inscientem Cn. Pompeium fecisse significat, -- quasi vero levius sit, cum in tanta re publica versere et maximis negotiis praesis, facere aliquid quod scias non licere, quam omnino non scire quid liceat! Etenim utrum *qui in* Hispania bellum acerrimum et maximum gesserat quo iure Gaditana civitas esse nesciebat, an, cum ius illius populi nosset, interpretationem foederis non tenebat? Id igitur quisquam Cn. Pompeium ignorasse dicere audebit quod mediocres homines, quod nullo usu, nullo studio praediti militari,quod librarioli denique scire *se* profiteantur? [conditional and alternate questions] [D.5]

For do you want him to have acted contrary to the treaties knowingly or unknowingly? If knowingly -- O renown of our empire! O exalted prestige of the Roman People! O praiseworthy reputation of Cn. Pompeius, which has been spread so far and wide that the proper home of his glory is bounded only by the borders of our empire! O tribes, cities, peoples, kings, tetrarchs, despots -- witnesses not only of Cn. Pompeius' courage in war but also of his scrupulousness in peace! You finally, silent regions, do I beseech, and ground of the most distant lands; you, seas, ports, islands, shores! For what shore is there, what haven, what place in which there are not present the imprinted marks not only of his courage but also of his culture, not only of his spirit but also of his judgment? Will anyone dare to say that this man, endowed with a certain incredible and unprecedented seriousness, courage, constancy, knowingly neglected, violated, sundered treaties? The prosecutor gratifies me with a gesture: he indicates that Cn. Pompeius did it unknowingly -- as if indeed this is less serious, when one is involved in the highest affairs of state and in the most important business, to do something which one knows is not allowed, rather than not to know at all what is allowed! He who had waged a very fierce and great war in Spain did not know the legal status of the city of Gades, or, although he knew the status of that people, did not grasp the interpretation of the treaty? Will someone then dare to say that Cn. Pompeius did not know that which common people, that which people endowed with no experience and no inclination in the military sphere, that which finally even secretaries declare that they know? (CPC)

Pis. 39: Nihil enim mea iam refert, utrum tu conscientia oppressus scelerum tuorum nihil umquam ausus sis scribere ad eum ordinem quem despexeras, quem adflixeras, quem deleveras, an amici tui tabellas abdiderunt idemque silentio suo temeritatem atque audaciam tuam condemnarint; atque haud scio an malim te videri nullo pudore fuisse in letteris mittendis, at amicos tuos plus habuisse et pudoris et consili, quam aut te videri pudentiorem fuisse quam soles, aut tuum factum non esse condemnatum iudicio amicorum. [alternate questions + aut...aut] [D.2]

For it makes no difference to my present argument whether it was that you could not bring yourself to write to the body which you despised, which you had outraged, and which you had nullified, or whether your friends concealed your dispatches and by their silence passed their condemnation upon your headstrong effrontery; and indeed I almost think I should prefer it to be supposed that you were sufficiently lost to shame to send dispatches, while your friends showed greater tact as well as a sense of shame, than that it should appear either that you acted under a sense of shame unusual with you, or that your conduct failed to be visited with the disapprobation of your friends.

Planc. 4: //Quae vero ita sunt agitata ab illis ut aut merita Cn. Planci erga me minora esse dicerent quam a me ipso praedicerentur, aut, si essent summa, negarent ea tamen ita magni ut putarem ponderis apud vos esse debere//, haec mihi sunt tractanda, iudices, et modice, ne quid ipse offendam, et tum denique cum respondero criminibus, ne non tam innocentia reus sua quam recordatione meorum temporum defensus esse videatur. [conditional + aut...aut] [E.4, E.5]

//But these matters have been so vigorously argued by the other side that they have either said that the services of Cn. Plancius towards me were less than I myself expected them to be, or they have said that, even if those services were the greatest, nevertheless they were not so great that I might think that they ought to carry some weight with you.// So I must treat these matters, gentlemen of the jury, both moderately, lest I myself somehow offend, and only at the point when I have answered the charges, lest the accused seem to have been defended not so much by his own innocence as by the recollection of my crisis. (CPC)

Planc. 6: Ita, si cedo illius ornamentis, quae multa et magna sunt, non solum huius dignitatis iactura facienda est sed etiam largitionis recipienda suspicio est; sin hunc illi antepono, contumeliosa habenda est oratio, et dicendum est id quod ille me flagitat, Laterensem a Plancio dignitate esse superatum. Ita aut amicissimi hominis existimatio offendenda est, si illam accusationis condicionem sequar, aut optime de me meriti salus deserenda. [conditional + aut...aut] [C.4, E.5]

Consequently, if I yield the palm to my opponent's endowments (and they are beyond question many and great), I must not merely jettison my client's honour, but I must lay myself open to the suspicion of corrupt collusion; if, on the other hand, I put the claims of my client before those of my friend, my speech must be devoted to vituperation, and I must state, since he importunes me for an answer, that the merits of Laterensis are surpassed by those of Plancius. So I am faced with the alternative of either damaging the reputation of a dear friend, if I pursue the line to which his speech has prompted me, or of betraying the cause of one to whom I am under a deep obligation.

Planc. 35: Nam quod primus scivit legem de publicanis tum cum vir amplissimus consul id illi ordini per populum dedit quod per senatum, si licuisset, dedisset, //si in eo crimen est quia suffragium tulit, quis non tulit publicanus? si quia primus scivit, utrum id sortis esse vis, an eius qui illam legem ferebat? Si sortis, nullum crimen est in casu; si consulis, statuis etiam hunc a summo viro principem esse ordinis iudicatum//. [conditional and alternate questions] [A.5, B.2, D.1]

As regards the fact that he was the first to vote for the law that dealt with the taxfarmers, on an occasion when a consul of supreme distinction accorded to that body through the medium of the popular assembly a privilege which he would have accorded them through the medium of the senate had he been permitted to do so, //if you say that his giving his vote is a chargeable offense, who was there among the tax-farmers who did not give his vote? If the offense lies in the fact that he was the first to vote, do you impute this fact to chance, or to the proposer of the law? If you impute it to chance, then you have nothing to charge *him* with; if to the consul, then you admit that our highest accounted Plancius to be the leading man of his order.//

APPENDIX I: DILEMMA FORMS IN CICERO'S ORATIONS

Planc. 44: Etenim quis te tum audiret illorum (sc. senatorum), aut quid diceres? //Sequestremne Plancium? Respuerent aures, nemo agnosceret, repudiarent. An gratiosum? Illi libenter audirent, nos non timide confiteremur.// [alternate questions] [A.1, A.2, A.3]

For then who of the those men (sc. senators) would listen to you, or what would you say? //That Plancius was a bribery agent? Their ears would shun this. No one would acknowledge it. They would reject it. Or that he was popular? They would gladly hear this. We would admit it without hesitation.// (CPC)

Planc. 46: Ego Plancium, Laterensis, et ipsum gratiosum esse dico et habuisse in petitione multos cupidos sui gratiosos, //quos tu si sodalis vocas, officiosam amicitiam nomine inquinas criminoso; sin, quia gratiosi sint, accusandos putas, noli mirari te id quod tua dignitas postularit repudiandis gratiosorum amicitiis non esse adsecutum.// [conditional] [A.1, A.2, A.3, D.5]

I tell you, Laterensis, that not only is Plancius himself popular, but that the host of ardent supporters who backed his candidature were also popular. //If you apply to these the name of "cronies," you are sullying disinterested friendship with a name that is a stain; but if you think that their popularity renders them amenable to prosecution, cease to wonder that by your refusal to cultivate the friendship of popular persons you should have failed to win that distinction which your merits demanded as their due.//

Planc. 54: nam quod questus es pluris te testis habere de Voltinia quam quot in ea tribu puncta tuleris, indicas aut eos testis te producere qui, quia nummos acciperent, te praeterierint, aut te ne gratuita quidem eorum suffragia tulisse. [aut...aut] [A.4]

I say this, because by complaining that you have more witnesses from the Voltinian tribe than the number of votes you got in that tribe, you show, either that those whom you are producing as witnesses are men who were bribed to withhold their vote from you, or even that you made it worth their while to vote for you.

Planc. 79: Distineor tamen et divellor dolore et in causa dispari offendi te a me doleo; sed me dius fidius multo citius meam salutem pro te abiecero quam Cn. Planci salutem tradidero contentioni tuae. [other] [C.4, E.5]

But I am torn by a painful dilemma, and in such a disparity of interests it goes to my heart to offer you an affront; but, upon my honour, I will far more readily sacrifice my existence as a citizen in your behalf, than surrender that of Plancius to your claims.

Planc. 83: Deridebor, si mentionem tensarum fecero, cum tu id praedixeris; sine tensis autem quid potero dicere? [conditional] [E.3]

Now that you have predicted my use of the sacred cars, I shall have but to breathe a word of them to arouse a smile; and if I cannot mention the sacred cars, how shall I be able to make a speech at all?

Planc. 84: 'Rhodi enim,' inquit, 'ego non fui' -- me volt fuisse --'sed fui,' inquit -- putabam in Vaccaeis dicturum-- 'bis in Bithynia.' //Si locus habet reprehensionis ansam aliquam, nescio cur severiorem Nicaeam putes quam Rhodum; si specatanda causa est, et tu in Bithynia summa cum dignitate fuisti et ego Rhodi non minore.// [conditional]

"For I," he says, "never went to Rhodes," implying that I did. "But," he adds, "I have been" -- I thought he was going to say "among the Vaccaei" -- "twice in Bithynia." //If localities give any handle for censure, I cannot understand why you should think that Nicaea is a place of stricter morals than Rhodes; if we are to consider our respective motives, the business that took me to Rhodes was just as highly respectable as the business that took you to Bithynia.

**Planc.* 88: Nihil dico amplius nisi illud: //victoriae nostrae gravis adversarios paratos, interitus nullos esse ultores videbam.// [other] [C.4, E.4]

I will say but one thing more on this matter: //I realized that, if we won, formidable adversaries would be set in array against us; but that, if we fell, there would be none to avenge us.//

**Planc.* 89(i): Hisce ego auxiliis salutis meae si idcirco defui quia nolui dimicare, fatebor id quod vis, non mihi auxilium, sed me auxilio defuisse; sin autem, quo maiora studia in me bonorum fuerunt, hoc eis magis consulendum et parcendum putavi, tu id in me reprehendis quod Q. Metello laudi datum est hodieque et semper erit maximae gloriae? [conditional] [C.4; cf. E.5]]

If I say that my motive in refusing to avail myself of the help of those who were ready to strike for my safety was a reluctance to fight, I shall make the confession you desire, that it was not my helpers who failed me, but I my helpers. But if I say that the more earnest good patriots showed themselves in my cause, the more careful of their interests and sparing of their efforts I thought it my duty to be, can you impute blame to me for that which in the case of Quintus Metellus has been counted to his credit, and today is, and ever will be, the fairest jewel in his reputation?

**Planc.* 89(ii): ego tantis periculis propositis cum, //si victus essem, interitus rei publicae, si vicissem, infinita dimicatio pararetur,// committerem ut idem perditor rei publicae nominarer qui servator fuissem? [conditional] [C.4, E.4]

...and in face of such grave peril, //and the prospect of the downfall of the state should I fall, and an endless series of struggles should I prevail,// was I, who had once been the saviour of the republic, now to gain for myself the name of its destroyer?

Lig. 23: 'Recepti in provinciam non sumus.' Quid, si essetis? //Caesarine eam tradituri fuistis an contra Caesarem retenturi? Vide quid licentiae, Caesar, nobis tua liberalitas det vel potius audaciae. Si responderit Tubero, Africam, quo senatus eum sorsque miserat, tibi patrem suum traditurum fuisse, non dubitabo apud ipsum te cuius id eum facere interfuit gravissimis verbis eius consilium reprehendere. Non enim, si tibi ea res grata fuisset, esset etiam approbata. (24) Sed iam hoc totum omitto, non ultra offendam tuas patientissimas auris quam ne Tubero quod numquam cogitavit facturus fuisse videatur.// [conditional and alternate questions] [D.5]

"We were refused admission into the province." And what if you had been admitted? Did you intend to hand it over to Caesar or to retain it against Caesar? Mark, Caesar,

APPENDIX I: DILEMMA FORMS IN CICERO'S ORATIONS 207

how great a measure of free speech, or rather of effrontery, your generosity accords us. If Tubero replies that Africa, whither the Senate and the lot had sent him, would have been handed over by his father to you, I shall have no hesitation, even in your presence, to whose interest it was the he should do so, to censure such a policy in the severest language. For welcome though it might have been, it would not have been approved by you. But I now dismiss the whole topic, not so much to avoid offending your long-suffering ears as that it may not appear that Tubero would ever have done what it never entered his head to do.

Lig. 29: Nunc quaero utrum vestras iniurias an rei publicae persequamini. Si rei publicae, quid de vestra in illa causa perseverantia respondebitis? si vestras, videte ne erretis qui Caesarem vestris inimicis iratum fore putetis, cum ignoverit suis. [conditional and alternate questions] [D.4]

As it is, what outrage, I ask, are you seeking to avenge -- your own or the state's? If the state's, what answer will you make with regard to your perseverance in that cause? If your own, beware how you fall into the blunder of thinking that Caesar will vent his wrath upon *your* foes, when he has pardoned his own.

*Phil.*2.16: O miser, sive illa tibi nota non sunt -- nihil enim boni nosti -- sive sunt, qui apud talis viros tam impudenter loquare. [sive...sive] [D.2]

Miserable wretch, whether you don't know what happened (wholesome knowledge does not come your way) or whether you do! Such shameless talk before an audience!

**Phil.*2.32: etenim vereor ne aut celatum me illis ipsis non honestum aut invitatum refugisse mihi sit turpissimum. [aut...aut] [E.3, E.5]

Frankly I am afraid that they may be criticized themselves for keeping me in the dark, or else that the refusal of an invitation to join may be highly discreditable to me.

*Phil.*2.54: o miserum te, si haec intellegis, miseriorem, si non intellegis hoc litteris mandari, hoc memoriae prodi, huius rei ne posteritatem quidem omnium saeculorum umquam immemorem fore, <propter unum te> consules ex Italia expulsos, cumque eis Cn. Pompeium, quod imperi populi Romani decus ac lumen fuit, omnis consularis qui per valetudinem exsequi cladem illam fugamque potuissent, praetores, praetorios, tribunos plebis, magnam partem senatus, omnem subolem iuventutis, uno[que] verbo rem publicam expulsam atque exterminatam suis sedibus! [conditional] [D.2]

What a miserable creature you are if you realize this! More miserable still, if you do not realize what is being recorded by historians, handed down to memory so that in all ages to come it will never pass out of men's minds: namely, that on your sole account the consuls were driven from Italy, and with them Gnaeus Pompeius, the pride and ornament of the Roman empire, as well as all consulars whose health allowed them to follow that disastrous exodus, the praetors, the praetorians, the tribunes of the plebs, a large part of the Senate, all our rising youth -- that in a word the Commonwealth was dirven out, banished from its home.

*Phil.*2.56: si severus, cur non in omnis? si misericors, cur non in suos? [conditional] [A.1, B.4, D.4]

If he is severe, why not to all? If compassionate, why not to his own kith and kin?

Phil.2.75: aut non suscipienda fuit ista causa, Antoni, aut, cum suscepisses, defendenda usque ad extremum. [aut...aut] [D.3, D.4]
You should either not have enlisted under that banner, Antonius, or having done so you should have fought for it to the end.

Phil.2.84: si nihil est cum augur eis verbis nuntiat quibus tu nuntiasti, confitere te, cum "alio die" dixeris, sobrium non fuisse; sin est aliqua vis in istis verbis, ea quae sit augur a collega requiro. [conditional] [B.2, D.1]
If it means nothing when an augur makes an announcement in the terms in which you made yours, admit that when you said "Meeting adjourned" you were not sober. On the other hand, if those terms have any force, as one augur to another I ask you to tell me what it is.

Phil.2.100: si sunt falsa, cur probantur? si vera, cur veneunt? 8 [conditional] [D.4]
If they are forgeries, why are they approved? If genuine, why are they for sale?

Phil.2.110(i): o detestabilem hominem, sive quod tyranni sacerdos es sive quod mortui! [sive...sive] [D.2]
Detestable man--whether because you are the priest of a tyrant or because you are the priest of a dead man! (CPC)

Phil.2.110(ii): aut undique religionem tolle aut usque quaque conserva. [aut...aut] D.4]
Either abolish religion altogether or approve it at every point.

Phil.3.21: //necesse erat enim alterutrum esse hostem; nec poterat aliter de adversariis ducibus iudicari. si igitur Caesar hostis, cur consul nihil refert ad senatum? sin ille a senatu notandus non fuit, quid potest dicere quin, cum de illo tacuerit, se hostem confessus sit?// quem in edictis Spartacum appellat, hunc in senatu ne improbum quidem dicere audet. [conditional and alternate questions] [B.2, D.4]
//For one of the two had to be an enemy; no other judgment was possible on two opposing commanders. If Caesar was the enemy, why does the consul not refer to the Senate? But if Caesar was not to be censured by the Senate, what can he say except that by keeping silent about Casear he admitted himself to be the enemy?// He calls Caesar a Spartacus in his manifestos, but in the Senate he dares not so much as call him disloyal.

Phil.5.5: hoc qui non videt, excors, qui cum videt decernit, impius <est>. [other] [cf. D.2]
Anyone who does not see this is a fool. Anyone who does, and makes the proposal all the same, is a traitor.

*Phil.9.6: at ille cum videret, //si vestrae auctoritati non paruisset, dissimilem se futurum sui, sin paruisset, munus sibi illud pro re publica susceptum vitae finem fore,// maluit in maximo rei publicae discrimine emori quam minus quam potuisset videri rei publicae profuisse. [conditional] [E.1, n.21]
But when he saw that //he would be unlike himself if he did not obey your authority, whereas if he did obey it that charge undertaken for the sake of the Commonwealth would be the end of his life,// he preferred at a public crisis of the utmost gravity to die

APPENDIX I: DILEMMA FORMS IN CICERO'S ORATIONS 209

outright rather than appear to have done less for the Commonwealth than he might have done.

*Phil.*11.5: oppressus Trebonius, si ut ab eo qui aperte hostis esset, incautus; si ut ab eo qui civis etiam tum speciem haberet, miser. [conditional] [E.1]

Trebonius was taken by surprise. He was careless if we think of his assailant as an open enemy; but if we think of him as still bearing the semblance of a fellow countryman, Trebonius is to be pitied.

*Phil.*11.19(i): //adsensus ero, ambitionem induxero in curiam; negaro, videbor suffragio meo, tamquam comitiis, honorem homini amicissimo denegavisse.// quod si comitia placet in senatu haberi, petamus, ambiamus, tabella modo detur nobis, sicut populo data est. cur committis, Caesar, ut aut praestantissimus vir, si tibi non sit adsensum, repulsam tulisse videatur aut unus quisque nostrum praeteritus, si, cum pari dignitate simus, eodem honore digni non putemur? [other] [E.5, n.24]

//Suppose I support the motion: I will be bringing electioneering into the Senate-house. Suppose I say no; it will look as though I have refused an honor to a close friend by my vote, as in an election.// Well, if elections are to be held in the Senate, let us present ourselves as candidates, let us canvass, but let us be given a ballot as are the people. Why put us in such a dilemma, Caesar? If your motion fails, it will appear that a most eminent personage has been rejected; or else each one of us will seem to have been passed over, if we are not deemed worthy of the same honor as an equal in rank.

*Phil.*11.19(ii): adsensus ero, ambitionem induxero in curiam; negaro, videbor suffragio meo, tamquam comitiis, honorem homini amicissimo denegavisse. quod si comitia placet in senatu haberi, petamus, ambiamus, tabella modo detur nobis, sicut populo data est. //cur committis, Caesar, ut aut praestantissimus vir, si tibi non sit adsensum, repulsam tulisse videatur aut unus quisque nostrum praeteritus, si, cum pari dignitate simus, eodem honore digni non putemur?// [conditional + aut...aut] [E.2]

Suppose I support the motion: I will be bringing electioneering into the Senate-house. Suppose I say no; it will look as though I have refused an honor to a close friend by my vote, as in an election. Well, if elections are to be held in the Senate, let us present ourselves as candidates, let us canvass, but let us be given a ballot as are the people. //Why put us in such a dilemma, Caesar? If your motion fails, it will appear that a most eminent personage has been rejected; or else each one of us will seem to have been passed over, if we are not deemed worthy of the same honor as an equal in rank.//

ALPHABETICAL LIST OF CITATIONS OF DILEMMA FORMS IN CICERO'S SPEECHES

Dilemma forms that do not meet Quintilian's definition are marked with an asterisk(*).

Citations are followed only by the numbers of pages where the dilemma forms are quoted in full. For a complete list of references to each citation, please see the index of passages cited.

Agr.
  1.11: 193
  *2.43: 194
  2.46: 194
  2.57: 194
  *2.61: 194

Balb. 13-14: 202-203

Caec.
  *3(i): 190
  3(ii): 190-191
  *4: 191
  *8: 191

Cael.
  35: 111, 200
  50: 112, 200
  52: 144, 200
  53(i): 114, 201
  53(ii): 114, 201
  53(iii): 116, 201
  58: 117, 201
  61: 118, 201
  62: 119, 201

*Cat.*1. 18: 195

Clu.
  *69: 192
  114: 193
  135: 193
  175: 193

Div. Caec.
  *4: 53, 185
  12: 55-56, 186
  *14: 56, 186
  31: 58-59, 186
  33: 59, 186
  58: 62-63, 186
  60: 63-64, 187

Dom.
  22(i): 197
  22(ii): 197
  *91: 197
  124: 197
  125(i): 198
  125(ii): 198-199
  134: 199

Flac.
  *39: 196
  53: 196
  58: 196
  59: 196
  84: 197

**Font.* 3: 190

Har. Resp. 5: 199

Lig.
  23: 206-207
  29: 207

Mur. 57: 195

*Phil.*2.
  16: 155, 207
  *32: 158, 207
  54: 158=159
  56: 159, 207

Phil.2. (cont.)
  75: 160, 207
  84: 162, 208
  100: 163, 208
  110(i): 164, 208
  110(ii): 164-165, 208

Phil.3. 21: 208

Phil.5. 5: 208

*Phil.9. 6: 208

Phil.11.
  *5: 209
  *19(i): 209
  19(ii): 209

Pis. 39: 203

Planc.
  *4: 129-130, 204
  *6: 130-131, 204
  35: 134, 204
  44: 135-136, 205
  46: 135-136, 205
  54: 137, 205
  *79: 139-140
  *83: 140, 205
  84: 140, 205-206
  *88: 141, 206
  *89(i): 141, 206
  *89(ii): 141-142, 206

Prov.
  46(i): 202
  46(ii): 202

Q. Rosc.
  9: 75, 191
  16: 79, 191
  25(i): 80, 192
  25(ii): 81, 192
  40: 83, 192
  43: 83-84, 192
  52: 84, 192
  55: 86, 192

Quinct.
  *32: 182
  41: 182
  *64-65: 182

  73: 182
  81: 183

S. Rosc.
  *30: 33, 183
  74: 34, 183
  79: 35-36, 184
  93: 37-38, 184
  *120: 38, 184
  *124: 39, 185
  128: 40, 185

Sest.
  32: 199
  *37: 199
  *44: 199

Sul.
  10: 92-93, 195
  21: 94, 195
  25(i): 95, 195
  25(ii): 96, 195
  39: 98, 195
  81: 100, 196

Tul.
  *32: 185
  38: 185

Vat.
  10: 200
  20: 200

Ver.
  *1.144: 187
  *2.74: 187
  *2.142: 187
  *2.144: 188
  2.150: 188
  2.177: 188
  2.191: 188
  *3.37: 188
  3.84: 188
  3.106: 189
  3.118: 189
  *3.135: 189
  3.169: 189
  3.182: 190
  5.135: 190

APPENDIX II: SYNTAX AND FUNCTION OF DILEMMA FORMS IN CICERO'S ORATIONS

The three basic questions about the syntax of dilemma forms are these: 1) What are the principal syntactical patterns that Cicero uses for dilemma forms? 2) How does Cicero's preference for various of those syntactical patterns change through time? 3) Are there any clear relationships between different syntactical patterns and different argumentative functions of the device?

It will be convenient to take the first two questions together. In the introduction, we noted that the rhetorical literature leads us to expect that the two choices offered in a dilemma will be presented either as alternate conditions ("si...si", etc.), or as alternate questions, direct or indirect ("utrum...an", etc.). Still, it is possible for a form to meet the criteria of Quintilian's definition without using either of these syntactical patterns; viewed as *exornatio*, dilemma falls among the figures of thought rather than the figures of speech. So, for example, the dilemmas that we noted at *Planc.* 54 and *Phil.* 2.110(ii) are true dilemmas in which the choices are offered in "aut...aut" syntax. Further, Cicero may combine alternate questions with conditionals, or "aut...aut" constructions with either alternate questions or conditionals, or even make a structure sufficiently elaborate simply to jumble these elements, as at *S. Rosc.* 74. Finally, it is possible (although very rare) for Cicero to construct a dilemma form without using any special signature conjunction, e.g. *Phil.*5.5.[1]

---

[1] The other examples are *Ver.*3.37 (against victims of Verres); *Agr.* 2.43 (both choices offensive to audience); *Planc.* 79 and 88, and *Phil.* 11.19(i) (directed against Cicero). None of these five examples directly targets the opponent.

Given these diverse possibilities, and the relatively small number of 126 examples of dilemma forms in the orations, elaborate statistical analyses of Cicero's syntactical preferences as they change through time are of dubious value, and might prove misleading. Instead I offer a simple division of eight syntactical possibilities, their total frequency, and a distribution following the four periods of Cicero's career defined by Schanz. In the first appendix, I have indicated the syntactical category to which each example belongs.

From Table I (p. 216), it is clear that the conditional form with two alternative "if...then" constructions, is the most common. Conditions, including those combined with alternate questions or "aut...aut" constructions, account for 73 of the 126 examples. Dilemmas that offer their choices in "aut...aut" syntax, rather than in alternate questions are in practice the second most common type. The first period shows both the greatest frequency and the most balanced use of different syntactical forms of the device. After that period, Cicero is more sparing in his use of dilemma forms, and more regular in using the conditional syntax.

Because of the small number of examples of each specific function defined in the typology in the concluding chapter, statistical generalization about the correlation of syntax and function would be absurd. For those who are interested, I offer in Table II (p.217) a distribution by syntactical category of the examples I have offered of each of the specific functions enumerated in the typology in the concluding chapter. In order to present the clearest possible picture, I have omitted the tangential comparanda (introduced by "cf." in the notes of the concluding chapter), as well as the syntactical classification of the types that are noted only for forming resonances in entire speeches (C.1-C.5).

I must stress that the meager numbers in Table II can lead to no substantial conclusions by themselves. They may only buttress speculation based upon our experience with the texts.

The largest single usage of synthetic dilemmas is in the form of conditions and alternate questions. This is so because of the repeated use in *Q. Rosc.* of an elaborate form of alternate questions chiastically arranged with the alternate conditions that follow them. We have already noted that these dilemmas are synthetic, and that their lack of forceful content perhaps accounts for their elaboration of form. We might similarly observe that dilemmas marking the beginning of a line of argument (B.1) tend towards a more ostentatious compound structure. On the other hand, dilemmas which point to an opponent's deficient character or mental state (D.2) are not regularly expressed in compound forms, and take special advantage of the shorter, purely subordinated "sive...sive" form. Narrative dilemmas (D.3) do not disrupt their narrative pace with elaborate compound structures. The fact that a dilemma asserting an opponent's lack of self-consistency (D.4) is regularly not a compound structure may be related to the fact that most of the examples come from the fourth period of Cicero's career, when he has little use for such elaboration. (The exceptions come in the sublimely ironic argument in the *Ligariana*). Dilemmas that make the opponent offensive rather than refuting him (D.5) also avoid compound structures, but this need not be due to any avoidance of elaboration for this particular function; one of the examples, *Balb.* 13-14, is among the most lengthily presented forms in the corpus. Perhaps the dominance of the textbook conditional form for this use reflects an attempt to cloak *obiter dicta* with the aura of substantial argument. Finally, Cicero's profession that he was in a dilemma, usually to justify his peaceful departure into exile (E.4) strongly favors the "aut...aut" form, which can be seen to make his untenable situation clear without seeming to protest too much.

These are speculations, nothing more. Finally, the syntactical choices that Cicero makes in creating dilemma structures do not allow convincing general identification of structure with specific function; those choices are more powerfully affected by the specific environments, both argumentative and syntactical, where they occur.

TABLE I, OVERVIEW OF CHRONOLOGICAL DISTRIBUTION OF SYNTACTICAL PATTERNS

Period	Conditional	Alt. Quest.	aut ... aut	Conditional & Alt. Quest.	Conditional & aut...aut	Alt. Quest. & aut...aut	sive ... sive	Other	Total
I (81-66)	12	12	11	7	4	0	1	2	49
II (66-59)	13	2	2	2	2	0	0	1	22
III (57-52)	16	2	6	3	5	2	2	2	38
IV (46-43)	6	0	3	3	1	0	2	2	17
TOTAL	47	16	22	15	12	2	5	7	126

APPENDIX II: SYNTAX AND FUNCTION OF DILEMMA FORMS 217

TABLE II, DISTRIBUTION OF SYNTACTICAL CATEGORIES BY FUNCTIONAL TYPE

	Cond.	Alt. Q.	aut ... aut	Cond. & Alt. Q.	Cond. & aut ... aut	Alt. Q. & aut ... aut	sive ... sive	Other
Synth.	3	3	3	5	0	0	0	0
A.1	7	6	4	7	3	0	0	0
A.2	5	3	1	3	1	0	0	0
A.3	5	1	1	1	1	0	0	0
A.4	1	0	1	0	0	0	0	0
A.5	0	0	1	1	0	0	0	0
B.1	1	3	0	3	0	0	0	0
B.2	6	3	4	3	3	0	0	0
B.3	0	0	1	0	0	0	0	0
B.4	1	0	0	0	0	0	0	0
D.1	3	1	0	1	0	0	0	0
D.2	2	0	1	0	0	1	3	0
D.3	3	2	2	0	0	0	0	0
D.4	6	0	3	3	0	0	0	0
D.5	5	1	0	2	0	0	0	1
E.1	2	1	0	0	1	0	0	1
E.2	1	0	1	0	2	0	0	0
E.3	1	0	1	0	0	0	0	0
E.4	1	0	5	0	1	0	0	1
E.5	1	0	3	0	2	0	0	2

BIBLIOGRAPHY

This bibliography includes both works cited above and other works that I have found helpful for understanding Ciceronian oratory, the tradition of classical rhetoric, and the roles of form as argument in Ciceronian persuasion.

I. TEXTS AND TRANSLATIONS QUOTED ABOVE

Axer, J., ed. *Oratio pro Q. Roscio Comoedo*. M. Tulli Ciceronis scripta quae manserunt omnia, 9. Leipzig: Teubner, 1976.

Bailey, D. R. Shackleton, ed. and trans. *Cicero: Philippics*. Chapel Hill and London: University of North Carolina Press, 1986.

Butler, H.E. ed. and trans. Quintilian. 4 vols. Cambridge, MA: Harvard University Press. 1960 [1921].

Caplan, H. ed. and trans. *[Cicero]: ad C. Herennium de ratione dicendi*. Cambridge, MA: Harvard University Press, 1954, 1977. *Loeb Classical Library*.

Clark, A. C., and W. Peterson, eds. *M. Tulli Ciceronis Orationes*. 6 vols. Oxford: Clarendon Press, 1905-1910.

Fedeli, P., ed. *In M. Antonium Orationes Philippicae XIV*. M. Tulli Ciceronis Scripta Quae Manserunt Omnia, 28. Leipzig: Teubner, 1982. (Apparatus criticus used in conjunction with Bailey's edition of the *Philippics*.)

Freese, J. H., ed. and trans. *Cicero, The Speeches, Pro Publio Quinctio, Pro Sexto Roscio Amerino, Pro Quinto Roscio Comoedo, De Lege Agraria I, II, III*. New York: G.P. Putnam's Sons, 1966 [1930]. *Loeb Classical Library*.

Gardner, R., ed. and trans. *Cicero, The Speeches, Pro Sestio, In Vatinium, Pro Caelio, De Provinciis Consularibus, Pro Balbo*. 2 vols. Cambridge, MA: Harvard University Press, 1965-1966 [1958]. *Loeb Classical Library*.

Greenwood, L. H. G., ed. and trans. *Cicero, The Verrine Orations*. 2 vols. Cambridge, MA: Harvard University Press, 1953 [1928-1935]. *Loeb Classical Library*.

Hodge, H. G., ed. and trans. *Cicero, The Speeches, Pro Lege Manilia, Pro Caecina, Pro Cluentio, Pro Rabirio Perduellionis*. New York: G.P. Putnam's Sons, 1927. *Loeb Classical Library*.

Hubbell, H. ed. and trans. *Cicero II, De Inventione, De Optimo Genere Oratorum, Topica*. Cambridge, MA: Harvard University Press, 1976. *Loeb Classical Library*.

Kennedy, G.A., trans. *Aristotle on Rhetoric: A Theory of Civic Discourse*. New York: Oxford University Press. 1991.

MacDonald, C., ed. and trans. *Cicero, The Speeches*. Vol. 10. Cambridge: Harvard University Press, 1977. *Loeb Classical Library*.

Maidment, K. J., ed. and trans. *Minor Attic Orators*. 2 vols. Cambridge, MA: Harvard University Press, 1953. *Loeb Classical Library*.

Malcovati, H., ed. *Oratorum Romanorum Fragmenta Liberae Rei Publicae*. 4th ed. 2 vols. Torino: Paravia, 1976.

Minors, R. A. B., ed. *P. Vergili Maronis Opera*. Oxford: Clarendon Press, 1972.

Norlin, G., ed. and trans. *Isocrates*. 3 vols. London: Heinemann. 1929. *Loeb Classical Library*.

Rabe, H., ed. *Hermogenes*. Stuttgart: Teubner, 1969 [1913].

Rand, E. K., J. J. Savage, H. T. Smith, G. B. Waldrop, J. P. Elder, B. M. Peebles, and A. F. Stocker, eds. *Servianorum in Vergilii Carmina Commentariorum editionis Harvardianae volumen II quod in Aeneidos libros I et II explanationes continet*. Vol. 2. Lancaster, PA: American Philological Association, 1946.

Stangl, T., ed. *Ciceronis Orationum Scholiastae*. Hildesheim: Georg Olms, 1964. reprint of the 1912 Vienna edition.

Sutton, E.W. and H. Rackham, ed. and trans. *Cicero, De Oratore*. 2 vols. Cambridge, MA: Harvard University Press. 1959 [1942]. *Loeb Classical Library*.

Thilo, G., and H. Hagen, eds. *Servii Grammatici qui feruntur in Vergilii carmina commentarii*. 3 vols. Hildesheim: Georg Olms, 1961. reprint of 1878-1902 Leipzig edition.

Vince, C. A., and J. H. Vince, ed. and trans. *Demosthenes II, De Corona and De Falsa Legatione*. Cambridge, MA: Harvard University Press, 1953. *Loeb Classical Library*.

Watts, B. A., ed. and trans. *Cicero, The Speeches, Pro T. Annio Milone, In L. Calpurnium Pisonem, Pro M. Aemilio Scauro, Pro M. Fonteio, Pro C. Rabirio Postumo, Pro M. Marcello, Pro Q. Ligario, Pro Rege Deiotaro.* New York: G.P. Putnam's Sons, 1931. *Loeb Classical Library.*

Watts, N. H., ed. and trans. *Cicero, The Speeches, Pro Archia Poeta, Post Reditum in Senatu, Post Reditum ad Quirites, De Domo Sua, De Haruspicum Responsis, Pro Plancio.* Cambridge, MA: Harvard University Press, 1935 [1928]. *Loeb Classical Library.*

Wilkins, A.S., ed. *Ciceronis Rhetorica.* 2 vols. Oxford: Clarendon Press, 1902-1903.

II. OTHER WORKS

Adamietz, J. "Ciceros Verfahren in den Ambitus-Prozessen gegen Murena und Plancius." *Gymnasium* 93 (1986): 102-17.

Afzelius, A. "Zwei Episoden aus dem Leben Ciceros." *Classica et Medievalia* 5 (1942): 209-17.

von Albrecht, M. "M.T. Cicero, Stil und Sprache." *Paulys Realencyclopädie der classischen Altertumswissenschaft* Supplementband 13 (1973): 1237-1347.

Alexander, M. C. "*Praemia* in the *Quaestiones* of the Late Republic." *Classical Philology* 80 (1985): 20-32.

---. *Trials in the Late Roman Republic, 149 BC to 50 BC.* Toronto, Buffalo, London: University of Toronto Press, 1990.

Arangio-Ruiz, V., E. Longi, and G. Broggini, eds. *Marco Tullio Cicerone, Le Orazioni.* Verona: Mondadori, 1964. *Pro Quinctio* and Pro Roscio Comoedo translated by Arangio-Ruiz, *Pro Roscio Amerino* by Longi, *Pro Tullio* by Broggini.

Auden, H. W., ed. *Cicero Pro Plancio.* London: MacMillan, 1897.

Austin, R. G., ed. *M. Tulli Ciceronis Pro M. Caelio Oratio.* 3rd ed. Oxford: Oxford University Press, 1960.

---. *The Style and Composition of Cicero's Speech Pro Roscio Comoedo, Origin and Function.* Studia Antiqua, 3. Warsaw: Wydawnictwa Uniwersytetu Warsawskiego, 1980.

---. "Tribunal-Stage-Arena: Modelling of the Communications Situation in M. Tullius Cicero's Judicial Speeches." *Rhetorica* 7 (1989): 299-311.

Ayers, D. M. "Cato's Speech against Murena." *Classical Journal* 49 (1954): 245-54.

Badian, E. "Three Non-Trials in Cicero: Notes on the Text, Prosopography and Chronology of Divinatio in Caecilium 63." *Klio* 66 (1984): 291-309.

Bailey, D. R. Shackleton, ed. and trans. *Cicero's Letters to Atticus.* Cambridge University Press: Cambridge, 1965-1970. 7 vols.

---. ed. *Cicero, Epistulae ad Familiares.* Cambridge: Cambridge University Press, 1977. 2 vols.

---. ed. *Cicero: Epistulae ad Quintum Fratrem et M. Brutum.* Cambridge, London, New York, New Rochelle, Melbourne, Sydney: Cambridge University Press, 1980.

---. *Onomasticon to Cicero's Speeches.* Norman and London: University of Oklahoma Press, 1988.

Barnes, J. "Is Rhetoric an Art?" *d.a.r.g. Newsletter (newsletter of the Discourse Analysis Research Group of the University of Calgary)* 2, no. 2 (Fall 1986): 2-22.

Bitzer, L. "The Rhetorical Situation." *Philosophy and Rhetoric* 1 (1968): 1-14.

Black, E. *Rhetorical Criticism, A Study in Method.* Madison: University of Wisconsin Press, 1978.

Bonino, G. B., ed. *L'Orazione di M. Tullio Cicerone in Difesa di Cn. Plancio.* Torino: Giovanni Chiantore, 1923. reprint of the 1886 edition.

Bonner, S. *Education in Ancient Rome.* Berkeley: University of California Press, 1977.

Boulanger, A., ed. and trans. *Cicéron: Discours.* Vol. 11. Paris: Société d'Édition "Les Belles Lettres," 1946. *Budé.*

Boulanger, A., and P. Weilleumier, eds. *Cicéron, Discours.* Budé. Vol. 19. Paris: Société d'Edition "les belles lettres," 1972.

Broughton, T. R. S. *Magistrates of the Roman Republic. American Philological Association Monographs.* revised ed. 3 vols. Chico, CA: Scholars Press, 1984-1986.

Brunt, P. A. "*Amicitia* in the Late Roman Republic." *Proceedings of the Cambridge Philological Society* 191 (1965): 1-20.

Buchheit, V. "Chrysogonus als Tyrann in Ciceros Rede für Roscius aus Ameria." *Chiron* 5 (1975): 193-211.

---. "Ciceros Kritik an Sulla in der Rede für Roscius aus Ameria." *Historia* 24 (1975): 570-71.

Burke, K. *A Grammar of Motives.* New York: Prentice-Hall, 1945. reprint Berkeley: University of California Press, 1963.

---. "The Nature of Form." In *Contemporary Rhetoric*, edited by W. R. Winterowd, 183-99. New York: Harcourt Brace Jovanovich, 1975. reprinted from *Counterstatement* (Los Altos: Hermes).

BIBLIOGRAPHY

Canter, H. "*Digressio* in the Orations of Cicero." *American Journal of Philology* 52 (1931): 351-61.

---. "Irony in the Orations of Cicero." *American Journal of Philology* 57 (1936): 457-64.

Ciaceri, E. "Il processo di M. Celio Rufo e l'arringa di Cicerone." *Atti della Reale Accademia di Archeologia, Lettere e Belle Arti, Napoli, nuova serie* 11 (1929-1930): 1-24.

---. *Cicerone e i suoi tempi*. 2nd ed. 2 vols. Genova, Roma, Napoli: Società Anonima Editrice Dante Alighieri, 1939-1941.

Clark, D. L. *Rhetoric in Greco-Roman Education*. New York: Columbia University Press, 1957.

Clarke, M. L. *Rhetoric at Rome*. London: Cohen & West, 1953.

Classen, C. J. "Ciceros Rede für Caelius." *Aufstieg und Niedergang der römischen Welt* 1, no. 3 (1973): 60-94.

---. "Ciceros Kunst der Überredung." Chap. 4 In *Éloquence et Rhétorique chez Cicéron*, edited by W. Ludwig, 149-84. Entretiens sur l'Antiquité Classique. Vol. 28. Vandoeuvres-Genève: Fondation Hardt, 1982. with discussion, 185-192.

---. *Recht - Rhetorik - Politik*. Darmstadt: Wissenschaftliche Buchgesellschaft, 1985.

Cole, Thomas. *The Origins of Rhetoric in Ancient Greece*. Baltimore: Johns Hopkins University Press, 1991.

Costa, E. *Cicerone giureconsulto*. 4 vols. Bologna: Gamberini e Parmeggiani, 1916. 2nd ed. = Bologna: Zanichelli, 1927, reprint 1964.

Craig, C. P. "The Role of Rational Argumentation in Selected Judicial Speeches of Cicero." Ph.D. diss., University of North Carolina, 1979.

---. "The *Accusator* as *Amicus*: An Original Roman Tactic of Ethical Argumentation." *Transactions of the American Philological Association* 111 (1981): 31-37.

---. "The Central Argument of Cicero's Speech for Ligarius." *Classical Journal* 79 (1984): 193-99.

---. "Dilemma in Cicero's *Divinatio in Caecilium*." *American Journal of Philology* 106 (1985): 442-46.

---. "The Structural Pedigree of Cicero's Speeches *Pro Archia*, *Pro Milone* and *Pro Quinctio*." *Classical Philology* 80 (1985): 136-37.

---. "Cato's Stoicism and the Understanding of Cicero's Speech for Murena." *Transactions of the American Philological Association* 116 (1986): 229-39.

---. "Reason, Resonance, and Dilemma in Cicero's Speech for Caelius." *Rhetorica* 7 (1989): 313-28.

---. "Cicero's Strategy of Embarrassment in the Speech for Plancius." *American Journal of Philology* 111 (1990): 75-81.

Crawford, J. M. *Tullius Cicero: The Lost and Unpublished Orations.* Göttingen: Vandenhoeck & Ruprecht, 1984.

Crook, J. *Law and Life at Rome.* Ithaca: Cornell University Press, 1967. corrected edition, 1984.

Delaunois, M. "Statistiques des Idées dans le Cadre du Plan Oratoire des *Philippiques* de Cicéron." *Les Études Classiques* 34 (1966): 3-34.

Denniston, J., ed. *M. Tulli Ciceronis in M. Antonium orationes philippicae prima et secunda.* Oxford: Clarendon Press, 1926.

Donkin, E. H., ed. *M. Tullii Ciceronis pro Sexto Roscio Amerino oratio ad Iudices.* 2nd ed. London: MacMillan, 1955. reprint of the 1916 edition.

Donnelly, F. *Cicero's Milo: A Rhetorical Commentary.* New York: Bruce, 1935.

---. *Cicero's Manilian Law: A Rhetorical Commentary.* New York: Fordham University Press, 1939.

Dorey, T. A. ""Cicero, Clodia, and the *Pro Caelio*"." *Greece & Rome* 5 (1958): 175-80. new series.

--- ed. *Cicero.* Studies in Latin Literature and Its Influence. London: Routledge & Kegan Paul, 1964.

Douglas, A. E. "A Ciceronian Contribution to Rhetorical Theory." *Eranos* 55 (1957): 18-26.

--- ed. *M. Tulli Ciceronis Brutus.* Oxford: Clarendon Press, 1966.

---. *Cicero.* Oxford: Clarendon Press, 1968.

---. "The Intellectual Background of Cicero's Rhetorica: A Study in Method." *Aufstieg und Niedergang der römischen Welt* 1, no. 3 (1973): 95-138.

Drexler, H. "Zu Ciceros Rede pro Caelio." *Nachrichten von der Akademie der Wissenschaften in Göttingen, Philologisch-Historisches Klasse* 1944 (1944): 1-32.

Dumont, M. J.-C. "Cicéron et le théâtre." In *Actes du IXe Congrès de l'Association Guillaume Budé, Rome 13-18 avril, 1973*, 424-30. Paris: Les Belles Lettres, 1975.

Dunkle, J. R. "The Greek Tyrant and Roman Political Invective of the Late Republic." *Transactions of the American Philological Association* 98 (1967): 151-71.

---. "The Rhetorical Tyrant in Roman Historiography: Sallust, Livy and Tacitus." *Classical Weekly* 65 (1971-1972): 12-20.

Enos, R. L. "The Epistemological Foundation of Cicero's Litigation Strategies." *Central States Speech Journal* 26 (1975): 207-14.

---. *The Literate Mode of Cicero's Legal Rhetoric*. Carbondale: Southern Illinois University Press, 1988.

Epstein, D. F. *Personal Enmity in Roman Politics, 218-43 BC*. London, New York, Sydney: Croom Helm, 1987.

Fabbri, Q. "Q. Cecilio e la Divinatio." *Historia: studi storici per l'antichità classica* 6 (1932): 292-96.

Fantham, E. "Ciceronian *Conciliare* and Aristotelian Ethos." *Phoenix* 27 (1973): 262-75.

Fortenbaugh, W. W. "*Benevolentiam conciliare* and *animos permovere*: Some remarks on Cicero's *De Oratore* 2.178-216." *Rhetorica* 6 (1988): 259-73.

---. "Cicero's Knowledge of the Rhetorical Treatises of Aristotle and Theophrastus." In *Cicero's Knowledge of the Peripatos*, edited by W. W. Fortenbaugh and P. Steinmetz, 39-60. Rutgers University Studies in Classical Humanities, 4. New Brunswick and London: Transaction Publishers, 1989.

Fraccaro, P. "Studi sull' eta dei Gracchi." *Studi Storici per l'Antichita Classica, nuova serie* 1 (1913): 42-136.

Frier, B. *The Rise of the Roman Jurists: Studies in Cicero's* Pro Caecina. Princeton: Princeton University Press, 1985.

Frisch, H. *Cicero's Fight for the Republic: The Historical Background of Cicero's Philippics*. Copenhagen: Glydendal, 1946.

---. "The First Catilinarian Conspiracy: A Study in Historical Conjecture." *Classica et Medievalia* 9 (1948): 10-36.

Gabba, E. "Cicerone e la Falsificazione dei Senatoconsulti." *Studi Classici e Orientali* 10 (1961): 89-96.

Game, J. B. "An Introduction to the Philippics of Cicero and to the Study of his Invective." Ph.D. diss., Yale University, 1909.

Geffcken, K. *Comedy in the Pro Caelio (with an appendix on the in Clodium et Curionem)*. Leiden: Brill, 1973.

Gelzer, M. *Cicero: ein Biographischer Versuch*. Wiesbaden: Steiner, 1969.

Giaro, T. "La "pro Roscio" interpretata." *Index: Quaderni comerti di studi romanistici* 12 (1983-1984): 566-69.

Glare, P.G.W., ed. *The Oxford Latin Dictionary*. Oxford: Clarendon Press. 1982.

Gossrau, W. G., ed. *M. Tullii Ciceronis pro Sexto Roscio Amerino Oratio*. Quedlinburgi: L.L. Frankius, 1853.

Gotoff, H. C. *Cicero's Elegant Style: An Analysis of the* Pro Archia. Urbana: University of Illinois Press, 1979.

---. "Cicero's Analysis of the Prosecution Speeches in the *Pro Caelio*: An Exercise in Practical Criticism." *Classical Philology* 81 (1986): 122-32.

Grant, M. A. *The Ancient Rhetorical Theories of the Laughable: The Greek Rhetoricians and Cicero*. University of Wisconsin Studies in Language and Literature. Madison: University of Wisconsin Press, 1924.

Green, L. D. "Aristotelian Rhetoric, Dialectic, and the Traditions of *Antistrophos*." *Rhetorica* 8 (1990): 5-27.

Greenidge, A. H. J. *The Legal Procedure of Cicero's Time*. Oxford: Clarendon Press, 1901.

Grimal, P., ed. *Cicéron, Discours*. Vol. 16.2. Paris: Association "les belles lettres," 1976. Budé.

Grube, G. "Educational, Rhetorical and Literary Theory in Cicero." *Phoenix* 16 (1962): 234-57.

Gruen, E. S. *Roman Politics and the Criminal Courts, 149-78 B.C.* Cambridge: Harvard University Press, 1968.

---. *The Last Generation of the Roman Republic*. Berkeley: University of California Press, 1974.

Habicht, C. *Cicero the Politician*. Ancient Society and History. Baltimore and London: Johns Hopkins University Press, 1990.

Hachtmann, K., ed. *M.T. Ciceronis Divinatio in Caecilium*. Gotha: Bibliotheca Gothana, 1891.

Halm, C. (=K.), ed. *Rhetores Latini Minores*. Leipzig: Teubner, 1863.

Halm, K., ed. *Ciceros Ausgewälte Reden*. 6th ed. Vol. 2. Berlin: Weidmann, 1874. *Rede gegen Q. Caecilius und der Anklagerede gegen C. Verres viertes und fünftes Buch.*

Halm, K., and G. Laubmann, eds. *Ciceros Ausgewälte Reden*. 4th ed. Vol. 7. Berlin: Weidmann, 1883. *für L. Murena, für P. Sulla.*

--- eds. *Ciceros Ausgewälte Reden*. 10th ed. Vol. 1. Berlin: Weidmann, 1886. *für Sex. Roscius aus Ameria; Das Imperium des Cn. Pompeius.*

--- eds. *Ciceros Ausgewälte Reden*. 7th ed. Vol. 6. Berlin: Weidmann, 1887. *erste un zweite Philippische Rede*.

Haury, A. *L'ironie et l'humeur chez Cicéron*. Leiden: Brill, 1955.

Heinze, R. "Ciceros Rede *Pro Caelio*." *Hermes* 60 (1925): 193-258.

---. "Ciceros politische Anfänge." In *Vom Geist des Römertums*. 3rd ed., edited by E. Burck, 87-140. Darmstadt: Wissenschaftlische Buchgesellschaft, 1960. 1909.

Heitland, W. E., and H. Cowie, eds. *M.T. Ciceronis in Q. Caecilium Divinatio et in C. Verrem Actio Prima*. Pitt Press Series. 2nd ed. Cambridge: Cambridge University Press, 1900.

Hinks, D. "Tria genera causarum." *Classical Quarterly* 30 (1936): 170-76.

Hollingsworth, J. *Antithesis in the Attic Orators From Antiphon to Isaeus*. Menasha, WI: Banta, 1915.

Holst, H. *Die Wortspiele in Ciceros Reden*. Oslo: Some & Co., 1925.

Hubbell, H. *The Influence of Isocrates on Cicero, Dionysius and Aristides*. New Haven: Yale University Press, 1913.

Humbert, J. *Les plaidoyers écrits et les plaidoiries réelles de Cicéron*. Paris: Presses Universitaires de France, 1925.

Huzar, E. G. *Marc Antony, A Biography*. Minneapolis: University of Minnesota Press, 1978.

Innes, D. "Cicero on Tropes." *Rhetorica* 6 (1988): 307-25.

Johnson, W. R. "Varieties of Narrative in Cicero's Speeches." Ph.D. diss., University of California at Berkeley, 1967.

---. *Luxuriance and Econonmy: Cicero and the Alien Style*. Berkeley: University of California Press, 1971.

Jones, A. H. M. *The Criminal Courts of the Roman Republic and Principate*. Oxford: Blackwell, 1972.

Kaser, M. *Römische Zivilprozessrecht*. München: C.H. Beck, 1966.

---. *Roman Private Law*. 3rd ed. trans. R. Dannenbring. Pretoria: University of South Africa, 1980.

Kennedy, G. A. *The Art of Persuasion in Greece*. Princeton: Princeton University Press, 1963.

---. "The Rhetoric of Advocacy in Greece and Rome." *American Journal of Philology* 89 (1968): 419-36.

---. *The Art of Rhetoric in the Roman World*. Princeton: Princeton University Press, 1972.

---. *Classical Rhetoric in its Christian and Secular Tradition from Ancient to Modern Times*. Chapel Hill: University of North Carolina Press, 1980.

Kenney, E. J., and W. V. Clausen, eds. *The Cambridge History of Classical Literature, Volume II, Latin Literature*. Cambridge, London, New York, New Rochelle, Melbourne, Sydney: Cambridge University Press, 1982.

Kinsey, T. E. "A Dilemma in the Pro Roscio Amerino." *Mnemosyne* 19 (1966): 270-71.

--- ed. *M. Tulli Ciceronis Pro P. Quinctio Oratio*. Sydney: Sydney University Press, 1971.

---. "Cicero's Speech for Roscius of Ameria." *Symbolae Osloenses* 50 (1975): 91-104.

---. "Cicero's Case against Magnus, Capito and Chrysogonus in the *Pro Sex. Roscio Amerino* and Its Use for the Historian." *L'Antiquité Classique* 49 (1980): 173-90.

---. "A Problem in *Pro Roscio Amerino*." *Eranos* 79 (1981): 149-50.

---. "The Case against Sextus Roscius of Ameria." *L'Antiquité Classique* 54 (1985): 188-96.

Kirby, J. T. *The Rhetoric of Cicero's Pro Cluentio*. London Studies in Classical Philology, edited by G. Giangrande, 23. Amsterdam: Gieben, 1990.

Koepke, E., ed. *Ciceros Rede für Cn. Plancius*. 3rd ed. Leipzig: Teubner, 1887. rev. G. Landgraf.

Kroll, W. "Das Epicheirema." *Sitzungsberichte der Akademie der Wissenschaften in Wien, Philosophisch-historische Klasse* 216, no. 2 (1936): 1-17.

---. "Ciceros Rede für Plancius." *Rheinisches Museum für Philologie* 86 (1937): 127-39.

---. "Rhetorik." *Paulys Realencyclopädie der classischen Altertumswissenschaft* Supplementband 7 (1940): 1039-1138.

Kumaniecki, K. "Ciceros Rede 'Pro Murena'." In *Acta Conventus XI "Eirene," Diebus xxi-xxv mensis Octobris Anni MCMLXVIII Habiti*, 161-79. Wratislaviae, Varsaviae, Cracvoviae, Gedani:, 1971.

Kytzler, B., ed. *Ciceros literarische Leistung*. Wege der Forschung, 240. Darmstadt: Wissenschaftliche Buchgesellschaft, 1973.

Lacey, W. K., ed. *Cicero: Second Philippic.* Warminster: Aris & Phillips, 1986.

Landgraf, G., ed. *Kommentar zu Ciceros Rede Pro Sex. Roscio Amerino.* 2nd ed. Berlin: Teubner, 1914.

Laurand, L. *Études sur le Style des Discours de Cicéron.* 4th ed. Amsterdam: A.M. Hakkert, 1965. three volumes in one, reprint of the 1936-1938 Paris edition.

Lausberg, H. *Handbuch der Literarischen Rhetorik.* München: Max Hueber Verlag, 1960. 2 vols.

Leeman, A. D. *Orationis Ratio: The Stylistic Theories and Practice of the Roman Orators, Historians, and Philosophers.* Amsterdam: A.M. Hakkert, 1963.

---. "The Technique of Persuasion in Cicero's Pro Murena." Chap. 5 In *Éloquence et Rhétorique chez Cicéron*, edited by W. Ludwig, 193-228. Entretiens sur l'Antiquité Classique. Vol. 28. Vandoeuvres-Genève: Fondation Hardt, 1982. with discussion, 229-236.

Leeman, A. D., and H. Pinkster. *M. Tullius Cicero, De Oratore Libri III, Kommentar.* Vol. 1. Heidelberg: Carl Winter, 1981. on I.1-165.

Leeman, A. D., H. Pinkster, and H. L. W. Nelson. *M. Tullius Cicero, De Oratore Libri III, Kommentar.* Vol. 2. Heidelberg: Carl Winter, 1985. on 1.166-265; 2.1-98.

Leeman, A. D., H. Pinkster, and E. Rabbie. *M. Tullius Cicero, De Oratore Libri III, Kommentar.* Vol. 3. Heidelberg: Carl Winter, 1989. on 2.99-290.

Leff, M. C. "Redemptive Identification: Cicero's Catilinarian Orations." In *Explorations in Rhetorical Criticism*, edited by G. P. Mohrmann, 158-77. University Park: Pennsylvania State University Press, 1973.

Leon, H. "The Technique of Emotional Appeal in Cicero's Judicial Speeches." *Classical Weekly* 29 (1935): 33-37.

Lincke, E. "Zur Beweisführung Ciceros in der Rede für Sextus Roscius aus Ameria." *Commentationes Fleckeisenianae* 1 (1890): 187-98.

Linderski, J. "Ciceros Rede Pro Caelio und die Ambitus- und Vereinsgesetzgebung der ausgehenden Republik." *Hermes* 89 (1961): 106-19.

Loutsch, C. "Ironie et Liberté de Parole: Remarques sur l'exorde *ad Principem* du *Pro Ligario* de Cicéron." *Revue des Études Latines* 62 (1984): 98-110.

Lovera, F. "Questioni riguardanti il processo de vi di M. Celio Rufo e l'orazione di Cicerone." *Il Mondo Classico* 6 (1936): 167-78.

Ludwig, W., ed. *Éloquence et Rhétorique chez Cicéron.* Entretiens sur l'Antiquité Classique. Vol. 28. Vandoeuvres-Genève: Fondation Hardt, 1982.

May, J. M. "The *Ethica Digressio* and Cicero's *Pro Milone*: A Progression of Intensity from *Logos* to *Ethos* to *Pathos*." *Classical Journal* 74 (1979): 240-46.

---. "The Image of the Ship of State in Cicero's *Pro Sestio*." *Maia (nuova serie)* 3 (1980): 259-64.

---. "The Rhetoric of Advocacy and Patron-Client Identification: Variation on a Theme." *American Journal of Philology* 102 (1981): 308-15.

---. *Trials of Character*. Chapel Hill and London: University of North Carolina Press, 1988.

McDermott, W. C. "In Ligarianam." *Transactions of the American Philological Association* 101 (1970): 317-47.

Merrill, N. W. "Cicero and Early Roman Invective." Ph.D. diss., University of Cincinnati, 1975.

Mette, H. J. "Der junge Anwalt Cicero." *Gymnasium* 72 (1965): 10-27.

Michel, A. *Rhétorique et Philosophie chez Cicéron*. Paris: Presses Universitaires de France, 1960.

Mitchell, T. N. *Cicero: The Ascending Years*. New Haven: Yale University Press, 1979.

---. *Cicero, the Senior Statesman*. New Haven: Yale University Press, 1991.

Mohrmann, G. P., C. J. Stewart, and D. J. Ochs, eds. *Explorations in Rhetorical Criticism*. University Park: Pennsylvania State University Press, 1973.

della Morte, P. M. *Studi su Cicerone Oratore*. Studi e Testi dell' Antichità, 8. Naples: Società Editrice Napolitana, 1977.

Müller, S., ed. *M. Tullio Cicero pro Sex. Roscio Amerino*. Heidelberger Texte, Lateinische Reihe, 15. Heidelberg: F.H. Kerle, 1949.

Neumeister, Chr. *Grundsätze der forensischen Rhetorik gezeigt an Gerichtsreden Ciceros*. Langue et parole, Sprach- und Literaturstrukturelle Studien, 3. Munich: M. Hüber, 1964.

Nicholas, B. *An Introduction to Roman Law*. Clarendon Law Series, edited by H. L. A. Hart. Oxford: Clarendon Press, 1962. reprinted with corrections, 1975.

Nisbet, R. G. M., ed. *M. Tulli Ciceronis De Domo Sua ad Pontifices Oratio*. Oxford: Clarendon Press, 1939. reprinted by Arno Press, Latin Texts and Commentaries, 1979.

--- ed. *M. Tulli Ciceronis in L. Calpurnium Pisonem Oratio*. Oxford: Clarendon Press, 1961.

---. "The Speeches." In *Cicero*, edited by T. A. Dorey, 47-79. Studies in Latin Literature and Its Influence. London: Routledge and Kegan Paul, 1964.

Nohl, H., ed. *Ciceros Rede für den Sex. Roscius aus Ameria*. 2nd ed. Leipzig: Freytag, 1897.

Norden, E. "Aus Ciceros Werkstatt." *Sitzungsberichte der Preussischen Akademie der Wissenschaften, philosophisch-historische Klasse* 1913 (1913): 12-32. reprinted in *Kleine Schriften zum Klassichen Altertum*, ed. B. Kytzler (Berlin: de Gruyter, 1966) 144-166.

Opelt, I. *Die lateinischen Schimpfwörter und verwandte sprachliche Erscheinungen: Eine Typologie*. Heidelberg: Carl Winter, 1965.

Osenbrüggen, E., ed. *Cicero's [sic] Rede für Sextus Roscius aus Ameria*. Braunschweig: Friedrich Vieweg, 1844.

Pacitti, G. "Cicerone al processo di M. Celio Rufo." In *Atti I Congresso Internazionale di Studi Ciceroniani*, 67-79. Vol. 2. Roma: Centro di Studi Ciceroniani, 1961.

Palmer, G. B. *The TOPOI of Aristotle's Rhetoric as Exemplified in the Orators*. Chicago: Private edition distributed by University of Chicago Libraries, 1934. Publication of a 1932 University of Chicago dissertation.

Perelman, Ch, and L. Olbrechts-Tyteca. *The New Rhetoric: A Treatise on Argumentation*. South Bend: University of Notre Dame Press, 1969. trans. J. Wilkinson and P. Weaver.

Preiswerk. "De Inventione Orationum Ciceronianarum." Ph.D. diss., Basel, 1905.

Rawson, E. *Cicero: A Portrait*. Ithaca: Cornell University Press, 1983. revised edition.

Reizenstein, R. "Ciceros Rede für Caelius." *Nachrichten von der Akademie der Wissenschaften in Göttingen, Philologisch-Historisches Klasse* 1925 (1925): 25-32.

Richter, F., ed. *Ciceros Divinatio in Q. Caecilium*. 2nd ed. rev. A. Eberhard. Leipzig: Teubner, 1884.

Richter, F., and A. Fleckeisen, eds. *Ciceros Rede für Sex. Roscius*. 4th ed. Leipzig and Berlin: Teubner, 1906. rev. G. Ammon.

Roby, H. J. *Roman Private Law in the Times of Cicero and of the Antonines*. 2 vols. Cambridge: Cambridge University Press, 1902.

Rohde, F. "Cicero, quae de inventione praecepit, quatenus secutus sit in orationibus generis iudicialis." Ph.D. diss., Königsberg, 1903.

Salzman, M. R. "Cicero, the *Megalenses* and the Defense of Caelius." *American Journal of Philology* 103 (1982): 299-304.

Schanz, M., rev. C. Hosius. *Geschichte der Römischen Literatur.* 4th ed. Vol. 1. München: C.H. Beck, 1959. reproduction of the 1927 edition.

---. *Geschichte der Römischen Literatur.* 2nd ed. Vol. 4. München: C.H. Beck, 1959. reproduction of the 1914 edition.

Sedgwick, W. B. "Cicero's Conduct of the Case *Pro Roscio.*" *Classical Review* 48 (1934): 13.

Settle, J. N. "The Publication of Cicero's Orations." Ph.D. diss., University of North Carolina, 1962.

Skinner, M. B. "Clodia Metelli." *Transactions of the American Philological Association* 113 (1983): 273-87.

Solmsen, F. "Aristotle and Cicero on the Orator's Playing upon the Feelings." *Classical Philology* 33 (1938): 390-404. reprinted in Kleine Schriften II (Olms, Hildesheim, 1968) 2-16-230.

---. "Cicero's First Speeches: A Rhetorical Analysis." *Transactions of the American Philological Association* 69 (1938): 542-56. reprinted in Kleine Schriften II (Olms, Hildesheim, 1968) 231-245.

---. "The Aristotelian Tradition in Ancient Rhetoric." *American Journal of Philology* 62 (1941): 35-50, 169-90. reprinted in Kleine Schriften II (Olms, Hildesheim, 1968) 178-215.

---. *Kleine Schriften.* Vol. 2. Hildesheim: Georg Olms, 1968.

Spengel, L., ed. *Rhetores Graeci.* 3 vols. Leipzig: B.G. Teubner, 1853-56.

Sternkopf, W. "Gedankengang und Gliederung der 'Divinatio in Caecilium'." *Gymnasium Dortmund Jahresbericht* (1904-1905): 4-17. reprinted in B. Kytzler, ed., *Ciceros literarische Leistung, Wege der Forschung* vol. 240 [Darmstadt: Wissenschaftliche Buchgesellschaft, 1973] 267-299.

Stock, St. George, ed. *Cicero Pro Sexto Roscio Amerino.* 2nd ed. Oxford: Clarendon Press, 1901.

Stockton, D. *Cicero, A Political Biography.* New York: Oxford University Press, 1971.

---. *The Gracchi.* Oxford: Clarendon Press, 1979.

Stroh, W. *Taxis und Taktik.* Stuttgart: Teubner, 1975.

---. "Die Nachahmung des Demosthenes in Ciceros Philippiken." Chap. 1 In *Éloquence et Rhétorique chez Cicéron*, edited by W. Ludwig, 1-31. Entretiens sur l'Antiquité Classique. Vol. 28. Vandoeuvres-Genève: Fondation Hardt, 1982. with discussion, 32-40.

BIBLIOGRAPHY

Süss, W. *Ethos: Studien zur älteren griechischen Rhetorik.* Leipzig and Berlin: Teubner, 1920. reprint Aalen: Scientia Verlag, 1975.

Syme, R. *The Roman Revolution.* Oxford: Clarendon Press, 1939.

Taddeo, D. J., Jr. "Signs of Demosthenes in Cicero's Philippics." Ph.D. diss., Stanford University, 1971.

Taylor, L. R. *Party Politics in the Age of Caesar.* Berkeley: University of California Press, 1949.

---. "Magistrates of 55 B.C. in Cicero's *Pro Plancio* and Catullus 52." *Athenaeum* 42 (1968): 12-28. new series.

Thierfelder, A. "Über den Wert der Bemerkungen zur eigenen Person in Ciceros Prozessreden." *Gymnasium* 72 (1965): 385-414.

Thomas, É., ed. *Cicéron, Verrines: Divinatio in Q. Caecilium et Actionis Secundae Libri IV et V,* De Signis *et* De Suppliciis. Paris: Hachette, 1894.

Thompson, L. A. "The Relationship between Provincial Quaestors and their Commanders-in-Chief." *Historia* 11 (1962): 339-55.

Toulmin, S. E. *The Uses of Argument.* Cambridge, London, New York: Cambridge University Press, 1958.

Vasaly, A. "The Masks of Rhetoric: Cicero's *Pro Roscio Amerino.*" *Rhetorica* 3 (1985): 1-20.

Venturini, C. "L'Orazione pro Cn. Plancio e la Lex Licinia de Sodaliciis." In *Studi in Onore di Cesare San Filippo,* 787-804. Vol. 5. Milano: Guiffrè, 1984.

Vickers, B. *In Defense of Rhetoric.* Oxford: Clarendon Press, 1988.

Wallach, B. P. "Cicero's *Pro Archia* and the Topics." *Rheinisches Museum für Philologie* 132 (1989): 313-31.

Warmington, E. H., ed. *Remains of Old Latin.* 4 vols. Cambridge, MA: Harvard University Press, 1936. *Loeb Classical Library.*

Weische, A. *Ciceros Nachahmung den Attischen Redner.* Heidelberg: Carl Winter, Universitätsverlag, 1972.

Wieacker, F. *Cicero als Advokat.* Berlin: Walter de Gruyter, 1965.

Wilkinson, L. P. "Cicero and the Relationship of Oratory to Literature." In *The Cambridge History of Classical Literature, vol. II, Latin Literature,* edited by E. J. Kenney and W. V. Clausen, 230-67. Cambridge, London, New York, New Rochelle, Melbourne, Sydney: Cambridge University Press, 1982.

Willard, C. A. *Argumentation and the Social Grounds of Knowledge*. Tuscaloosa: University of Alabama Press, 1983.

Winterowd, W. R., ed. *Contemporary Rhetoric*. New York: Harcourt Brace Jovanovich, 1975.

Wiseman, T. P. *Catullus and his World: A Reappraisal*. Cambridge: Cambridge University Press, 1985.

Wisse, J. *Ethos and Pathos from Aristotle to Cicero*. Amsterdam:, 1989.

Wood, N. *Cicero's Social and Political Thought*. Berkeley, Los Angeles, London: University of California Press, 1988.

Wooten, C. W. *Cicero's Philippics and Their Demosthenic Model*. Chapel Hill and London: University of North Carolina Press, 1983.

Wunder, E., ed. *M. Tulli Ciceronis Oratio pro Cn. Plancio*. Leipzig: C.H.F. Hartmann, 1830.

BRIEF GLOSSARY OF RHETORICAL AND LEGAL TERMS

Every effort has been made to translate and otherwise to explain any technical terms as they occur in the text. This brief glossary includes only these items: a) English technical terms defined and used in some unique sense in this study; b) Latin terms of special importance that may still be puzzling to non-classicists; c) Roman legal terms, especially those relating to the discussion of *Pro Roscio Comoedo*, that may seem foreign even to some classicists. For a fuller treatment of Latin rhetorical terms, the reader is referred especially to Caplan's *Loeb* edition of the *Rhetorica ad Herennium*, to Hubbell's *Loeb* edition of *De Inventione*, and to the compendium of H. Lausberg, *Handbuch der Literarischen Rhetorik*, 2 vols. (Munich: Max Hüber Verlag, 1960).

For the terminology of Roman private law, basic works are those of Max Kaser cited in the bibliography. The reader may also find useful Barry Nicholas' fine *An Introduction to Roman Law*. (Oxford: Clarendon Press, 1962. reprinted with corrections, 1975).

N.B.: In this list, the phrase "Roman civil law" is used in the broadest sense to distinguish private from criminal law.

accusator: A principal accuser in a criminal trial. There is no public prosecutor, so this person is always a private individual who feels moved to undertake such an act.

actio certae creditae pecuniae: A civil action for the recovery of a fixed sum of money. The judge, called *iudex* rather than *arbiter*, must determine that the specific amount stipulated by the plaintiff is owed, or he must find for the defendant.

actio furti manifesti: a civil action for the recovery of stolen property that is in the possession of the thief. Theft was be construed very broadly; it might include fraud, embezzlement, or avoiding payment of a contractual obligation.

adiunctum negotio: An argument based upon the circumstances surrounding a crime. A subspecies of the *argumentum ex negotio*. See *Inv.* 1.41-42.

advocatus: a personage of importance who is present to support a defendant, but who is not a pleader. See pp. 101-102 and n20.

ambitus: criminal charge of bribing the electorate.

antikategoria: The turning of the accusation back on the accuser. See Quintilian 7.2.9, 18-25, and 3.10.4., and p. 153 with n17.

arbiter: 1) In Roman civil law, an individual who renders judgement in certain types of action, such as an arbitration to divide the assets of a partnership or an arbitration to apportion shares of an inheritance among the heirs.
2) an individual appointed by the praetor to provide binding arbitration in a financial dispute between two parties. The arbiter is regularly appointed only with the consent of the two opposing parties.

arbitrium (actio) pro socio: a civil action to settle the share that a partner has in the assets of a defunct partnership.

argumentum ex causa: In judicial rhetoric, the argument from the motive of a defendant. See *Inv.* 2.17-28.

argumentum ex negotio: In judicial rhetoric, an argument based upon physical evidence or other circumstances surrounding a crime. This stands in contrast to the *argumentum ex persona*. See *Inv.* 1.37-43 and 2. 38-44.

argumentum ex persona: In judicial rhetoric, an argument based upon the attributes of individuals rather than upon physical evidence or other circumstances surrounding a crime. In a question of fact, all such considerations, no matter how far removed from the alleged crime, are considered relevant. See *Inv.* 2.28-39 and 1.34-36.

cognitor: In Roman civil law, a representative formally appointed by either plaintiff or defendant to act in his behalf.

coitio: The agreement of two political candidates to join forces to block out other candidates. See pp. 124-125n7.

complexio: Cicero's word for dilemma at *Inv.* 1.44-45. See pp. 9-10.

comprehensio: Cicero's word for dilemma at *Inv.* 83-84. See pp. 12-13.

conclusio, duplex: See "*duplex conclusio.*"

conclusio, simplex: See "*simplex conclusio.*"

consilium: An advisory group to the praetor for a *divinatio*. This group was composed of people from the established pool of prospective jurors.

constitutio coniecturalis: the *status*, or stasis, or question, of fact. Did the defendant commit the act in question or not? This is the stasis of all five of the criminal cases considered above. Its principal content *loci* are those of motive, character, and the circumstances surrounding the fact itself (*argumenta ex causa, ex persona, ex negotio*). See *Inv.* 1.10; 2. 14-51 and 1.34-43.

GLOSSARY OF RHETORICAL AND LEGAL TERMS 237

contentio dignitatis: The Roman locus in which the *accusator* in an *ambitus* trial, if he was the person who had been defeated by the defendant in the election, would compare his own merits to those of the defendant in order to demonstrate that the defendant was obviously inferior in prestige. From this, the *accusator* would argue that the defendant could have won the election through bribery.

corona: the crowd of spectators who would surround the open-air tribunal where legal cases were pled and serve as the speakers' larger audience.

dilemma form: any dilemma or dilemma structure. See p. 26.

dilemma structure: a dilemma form that does not fulfill all of the requirements of the definition at Quintilian 5.10.69. Examples are narrative dilemmas and dilemmas directed at someone other than the opponent. See p. 26.

dilemma: To use Quintilian's definition (5.10.69, s.v. *divisio*): "...we may give our opponent the choice between two alternatives of which one must necessarily be true, and as a result, whichever he chooses, he will damage his case." See pp. 8-26, esp. p. 17.

divinatio: a procedure for determining which of several prospective *accusatores* is to be allowed to prosecute a criminal case. See pp. 48-49.

divisio: Quintilian places dilemma under this head. More broadly, it is simply a division, or enumeration, of possible grounds for inference. It is a figure of speech in *Rhet. Her.* 4.52, a form of argument at Quintilian 5.10.69. See pp. 16-17.

duplex conclusio: the word for dilemma at *Rhet. Her.* 2.38. See pp. 14-15.

ethical argument: Originally, Aristotle's *ethike pistis* (*Rhet.* 1.2.1356a4-8), the persuasive power that inheres in the speaker's self-presentation in the course of a speech. In this study, ethical argument has the more conventional modern meaning of the characterization of any individual or group in a rhetorical situation when that characterization serves to move the audience towards the orator's persuasive goal.

iudex: 1) In Roman civil law, a single individual appointed by a magistrate to pronounce judgement in a given suit. Although the distinction is often blurred, originally, a *iudex* would judge a suit where a fixed amount of money was at issue, while an *arbiter* would be appointed for a suit in which a fair distribution of assets was the goal.
2) A juror in a criminal case.

locus, pl. *loci* (Gr. *topos*): a "place" in which an argument is located. A *locus* may refer to the content of a certain passage, as a "*locus* on the reliability of witnesses," or, less commonly, it may refer to the form of an argument, such as the *locus* of the more and the less. See p. 1n3.

narrative dilemma: A dilemma structure referring to past time, and thus leaving the target no choice in the present. See p. 26 and n56; p. 176 and n17.

patronus, pl. *patroni*: A pleader who speaks in defense of another in court. One defendant may have several *patroni* in the same case. In theory, *patroni* are not paid for their services.

praeteritio (*occultatio*): Paralipsis. A device in which the speaker mentions something by saying that he will not mention it. The *auctor ad Herennium* (4.37) gives this example: "I do not mention that you have taken monies from our allies; I do not concern myself with your having despoiled the cities, kingdoms and homes of them all. I pass by your thieveries and robberies, all of them."

praevaricatio: collusion between an *accusator* and the defense with the aim of seeing the defendant acquitted.

promissio - repromissio: See "*stipulatio - restipulatio.*"

quaestio de ambitu: See "*quaestiones perpetuae.*"

quaestio de rebus repetundis: See "*quaestiones perpetuae.*"

quaestio de vi: See "*quaestiones perpetuae.*"

quaestiones perpetuae: the standing criminal courts. There were at least seven of these courts, designated to hear cases of provincial misgovernment (*de rebus repetundis,* or *repetundarum*), murder (*de veneficis ac sicariis*), embezzlement of public funds (*de peculatu*), treason (*de maiestate*), forgery (*de falsis*), corrupt election practices (*de ambitu*) and seditious violence (*de vi*). Their juries, after 70, did not consist solely of senators, but were composed equally of persons belonging to the three wealthiest groups in the state, senators, equites, and *tribuni aerarii*. The jury might consist of fifty-one to seventy-five *iudices*, under the president of the court, who was either a praetor or an appointed *iudex quaestionis*.

question of fact: See "*constitutio coniecturalis.*"

reus: a defendant in a criminal or civil suit.

simplex conclusio: a simple inference in *Inv.* 1.44-45. See pp. 9-10.

sodalicia: societies used illegally as organizational units for bribing the electorate.

stipulatio - restipulatio: In Roman civil law, a formal oral procedure for entering into a contract.

subscriptor: A secondary prosecutor in a criminal trial.

topos: See *locus*.

tribuni aerarii: See "*quaestiones perpetuae.*"

vis: a criminal charge of seditious violence.

INDEX OF NAMES

This index contains only the names of human individuals who lived during classical antiquity. Cicero is omitted, since his name occurs on virtually every page of the text. Citations of the names of authors in conjunction with their works are included in the index of passages cited.

Roman men's names are alphabetized according to gentile ("-ius") name. There are are sufficient cross-references to keep this convention from hindering those less familiar with gentile names. Non-classicists may also be puzzled by the parentheses following the names of some Roman men. These indicate the highest office that a Roman attained, along with the year of office. The standard abbreviations are as follows: cens. = censor; cos. = consul; cos. design. = consul designate; cos. suff. = suffect consul; pr. = praetor; tr. pl. = tribune of the plebs; aed. cur. = curule aedile; q. = quaestor; leg. = legate.

For individuals mentioned in Cicero's speeches, the basic research tool, keyed to the standard reference works, is D. R. Shackleton Bailey's *Onomasticon to Cicero's Speeches* (London and Norman: University of Oklahoma Press, 1988). In doubtful matters, I regularly follow Professor Bailey.

Abbius Oppianicus, Statius: 192, 193

Acilius Glabrio, M' (cos. 67): 48

Aelius Paetus Staienus, C. (q. 77): 176n17

Aelius Tubero, L. (leg. 61-59): 206

Aelius Tubero, Q. (son of the preceding, accuser of Ligarius): 206-207

Aemilius Lepidus, M. (triumvir): 157

Aeschines: 20, 153n17

Antonius Hybrida, C. (cos. 63): 159

Antonius, M. (triumvir): 147-168 *passim*, 207

Apronius, Q.: 189

Aquilius, C. (pr. 66): 182

Aristotle: 11; see also index of passages cited

Atratinus: see "Sempronius Atratinus"

Atticus: see "Pomponius Atticus"

Attius, T: 193

Augustus: see "Iulius Caesar Octavianus"

Aurelius Cotta, L. (cos. 65): 89

Autronius Paetus, P. (cos. design. 65): 89, 92, 93, 94, 98, 195

Brutus: see "Iunius Brutus"

Caecilia Metella (daughter of Baliaricus): 29, 36

Caecilius Metellus Celer, Q. (cos. 60): 117

Caecilius Metellus Nepos, Q. (cos. 57): 91

Caecilius Metellus Numidicus, Q. (cos. 109): 141, 178n24, 199, 206

Caecilius Niger, Q. (q. 73 or 72): 47-66 *passim*, 186, 187

Caelius Rufus, M. (aed. cur., 50): 105-121 *passim*, 200, 201.

Caelius, M. (father of Caelius Rufus): 110n12

Caesar: see "Iulius Caesar, C. (dictator)"

Caesernius, C.: 107n4

Calpurnius Piso Caesoninus, L. (cos. 58): 126n10, 148n4, 167

Calpurnius Piso, C.(cos. 67) (arbiter of the dispute between Roscius and Fannius): 68-86 *passim*.

Camurtius, M.: 107n4

Capito: see "Roscius Capito"

Cassius Longinus, L. (pr. 66, Catilinarian): 98, 99, 195

Cassius Longinus, L. (tr. pl. 44) (*subscriptor* vs. Cn. Plancius): 124, 127n16, 128 and n17, 132n22, 138, 139, 141

Catiline: see "Sergius Catilina"

Cato: see "Porcius Cato"

Chrysogonus: see "Cornelius Chrysogonus"

Cimber: see "Tillius Cimber"

Claudius Caecus, Ap. (cens. 312): 111

Claudius Marcellus, C. (pr. 80): 56

Claudius Marcellus, M. (aed. cur. 91?) (guardian of Iunius): 187

INDEX OF NAMES 241

Clodia Metelli: 106-121 *passim*, 174, 176n19, 200, 201

Clodius Pulcher, P. (aed. cur. 56): 91, 106, 111, 150, 153, 167, 202

Clodius, P. (*subscriptor* vs. Caelius): 106

Cluvius, C: 71n11, 83, 84, 192

Cornelius (*subscriptor* vs. P. Sulla): 90

Cornelius Chrysogonus, L.: 28-45 *passim*, 185.

Cornelius Dolabella, P. [Cn.?] (cos. suff. 44): 160, 161 and n30, 162

Cornelius Lentulus Marcellinus, Cn. (cos. 56): 56

Cornelius Sulla Felix, L. (dictator): 28-32 *passim*, 37, 40, 47, 48, 49

Cornelius Sulla, P. (cos. design. 65): 89-102 *passim*, 195

Crassus: see "Licinius Crassus"

Demosthenes: 19, and see the index of passages cited

Dio of Alexandria: 106, 107n4, 115, 116, 117

Dolabella: see "Cornelius Dolabella"

Egnatius, Cn.: 193

Erucius, C. (*accusator* of Sex. Roscius): 29, 31-37 *passim*, 45n1, 184

Fannius Chaerea, C. (opponent of Q. Roscius): 67-88 *passim*, 191-192.

Flavius, Q. (of Tarquinii): 68-86 *passim*, 192

Gabinius, A. (cos. 58): 126n10, 198

Herennius Balbus, L. (*subscriptor* vs. Caelius): 106, 113n20, 114, 115

Hermagoras: 1n3

Hermogenes: 19, and see the index of passages cited

Hiempsal (king of Numidia): 193

Hortensius Hortalus, Q. (cos. 69): 48 and n4, 51, 52, 57, 60, 62 and n29, 63, 64, 66, 90, 92, 93, 124 and n4

Iulius Caesar Octavianus, C. (Caesar Augustus): 148 and n3, 151, 168n44

Iulius Caesar Strabo, C. (aed. cur. 90) (interlocutor in *De Oratore*): 13n31

Iulius Caesar, C. (dictator): 133-168 *passim*, 177n20, 197, 202, 206, 207, 208

Iulius Caesar, L. (cos. 64): 209

Iunius Brutus, Decimus (cos. 77): 187

Iuventius Laterensis, M. (pr. 51) (accuser of Plancius): 124-143 *passim*, 204, 205

Julius Caesar: see "Iulius Caesar, C."

Laterensis: see "Iuventius Laterensis"

Lentulus: see "Cornelius Lentulus"

Licinius Crassus, L. (cos. 95) (interlocutor in *De Orat.*): 13n31

Licinius Crassus, M. (cos. 70, 55) ("triumvir"): 48, 107, 126n11, 133

Licinius Lenticula (gambler): 159

Licinius Sacerdos, C. (pr. 75): 187

Licinius, P. (alleged agent of Caelius): 117, 118

Lucceius, L. (pr. 67): 114, 116

Luscius Ocrea, C. (witness for Q. Roscius): 83, 84

Maccius Plautus, T. (comic poet): 73, 84

Maeandrius: 196

Magnus: see "Roscius Magnus"

Manilius, T. (witness for Q. Roscius): 83, 84, 192

Manlius Torquatus, L. (cos. 65) (father of the following): 89, 90, 91, 99, 100, 101, 102

Manlius Torquatus, L. (pr. 49) (accuser of P. Sulla): 89-102 *passim*

Marcellus: see "Claudius Marcellus"

Metellus: see "Caecilius Metellus"

Munatius Plancus Bursa, T. (tr. pl. 52): 48n3

Ninnius, L. (pr. 58): 198

Numa (second king of Rome): 95

Octavian: see "Iulius Caesar Octavianus"

Oppianicus: see "Abbius Oppianicus"

Panurgus (slave actor trained by Q. Roscius): 67, 78

Piso: see "Calpurnius Piso"

Plancius, Cn. (Cicero's client): 123-143 *passim*, 204, 205

Plancius, Cn. (father of following): 124, 126 and nn11-12, 132, 133 and n25, 134, 135

Plautus: see "Maccius Plautus"

Plotius, A. (pr. 51): 125n7, 137 and n31

Pompeius, Cn. (cos. 70, 55, 52) ("triumvir"): 48 and n.4, 89, 90, 93, 107 and n4, 108, 133, 141n37, 150 and n8, 158, 160, 194, 202, 203, 207

Pompey the Great: see "Pompeius"

Pomponius Atticus, T.: 149, 161n30

Popilius Laenas, P. (cos. 132): 23

Porcius Cato, M. (pr. 54): 126n14, 133, 197

Ptolemy XII Auletes (king of Egypt): 106, 107, 108

Quinctius, P. (Cicero's client): 182

Romulus (first king of Rome): 200

Roscius Capito, T. (enemy of Sex. Roscius): 28-38 *passim*, 44

INDEX OF NAMES
243

Roscius Gallus, Q. (comic actor and defendant): 67-87 *passim*, 192

Roscius Magnus, T. (enemy of Sex. Roscius): 28-41 *passim*, 44, 183

Roscius, Sex. (of Ameria. Defended by Cicero.): 28-45 *passim*, 183, 184

Roscius, Sex. (of Ameria. Father of following.): 28-45 *passim*

Rullus: see "Servilius Rullus"

Sacerdos: see "Licinius Sacerdos"

Saturius, P. (advocate of Fannius against Q. Roscius): 69, 71, 72, 75, 77, 81, 82, 83, 86

Sempronius Atratinus, L. (cos. suff. 34) (accuser of Caelius): 106

Sempronius Gracchus, C.: 23, 24, 25, 33n15, 155n22, 166n37, 178n22

Sergius Catilina, L. (pr. 68) (conspirator): 89-94 *passim*, 99, 100, 101, 102, 141n37, 150, 155, 177n20

Servilius Rullus, P. (tr. pl. 63): 194

Sopater (of Halicyae): 187

Spartacus (gladiator and leader of slave revolt): 208

Staienus: see "Aelius Paetus Staienus"

Sulla: see "Cornelius Sulla"

Sulpicius Rufus, Ser. (cos. 51): 126n14, 131n22, 178n21

Tarquinius Priscus, L. (fifth king of Rome): 95

Tillius Cimber, L. (proconsul 44-43): 157

Torquatus: see "Manlius Torquatus"

Trebonius, C. (cos. suff. 45): 157, 178n21, 209

Tullius, M. (*pro Tullio*): 185

Valerius Flaccus, L. (cos. suff. 86) (father of the following): 196

Valerius Flaccus, L. (pr. 63) (*pro Flacco*): 196, 197

Vatinius, P. (cos. 47) (*in Vatinium*): 126

Verres, C. (pr. 74) (*in Verrem*): 48-64 *passim*

Verrucius, C. (= C. Verres): 188

Xenophanes of Colophon: 11, 12, 24

INDEX OF PASSAGES CITED

The index is divided into two sections, the first for works of Cicero and the second for other authors. Cicero's works are further divided into sections on the Orations, the *Rhetorica*, the *Philosophica*, and the Letters. Abbreviations of Latin works are those in the *Oxford Latin Dictionary*. Page numbers in boldface give citations where the texts of dilemma forms and other key passages are given.

I. CICERO

A. ORATIONS

Agr.
   1.11: 175n15, **193**
   2.43: 177n20, **194**, 213n1
   2.46: 177n20, **194**
   2.57: 177n19, **194**
   2.61: 177n20, **194**

Balb. 13-14: 177n20, **202-203**, 215

Caec.
   3(i): 178n24, **190**
   3(ii): 178n24, **190-191**
   4: 176n17 & n18, **191**
   8: 178n22, **191**

Cael.: 6, 87, 88, chapter six, 105-121, 143, 144 and n43, 174 and n11, 175 and n14
   1-2: 110
   3-50: 110
   3-20: 106
   3: 110n12
   21-22: 105n2
   22: 116
   23-24: 106, 107n4
   23: 106
   25-29: 106
   26: 106
   28: 106n2
   29: 109n10
   30: 107
   30b-32: 113n21
   31-50: 112n19

Cael. (cont.)
  35: 106, **111** and n15, 113, 120, 143n42, 144n44, 171n2, 172n3 & n4, 176n19, **200**
  38: 106n2, 113n20
  39-50: 112n19
  41-43: 106n2
  44-47: 109
  48-50: 106n2
  50: 106, **112**, 113, 115, 117, 120-121, 143n42, 144n44, 166n38, 170, 171n2, 172n3 & n4, 173n8, **200**
  51-69: 110
  51-55: 106
  51: 107
  52-53a: 113
  52: 106, **114**, 115, 120, 143n42, 171n2, 172n3 & n4, **200**
  53: 106, 116
  53(i): 106, **114**, 120, 143n42, 171n2, 172n3 & n4, **201**
  53(ii): 106, **114**, 143n42, 171n2, 172n3 & n4, **201**
  53(iii): 106, **116**, 120, 173n5, **201**
  53b-54: 116
  55: 105n2
  56-59: 106, 117
  57: 113n20
  58: 106, **117**, 118, 120, 144, 171n2, 172n5, **201**
  61-69: 118
  61: 106, **118**, 120, 171n2, 172n3 & n4, **201**
  62: 106, **119**, 120, 171n2, 174, 175n15, **201**
  66: 116
  70-80: 110
  71: 107 and n4
  72-77a: 110
  75: 110n13

Cat. 1.18: 177n20, **195**

Clu.
  176n17, **192**
  114: 173n8, 177n19, **193**
  135: 173n8, 177n19, **193**
  175: 171n1, **193**

Clu.: 153n17

64: 11n27

Div. Caec.: 5, chapter three, 47-66, 103, 120, 168, 174n10
  1-11a: 52
  1-3: 53
  1-5: 49-55
  1: 51n11
  2-5: 52
  4: 47, **53**, 55, 58, 64, 65, 86n26, 102n23, 120n31, 130n21, 144n46 & n47, 166n39, 178n24, 179n25, **185**
  5: 54
  6-9: 49, 54, 57
  8-9: 54-59
  10: 52, 54
  11a-22a: 49, 52
  11b-72: 52
  11-12: 55-56
  12-16: 56
  12-13: 49, 56
  12: 47, **55-56**, 60, 64, 86, 87, 101n21, 102n22, 120n29, 173 and n7, 175n15, **186**
  13: 56
  14: 47, 55n17, **56**, 64, 65, 86n26, 102n23, 120n31, 144n46 & n47, 166n39, 178n24, 179n25, **186**
  16: 56
  17-22a: 55
  17: 11n27
  18: 55
  19: 55
  20: 55
  21-22a, 55, 58
  22b-26: 57
  22-24: 49n6
  23: 49
  26: 49
  27-47a: 49, 52, 57
  27b-35a: 52
  27b-28: 57
  28: 49, 58
  29-35a: 57
  29: 49, 58, 61
  30-33a: 58
  31: 47, **58-59**, 60, 63, 64, 87, 120n27, 144n43, 171n2, **186**
  33: 47, **59**, 60, 63, 64, 120n27, 144n43, 171n2, **186**

INDEX OF PASSAGES CITED

35-47a: 52, 59
35b-43: 57
36: 51n12
37-39: 59
40-43: 59
44-47a: 57, 60
44: 60
45-47a: 60
45: 47n1, **60**, 63, 64
46: 60n25, 62 and n29
47: 53n14, 63
47b-50: 52, 61
49-50: 50
50-51: 52, 61
51: 61
52-63a: 53, 58
52: 61
53-54; 49
53: 61n27
54: 61
55-58: 58n21, 62
56-63: 63
58: 47, 49, **62-63**, 64, 86, 101n21, 120n27, 144n43, 171n2, 173n8, **186**
59-63a: 62
60: 47, **63-64**, 187
61-63a: 64
63b-73: 64
63b-72: 53
69-70: 50
70-71: 49
71: 53n14
73: 49, 52, 53, 54

Dom.
22(i): 177n20, **197**
22(ii): 156n23, 167, 176n16, **197**
91: 144n46, 178n24, **197**
124: 176n19, **197**
125(i): 176n19, **198**
125(ii): 176n19, **198-199**
134: 175n16, **199**

Flac.
39: 176n17 & n18, **196**
53: 173n8, **196**
58: 173n8m 177n20, **196**
59: 173b7, **196**
84: 171n1, **197**

Font. 3: 171n1, **190**

Har. Resp. 5: 121, 167n42, 175n16, **199**

Lig.: 153n17, 215
23: 177n20, **206-207**
29: 176n19, **207**

Mur.: 123, 126n14
11-13: 132
15-17: 95
21-30: 138n34
21: 131n22
24: 138n34
57: 123, 173n8, **195**
67-77: 135n28

Op.: 17, 21n41

Philippics: 147n1, 148, 149n6, 168n44

*Phil.*1: 148
4-10: 150n9
7-9: 148
10: 148n4
12: 148
16-24: 148
32: 156n24
35: 156n24

*Phil.*2: 6, chapter eight, 147-168, 174n10 & n12
1-10: 155
2: 154n18
3-10: 150
3: 152n14
6: 152n14
8b-10a: 151
9: 154n20
10: 154n20
11-43: 155
11-19: 150
14: 152n14
15: 152n14
16: 148, 154n20, **155**, 159, 164, 166, 167, 175n16, 176n16, **207**
18: 152n14 & n18, 155
19: 153, 154n18, 155
20: 150, 152n14
21-22: 150

Phil. 2 (cont.)
21: 153
23-24: 150, 153, 158
24: 152n14
25-36: 150, 152, 156
25-27: 157
25: 154n20
27: 157
28: 154n20, 157
29: 154n20, 157
30-32a: 157
30: 153n16, 154n20
31-32: 154n20, 157n26
32b-34: 157
32: 144n46, 148, **158**, 166, 178n23, 179n25, **207**
34b-36a: 153, 158, 160
34b: 154n21
35: 152n14
37-39: 150
39-40a: 150
40b-42a: 151
41: 142n14
42-43: 154n20
42: 152n14, 153n16
43: 151n10, 152n14, 154n21
44-114: 155
44-46: 152n14
44: 152n14
48: 152n14
49: 153
50: 152n14
51-55a: 158
51-53: 158
54: 148, 154n20, 156, **158-159**, 164, 167, 175n16, **207**
55b-56: 159
55b: 159
56: 148, 152n14, **159**, 160, 166, 168, 171n2, 174, 176n17, **207**
57: 152n14
59: 152n14, 160
61-70a: 160
62: 152n14, 153n16
63: 152n14, 153n16
65-67: 152n14
65: 154n20
67: 153n16
70b: 152n14
70b-72: 153
71-74a: 154n21, 160

71: 160
74a: 153
74b-75: 152n14, 154n21
75: 148, **160**, 167, 168, 176n17, 176n19, **207**
76: 150, 152n14, 153n16
78b: 152n14
79-84a: 161 and n31
80-81: 154n20
80: 154n21
81: 153n16, 162
84: 148, 153n16, **162**, 166, 167, 168, 171n1, 173n8, 175n15, **208**
86: 152n14
87: 153n16, 162
88: 154n21, 161n32
90: 152n14
91: 154n21
92-97: 163
93: 152n14
94-95: 154n21
97: 152n14, 154n20 & n21
98-99: 152n14
98: 154n21
99: 152n14
100b-107: 163
100: 148, 154n21, **163**, 166, 168, 176n19, **208**
103-104: 152n14, 154n21
104: 153n16
105-107: 152n14
105: 152n14
108-110a: 163
109: 154n21, 163
110-111: 154n21, 164-165
110(i): 148, 156n23, **164**, 166, 167, 168, 175n16, 176n16, **208**
110(ii): 148, **164-165**, 166, 168, 176n19, **208**, 213
111: 152n14, 165
115-119: 155
116-117: 154n21, 165n36

Phil. 3: 168n44
21: 148n2, 173n8, 176n19, **208**

Phil. 5
5: 148n2, 175n16, **208**, 213
19: 149

INDEX OF PASSAGES CITED

Phil. 9
  6: 148n2, 178n21, **208**

Phil. 11
  5: 148n2, 178n21, **209**
  19(i): 144n46, 148n2, 179n25, **209**, 213n1
  19(ii): 148n2, 178, **209**

Pis.: 151n10, 152 and n14, 167
  25: 126n10
  39: 148n2, 167n43, 175n16, **203**

Planc.: 6, chapter seven, 123-146, 174n13
  1-6a: 129
  1-5: 126
  2: 127
  3-4: 129-130
  3: 139
  4: 123, 126n12, **129-130**, 139, 144 and n46, 166n39, 178n24, 179n25, **204**
  5-6: 130-131
  5: 138
  6b-100: 129
  6b-26: 131
  6: 123, 127 and **n17**, **130-131**, 132, 142, 143n41, 144 and n46, 166n39, 179n25, **204**
  13: 125, 127n17
  18: 138
  19-23: 95
  24b-26: 131
  25-26: 129
  27-35: 132
  29: 132
  30a: 132
  30b-31a: 132
  31-35: 126n11, 132
  31: 133
  32: 133
  33-34: 133
  34: 133 and n25
  35: 123, **134**, 143, 166n38, 173n6, 173n8, 175n15, **204**
  36-55: 135
  36-47a: 135n27
  36-41: 125
  37: 124n4
  44-47a: 135
  44: 123, **135-136**, 143, 171n2, 172n3 and n4, **205**
  45-46: 136n29
  45: 124, 137
  46: 123, **135-136**, 143, 171n2, 172n3 & n4, 177n20, **205**
  47: 124n7
  53b-57: 126n13
  53b-55a: 137
  53b-54: 124
  54: 123, 125, **137** and n31, 144, 172n5, **205**, 213
  55b-56: 138
  55: 126
  56: 138n33
  57: 138
  58-71: 138
  58-67: 127n16, 132n23, 138
  58: 139
  59-62: 138
  62-67: 138
  63: 127n13
  68-99: 139
  68-90: 139
  68-74: 129
  68-69: 128
  68: 139
  70: 139
  71: 139
  72: 127 and n13, 139n35
  73: 125, 127, 128n17
  78: 127n17
  79: 123, 127, 128n17, **139-140**, 144 and n46, 166n39, 179n25, **205**, 213n1
  80-81: 128, 140
  80: 128
  83: 123, **146**, 144 and n46, 158n27, 166, 178n23, **205**
  84: 123, **140**, 144, 171n1, **205-206**
  85: 141 and n37
  86-90: 129, 141
  88: 123, **141**, 144 and n46, 166n39, 178n24, **206**, 213n1
  89(i): 123, **141**, 144 and n6, 166n39, 179n25, **206**
  89(ii): 123, **141-142**, 144 and n46, 166n39, 178n24, **206**
  91-94: 141n37, 142
  91: 126n11

Planc. (cont.)
  95-100: 129, 142
  96-100: 128
  100-104: 139
  101-104: 129, 142
  101: 142n39

Prov.
  46(i): 171n1, 178, **202**
  46(ii): 178, **202**

Quinct.: 27
  32: 177n21, **182**
  41: 171n2, 173n8, **182**
  64-65: 171n1, 173n8, **182**
  73: 171n2, **182**
  81: 170, 171n1, **183**

Q. Rosc.: 5, chapter four, 67-88, 103, 121, 144, 153n17, 175n14
  1-13: 69, 70, 71, 73, 74, 75, 81, 82, 86, 174n9
  1-2: 74
  2-5: 75
  4: 68, 69, 70
  5-9a: 75
  8: 68-69
  9: 67, **75**, 86, 87, 101n21, 120n30 & n31, 166n38, 171n1 & n2, 173n8, 175n14, **191**
  9b-13a: 76
  10-11: 69
  11: 68
  12: 69
  13b-14: 77
  13: 74
  15: 78 and n15
  16-56: 73, 78
  16-19: 78
  16: 67, **79**, 86, 87, 101n21, 102n22, 120n29, 171n1 & n2, 173n7, 175n14, **191**
  17-25: 81, 87
  17-23: 80
  20: 73
  20-21: 78
  22-23: 78
  22: 68
  24-31: 67
  24-25: 78-80
  25-26: 73, 81
  25(i): 67, **80**, 86, 87, 101n21, 102n22, 120n29 & n30, 143n40, 166n38, 171n1 & n2, 173n6, 173n8, 175n14, **192**
  25(ii): 67, **81**, 86, 87, 102n22, 120n29 & n31, 171n1 & n2, 174n9, 175n14, **192**
  26: 69, 70, 71 and n9, 78
  27-34a: 82
  27-31: 78
  27: 78
  32-51: 73
  32-39: 78
  32: 68, 69, 79
  34-51: 82
  34: 71, **82**
  35-37a: 82
  37a-39: 82
  37: 67, 68
  38-51: 68
  38: 68, 69, 70
  39-51: 72, 73, 79, 82, 86, 174n9
  40:67, **83**, 86, 87, 101n21, 102n22, 171n1 & n2, 172n3, 173n7, 175n14, **192**
  42: 68
  43-45: 83
  43: 67, **84**, 120n29, 177n20, **192**
  46-47: 84
  51-56: 73, 79
  51-52: 84
  52: 67, **84**, 86, 87, 101n21, 102n22, 120n29, 171n1 & n2, 172n3, 173n7, 175n14, **192**
  53-54: 85
  55: 67, **85**, 86, 87, 102n22, 120n29, 171n1 & n2, 172n3, 175n14, **192**

S. Rosc.: 6, chapter two, 27-45, 64, 65
  1-14: 33
  1-4: 29
  5-6: 29
  6: 28
  15-34: 33
  15-16: 28
  18: 28
  19: 28
  20-22: 28
  21: 28, 45n1

INDEX OF PASSAGES CITED

23-26: 28
26: 29
27: 29
28-29a: 29
29b-34: 33
30: **33**, 39, 42, 177n21, **183**
35-36: 33
37-82: 34
40: 29
42: 29
52: 29
55: 29
58: 29
71-73a: 34
74-79: 41
74: **34**, 35, 63, 116, 120n32, 144n43, 171n2, 173n5, **183**, 213
77-79: 39
77-78: 35
79: **35-36**, 63, 143n43, 171n2, **184**
80: 29
82: 29
83-123: 36
83: 36
86-88: 37
86: 37
89-91: 37
91: 38
92: 37
93: **37-38**, 42, 63, 120n27, 144n43, 171n2, **184**
96-98: 28
105-107: 28
108: 28
109-110: 28
119-123: 38, 39
120: **38**, 42, 176n17, **184**
124-142: 134
124: **39**, 41, 53n15, 64, 102n23, 130n21, 144n46, 166n39, 179n25, **185**
125-126: 40
127: 44
128-129: 41
128: 28, **40**, 42, 45n1, 65, 173, **185**
130: 41
132: 29

Sest.
32: 156n23, 167, 175n16, 176n16, **199**
37: 178n24, **199**
44: 144n46, 178n24, **199**

Sul.: 5, chapter four, 89-103, 124, 126, 142, 145
1-2: 92
1: 92
2: 91-92
3-35: 91, 92, 99
3-11: 92
3-9: 93
3-5: 92
6-7: 92
7-8: 92
9: 92
10: 89, **92-93**, 101, 103, 120n28 & n30, 143n42, 166n38, 172n3, 173n8, **195**
11-14a: 93
11: 90
12-14: 90
13-14: 99
13: 90n5, 93
14b-20: 93
18-19: 94
20: 94
21: 89, **94**, 101, 102, 103, 120n29, 171n1, 173n7, 176n19, **195**
22-29: 95
22: 95
23: 95
24: 95
25(i): 89, **95**, 102, 103, 171n1, 173n8, 176n19, **195**
25(ii): 84, **96**, 102, 103, 171n1, 173n8, 179n25, **195**
26-29: 97
29: 96n15
30-35: 95
30-31: 91
30: 91
31: 97
36-68: 92, 99
36-39: 97
39: 89, **98**, 101, 120n28, 143n42, 171n2, 172n3, **195**
40-44: 97

Sul. (cont.)
  46-47: 91
  49: 91
  50: 89, 91
  51: 90
  69-79: 92, 99
  80-87: 91, 92, 99
  81-82: 92, 99
  81: 89, **100**, 102, 103, 172n4, **196**
  86-87: 99
  88-93: 92, 99

Tul.
  32: 156n23, 176n16, **185**
  38: 87, 171n1, 173n7, **185**

Var: 17, 21n41, 36

Vat.: 126
  10: 171n1, **200**
  20: 173n8, 176n17, **200**

Verrines: 48
  first Verrine
    16-32: 49n6
    45: 48
  second Verrine
    1.15: **49** and n6
    1.144: 175n16, **187**
    2.15: 55n17
    2.74: 176n17, **187**
    2.96: 48
    2.114: 55n17
    2.142: 177n20, **187**
    2.144: 171n1, **188**
    2.150: 170, 171n1, **188**
    2.177: 171n1, **188**
    2.191: 173n8, **188**
    3.37: 178n21, **188**, 213n1
    3.84: 171n1, **188**
    3.106: 171n1, **189**
    3.118: 173n5, **189**
    3.135: 176n17, **189**
    3.169: 173n8, **189**
    3.182: 177n20, **190**
    4.3: 55n17
    4.140: 55n17
    5.135: 173n8, **190**

B. RHETORICA
Brut. 190: 90, 107

De Orat.
  2.43-50: 152n12
  2.105: 135n28
  2.162-173: 2n3
  2.367: 13n31
  3.214: 24, 33n15

Inv. 1 and n1 & n3, 12, 22, 25, 26, 33
  1.9: 1 and n2
  1.10: 237
  1.11: 2n3
  1.34-43: 2n3, 34, 237
  1.34-36: 43, 132, 236
  1.37-43: 236
  1.41-42: 236
  1.41: 2n3
  1.44-45: 2n4, **9-10**, 11, 12, 13, 15, 20, 22, 24, 25n54, 36, 142, 155n22, 166n37, 176n19, 236, 238
  1.49: 2n4, 3n4
  150: 2n4
  1.51-56: 2n4, 9
  1.57-77: 2n4, 8
  1.74-75: 2n4
  1.79: 2n4
  1.83-84: 2n4, **12-13**, 42, 178n24, 236
  1.84-85: 2n4
  2.14-51: 237
  2.16-51: 2n3, 34
  2.17-39: 80n19
  2.17-28: 236
  2.28-37: 43
  2.28-39: 236
  2.32-37: 106n3, 132
  2.38-44: 236
  2.52-56: 2n3
  2.177-178: 153

Opt. Gen.: 1n1

Orat.: 130: 90, 107

Top.: 1n1
  8: 2n3
  44-45: 2n4
  53-57: 2n4, 8

INDEX OF PASSAGES CITED

C. PHILOSOPHICA
Off.
  2.26: 91n9
  2.51: 31

D. LETTERS
ad Atticum
  1.2: 99n19
  3.15.1: 141n38
  4.5: 125
  4.18.3: 90
  14.1.1: 148
  14.13B: 151
  15.13.1: 149
  16.7.1: 148
  16.7.5: 148n4
  16.11.1-3: 149
  16.11.2: 161n30

ad Familiares
  9.10.3: 91n9
  12.2.1: 148n4, 149, 156n24
  15.17.2: 91n9

II. OTHER ANCIENT WORKS

Aeschines
  2.163: 22n42

Andocides
  2.2-3: 22 and n42, 25n54, 175n16
  2.7-8: 23, 178n24
  2.22: 22n42

Antiphon
  1.1: 26n55, 42n21, 179n25
  Tetralogies 1.beta.3: 23n46, 26n56, 178n24

Apsines
  Spengel I.376.25: 19n38

Aristotle
  Rhetoric
  1.1.1355a3-14: 8
  1.1.1357a1-4: 8
  1.2.1356a4-8: 237
  2.22.1395b21-23: 8
  2.23.1399a19-29: 11, 13, 25n54
  2.23.1400b5-8: 11, 24, 25n54, 155n22, 166n37

Cassius Dio 39.13-14: 106

Catullus: 109n10

Demosthenes: 147n1, 152 and n13, 153
  4.18: 22n42
  15.24: 22n42
  15.28: 22n42
  16.30: 22n42
  18.4: 26n55, 42n21, 179n25
  18.17-52: 153n17
  18.24: 22n42
  18.136: 153n17
  18.139: 22n42
  18.196: 20, 22n42
  18.217: 19-20, 21-22, 22n42, 176n19
  20.24: 22n42
  20.102: 22n42, 25n54, 175n16
  20.113: 22n42
  20.121: 24n49
  20.145: 22n42
  22.40-41: 22n42, 25n54, 175n16, 176n19
  22.62: 22n42, 25n54
  23.43: 24n49
  23.133-134: 22n42, 25n54, 175n16
  23.195: 24n49
  24.122: 22n42, 25n54, 175n16
  24.188-89: 22n42, 25n54
  25.38: 22n42, 25n54
  25.64-68: 22n42, 177n20
  26.14: 22n42, 25n54, 155n22, 166n37, 176n19
  27.53: 26n55, 42n21, 179n25
  27.55: 22n42, 25n54
  29.47: 22n42
  32.16: 22n42
  37.8: 22n42
  49.41: 22n42
  51.16: 22n42, 176n19
  56.32: 22n42
  58.12: 22n42, 176n19
  58.45-47: 22n42

Dio: see "Cassius Dio"

Euripides, *Medea*: 24

Aulus Gellius, *Noctes Atticae*
  2.4.1: 49n5
  11.13.1: 24 and n48, 25n54, 155n22, 166n37, 178n22
  12.12.2: 91n7

(pseudo-) Hermogenes
  De Inventione 4.6: 19-20, 156n23, 167, 176n16

Hieronymus (Jerome)
  contra Rufinum 3.3: 18n36

Hyperides
  For Euxennippus 14-15 and 17: 22n42
  Against Philippides 10: 24n49

Isaeus
  1.21: 22n42
  6.58: 22n42, 176n19

Isocrates
  6.70 26n55, 42n21, 179n25
  11.42-43: 22n42
  14.46-47: 25n52, 26n55, 179n25
  15.83: 26n55
  15.94-96: 22n42
  17.6 and 10: 23n46, 26n56, 178n24
  17.27-28: 22n42, 23, 26n56, 39, 176n17
  19.32: 22n42

Luke
  20.1-8: 25n53

Lycurgus, *Against Leocrates* 34, 63 and 75-76: 22n42

Lysias
  13.75-76: 22n24
  15.8: 24n49
  25.14: 22n24
  27.6: 24n49, 176n20

Mark
  11.27-33: 25n53

Matthew
  21.23-27: 25n53

Pseudo-Hermogenes: see Hermogenes

Quintilian, *Institutio Oratoria*
  3.10.4: 31, 153n17
  4.1.56: 51
  4.2.27: 107
  5.10.69: **17**, 21n41, 36, 42, 237
  5.10.120-121: 22
  7.2.9: 31, 236
  7.2.18-25: 31, 236
  7.4.34: **50**, 53, 55, 61
  8.6.52: 119n26
  9.3.93: 17n34
  11.1.15: 51

Rhetorica ad Herennium
  2.28-30: 2n4, 9n22, 14, 22, 25
  2.31: 14
  2.33-34: 2n4
  2.38-39: 2n4, **14**, 25n54, 155n22, 166n37, 178n24, 237
  3.10-15: 153
  3:13-15: 151n10
  3.15: 152n12
  4.37: 238
  4.52: 2n4, **16**, 17 and n34, 20, 26, 179n25, 237

Scholia
  Pseudo-Asconius
    p. 185 Stangl: 50
    p. 186 Stangl: 49n5
    p. 190 Stangl: 100n20
  Scholia Bobiensia
    p. 77 Stangl: 93n11
    pp. 79-80 Stangl: 95
    p. 152 Stangl: 127n7
  Scholia Gronoviana
    p. 314 Stangl: 29n3

Servius
  on *Aen.* 2.675-78: **18**, 19
  on *Aen.* 10.449-51: **18**

Vergil, *Aeneid*
  2.675--78: **18**
  10.449-51: **18**

Victorinus, *De Inventione*, p.233.11 Halm: 20n39

www.ingramcontent.com/pod-product-compliance
Ingram Content Group UK Ltd.
Pitfield, Milton Keynes, MK11 3LW, UK
UKHW041431180426
11947UKWH00007B/378